www.letsgo.com

LONDON, OXFORD, CAMBRIDGE & EDINBURGH

researcher-writers
Asa Bush
Rachel Lipson
Benjamin Naddaff-Hafrey

staff writers
Simone Gonzalez
Meghan Houser
Dorothy McLeod
Alexandra Perloff-Giles
Qichen Zhang

research manager
Matthew Whitaker

editor
Meagan Michelson

managing editor
Daniel C. Barbero

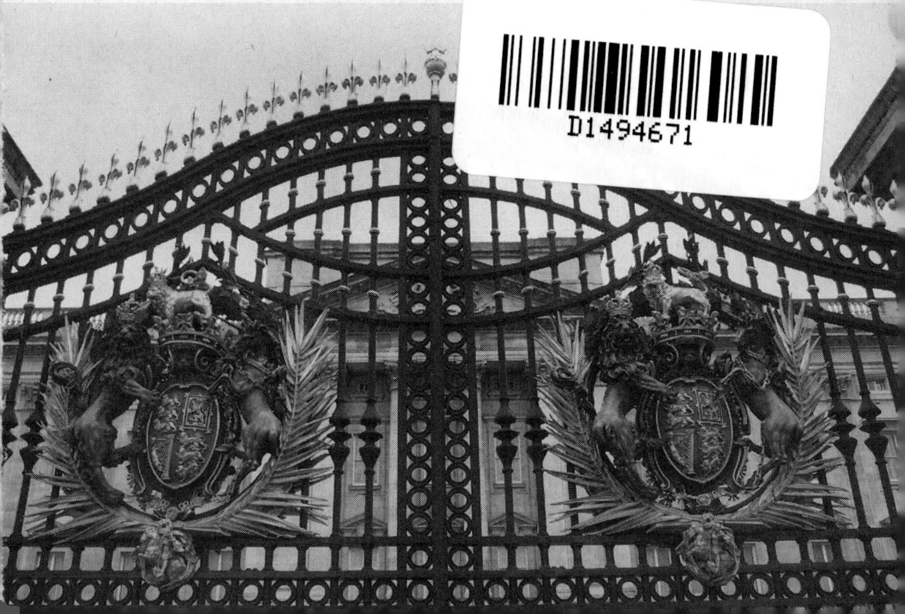

RESEARCHER-WRITERS

ASA BUSH. This *Let's Go* veteran kept us laughing with his witty writing and quirky photos from Scotland and Ireland. From a tour of the Jameson Irish Whiskey Factory to "Bloomsday" celebrations with fellow James Joyce fanatics, Asa's eye for excitement found him plenty of kindred—and distilled—spirits during his stay in Dublin.

RACHEL LIPSON. Britain's confusing accents and dreary weather couldn't put a damper on this New York native and first-time *Let's Go* RW. Whether chatting with Vikings or pretending to be an Oxford student, Rachel showed an incredible thirst for adventure (and cider!) as she traveled all across England.

BENJAMIN NADDAFF-HAFREY. Though some travel to London for prestige and tradition, this feisty freshman came to the British capital with a different mission: to get into his first bar fight. Lucky for us, Ben decided to play it safe while he single-handedly navigated London, even as World Cup mania brought out the hooligan in every Englishman.

CONTENTS

DISCOVER LONDON, OXFORD, CAMBRIDGE & EDINBURGH....1
- when to go 2
- what to do 2
- suggested itineraries 6
- how to use this book 10

LONDON....13
- orientation 14
- accommodations 21
- sights 31
- food 59
- nightlife 72
- arts and culture 85
- shopping 95
- essentials 101

OXFORD....105
- orientation 108
- accommodations 110
- sights 113
- food 120
- nightlife 124
- arts and culture 126
- shopping 127
- essentials 130

CAMBRIDGE....133
- orientation 135
- accommodations 135
- sights 136
- food 141
- nightlife 144
- arts and culture 147
- shopping 149
- essentials 151

EDINBURGH....153
- orientation 154
- accommodations 155
- sights 160
- food 165
- nightlife 172
- arts and culture 179
- shopping 181
- essentials 185

ESSENTIALS....187

LONDON, OXFORD, CAMBRIDGE & EDINBURGH 101....201
- people and customs 202
- food and drink 202
- town and gown 203
- sports and recreation 203
- media 205
- fine arts 206
- holidays and festivals 207

BEYOND TOURISM....209
- studying 210
- volunteering 213
- working 215

INDEX....219

MAP INDEX....221

QUICK REFERENCE....228

LONDON, OXFORD, CAMBRIDGE & EDINBURGH

"When a man is tired of **London,** he is tired of life; for there is in London all that life can afford."
—author Samuel Johnson

"But a girl of seventeen is not always thinking of books, especially in the **Oxford** summer term."
—novelist Mary A. Ward

"Living in **Cambridge,** with nature and everything, it's so clean."
—Syd Barret, frontman of *Pink Floyd*

"He said I was a *radge wee midden*, which I am told means a sexy little lady, so I will take it like that."
—singer Christina Aguilera on a compliment received at the MTV Europe Awards, **Edinburgh**

when to go

High season in London, Oxford, Cambridge, and Edinburgh tends to be June through August, but expect a steady influx of tourists almost year-round. Low (or at least lower) seasons are spring, April-May and fall, September-October. During these months, you'll likely find cheaper flights, though be warned that sights and accommodations may have reduced hours.

With few exceptions, weather tends to be mild throughout the central parts of England, Ireland, and Scotland, and climatic extremes are few and far between. In fact, in London it so rarely snows substantially that if a few inches fall university students frolic outside and make snow angels. In the spring, expect any green patches to be blanketed by daffodils. And as much as we'd like to tell you it's all flowers and frolicking, there's one element we can't escape: the rain. No matter when you're going to Britain, be sure to bring along your waterproof duds.

what to do

DOMES, THRONES, AND BONES

Even if history class isn't your cup of tea, it's hard not to acknowledge the rich past saturating London, Oxford, Cambridge, and Edinburgh. You can't possibly walk through any of these cities without stumbling upon a grand structure commemorating an even grander history.

- **INTO PARLIAMENT YOU SHALL GO:** Stop by the **Houses of Parliament** (p. 20) and maybe you too can wear one of those awesome wigs.
- **DEAD POET'S SOCIETY:** Be sure to visit the **Poet's Corner** at **Westminster Abbey** (p. 54), but you better not step on Alfred Lord Tennyson.
- **WHISPER SWEET NOTHINGS:** The legendary **Whispering Gallery** of **St. Paul's Cathedral** (p. 41) has unique acoustics that make it really hard to tell a secret.
- **PRIMING MINISTERS:** Cambridge University's **Corpus Christi College** was founded to quickly prepare new pontiffs after the Black Death left a shortage of priests in England.
- **PRIMING PRIME MINISTERS:** Oxford University's **Christ Church College** (p. 113) boasts a roster of distinguished alumni, including 13 prime ministers.
- **LIGHTS, CAMERA, ACTION:** Climb Outlook Tower in Edinburgh to see the 150-year-old **camera obscura** (p. 162), which captures dazzling images of the street below.

GET YOUR NERD ON

Admit it, one of the reasons you're visiting Britain is to hit up its literary and academic hotspots. And who can blame you? Throw back ale at the haunts of literary greats in Edinburgh. In London, experience a traditional Shakespearean performance as a groundling or take a Woolfian promenade down the Strand. Then head to Oxford and Cambridge where you can channel the spirits of famous alumni of yore.

- **MISERABLE ORPHANS:** Make pit stops at London landmarks like Bernard's Inn and Newgate Prison, famously featured in **Charles Dickens'** novels of the nitty gritty city.
- **MAGICAL ORPHANS: Harry Potter** enthusiasts flock to such London sights as Leadenhall Market, the Boa Constrictor tank at London Zoo, and Platform 9¾ at King's Cross Tube station (you know, for when you're out of Floo Powder).

- **BILLY SHAKES:** Hit up a performance at **Shakespeare's Globe Theatre** (p. 92) in London, and you might be lucky enough to get a pre-show serenade.
- **WHO'S AFRAID?:** Meander through **Bloomsbury** (p. 14) in London where Woolf and her Modernist cohorts shot the intellectual breeze.
- **NOTABLE AND QUOTABLE OXONIANS:** Eleven of Britain's poet laureates studied at Oxford. Among the university's literary luminaries are **John Donne** (Hertford), **Richard Lovelace** (Merton), **Percy Bysshe Shelley** (University), **T.S. Eliot** (Merton), **W.H. Auden** (Christ Church), **Oscar Wilde** (Magdalen), **Aldous Huxley** (Balliol), and **Dr. Seuss**.
- **ALES AND TALES:** Oxford alums **J.R.R. Tolkien** and **C.S. Lewis** contrived wizards and wardrobes over pints at **The Eagle and Child** (p. 124).
- **POETICAL CANTABRIGIAN PUPILS:** Drop by the alma maters of Cambridge's particularly well-versed graduates including **Edmund Spenser** (Pembroke), **Christopher Marlowe** (Corpus Christi), **John Milton** (Christ's), **William Wordsworth** (St. John's), **Samuel Taylor Coleridge** (Jesus), **Sylvia Plath** (Newnham), and **Ted Hughes** (Pembroke).
- **METHODICAL CANTABRIGIAN PUPILS:** Evolutionary revolutionary **Charles Darwin** (Christ's) is a Cambridge alum, along with **Sir Isaac Newton** (Trinity), **James Watson** (Clare) and **Francis Crick** (Caius), who announced the discovery of DNA at the Eagle pub (p. 144).
- **DEEP IN THE HUNDRED ACRE WOOD:** At Cambridge University, visit **Trinity's Wren Library** (p. 137), which houses handwritten copies of A.A. Milne's *Winnie the Pooh* books.
- **SCOTTY BOY:** Scattered throughout **Edinburgh** (p. 153) you'll find monuments commemorating locals' favorite literary hometown boy, **Sir Walter Scott.**

top five places to bridge the gap

5. FORTH BRIDGE: Famous railway bridge (and prospective UNESCO World Heritage site) linking Edinburgh with Fife.

4. MATHEMATICAL BRIDGE: Legend has it that Newton designed this modest bridge across the River Cam without using nuts or bolts.

3. BRIDGE OF SIGHS (OXFORD AND CAMBRDIGE): Both British universities ripped off the Venetian version of this structure.

2. TOWER BRIDGE: A spectacular suspension bridge that everybody mistakes for the rather anticlimactic London Bridge.

1. MILLENNIUM BRIDGE: A steel footbridge in London with St. Paul's Cathedral on one end and Shakespeare's Globe Theatre on the other.

Humped
Zebra
Crossing

LET'S GOAL!

Football (soccer, if you must) fanatics are everywhere in Britain: the queen is an Arsenal fan, and the police run a national hooligan hotline. Sports like rugby, cricket, and horseracing also have loyal fans—though they're not nearly as insane as their football counterparts.

- **FOOTBALL:** In London, don **Chelsea** blue at Stamford Bridge or spur on the **Spurs** at White Hart Lane.
- **"THE GENTLEMAN'S GAME":** Men in white play their endless games at **Lord's Cricket Ground** in St. John's Wood in London. The world's longest cricket marathon was played by the Cheriton Fitzpaine Club in Devon for 24hr. and 34min.
- **40-LOVE:** A fierce competition masquerading as a garden party, **Wimbledon** (p. 204) is the world's oldest annual tennis tournament.
- **GIDDY-UP!:** Saddle up for the annual **Royal Ascot horse race**, a train-ride or 1hr. drive away from London. Dress code depends upon where you're sitting for the events. Want to come looking like a frump? Neigh!
- **TO A TEE:** In Edinburgh, **golf** is probably the most popular sport–though Edinburghers are not quite as obsessed with the pastime as their St. Andrews counterparts.
- **STUCK IN THE MUD:** Punting is a popular pastime at **Oxford** (p. 105) and **Cambridge** (p. 133). How does one "punt," you ask? You literally navigate a boat by jabbing a pole in the mud. As long as you're not the one steering, it's quite a tranquil experience.

TAKE A BOW, BRITAIN

London is known for vibant, sparkling theater, while Edinburgh is renowned for its world-class arts festivals. And who ever said thespians couldn't be studious? Oxford and Cambridge also host hip performing arts scenes, perfect for the theater- and music-hungry traveler.

student superlatives

- **BEST PLACE FOR MONK-Y BUSINESS:** Westminster Abbey (p. 54).
- **BEST PLACE TO GET AN ARSE-ACHE:** Shakespeare's Globe Theatre (p. 49).
- **BEST WAY TO REPLACE YOUR STAIR MASTER:** Climbing to the Dome of St. Paul's Cathedral (p. 41).
- **BEST PLACE TO GET YOUR STICK STUCK IN THE MUD:** The River Thames at Oxford (p. 105) or the River Cam at Cambridge (p. 133).
- **BEST PLACE TO SMELL THE FLOWERS:** Oxford Botanic Garden (p. 119).
- **BEST PLACE TO GET ROW-DY:** The Race (p. 127) between Oxford and Cambridge.
- **BEST PLACE TO WEAR PLAID:** Edinburgh (p. 153).
- **BEST PLACE TO GET FRISKY WITH WHISKEY:** The Scotch Whisky Experience (p. 160) in Edinburgh.

- **THEATER OUT THE WEST END:** From Billy Shakespeare to *Billy Elliot*, you're bound to find a show that tickles your fancy in **London's West End,** where the bustling theater community rivals that of New York City's Broadway.
- **'TIL THE FAT LADY SINGS:** Classical music aficionados flock to the **London Coliseum,** home of the **English National Opera,** and the **Royal Opera** (p. 87) in Covent Garden.
- **ALL THAT JAZZ:** Head to **Jazz Café** (p. 89) in London's Camden Town for some quality crooning.
- **MUSIC OVER EASY:** There's nothing like music in the morning time. Pry yourself away from the library (yeah right), and attend one of the **Oxford Coffee Concerts** (p. 126), top-notch chamber music performances held every Sunday morning in Holywell Music Hall.
- **BARDY PARTY:** The **Cambridge Shakespeare Festival** (p. 149) takes place every year throughout July and August and features several plays by the man himself.
- **FRINGE BENEFITS:** The **Edinburgh Festival Fringe** (p. 179), the world's largest arts festival takes place over the course of three weeks every August.

BEYOND TOURISM

Those craving an international adventure that involves more than just sightseeing ought to explore the study, work, and volunteer opportunities available in Great Britain, Ireland, and Scotland. Especially in Anglophone countries, it's possible to dive into academic and professional programs headfirst and get a full immersion experience.

- **STUDY ABROAD:** Whether you're a Shakespearean or a biologist, you're bound to find a titillating program at one of England, Ireland, or Scotland's premiere universities. Get your Econ on at **LSE**, be "supervised" in one of **Cambridge's** small tutorials, or study with the Scottish Parliament at the **University of Edinburgh** (see **Studying,** p. 210).
- **VOLUNTEER ABROAD:** If you'd rather get in touch with your philanthropic side, not to fear. There are countless possibilities in Great Britain, Ireland, and Scotland, from offering urban families financial advice to creating **sustainability** projects (see **Volunteering,** p. 213).
- **WORK ABROAD:** If you want to rake in any kind of dough during your time abroad, you should plan ahead. With the right qualifications you might wind up **teaching** your subject of choice at a British grammar school. Events like the **Edinburgh Festival Fringe** (p. 179) are teeming with short-term employment opportunities (see **Working,** p. 215).

suggested itineraries

THE BEST OF LONDON, OXFORD, CAMBRIDGE, AND EDINBURGH

LONDON (1 WEEK). First, be inspired to belt out a riveting rendition of "God Save the Queen" at **Buckingham Palace**. At **Westminster Abbey**, pay homage to Tennyson, Dickens, and Hardy in the **Poet's Corner.** While you're in the neighborhood, take a gander at the **Houses of Parliament**, where all those guys in wigs make important decisions. Straddle a lion in **Trafalgar Square.** Then visit the Impressionist exhibit in the **National Gallery**. Next, marvel at **St. Paul's Cathedral**, a domed marble masterpiece. Next, trek over to Bloomsbury and **The British Museum,** where the **Rosetta Stone** isn't even the climax. Enjoy an interactive medieval experience at the **Tower of London**.

OXFORD (4 DAYS). Hit up each of the **colleges** oozing with history—from **Christ Church** to **Queen's** to **Trinity**. But don't be sheisty, or the "bulldogs" will getcha. If they reprimand you, book it to **Oxford Castle.** Castle? Prison? Restaurant, theater, and luxury hotel complex? Yes, yes, yes, yes, and yes. If you're feeling studious and whimsical, skip on over to **Bodleian Library,** the best place to go down the rabbit hole.

CAMBRIDGE (3 DAYS). The **colleges** are surprisingly identical to those of Oxford, but with their own pasts to brag about, including Henry VI, Henry VIII, and *Winnie the Pooh.* The second oldest building in Cambridge, **Round Church** even outdates the university. Meanwhile, **Great Saint Mary's Church** provides awesome views of the city, but pray that the 12 bells don't ring while you're schlepping up the 123 spiral steps.

EDINBURGH (1 WEEK). Start off at **Edinburgh Castle**, which includes the palace where Mary, Queen of Scots, became Mommy, Queen of Scots. It's a James! Climb Outlook Tower to see the **camera obscura** (p. 162), which offers a spectacularly baller view of the street below. If you're looking for a place that's like Disney World, with alcohol, hit up the **Scotch Whisky Experience.** Once the buzz wears off (you *are* responsible adults, aren't you?) visit the **National Gallery of Scotland**—Raphael, Titian, El Greco, Turner, Gauguin, Monet, Poussin. 'Nuff said. Finally, visit **Thistle Chapel** at the **High Kirk of Saint Giles** and garner some scraps of hope that chivalry is not dead.

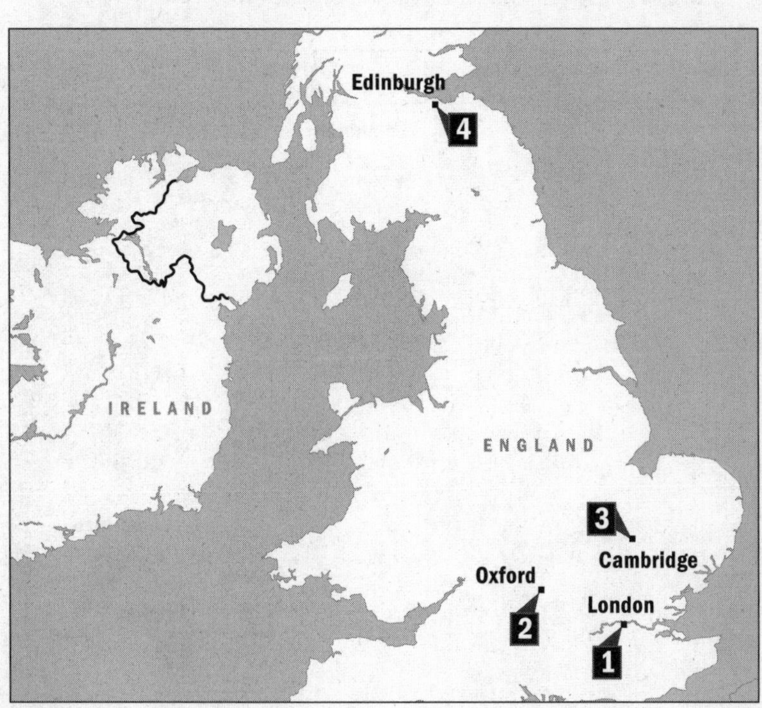

THE BEST OF THE OUTDOORS

LONDON. Take the Tube to northern London and head to **Hampstead Heath**, the best place for simultaneously frolicking on the hills and spotting celebs. Closer to the center of London, in the posh part of town (and certainly not without spice), are **Hyde Park** and **Kensington Gardens**. Hear proselytizers and politicos at **Speakers' Corner** and visit the iconic **Peter Pan** statue. Do *you* believe in fairies? Yes! Clap, clap. Finally, **Regent's Park** is the perfect place for prim and proper dallying. Don't miss Queen Mary's Gardens or Primrose Hill. The famous Open Air Theatre hosts Shakespearean productions May-September.

OXFORD. Take a good whiff of the university **botanic garden**. Then, gambol along the path connecting the garden to Christ Church Meadow and catch a glimpse of the Thames and the cricket grounds on the opposite bank. Take to the water and go **punting on the Thames.** A punt is like the British version of a gondola.

CAMBRIDGE. With over 8000 plant species, Cambridge University's **botanic garden** offers the best kind of aroma therapy. After a jaunt in the garden, get your poles ready for action and go **punting on the Cam**. If you're here the third week in June, screw the library and head to the **Midsummer Fair.**

EDINBURGH. The **Nelson Monument,** the **City Observatory,** and the **National Monument** sit atop **Castle Hill**, which offers beautiful panoramas of the Scottish capital. Roll down the hill (not really) and head to the **Royal Botanic Gardens**, a veritable herbaceous oasis smack-dab in the middle of Scotland.

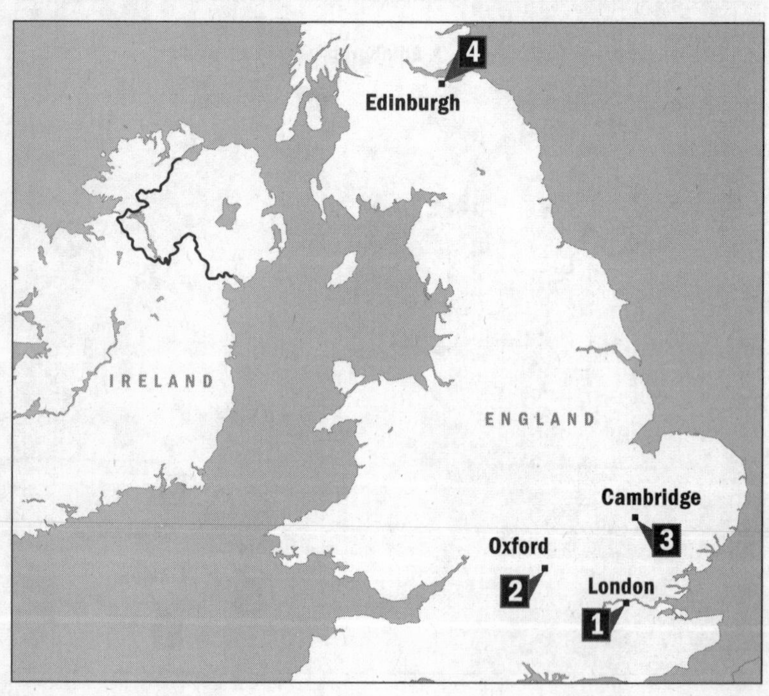

CAMPUS CRASHING: A TOUR OF OXFORD AND CAMBRIDGE

OXFORD. 9am: Start the day with a bit of reflection at **University Church of Saint Mary the Virgin**. **10am:** Dawdle through **Christ Church Meadow**. **Noon:** Grab a fresh bite to eat at **Gloucester Green Market**. **3pm:** Go punting on the **River Cam. 5pm:** Hit the books in **Bodleian Library**. **7pm:** Satisfy your appetite (no need to analyze—we're talking dinner) at **Freud**, an interesting combination club, bar, cafe, and art gallery. **8pm:** Grab a pint at **The Turf Tavern,** where Bill Clinton allegedly "didn't inhale" as a Rhodes Scholar. **9:05pm:** Head to Tom's Quad to hear the 7-ton bell, **Big Tom,** toll 101 times. Then dabble in a little lily-pond dunking.

CAMBRIDGE. 9:30am: Take a moment to meditate in **King's College Chapel**. **10am:** At **Trinity College**, walk through Nevile's Court and sit by the fountain—but we don't advise you to bathe nude, even if it was a favorite pastime of Lord Byron. **Noon:** Munch on lunch at **The Regal**, the largest pub in the UK. **3pm:** Go punting on the River Thames. **5pm:** Get your study on at **The Wren Library**. **7pm:** If you're willing to splurge a bit, grab some grub at **CB2. 8pm:** Join your fellow pupils for a pint at **The Free Press.**

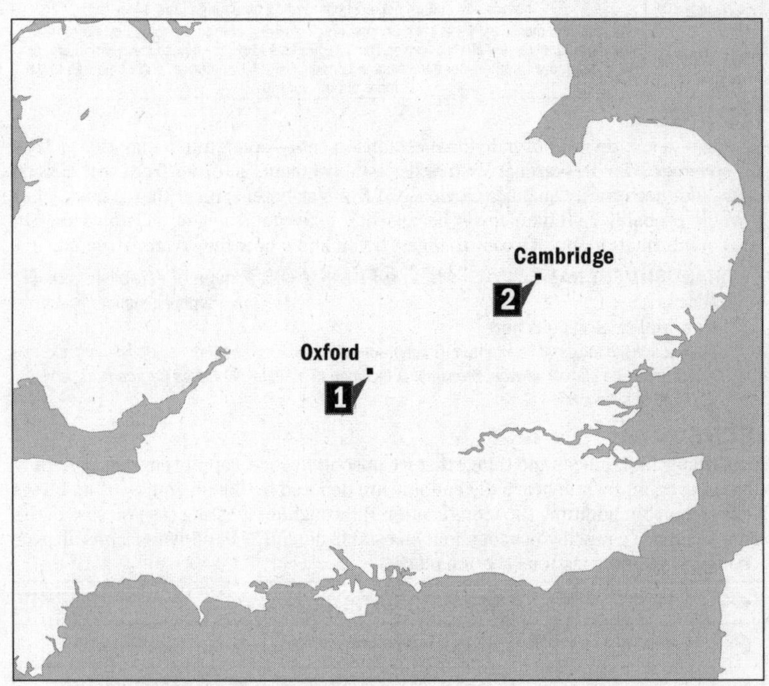

how to use this book

CHAPTERS

In the next few pages, the travel coverage chapters—the meat of any *Let's Go* book—we begin with **London.** After a visit to Big Ben and a romp through Hampstead Heath, we venture to **Oxford** and **Cambridge,** the world's most famous college towns. The journey concludes in Scotland's capital, **Edinburgh,** which boasts a castle *and* a whiskey factory.

But that's not all, folks. We also have a few extra chapters for you to peruse:

CHAPTER	DESCRIPTION
Discover London, Oxford, Cambridge & Edinburgh	Discover tells you what to do, when to do it, and where to go for it. The absolute coolest things about any destination get highlighted in this chapter at the front of all *Let's Go* books.
Essentials	Essentials contains the practical info you need before, during, and after your trip—visas, regional transportation, health and safety, phrasebooks, and more.
London, Oxford, Cambridge & Edinburgh 101	London, Oxford, Cambridge, and Edinburgh 101 is just what it sounds like—a crash course in where you're traveling. This short chapter on London, Oxford, Cambridge, and Edinburgh history and culture makes great reading on a long plane ride.
Beyond Tourism	As students ourselves, we at *Let's Go* encourage studying abroad, or going beyond tourism more generally, every chance we get. This chapter lists ideas for how to study, volunteer, or work abroad with other young travelers in London, Oxford, Cambridge, and Edinburgh to get more out of your trip.

LISTINGS

Listings—a.k.a. reviews of individual establishments—constitute a majority of *Let's Go* coverage. Our Researcher-Writers list establishments in order from **best to worst value**—not necessarily quality. (Obviously a five-star hotel is nicer than a hostel, but it would probably be ranked lower because it's not as good a value.) Listings pack in a lot of information, but it's easy to digest if you know how they're constructed:

ESTABLISHMENT NAME type of establishment ❶

Address ☎phone number website

Editorial review goes here.

Directions to the establishment. ℹ Other practical information about the establishment, like age restrictions at a club or whether breakfast is included at a hostel. Ⓢ Prices for goods or services. Hours or schedules.

ICONS

First things first: places and things that we absolutely love, sappily cherish, generally obsess over, and wholeheartedly endorse are denoted by the all-empowering **Let's Go thumbs-up.** In addition, the icons scattered throughout a listing (as you saw in the sample above) can tell you a lot about an establishment. The following icons answer a series of yes-no questions about a place:

Credit cards accepted	Cash only	Wheelchair-accessible
Not wheelchair-accessible	Internet access available	Alcohol served
Air-conditioned	Outdoor seating available	▼ GLBT or GLBT-friendly

The rest are visual cues to help you navigate each listing:

☎ Phone numbers	Websites	Directions
ℹ Other hard info	Ⓢ Prices	Hours

Let's Go
www.letsgo.com

OTHER USEFUL STUFF

Area codes for each destination appear opposite the name of the city and are denoted by the ☎ icon. Finally, in order to pack the book with as much information as possible, we have used a few **standard abbreviations.** Note that "concession" is the British version of discount. Concessions are usually granted to students and senior citizens (65+), and sometimes to the disabled and unemployed.

PRICE DIVERSITY

A final set of icons corresponds to what we call our "price diversity" scale, which approximates how much money you can expect to spend at a given establishment. For **accommodations,** we base our range on the cheapest price for which a traveler can stay for one night. For **food,** we estimate the average amount one traveler will spend in one sitting. The table below tells you what you'll *typically* find in London, Oxford, Cambridge, and Edinburgh at the corresponding price range, but keep in mind that no system can allow for the quirks of individual establishments.

ACCOMMODATIONS	LONDON	OXFORD, CAMBRIDGE, EDINBURGH	WHAT YOU'RE LIKELY TO FIND
❶	under £26	under £20	Campgrounds and dorm rooms, both in hostels and actual universities. Expect bunk beds and a communal bath. You may have to provide or rent towels and sheets.
❷	£26-42	£20-27	Upper-end hostels and lower-end B and Bs. You may have a private bathroom, or there may be a sink in your room and a communal shower in the hall. Breakfast and some amenities, like TVs, may be included.
❸	£42-57	£27-34	A small room with a private bath, probably in a budget hotel. Should have decent amenities, such as phone and TV. Breakfast may be included in the price of the room.
❹	£57-77	£34-42	Similar to a ❸, though maybe a bit larger. A room in this range will probably have more amenities or be more centrally located. It should have some charm, too.
❺	over £77	over £42	Large hotels or upscale chains, nice B and Bs, and even castles. A splurge for budget travelers, but you deserve to be pampered once in a while.
FOOD	**RANGE**		**WHAT YOU'RE LIKELY TO FIND**
❶	under £6	under £6	Mostly street-corner stands, food trolleys, sandwiches, takeaway, and tea shops. Rarely a sit-down meal.
❷	£6-12	£6-12	Pub grub, fish 'n chips, and cheap ethnic eateries. Sandwiches, pizza, appetizers at a bar. Could be sit-down or takeaway.
❸	£12-18	£12-18	Mid-priced entrees, fancier pubs and higher quality ethnic food. Most Indian places are in this range. You'll probably have a waiter or waitress, so the tip will bump you up a few £s.
❹	£18-24	£18-24	May have heartier and more elaborate food, but the real draw is the ambience. As in ❸, higher prices are usually related to better service. Includes some fancier restaurants, and most gastro-pubs (fish 'n *frîtes*, anyone?).
❺	over £24	over £24	Elegant restaurants. You'll probably need to take off your T-shirt. Don't keep it off! Put on one of those nice shirts, with buttons.

LONDON

Most people have a well-defined idea of "London:" staid tradition, afternoon tea, stuffy Englishmen with cultured accents, heavy ales, and winding lanes—all of it decorated in styles that were popular back when high foreheads were also fashionable. People with this notion of London can easily complete their vacation in 3min. by working their way to the bank of the Thames and staring pointedly at the gilded heights of **Big Ben,** but to employ this tactic is to miss the true charm of the foggy city.

Despite London's weighty history and culture, the city today is not all **ghost tours, beefeaters,** and **double-decker buses.** In London, there's always an underground scene to be found, and a modern pulse beats behind every beautiful old surface.

History is written on the face of every Blitz-scarred building, but take the time to wander and talk to the people inside them. Immerse yourself in the culture, especially if you're from a superficially similar English-speaking country; the difference will only be more poignant when you realize it. Now, finish your **pint** and *Let's Go.*

greatest hits

- **MAMMA MIA!** Satisfy your *buon appettito* with some of the most epic sandwiches in London at Spianata (p. 64).
- **CHALLENGE THE STATUS QUO.** Or at least hear others with more gumption do so at the Speakers' Corner in Hyde Park (p. 32).
- **DRINK WITH ANIMALS.** Triumph over a fake rhinoceros in the weekly pub quiz at The Three Kings (p. 76).
- **YA DIG IT?** Get your jazz on in the smooth surroundings of Ronnie Scott's in Soho (p. 88).

student life

Face it. Over the past few centuries, the Parliament's lost its funk. If you want to experience the best student life in London, head to Bloomsbury. The home of University College London also hosts countless student backpackers looking for the cheapest hostels in the city. Bloomsbury may not have the best clubs in town, but the bar scene is young and vibrant. Tired of British pub grub? Well, Bloomsbury also has some of the best ethnic restaurants in London, so you can satisfy your craving for tapas and souvlaki without leaving the neighborhood. Bloomsbury also has some of the city's most beautiful gardens, so you and your roommates can make your own picnic and enjoy the scenery (for free!). Throw off your backpack and set up shop in Bloomsbury.

orientation

BAYSWATER

Formerly a watering hole for livestock, Bayswater was built up from a small hamlet in the late 18th and early 19th centuries. In the late 19th century, the neighborhood took on a wealthier set of inhabitants before increased immigration to London spiced up its character and cuisine a bit. It's nestled close to Notting Hill but has much cheaper housing. Get off the Tube at the ⊖**Bayswater** stop for the west of the neighborhood, and at ⊖**Paddington** or ⊖**Lancaster Gate** for the east. Bayswater is east of Notting Hill and west of Marylebone.

BLOOMSBURY

Once famous for the manor houses, hospitals, universities, and museums that made the area a cultural landmark, Bloomsbury is now a haven for student travelers seeking cheap accommodations in a central location. Providing easy access to the British Museum and the rest of London, Bloomsbury is a perfect location from which to see the city. The borough features a wide range of ethnic restaurants, providing a welcome respite from British specialties like the inimitable "bubble and squeak" (fried leftovers). Especially pleasant are the many beautiful gardens and parks sprinkled throughout the neighborhood. Where once you might have seen **Virginia Woolf** and **John Maynard Keynes,** members of the bohemian Bloomsbury Group, you may now see Ricky Gervais. To reach Bloomsbury, west of **Clerkenwell,** take the Tube to ⊖**Tottenham Court Rd.** or ⊖**Russell Square.**

CHELSEA

Chelsea once gained a reputation as a punk hangout, but there is nothing punk about the neighborhood today. Overrun by rich "Sloanes" (preps, in British parlance), Chelsea now has sky-high prices, expensive clubs, and absurd cars. Just about the only thing that's still edgy about the neighborhood is the **Saatchi Gallery.** Current home of **Mick Jagger** and former home of **Oscar Wilde,** most of the action can be found in **Sloane Square, King's Road,** and **Royal Hospital Road.** Visit for the restaurants and the sights, but find your home and nightlife elsewhere. Chelsea is between **Westminster** and **Hammersmith** and beneath **Kensington.** Take to the Tube to ⊖**Sloane Square** to access it.

THE CITY OF LONDON

One of the oldest and most historic parts of London, the City of London, often referred to as "the City," houses many of London's finest and most crowded tourist attractions, as well as the city's financial center. Written in the histories of many of the buildings are the devastating tragedies of German bombing during the Blitz and the Great Fire of London in 1666. The fire spread rapidly, destroying 80% of the City of London in five days. Much of the current city was rebuilt after both of these tragedies, and its fantastic architecture stands as a monument to the resilient London spirit. "The City" also holds many of London's Roman artifacts, as well as vestiges of the ancient London Wall. It is a neighborhood where the spires of famous churches stretch up with the towers of powerful insurance companies. The City borders the northern bank of the **Thames** and is east of **Holborn.** Take the Tube to **⊖St. Paul's.**

HOLBORN AND CLERKENWELL

In the 18th century, Holborn was home to **Mother Clap's Molly House,** a gay brothel. Today, however, it houses many banks, law firms, and upscale pubs, so things are a little bit different. Clerkenwell is a former monastic center, defined by the Priory of St. John, before Henry VIII began the reformation. It has since become a popular spot for excellent meals and hardy night life. Holborn is west of the City of London; Clerkenwell is north of Holborn, with Charterhouse St. serving as part of its southern boundary. Take the Tube to **⊖Farringdon** or **⊖Temple.**

KENSINGTON AND EARL'S COURT

Once a Saxon settlement, Kensington has since developed into one of the most pleasant parts of London. Known as **The Royal Borough of Kensington and Chelsea,** it is sometimes pretentiously referred to as "The Royal Borough." Filled with some of the best museums, nicest bars and swankiest residences in London, Kensington may have more Lamborghinis, Maseratis, and Ferraris per capita than most London neighborhoods. Notable for its museums, ease of access to **Hyde Park,** and laid-back nightlife, Kensington is well worth a visit. Kensington is south of **Notting Hill** and north of **Knightsbridge.** Use **⊖High Street Kensington** for Kensington High St. and Hyde Park, and **⊖South Kensington** for Old Brompton Rd. and the museums. Earl's Court is just up Old Brompton Rd. from Kensington, but it feels worlds apart, and is a much better neighborhood for a quiet evening out.

KNIGHTSBRIDGE AND BELGRAVIA

Once a dangerous neighborhood, Knightsbridge has since improved its rep. Appealing mostly thanks to its selection of undercrowded and enjoyable sights and fantastic department stores, this neighborhood between **South Kensington** and **Kensington** merits at least a short visit. Use **⊖Knightsbridge** and **⊖Hyde Park Corner** if you travel here. **Belgravia** is a rich neighborhood bordered by **Chelsea** and **Westminster.** It features many fantastic restaurants and a reasonable selection of accommodations, but not much else. Take the Tube to **⊖Sloane Square** or **⊖Victoria** to get to Belgravia.

MARYLEBONE AND REGENT'S PARK

Pronounced (*Mar*-leh-bone), Marylebone is a classic London neighborhood. From the winding, pub-lined **Marylebone Lane** to the gorgeous and romantic **Regent's Park,** the neighborhood offers a complete British experience. The city's diverse population is represented on Edgware Road, where a predominantly Lebanese community boasts many Middle Eastern restaurants. The area surrounding **Baker Street** features some of the city's more touristy attractions, including the Sherlock Holmes Museum and Madame Tussaud's. Take **⊖Bond Street** to reach the south, **⊖Edgware** for the Lebanese area. **⊖Baker Street** or **⊖Regent's Park** will get you to Regent's Park. Shocking, no?

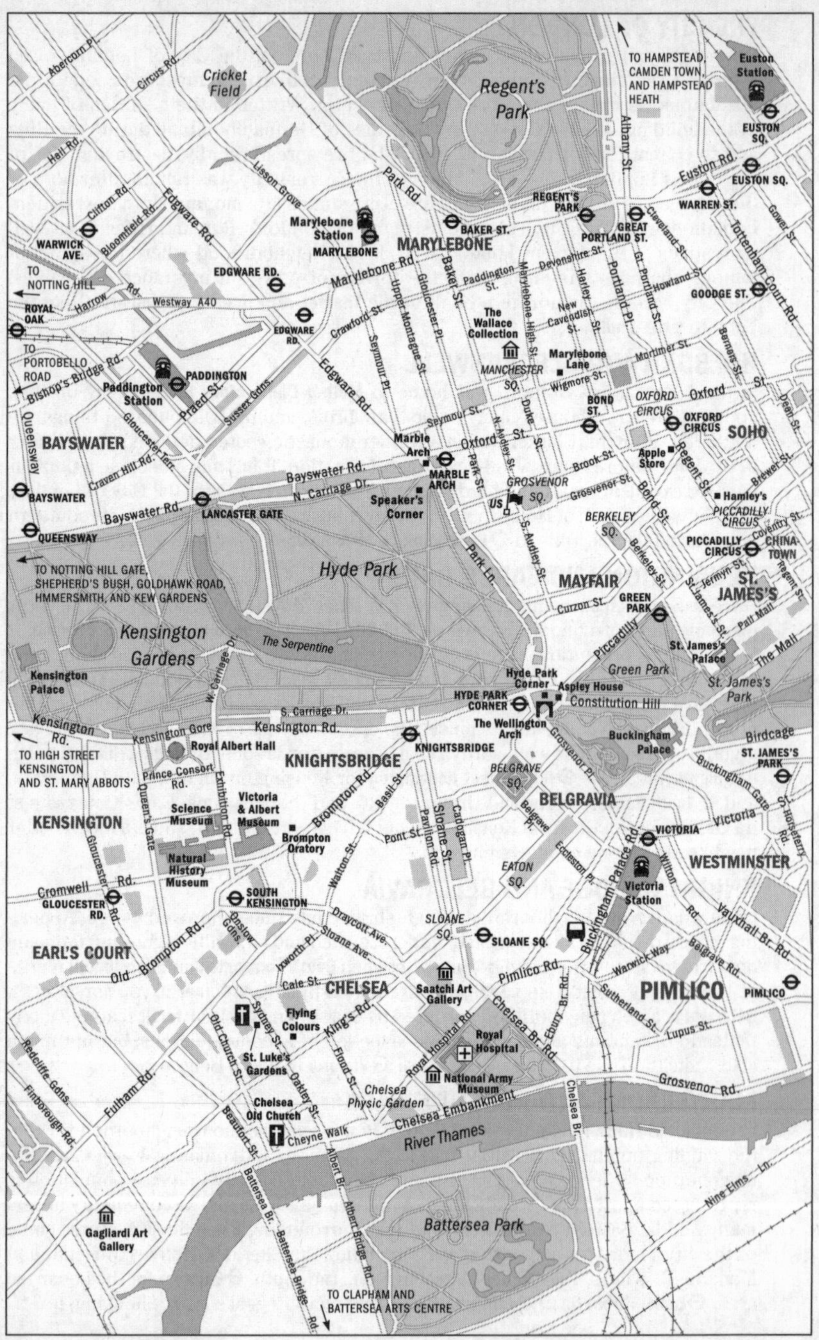
Regent's Park
Cricket Field
TO HAMPSTEAD, CAMDEN TOWN, AND HAMPSTEAD HEATH
Euston Station
EUSTON SQ.
MARYLEBONE
Marylebone Station
PADDINGTON
Paddington Station
BAYSWATER
TO NOTTING HILL
TO PORTOBELLO ROAD
The Wallace Collection
MANCHESTER SQ.
Marble Arch
Speaker's Corner
OXFORD CIRCUS
SOHO
Apple Store
Hamley's
PICCADILLY CIRCUS
CHINA-TOWN
GROSVENOR SQ.
BERKELEY SQ.
MAYFAIR
ST. JAMES'S
Hyde Park
The Serpentine
Kensington Gardens
Kensington Palace
TO NOTTING HILL GATE, SHEPHERD'S BUSH, GOLDHAWK ROAD, HMMERSMITH, AND KEW GARDENS
Green Park
St. James's Palace
St. James's Park
Hyde Park Corner
Aspley House
The Wellington Arch
Buckingham Palace
Royal Albert Hall
TO HIGH STREET KENSINGTON AND ST. MARY ABBOTS'
KNIGHTSBRIDGE
BELGRAVIA
KENSINGTON
Science Museum
Victoria & Albert Museum
Brompton Oratory
Natural History Museum
WESTMINSTER
Victoria Station
EARL'S COURT
CHELSEA
PIMLICO
Saatchi Art Gallery
Flying Colours
St. Luke's Gardens
Royal Hospital
National Army Museum
Chelsea Physic Garden
Chelsea Old Church
River Thames
Battersea Park
Gagliardi Art Gallery
TO CLAPHAM AND BATTERSEA ARTS CENTRE

london

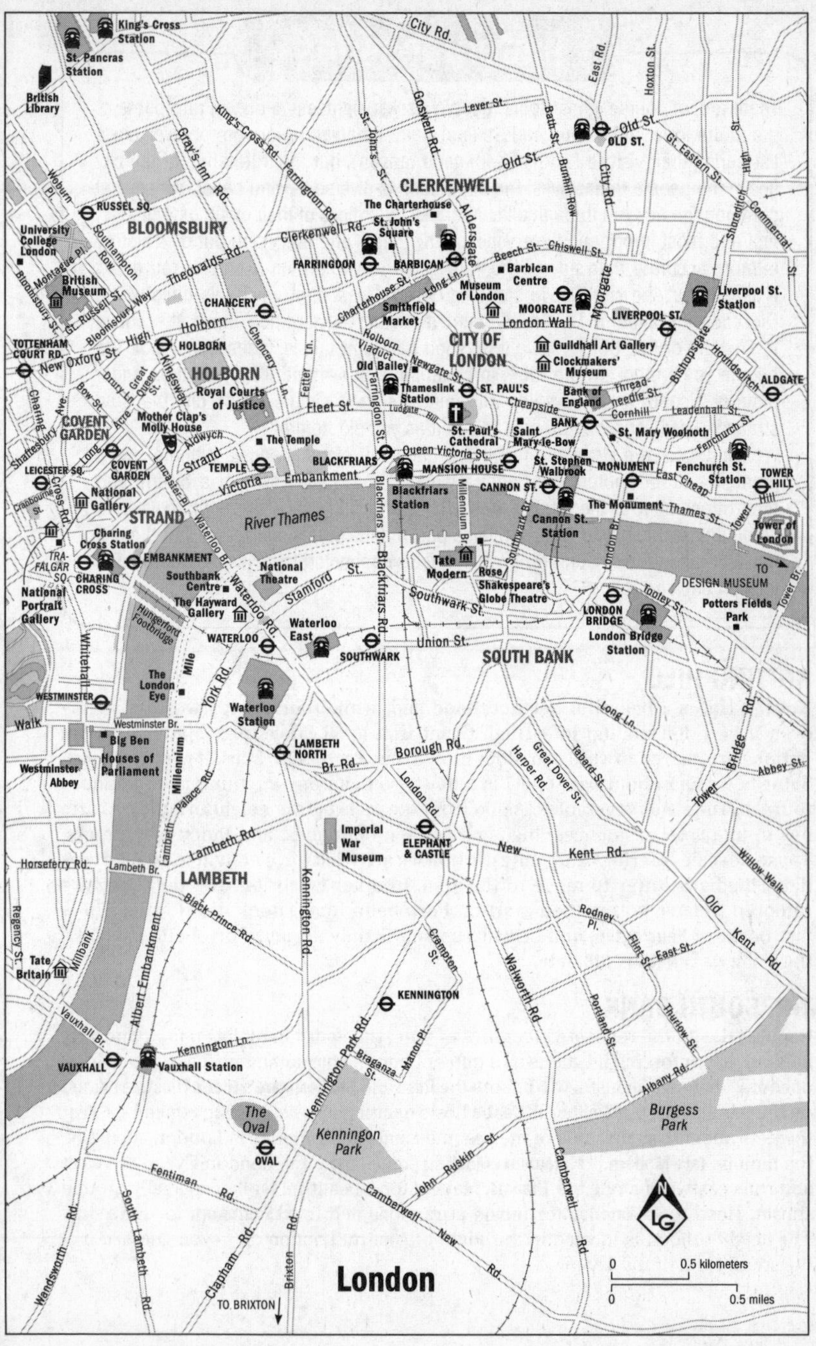
London
King's Cross Station
St. Pancras Station
British Library
City Rd.
East Rd.
Hoxton St.
Lever St.
Goswell Rd.
St. John's St.
King's Cross Rd.
Farringdon Rd.
Gray's Inn Rd.
Bath St.
Bunhill Row
City Rd.
OLD ST.
Old St.
Gt. Eastern St.
High St.
Shoreditch
Commercial St.
CLERKENWELL
The Charterhouse
St. John's Square
Aldersgate
Clerkenwell Rd.
FARRINGDON
BARBICAN
Beech St.
Chiswell St.
Barbican Centre
Woburn Pl.
RUSSEL SQ.
BLOOMSBURY
Southampton Row
University College London
Montague Pl.
Bloomsbury St.
British Museum
Gt. Russell St.
Bloomsbury Way
Theobalds Rd.
CHANCERY
Charterhouse St.
Long Ln.
Smithfield Market
Museum of London
MOORGATE
Moorgate
Liverpool St. Station
LIVERPOOL ST.
London Wall
CITY OF LONDON
Guildhall Art Gallery
Clockmakers' Museum
Bishopsgate
Houndsditch
ALDGATE
TOTTENHAM COURT RD.
New Oxford St.
High Holborn
HOLBORN
Kingsway
Chancery Ln.
Fetter Ln.
Holborn Viaduct
Newgate St.
Old Bailey
Thameslink Station
ST. PAUL'S
Bank of England
Threadneedle St.
Cheapside
Cornhill
Leadenhall St.
Charing Cross Rd.
Shaftesbury Ave.
Bow St.
Drury Ln.
Great Queen St.
HOLBORN
Royal Courts of Justice
Fleet St.
Farringdon St.
Ludgate Hill
COVENT GARDEN
Long Acre
Mother Clap's Molly House
Aldwych
The Temple
St. Paul's Cathedral
Saint Mary-le-Bow
BANK
St. Mary Woolnoth
Fenchurch St.
COVENT GARDEN
Strand
Lancaster Pl.
TEMPLE
BLACKFRIARS
Queen Victoria St.
MANSION HOUSE
St. Stephen Walbrook
MONUMENT
Fenchurch St. Station
TOWER HILL
LEICESTER SQ.
Cranbourne St.
National Gallery
Victoria Embankment
Blackfriars Station
CANNON ST.
East Cheap
The Monument
Thames St.
Tower Hill
STRAND
River Thames
Millennium Br.
Southwark Br.
London Br.
Cannon St. Station
Tower of London
Charing Cross Station
TRAFALGAR SQ.
EMBANKMENT
CHARING CROSS
Waterloo Br.
National Theatre
Stamford St.
Blackfriars Br.
Blackfriars Rd.
Tate Modern
Rose/Shakespeare's Globe Theatre
TO DESIGN MUSEUM
Tooley St.
Tower Br.
National Portrait Gallery
Southbank Centre
Waterloo Rd.
Southwark St.
LONDON BRIDGE
Potters Fields Park
The Hayward Gallery
Hungerford Footbridge
Waterloo East
WATERLOO
SOUTHWARK
Union St.
London Bridge Station
SOUTH BANK
Whitehall
The London Eye
Mile
York Rd.
Waterloo Station
WESTMINSTER
Walk
Westminster Br.
Big Ben
Houses of Parliament
Millennium
LAMBETH NORTH
Borough Rd.
Br. Rd.
Long Ln.
Great Dover St.
Tabard St.
Harper Rd.
Tower Bridge Rd.
Abbey St.
Westminster Abbey
Palace Rd.
Lambeth
London Rd.
Imperial War Museum
ELEPHANT & CASTLE
New Kent Rd.
Horseferry Rd.
Lambeth Br.
Lambeth Rd.
LAMBETH
Kennington Rd.
Willow Walk
Old Kent Rd.
Regency St.
Black Prince Rd.
Rodney Pl.
Flint St.
East St.
Millbank
Tate Britain
Albert Embankment
Crampton St.
Walworth Rd.
KENNINGTON
Portland St.
Thurlow St.
Vauxhall Br.
VAUXHALL
Vauxhall Station
Kennington Ln.
Kennington Park Rd.
Manor Pl.
Braganza St.
Albany Rd.
Burgess Park
The Oval
Kennington Park
John Ruskin St.
OVAL
Fentiman Rd.
Camberwell New Rd.
Camberwell Rd.
Wandsworth Rd.
South Lambeth Rd.
Clapham Rd.
Brixton Rd.
TO BRIXTON
N
LG
0
0.5 kilometers
0
0.5 miles

history lessons

There are, of course, ghost tours, double-decker sightseeing buses, and beefeaters at the Tower of London, and St. Paul's and Trafalgar Square are on everyone's list during their visit to London (with good reason), but the true fabric of the city lies in the people themselves. The population is diverse beyond belief, but several common threads run through all Londoners, regardless of their origin or language: first and most importantly, everyone is a historian, and every pub pundit's history is more accurate than any textbook or guide you'll find. An example: You didn't realize it, but the spot you're standing on now (yes, right now) was once where Dickens sold opium to Queen Elizabeth. It doesn't matter when, or whether you're in England or not, but we have it on good faith that this is, indeed, the spot. The people you'll meet on the Tube, in restaurants and–more likely–in pubs under pints of alcohol and heavy-lids will paint a slurred picture of the city that's so strangely vivid you won't be able to see it as you did before.

Londoners are doggedly persistent under all circumstances. Whether it's a grunting call for another beer after a World Cup bid goes awry or a bizarre and total attachment to the phrase "Keep Calm and Carry On," Londoners believe in continuity and consistency. It's in large part thanks to this conviction that the city has an authentic spirit and essence that feels connected to its history, rather than looking back on it.

NOTTING HILL

Notting Hill is a beautiful neighborhood and, while touristy, it's worth a visit—even if you don't bump into Hugh Grant in a local bookstore. Many shopping options are geared towards an older crowd, but Portobello Market (**Portobello Rd.**, Saturdays from about 6am-6pm) is a blast; you can buy anything from antiques to fresh fruits and vegetables. Aside from the market, the neighborhood's charm lies in its pastel residences, high-end fashion boutiques, and fancy restaurants. These upscale offerings and fantastic houses are what have convinced celebrities like Claudia Schiffer to move to the area. In other celebrity lore, the Clash are rumored to have gotten their start on Portobello Road. Rock on. Notting Hill is just north of **Kensington**, and organizes itself mainly around Portobello Rd. Take the Tube to **⊖Notting Hill Gate.**

THE SOUTH BANK

Populated with the renovated factories of yore, the South Bank has undergone a renaissance, reinforcing its status as a hub of London entertainment. This status does, of course, have some history to it: both the **Rose** and **Shakespeare's Globe Theatre** resided on the bank. Now, the **Southbank Centre** hosts exciting classical music concerts. Great theaters abound, as do some of the best museums and galleries in London, including the famous **Tate Modern.** **"Millennium Mile"** stretches from the London Eye in the west and runs eastward along the **Thames,** making for a beautiful walk, especially around sunset. Head to **⊖Waterloo** for inland attractions and to **⊖Southwark** for Bankside. The neighborhood is located in the south of Central London on —you guessed it—the south bank of the Thames.

THE WEST END

The West End is one of the largest, most exciting parts of London. Comprised of **Soho, Covent Garden, Mayfair and Saint James's,** and **Trafalgar Square,** the West End has some of the most affordable shopping in London, as well as arguably the city's best (free!) public museums, such as the **National Gallery,** and the **National Portrait Gallery,** among others. Known by many as the Broadway of London, the West End offers a host of excellent theater options close to Trafalgar Square, accessible by **⊖Charing Cross.**

Soho, most easily accessed via **⊖Tottenham Court Road** is one of the hipper and seedier parts of London. Home to one of the most prominent gay communities in London, Soho is teeming with nightlife for the GLBT and straight clubgoers alike. During the day, however, Soho is known for its excellent restaurants. **Chinatown** in particular offers many popular options. It's located off Gerrard St. and is easily accessed from Leicester Square or Piccadilly Circus. The **⊖Oxford Circus** Tube stop exits onto Regent St. which is one of the more famous and beautiful streets in London, and is home to many chains and famous shops. Most notable here are the gorgeous Apple store and the famous **Hamley's** toy store, which will help anyone rediscover their inner child.

Covent Garden (accessible via **⊖Covent Garden**—go figure!) is famous for its shops and the Covent Garden Piazza, recognizable from Hitchcock's *Frenzy* and the opening scene of *My Fair Lady.* Though no longer a Cockney flower market or a place where merchants burst spontaneously into song, Covent Garden is known for its rich history of street performers. One could spend a fulfilling trip in the West End only. It should be noted, however, that as the West End is a prime tourist location as well as a nightlife location, it can be quite dangerous. When going out, people should try to travel in groups and stick to the crowded, well-lit streets. If you get tired of walking on foot, you can also travel by rickshaw. Also note that false store fronts with paper signs inside advertising "model" or "girl" are poorly-concealed brothels. If taken in the right spirit, however, and with proper precautions, The West End's relative sketchiness only adds to its color. We prefer to think of it as Dickensian rather than depressing.

WESTMINSTER

After the City of London, Westminster lays claim to London's most famous sites. Between the **Houses of Parliament, Buckingham Palace,** and **Westminster Abbey** (as well as many of the modern centers of government), Westminster feels like the seat of the royal empire. Be warned that, outside of the sites, however, there isn't a lot to do. South of Victoria lies Pimlico, a residential neighborhood with several accommodation options, many of them on Belgrave Rd. The **⊖Westminster** Tube stop is near most sights, but exit at the **⊖Victoria** or **⊖Pimlico** stops if you're looking for hostels. Westminster is north of the **Thames** and West of **Belgravia** and **Pimlico**.

NORTH LONDON

North London is a sprawling expanse north of central London. **Hampstead** and **Camden Town** are the two most popular draws. Hampstead provides pleasant dining and a properly British small-town feel. It also offers the glorious and meandering **Heath,** a must for all nature-lovers. Camden was once punk central, but is now more upscale. Still worth a visit, it contains some underground culture and many upscale restaurants and boutiques. Hampstead is accessible via **⊖Hampstead** and **⊖Golders Green** on the northern line, and **⊖Hampstead Heath** via the **National Rail. Camden Town** is accessible on the **Northern Line.** Hampstead is just north of Camden.

SOUTH LONDON

South London has been maligned historically as one of London's dodgier neighborhoods. While the area has enjoyed something of a renaissance in recent years, it's still not as safe as many of the areas in London proper; **Clapham** is one of the best neighborhoods to find young professionals who patronize its pub and restaurant scene. Now a cultural center as well, Clapham houses the **Battersea Arts Centre,** renowned for its revolutionary productions. **Brixton** is less quaint than nearby Clapham. Bible-thumpers preach the Apocalypse from convenience store pulpits, and purveyors of all goods at the nearby Afro-Caribbean market make sales despite the overpowering smell of fish. Brixton is also a good place to be if you've been missing fast food. **Stockwell** and **Vauxhall** are less accessible and interesting than the other two neighborhoods in South London, but Vauxhall does claim the **City Farm** in the town park. The local underground stations in many of the southern neighborhoods play classical music, thought by many to be a tactic for keeping young people from accumulating in the Underground, *Clockwork Orange*-style. Access Clapham via **⊖Clapham North, ⊖Clapham Common** or **⊖Clapham South** or take the **National Rail** services to Clapham Junction. Brixton is accessible via **⊖Brixton** on the **Victoria Line,** and Stockwell can be easily reached via **⊖Stockwell.** Those looking to visit Dulwich can take the P4 bus from **⊖Brixton Station.** Vauxhall is southwest of the **City of London,** Clapham is south of Vauxhall, Brixton is east of Clapham and south of Stockwell.

EAST LONDON

East London, and especially the **East End,** is known for its cutting-edge galleries and its deliciously affordable markets and restaurants. The neighborhood has all of the spark and edge that **Chelsea** used to, and its massive immigrant community rounds out the culinary landscape nicely. **Brick Lane,** named after the brick kilns brought by Flemish immigrants and defined by the waves of Huguenot, French, Russian, Bengali, and Muslim immigrants who came after, is packed to the gills with fantastic and cheap ethnic cuisine as well as some of the most exciting and youthful nightlife in London. Further east, Greenwich features some of London's more famous sites. Use the **Docklands Light Railway (DLR)** to get to Greenwich, Old St., and Liverpool St. for the East End, **⊖Aldgate East** for Brick Lane.

WEST LONDON

West London is one of the more shape-shifting areas of London. **Shepherd's Bush** is a crush of ethnic life, which is evident in the varied restaurants lining **Goldhawk Road,** culminating in the veritable World's Fair that is **Shepherd's Bush Market.** Also unique to Shepherd's Bush is Westfield's, the 43-acre monument to shopping that makes American strip malls look like rinky-dink corner stores. It's essentially a shopping city, and one of those structures where a wavy ceiling constitutes a viable design aesthetic and makes a bold architectural statement. The name Shepherd's Bush is derived from a thorn tree that is deformed by shepherds lying in it while watching their flock. **Hammersmith** is removed from the bustle, feeling more like a seaside resort than a corner of London. The **Thames** provides many water views that would be impossible in the city proper. A good place for a good meal and a quiet day, **Kew** feels like rural London. It is, however, a bit touristy because of the gorgeous **Kew Gardens,** which is the world's largest collection of living plants. (*i Wheelchair-accessible. Ⓢ £13.50, concessions £11.50, under 17 free. ⏰ Open M-F 9:30am-6:30pm, Sa-Su 9:30am-7:30pm.*) Hammersmith is accessible via the **⊖Hammersmith and City Line** (last stop), and Shepherd's Bush is accessible via the **⊖Central Line.** Kew is on the **Richmond** branch of the **⊖District Line** and is the penultimate stop.

internet cafes

Many restaurants and cafes offer Wi-Fi, but there are a few surefire ways to get Internet in London.Travelling with a laptop has its challenges and its unexpected joys. No matter how heavy the computer, or how total the hard drive crash after your hostelmate spills beer and vodka, which he, for some reason, thought would "taste really good together, bro," few things compare to the thrill of finding cheap Internet somewhere other than the Internet cafe. Some sure bets include chains like Starbucks, but a true laptop adventurer won't stop there. Sure, you can hit up a Starbucks (and, if it has two floors like the one in Victoria Station, you can camp on the second floor for hours without anyone realizing you're there), but what happens after it closes? That's when you find the cheesiest, most touristy pub you can, and ask if they have Wi-Fi. If they do, you've got internet until 11pm or midnight, plus a killer soundtrack. If, however, that's just not your thing, www.easyinternetcafe.com allows users to search for nearby Internet cafes. Search London for a list of most internet cafes, and to add ratings.

accommodations

London is an infamously expensive city, and accommodations are no exception to this rule. The cheapest options are the city's hostels, and there are quite a few, especially in **Bloomsbury, Kensington,** and **Earl's Court** and **Bayswater** (extra emphasis on Bloomsbury). Travelers looking for long-term accommodations should look into rooms at the colleges. Those unwilling to stay in a hostel can stay in bed and breakfasts as they can offer the privacy and comfort of a hotel at close-to-hostel prices.

BAYSWATER

THE PAVILION — THEMED HOTEL ❺

34-36 Sussex Gardens — ☎020 7262 0905 www.pavilionhoteluk.com

All you really need to know about the Pavilion is that the most popular room is named "Honky Tonk Afro." Maybe you need to know more. No, the Pavilion is not a blaxploitation film, but rather a themed hotel with rooms ranging from '70s decor to a Casablanca theme. Many famous and half-naked celebrities have posed here and the hotel is often used by modeling companies.

 # ⊖Paddington. Left onto Praed St., right onto London St., left onto Sussex Gardens. i Continental breakfast delivered to your room. $ Small singles £60, large singles £85, doubles £100, triples £120, family (4 people) £130. 4% extra charge when you pay with a credit card.

ASTOR QUEST — HOSTEL ❷

45 Queensborough Terr. ☎020 7229 7782 www.astorhostels.com

A homey and friendly hostel with a chummy staff that lives on-sight. The rooms are par for the course in hostel-land, but everything is cleaned and beds are made with fresh sheets daily. Breakfast included and served in a room by the kitchen, which is freely available for use. Hostel-weary travelers have the unique experience of dining under Sid Vicious's drugged-out gaze. Be sure to ask the 24hr. receptionist for deals on clubs.

 # ⊖Bayswater. Take right onto Queensway, left onto Bayswater Rd., and left onto Queensborough Terr. i Age limit is 18-35. 4-bed dorms and twin rooms have shared bathroom. Free luggage storage. Padlocks £2. 1 female-only room available; 6 beds; £19. Laundry wash £2.50, dry £1. Check-out 10am. Check-in any time after 2pm. Hostel renovations should be completed in Jan 2011. $ 4-bed dorm £20, 8-bed £17.00, 6-bed with ensuite bathroom £19, 4-bed with ensuite £21.

HYDE PARK HOSTEL — HOSTEL ❶

2-6 Inverness Terr. ☎020 7727 9163 www.hydeparkhostel.net

Ramshackle glory seems a fitting description for this aging, battered but grand hostel. Ten-bed dorms have high ceilings with intricate woodwork and lots of open space. While it doesn't seem a particularly convivial hostel, the rooms are well-suited to a debauched weekend in the city. Shared bathrooms.

*Bayswater. Take right onto Queensway, left onto Bayswater and left onto Inverness Terr. **i** Must be above 18. 2-week max. stay. Wi-Fi £1 per hr. Lockers £1.50 per day. Free bed sheets are given daily upon request. 14-bed dorm £7.99, 4-bed £14, 6-bed £13, 8-bed £12.50, 12-bed £11, 10-bed £10, singles £40. Reception, kitchen, laundry, TV room 24hr.*

GARDEN COURT HOTEL — HOTEL ❹

30/31 Kensington Gardens Sq. ☎020 7229 2553 www.gardencourthotel.co.uk

The Garden Court Hotel offers a bed and breakfast level of comfort, cleanliness, and isolation within the bustle of London. The gardens make the Garden Court feel tucked away, but it is actually phenomenally close to Bayswater's attractions. The Garden Court has spacious and reasonably furnished rooms at a price. To save money, you may book a room without a bathroom.

*Bayswater. Left onto Queensway, left onto Porchester Gardens, right onto Kensington Gardens Sq. **i** Wi-Fi £1 per hr. Singles without facilities £49, with facilities £74; doubles without facilities £78, with facilities £119; triples with facilities £150; family with facilities £170.*

THE ADMIRAL HOTEL — HOTEL ❺

143 Sussex Gardens ☎020 7723 7309 www.admiral-hotel.com

Though the art lining the walls tries to be as suave and modern as the blue lights throughout the hotel, the presence of glitter in the paintings sort of ruins the effect. The rooms are modern and sophisticated and are spacious enough, well-furnished, and lit by large windows. The glass door in the lobby leads to a breakfast room where a picture of Sinatra hangs on the wall: yup, **Old Blue Eyes** in Britain.

*Paddington. Left onto Praed St., right onto London St., left onto Sussex Gardens. **i** Check-in at 139 Sussex Gardens. Singles £59-69, doubles £69-79, triples £89-99, quads £99-119.*

BLOOMSBURY

ASTORS MUSEUM HOSTEL — HOSTEL ❶

27 Montague St. ☎020 7580 5360 www.astorhostels.com

This is a true backpackers' hostel, quiet but centrally located. The incredibly friendly staff live on site and are always ready with a pub-crawl, a good song on the reception speakers, a discount on local sights, and themed parties once a week. Astors is welcoming, comfortable, and exciting all at once. The rooms are spacious and clean, the kitchen is open for guest use, and everything is cleaned at least once a day.

*Russell Square. Go down Guilford toward Russell Sq., turn left onto the square and follow it around until you reach Montague St. Turn left onto Montague St. **i** Continental breakfast included. Bring a padlock for the locker under the bed or borrow one with a £3 deposit and a £2 rental. Luggage storage free. Laundry £2.50 to wash, £0.50 dry. Wi-Fi throughout building, 40min. free upon arrival, £5 per day, £8 per week. Recommend that you book 2 weeks in advance and 3 weeks in advance for weekends. No ensuite rooms. 4-bed, 6-bed, 8-bed, 10-bed, and 12-bed dorms range £15-25, but prices vary. Double/twin £70 for 2 people per night, but price subject to change.*

GENERATOR HOSTEL — PARTY HOSTEL ❶

37 Tavistock Pl. ☎020 7388 7666 www.generatorhostels.com

Upon waking up in the Generator Hostel after a night of revelry, you may wonder if you forgot to leave the club. The likely answer is that you never went to a club but stayed in to partake in one of the hostel's nightly parties which occasionally feature DJs. Equipped with a bar open late and a 24hr. reception that plays 24hr. of music, the Generator is generating some very good times. The cafeteria-like common spaces and the fact that the staff doesn't live on-site prevents it from feeling homey, but the neon blue lights and steel panels make it look like a hell of a party. Plus, the money you save here will make your evenings just better.

Russell Sq. Go down Colonnade away from Russell Sq. and turn left onto Grenville St.; follow it onto Hunter St. and turn left onto Tavistock Pl. i Bring your own padlock. Laundry £2 wash, £0.50 per 10min. in dryers. Free Wi-Fi. No private baths. 4-6 bed dorms £20-25; 8-12 bed dorms £17.50-22.50. Singles £55-60; doubles £25-30; triples £17.50-25.00; quads £17.50-20. Call ahead as prices change. Bar open 6pm-2am. Happy hour 6-9pm.

CLINK 261 HOSTEL 1

265 Gray's Inn Rd. 020 7833 9400 www.ashleehouse.co.uk

If you dream of a hostel where every night is movie night (and the film is picked by majority vote and watched from comfortable pleather chairs), where cube chairs fill the entry, and where sleek, retro plastic coverings blanket every surface, then you have dreamed of quirky Clink 261. Centrally located in Bloomsbury, Clink 261 has style, relative grace, and clean and simple rooms that are well-suited to hostelgoers unwilling to commit to grungier options.

King's Cross/St. Pancras. Turn left onto Euston Rd. and follow it as it curves right into Gray's Inn Rd. i Continental breakfast included. Lockers free, but bring your own padlock. Luggage storage and linens included. The hostel is cleaned and fresh sheets are distributed daily. Laundry £2 wash, 50p per 20min. in the dryer. Wi-Fi £1 per 30min., £2 per hr., £5 per day. Rooms available in 18-bed, 10-bed, 8-bed, 6-bed, 4-bed and private. Shared bath. Dorms £18-25; private rooms £50-60. Call ahead for current prices. Breakfast M-F 7:30-9:30am, Sa-Su 8-10am. Free walking tour daily 10:10am.

YHA ST. PANCRAS HOSTEL 3

79-81 Euston Rd. 020 7388 9998 www.yha.org.uk

The large YHA is home to guests of all ages, making it feel more like a hotel than a hostel. YHA is clean, efficient, and very modern in its design. Decked out with a few classy lounges filled with books such as Chabon's *The Yiddish Policeman's Union*, YHA is a bit more institutional than the average hostel, but also a bit cleaner.

King's Cross/St. Pancras. Turn right onto Euston Rd. i The Meal Deal (breakfast basket and a hot snack) £5. Laundry £4.50. Wi-Fi access from lounges £5 per 24hr., £9 per week. 80% of rooms have ensuite bath. Only one room is wheelchair-accessible, so call ahead if you need to use it. Doubles £45-72; quads £79-127; quints £99-159; 6-person rooms £116-191. Breakfast 7:30-10:00am. Bar open 24hr., alcohol served until 1am.

THANET HOTEL HOTEL 4

8 Bedford Pl. 020 7636 2869 www.thanethotel.co.uk

The charm of this hotel lies in its proximity to the beautiful Russell Square Gardens. Rooms are clean and the hotel is quiet. Guests on the lower floors have views through windows that stretch to the ceilings, which in this hotel are quite high. Enjoy breakfast in the pleasant breakfast room decorated with blue and teal curtains and fresh flowers on every table. In short, Thanet is a family-run, budget hotel whose accommodations hardly feel budget.

Russell Square. Turn onto Guilford going toward Russell Sq. Turn left onto Russell Sq. and follow it around until you reach Bedford Pl. i Wi-Fi is not guaranteed in all rooms, but it is free. Singles £82; doubles £110; triples £135; quads £150 Breakfast M-Sa 7:45-9:15am, Su 8:30-9:30am.

THE GEORGE HOTEL 4

58-60 Cartwright Gdns 020 7387 8777 www.georgehotel.com

The rooms at the George are a bit old, but they're quite spacious and well furnished. In a secluded part of busy Bloomsbury, the George is a quiet and cozy hotel that'll keep you rested without keeping you away from the action. All 40 rooms have digital TV and tea and coffee machines. Also, there's a **fish tank.**

Russell Sq. Go down Colonnade away from Russell Sq. and turn left onto Grenville St.; follow it onto Hunter St. and turn left onto Cartwright Gdns. i Full English breakfast included. Free

Wi-Fi. Ⓢ Singles £55, with bath £75; doubles £68/89; triples £79/99; quads with bath £89. Discounts for stays longer than 5 nights. ⏰ Breakfast M-F 7:30-9am, Sa-Su 8-9:30am.

THE WARDONIA HOTEL — BUDGET HOTEL ❸

46-54 Argyle St. ☎020 7837 3944 www.wardoniahotel.com

Located close to King's Cross, the Wardonia offers Spartan accommodations for correspondingly low prices. Don't come here if you're looking for community or "luxury" amenities like breakfast.

*⊖King's Cross/St. Pancras. Cross Euston Rd. and go down Belgrove St. with your back to King's Cross. Turn right onto Argyle St. **i** Luggage room. Ensuite bath. TV in room. Ⓢ Singles £45; doubles £60-65; triples £80.*

CHELSEA

No longer a punk-rock haven, Chelsea is now overrun with Ferraris, Benzes, and Porsches, and the hotels have adjusted accordingly. Budget accommodations here are short-stay apartment rentals.

IES RESIDENCE HALLS — STUDENT RESIDENCE HALLS ❶

Manresa Rd. ☎020 7808 9200 www.iesreshall.com

Simple but highly affordable and value-packed (as Chelsea accommodations go), IES Residence Halls fill a large void in the Chelsea housing market, which is dominated by four- and five-star hotels. Three rooms share one spacious kitchen that has chairs, a table, a couch, and a fridge. The style is modern, the concept is simple, and the rates are low. Common rooms on each floor house a TV and the six RAs organize occasional events.

*⊖Sloane Sq. Exit the Tube and go straight down Sloane Sq. The street slanting gently left is King's Rd. If you don't want to walk the road (it's manageable but long), the following buses service the area: 11, 19, 22, 211, 319, right on Manresa Rd. **i** Laundry £2 for washer and £1.20 for soap, £1 dryer. No Wi-Fi, but ethernet in every room. Bathrooms cleaned once a week, kitchens cleaned twice a week. Bathrooms ensuite. Ⓢ 1-16 weeks, weekly rates: singles £331-397; twin shared £207. Rates for 16-36 weeks and 36-50 weeks also available. Daily rates: singles: £52.86, twin £58.75. ⏰ Security 24hr.*

SYDNEY HOUSE CHELSEA — LUXURY HOTEL ❹

9-11 Sydney St. ☎020 7376 7711 www.sydneyhousechelsea.com

A luxury hotel that's graceful rather than obnoxious. The rooms are beautiful and bright, all light wood and clean surfaces. The lobby contains a lovely tapestry and the common spaces are bedecked in cool modern paintings and sketches. The breakfast room is pleasant and lit by lights with a patterned surface that looks like the guys from Tron have been racing on it. Not exactly directed toward students, but a very pleasant, four-star hotel.

*⊖ Sloane Sq. Exit the Tube and go straight down Sloane Sq. The street slanting gently left is King's Rd., go onto it and turn right at Sydney St. **i** Breakfast of pastries, poilane bread, and coffee or tea £5.50. English breakfast £11. Everything is cleaned daily. Bathrooms ensuite. Ⓢ Prices change, but rooms range £150-295. Call in advance.*

THE SLOANE SQUARE — LUXURY HOTEL ❹

7-12 Sloane Sq. ☎020 7896 9988 www.sloanesquarehotel.co.uk

These rooms preside over gorgeous (and expensive) Sloane Square with elegance. If you're going for the luxury Sloane experience, might as well go all the way. This hotel provides some rooms with bay windows veiled by soft curtains and some with large bathtubs. They're well furnished and comfortable, each with a free locker, a laptop, and an iPod station. Pay for breakfast separately and enjoy it in the sleek breakfast room.

*⊖Sloane Sq. **i** Discounts at some local restaurants given. Wi-Fi £4.50 per 1hr., £14.99 per day. Ⓢ Singles £147; doubles £173; "superior" £214; club room £239. Rates exclusive of VAT; check online for weekend rates.*

CHELSEA CLOISTERS SHORT STAY APARTMENTS ❸

Sloane Ave. ☎020 7584 1002 www.chelseacloisters.co.uk

Though a bit old and worn, Chelsea Cloisters offers a viable alternative to the high-cost hotels that might otherwise prohibit a stay in Chelsea. The rooms are clean and efficient, each with its own kitchen and bathroom. It's not the swankiest or brightest building, but the apartments are clean and serviceable. Check carefully what you're paying before you book, as there are a few compulsory charges (cleaning and deposit) not included in the rates. Because of the deposits, it might be wise to book only for very long stays or for stays under a week, in which case no deposit is needed.

*Sloane Sq. Exit the Tube and go straight down Sloane Sq. The street slanting gently left is King's Rd., go onto it and turn right onto Sloane Ave. **i** Luggage room. BT Openzone vouchers (for Wi-Fi) sold at the desk; £40 per month, £27 per 5 days, £10 per 24hr. Book at least a week in advance. Ⓢ Compulsory 5-day maid service and linen change £58.75 for a studio, £70.50 for 1 bed, £82.25 for 2 beds. 1-week prices: standard studio apartment £53; large studio apartment £590; 1-bedroom apartment £785. 2-bedroom apartments: doubles and singles £1,025; doubles and twins £1,075. Deposit: studio £600; 1-bedroom £600; 2-bedroom £800.*

KENSINGTON AND EARL'S COURT

ASTOR HYDE PARK HOSTEL ❶

191 Queen's Gate ☎020 7581 0103 www.astorhostels.co.uk

Built in the 1800s as a grand Victorian House, the Astor Hyde Park was also a hotel once upon a time. The flagship among Astor Hostels, the Hyde Park location is all high ceilings, aged grandeur, and comfort. The hostel is very close to beautiful Hyde Park. The six-floor hostel has no maximum stay, but it's not meant for long-term stays. Everything is cleaned twice a day, and the kitchen is cleaned three times daily. Careful, though—backpackers subject to delusions of grandeur could easily mistake the other residents for servants in their personal mansion. The hostel keeps some of that old grandeur in the teas with live music and the spacious common room.

*High Street Kensington. Turn right onto Kensington High St., then turn right onto Queen's Gate. **i** Free linens and beds are made fresh daily. Laundry: washing machine £2.50, washing powder £1, dryer £1 per 40min. Lockers £1.50 per day, £7 per week. Free Wi-Fi. Coin-operated computers for those without laptops. Every room is ensuite, except 3- to 4-bed rooms, which still have private bathrooms. Ⓢ Winter prices around £15-20. Summer weekday dorm prices £20-£26; doubles £80 per night; twin £70. Weekend rates go up by £5 per dorm bed and £10 per double. Reception 24hr.*

VICARAGE HOTEL BED AND BREAKFAST ❹

10 Vicarage Gate ☎020 7229 4030 www.londonvicaragehotel.com

Posh and warm, the Vicarage Hotel provides an affordable experience of superb comfort. Each room is individually decorated, and the walls are bedecked with ornately framed, original paintings. The red-and-white-striped chairs on the landings are perfect reading chairs, and the rich red carpet only adds to the comfortable atmosphere of this simple B and B.

High Street Kensington. Turn right onto Kensington High St., left onto Kensington Church St., and continue straight onto Brunswick Gardens and right onto Vicarage Gate. Ⓢ Singles £56, with bath £95; doubles/twins £95, with bath £125; triples £120, with bath £160; quads £130, with bath £176. Reception 7:30am-7:30pm. Breakfast 7:30am-9am.

YHA EARL'S COURT LONDON HOSTEL ❷

38 Bolton Gdns. ☎020 7373 7083 www.yha.org.uk

In one of the pleasant in-between spaces of London which are central yet oddly removed, YHA Earl's Court London is a fairly spacious hostel which, despite its shared bathrooms, grants everyone their own space. Some of the rooms even have their own areas for storage. Frequented by families as well as backpackers, the hostel is welcoming and affordable.

West Brompton. Turn right on Old Brompton Rd., left onto Earl's Ct. Rd., right onto Bolton Gardens. Continental breakfast £2.95. Sheets are included, beds are made daily. Shared bathrooms. Laundry: washer, dryer, and detergent £4.50. Lockers in room, padlocks £3. Internet £5 per 24hr., £9 per week. Check ahead, but generally beds in singles sex 4-, 6-, and 10-bed dorms £20-24.50.

YHA LONDON HOLLAND PARK — HOSTEL ❷

20 Holland Wk. ☎020 7937 0748 www.yha.org.uk

A patchwork hostel of three buildings (one of which used to be a noble's house), the Holland Park YHA doesn't feel like a typical hostel. This bizarre otherness is furthered by its location at the rear of Holland Park, making it feel like a Park Ranger's office. The tranquil garden space, which features a fountain inhabited by fish and weird-looking duck-like creatures, is particularly peaceful when there's a classical music concert in the park. The Hostel frequently hosts school groups, but, despite the crowded rooms, for some it will be a welcome deviation from the norm.

High St. Kensington. Turn left onto Kensington High St. right down Holland Walk in Holland Park. Use night gate at the rear after 10pm as the park closes. Breakfast included. Free linens. Towels £4. Laundry: washer £1, dryer £.20 per 15min. drying cycle. Wi-Fi £1 per 20min., £3 per hr., £5 per 24hr., £9 per week. £21-27.50 per bed for adults; £16.50-21.50 for under 18. Breakfast 7:30-9:30am. Dinner is 5-8pm. Kitchen open until 10pm. 7-day max. stay.

OXFORD HOTEL — HOTEL ❸

16-18, 24 Penywern ☎020 7370 1161 www.the-oxford-hotel.com

A comfortable, simple hotel seconds away from the Tube, the Oxford Hotel provides amenities like fridges, LCD TVs, safes, and ensuite bathrooms with every room. The two breakfast rooms are bright yellow and pleasant. One is sometimes partially used to store luggage, and the other looks out onto a simple back patio with wooden stairs and a few chairs.

Earl's Court. Right onto Earl's Court, right onto Penywern. Reception is at 16-18 Penywern. Wi-Fi £5 per 3hr., £2 per 1hr., £8 per 5hr., £20 per 24hr. Luggage room £5 per day per room (to be used within reason). Singles £75; doubles/twins £85; triples £95; quads £105. Rates change, so check in closer to your stay. Reception 24hr.

BADEN-POWELL HOUSE (MEININGER HOSTEL) — HOSTEL ❷

65-67 Queen's Gate ☎020 7590 6900 www.meininger-hotels.com

A clean, simple urban hostel, the Baden-Powell House's Meininger Hostel is located close to the Tube. With a ping-pong table on the roof terrace and a foosball table in the lobby, you might not even need such easy access to the Tube to have a good time.

Gloucester Rd. Left onto Gloucester Rd. Right onto Queen's Gate.. Continental breakfast £5 per day. Laundry is £2.50 for washing and drying. Linens included. Each room has lockers. Free luggage room downstairs. Wi-Fi £1 per 20min., £5 per 24 hr., £8 per week. Dorms with shared facilities £15; max. 14-bed (coed) dorm £21; 14-bed-max. (single-sex) dorm £23; 3-to-8-bed £24. Singles £69; doubles £45. Breakfast M-F 7-10am, Sa-Su 7:30-11am.

KNIGHTSBRIDGE AND BELGRAVIA

MORGAN GUEST HOUSE — GUEST HOUSE ❷

120 Ebury St. ☎020 7730 2384 www.morganhouse.co.uk

This cozy guest house feels just like a home. Most rooms have a fireplace and all are clean and well decorated, occasionally decked out with chandeliers, huge mirrors, and fresh flowers. In the back, guests can enjoy a patio that's like the Secret Garden. For a pleasant budget stay in Belgravia, you could do worse than the Morgan Guest House.

Victoria. Turn left onto Buckingham Palace Rd. With your back to Buckingham Palace Rd., turn right onto Elizabeth, then left onto Ebury St. Singles £58; doubles £78, with bath £98; triples £98/138; quads with bath £148. Breakfast M-F 7:30-9am, Sa-Su 8-10am.

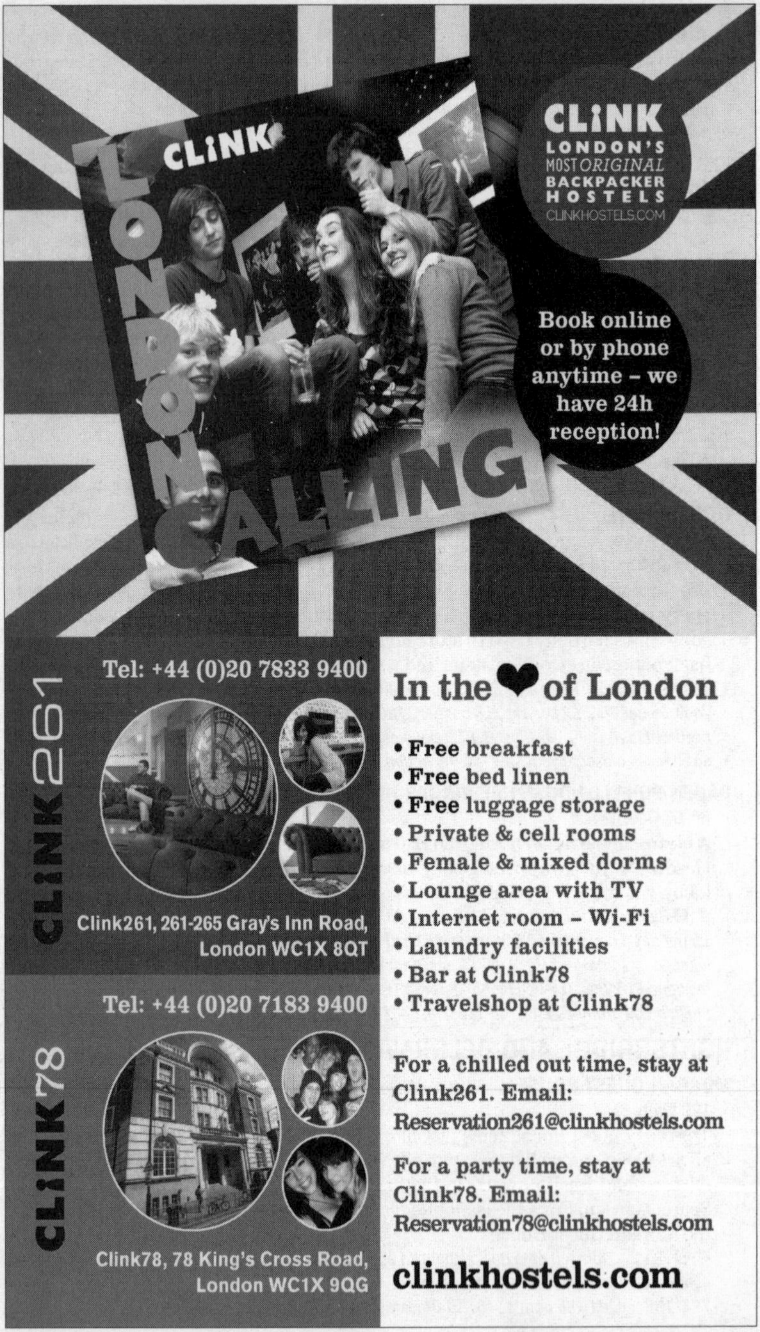
CLINK
LONDON CALLING
CLINK
LONDON'S
MOST ORIGINAL
BACKPACKER
HOSTELS
CLINKHOSTELS.COM
Book online or by phone anytime – we have 24h reception!
CLINK261
Tel: +44 (0)20 7833 9400
Clink261, 261-265 Gray's Inn Road, London WC1X 8QT
CLINK78
Tel: +44 (0)20 7183 9400
Clink78, 78 King's Cross Road, London WC1X 9QG
In the ❤ of London
• Free breakfast
• Free bed linen
• Free luggage storage
• Private & cell rooms
• Female & mixed dorms
• Lounge area with TV
• Internet room – Wi-Fi
• Laundry facilities
• Bar at Clink78
• Travelshop at Clink78
For a chilled out time, stay at Clink261. Email: Reservation261@clinkhostels.com
For a party time, stay at Clink78. Email: Reservation78@clinkhostels.com
clinkhostels.com

WEST END

FIELDING HOTEL

HOTEL ❸

4 Broad Court ☎020 7836 8305 www.thefieldinghotel.co.uk

Named after the novelist Henry Fielding, who worked next door at Bow St. Magistrate's Court where Oscar Wilde was later tried, the Fielding Hotel is located in pleasant Broad Court. A short walk from the Royal Opera House, the hotel is in one of the most exciting parts of town, but the Fielding doesn't use that as an excuse for poor rooms or exorbitant prices. Book a room at this comfortable, classy, well-located, and reasonably-priced hotel.

Covent Garden. Right onto Long Acre. Right onto Drury Ln. Right onto Broad Court. i Book around a month in advance. Singles £90; doubles £115.00; superior twins/doubles £140.00, with sitting room £160; suite (sleeps 3) £200. Rates do not include VAT. Call ahead because rates change.

YHA OXFORD ST.

HOSTEL ❶

14 Noel St. ☎020 7734 1618 oxford@yhalondon.org.uk

The big appeal of YHA Oxford St. is the location, with prime placement in the West End. There are prettier and friendlier accommodations in this city, but you can't complain about the price. Two washer-dryers service 76 beds, and the rooms begin on the third floor, with a battered lift as an alternative to the stairs; don't buy too much of the alcohol served behind reception, as you might not make it up.

Oxford Circus. Turn left down Regent St., left onto Noel St.. N13, N15, N18, N136, N159 available from the Oxford Circus Station Bus Stop. i 7-night max. stay. Wi-Fi: £1 per 20min., £5 per 24hr., £9 per 7 days, available in the lounge and some of the rooms. £1.60 for washing, 50p for a 15-20min. drying cycle. 3- to 4-bed dorms £23-32; doubles £56-76; triples £84-117. Alcohol served behind reception: Bottles of beer £2.10-2.75, Irish apple cider £3, Smirnoff Ice £2.85. Alcohol served 10am-11:30pm.

WESTMINSTER

ASTOR'S VICTORIA

HOSTEL ❸

71 Belgrave Rd. ☎020 7834 3077 www.hostelworld.com

A franchise in a chain, Astor's Victoria is especially popular with students. Rooms feel small and run-down but great to live in. Bathrooms are cleaned twice daily, and linens are changed daily. The walls are covered with friendly tips for travelers and low-cost (and specially discounted) outing opportunities. The staff hosts movie nights and pub crawls, and the hostel's excellent location only makes going out easier.

Victoria. Left onto Buckingham Palace Rd. Left on Belgrave Rd. i Breakfast included. Storage available. Personal safes £1.50. Wi-Fi £1 for 40min., £5 for 24hr. Common room open until 1am. Check-in after 2pm and before 8am. Check-out by 10am. Prices for rooms range wildly; call well in advance. Breakfast 8am-10am.

VICTOR HOTEL

HOTEL ❸

51 Belgrave Rd. ☎020 7592 9853 www.victorhotel.co.uk

A basic, clean, and—depending on the day—cheap hotel, the Victor is one of the many townhouse establishments lining Belgrave Rd. Boasting a convenient location near the heart of Westminster, the Victor provides well-kept rooms that, while not large, are not nearly as cramped as those of some of the hotels on the same street.

Victoria. Left onto Buckingham Palace Rd. Left onto Belgrave Rd. i All rooms have an ensuite bathroom. All room prices subject to change based on dates, season, and local events, so check online. Doubles M-F £75-85, Sa-Su up to £95. Reception 24hr.

london

NOTTING HILL

Notting Hill isn't an ideal place to find budget accommodations—although there are many beautiful residences, travelers short on funds aren't welcome to stay in many of them. Prices hover around £80-120 for doubles. Nearby Bayswater is a much better bet for the penny-pinching traveler.

BOWDEN COURT — HOSTEL ❷

24 Ladbroke Rd. ☎020 7727 5665 www.lhalondon.com

This four-floor hostel is just about the only budget-friendly option for people looking to stay in Notting Hill, but luckily, it's close to all the action. In the basement lies a clean and spacious dining room. The food is decent but not terribly healthy. Also in the basement are a laundry room, study room with computers, and TV room. Bathrooms are communal.

⊖Notting Hill Gate. Exit north, take a right onto Pembridge Rd., and turn left onto Ladbroke Rd. ***i*** *Lockers £1 per day, £3.50 per week, £10 per month. Washers £3; dryers £1. Ⓢ 2-bed dorms £25; 3-bed £23.50. Singles £28-29; doubles £52.00. Weekly 2-bed dorms £114; 3-beds £94.50. Weekly singles £159.50-179.50; doubles £250. ⏰ Breakfast M-F 7am-8:15am; Sa-Su and bank holidays 9:30-10:30am. Dinner M-F 6:30-8pm. Lunch Sa-Su and bank holidays 12:30-1:30pm.*

THE PORTOBELLO GOLD — HOTEL ❹

97 Portobello Rd. ☎020 7460 4910 www.portobellogold.com

Your life has been incomplete until you discover the Portobello Gold. While expensive, the Portobello Gold has such a good location that it might be worth it—not to mention access to a roof terrace complete with a putting green. Rooms are small but well kept. They might be noisy, since the pub is downstairs, but residents get a special fixed price menu at the pub, as well as an included continental breakfast. If you've come to London but don't actually want to leave your building, this is your deal.

Notting Hill Gate. Exit North, turn right onto Pembridge Rd. and left onto Portobello Rd. Doubles £80-£100; 4-poster bed, capacity to fit 3 mattresses on floor £135; apartment £180. Stay over 7 days and get a discounted rate.

THE ABBEY COURT HOTEL HOTEL ❺

20 Pembridge Gardens ☎020 7221 7518 www.abbeycourthotel.co.uk

If it's raining out—which is likely—cuddle up with a good book in a spacious, clean, and comfortable room at the Abbey Court Hotel. The centrally located and reasonably priced hotel boasts a sunlit breakfast room and a lavish lounge that feels properly British.

Notting Hill Gate. Exit South. Singles, doubles and four poster rooms available, but prices change on a regular basis, so be sure to call ahead.

THE GATE HOTEL ❹

6 Portobello Rd. ☎020 7221 0707 www.gatehotel.co.uk

At the top of busy Portobello Rd., The Gate enjoys the luxury of a centralized location, while maintaining the relative solitude of less active areas. The rooms are simple, with thick carpets and clean facilities.

Notting Hill Gate. Exit North, take right on Pembridge Rd., left onto Portobello Rd. i Wi-Fi £10 for your stay. Week rates/Weekend rates: Singles £60/70, doubles £85/95, doubles lux £95/105, triples £115/135.

NOTTING HILL HOTEL HOTEL ❸

2 Pembridge Sq. ☎020 7727 1316 www.nottinghillhotel.com

If you've been traveling for weeks and you are self-conscious about your body odor, stay here—the smell got here hours before you did, and no one will blame you for it. The only appealing thing about this place is its location; the rooms are in disrepair, and aren't that large. Still, if this is your only option, it's very close to the action on Notting Hill.

Notting Hill Gate. Exit North, take right on Pembridge Rd., turn right at Pembridge Sq. Notting Hill Hotel will be on your right. i Breakfast included. Midweek rates: singles from £50; doubles from £60; family rooms for 3 from £80. Weekend and holiday rates: singles from £55; doubles from £70; family rooms for 3 from £90.

sights

From the hints of the city's Roman past at the London Wall to the memories of WWII or the unforgettable Great Fire of London, London's long past has not only been documented in stone but also in its art scene, from the masterworks in the West End's National Gallery and the Tate Modern to the cutting edge galleries of Chelsea and the South Bank. And not to worry—this artistic splendor is totally accessible to travelers on a budget, especially those who carry their student IDs. When trying to see a church, look for service times, as you can frequently get in free during masses, Evensong, etc. If you can't afford to visit all of the sights individually, buy a ticket up to the top of St. Paul's—the view from the Golden Gallery is magnificent and the cathedral itself is worth every pence.

Don't limit your experience to the ticketed sights either. Once you realize that London's history is everywhere, you won't be able to escape it. No matter what path you choose, whether you're strolling down the winding lanes of Marylebone, ducking your way through the growth in Hampstead Heath, or navigating the thousands of roses in Regent's Park, your exploration will be rewarded. There is no wrong turn. Unless you're on the heath and you hear a strange growling noise to your left. In that case, a left turn may be the wrong turn.

BAYSWATER

SPEAKERS' CORNER — HISTORICAL SITE, PERFORMANCE SPACE

Hyde Park, Park Lane. London. W1K 1QB

This innocuous corner of Hyde Park is the stage for political, religious, and social debates. Speakers present ideas, challenge each other, and take questions from the audience. There are no set hours, and anyone is welcome to speak. Come watch free speech in action!

Lancaster Gate. Take left onto Bayswater Rd. Go in through Victoria Gate and continue left down Hyde Park. Stay close to Bayswater Rd. Free. Hours vary, but can be 9am-10pm in summer.

ALEXANDER FLEMING MUSEUM — MUSEUM

St. Mary's Hospital Praed St. — 020 7886 6528

Walk the same steps Alexander Fleming walked on the day in 1928 when he discovered Penicillin. The museum is small, but it successfully recreates the original conditions of the laboratory. Worth a visit if only to see the room where a discovery that completely changed the entire last century was made. Informative film and a room with facts about the discovery can be found upstairs.

Edgware Rd. Right on Chapel St. and continue onto Praed St. Look for St. Mary's. There will be a gate and a passageway. The museum is on your left with a picture of the petri dish in which penicillin was discovered. i Tours by request. £4, students and seniors £2. Open M-Th 10am-1pm.

SUBWAY GALLERY — GALLERY

Joe Strummer Subway — 078 1128 6503 www.subwaygallery.com

Bringing a new meaning to the term "underground art" (their joke), the Subway Gallery features installations from local artists often dealing with pop culture or music. Check the website for exhibit information. Exhibits change monthly. If you're in the area, it's definitely worth stopping by this very cool venue, but don't go out of your way to get here. And we wouldn't recommend traveling here at night.

Edgware Rd. Exit, take sharp right down Cabbell St., left before the flyover and then go down the stairs into Joe Strummer Subway. Free. Open M-Sa 11am-7pm.

concessions

The British word "concession" is the equivalent of the American "discount." It usually applies to fees for students, seniors, the unemployed with proof of unemployment and, sometimes, the disabled.

BLOOMSBURY

THE BRITISH MUSEUM — MUSEUM

Great Russell Street. — 020 7323 8299 www.british-museum.org

The funny thing about the British Museum is that there's almost nothing British in it. Founded in 1753 as the personal collection of Sir Hans Sloane, the museum juxtaposes Victorian Anglocentricism with more modern, multicultural acceptance. The building itself, in all its Neoclassical splendor, is magnificent; a leisurely stroll through the less crowded galleries is well worth an afternoon visit. The many visitors who don't make it past the main floor miss out—the galleries above and below are some of the museum's best, if not most famous.

The **Great Court** is the largest covered square in Europe, and has been used as the **British Library** stacks for the past 150 years. The blue chairs and desks of the **Reading Room,** set inside a towering dome of books, have shouldered the weight of research by Marx, Lenin, and Trotsky, as well as almost every major British writer and intellectual—and minor ones as well! From the main entrance, the large double doors to the left of the Reading Room lead to the Museum's most popular wing, the **West Galleries.** The **Rosetta Stone** takes center stage in the **Egyptian sculpture** rooms, while the less iconic but enduringly huge monumental friezes and reliefs of the Assyrian, Hittite, and other Ancient Near East civilizations are worth more than a glance. Most famous (and controversial) of the massive array of Greek sculptures on display are the **Elgin Marbles** from the Parthenon, statues carved under the direction of Athens's greatest sculptor, Phidias (Room 18). The Greek government technically bought the Marbles (albeit for a measly price). Other Hellenic highlights include remnants of two of the seven Wonders of the Ancient World: the **Temple of Artemis** at Ephesus and the **Mausoleum of Halikarnassos** (Rooms 21-22).

Upstairs, the **Portland Vase** presides over Roman ceramics and house wares (Room 70). When discovered in 1582, the vase had already been broken and reconstructed, and in 1845, it was shattered again by a drunk museum-goer. When it was put back together, 37 small chips were left over; two reconstructions have reincorporated more and more leftover chips, though some are still missing from the vase. Egyptian sarcophagi and mummies await in the **North Galleries** (rooms 61-66). The newer **African Galleries** display a fabulous collection accompanied by soft chanting, video displays, and abundant documentation (Room 25, lower floor). In Rooms 51-59, musical instruments and board games from the world's first city, Ur, show that leisure time is a historical constant, while Mexico dominates the **Americas** collection with extraordinary Aztec artifacts (Rooms 26-27). **Islamic** art resides in Room 34, and above it, the largest room in the museum holds **Chinese, South Asian,** and **Southeast Asian** artifacts alongside some particularly impressive Hindu sculpture (Room 33). The highlight of the Korean display, in Room 67, is a *sarangbang* house built on-site, while a tea house is the centerpiece of the **Japanese** galleries (Rooms 92-94).

In the **South and East Galleries,** the **King's Library** gallery holds artifacts gathered from throughout the world by English explorers during the **Enlightenment.** While the labeling is poor (and in some places nonexistent), the collection itself is spectacular. The upper level of the museum's southeast corner is dedicated to ancient and medieval Europe, and includes most of the museum's British artifacts. A highlight of the collection is the treasure excavated from the **Sutton Hoo Burial Ship;** the magnificent inlaid helmet is the most famous example of Anglo-Saxon craftsmanship. Along with the ship is the **Mildenhall Treasure,** a trove of brilliantly preserved Roman artifacts (Room 41). Next door are the enigmatic and beautiful **Lewis Chessmen,** an 800-year-old Scandinavian chess set mysteriously abandoned on Scotland's Outer Hebrides (Room 42). Collectors and enthusiasts will also enjoy the comprehensive **Clocks and Watches Gallery** (Rooms 38-39) and **Money Gallery** (Room 68).

⊖Tottenham Court Rd., Russell Square, or Holborn. ***i*** *Tours by request.* *Free. Small suggested donation. Prices for events and exhibitions vary.* *Museum open daily 10am-5:30pm. Select exhibitions and displays open Th and F until 8:30pm. Paul Hamlyn Library open M-W 10am-5:30pm, Th 10am-8:30pm, F noon-8:30pm, Sa 10am-7:30pm.*

THE BRITISH LIBRARY

♿ LIBRARY

96 Euston Rd. ☎020 7412 7676 www.bl.uk

Castigated during its long construction by traditionalists for being too modern and by moderns for being too traditional, the new British Library building (opened in 1998) now impresses all nay-sayers with its stunning interior. The 65,000 volumes of the King's Library, collected by George III and bequeathed to the nation in 1823 by his less bookish son, George IV, are displayed in a glass cube toward the rear. The sunken plaza out front features an enormous and somewhat strange statue of Newton, and also hosts a series of free concerts and events. The heart of the library is underground, with 12 million books on 200 miles of shelving; the above-ground brick building is home to cavernous reading rooms and an engrossing museum. In the **Literature Corner** of the museum, find **Shakespeare's** first folio, **Lewis Carroll's** handwritten manuscript of *Alice in Wonderland* (donated by Alice herself), and **Virginia Woolf's** handwritten notes to *Mrs. Dalloway* (then called *The Hours*). Music-lovers visiting the museum will appreciate **Handel's** handwritten *Messiah*, **Mozart's** marriage contract, **Beethoven's** tuning fork, and a whole display dedicated to the **Beatles,** including the original handwritten lyrics to "A Hard Day's Night"—scrawled on the back of Lennon's son Julian's first birthday card. In the museum, the original copy of the **Magna Carta** has its own room with accompanying Papal Bull that Pope Innocent III wrote in response. **Leonardo da Vinci's** notebooks are in the **Science** section, while one of 50 known **Gutenberg Bibles** is in the **Printing** section.

⊖Euston Sq. or King's Cross St. Pancras. i Free Wi-Fi. To register for use of reading room, bring 2 forms of ID—1 with a signature and 1 with a home address. Open M 9:30am-6pm, Tu 9:30am-8pm, W-F 9:30am-6pm, Sa 9:30am-5pm, Su 11am-5pm. Group tours (up to 15 people) Tu and Th at 10:30am and 2:30pm, £85 per group; call ☎ 020 7412 7639 to book. Individual tours M, W, and F 11am, free; booking recommended; call ☎ 019 3754 6546 to book.

the many haunts of london

If you believe all the stories, London is absolutely infested with ghosts. From the Tower of London to the Underground, here are some of the more interesting ghouls:

- **BACON'S CHICKEN:** Near the spot where Francis Bacon first put his idea of refrigeration to the test, a featherless, panicky chicken phantom, presumably the thing he refrigerated, has been known to roam.
- **THE PHARAOH IN THE TUBE:** The British Museum once had a Tube stop of the same name. However, it closed down in 1933, and if you believe the rumors, the reason was the presence of an escaped museum Egyptian. And that's not the end of the story—later, the comedy/thriller film *Bulldog Jack* included a secret tunnel from the station to the Egyptian room at the museum. The very night the film was released, two women disappeared from Holborn, the next station over from where the British Museum stop used to be.
- **THE SUBTERRANEANS:** Though not technically a ghost story, it's still disturbing: the idea that a group of Londoners who took to living in the subway tunnels have since mutated into half-wild humans who eat discarded junk food and the occasional solo traveler.
- **WAX PHANTOMS:** The Chamber of Horrors at Madame Tussaude's Wax Museum, which boasts replicas of dictators and the decapitated, is regularly reported to be haunted by the spirits of the models (as if a room full of bloody wax heads isn't creepy enough). Some say the perfectly coiffed hair on the wax head of Hitler grows noticeably!

CHELSEA

SAATCHI ART GALLERY — ♿ ART GALLERY

Duke of York Sq. ☎020 7811 3085 www.saatchigallery.co.uk

It's rare to find a free gallery of this caliber. The rooms are cavernous and bright, providing ample space for each installation. The gallery focuses on contemporary art, all taken from Charles Saatchi's collection. If you see something you really like, be sure to check out the shop where many of the works are condensed into pocket-sized forms. There are 3-4 shows a year, and the pieces run the gamut from paintings, to sculptures, to really frightening installations of plaster people hunched in corners. If you really want to experience the Saatchi Gallery, stand next to one of the wax/plaster humanoid sculptures and argue with it. Sure, it's weird, but is it art?

Sloane Sq. Go straight once out of the Tube and continue onto King's Rd. Free as the wind. Open M-F 10am-5:50pm, Su-Sa 10am-5:45pm.

CHELSEA PHYSIC GARDENS BOTANICAL GARDENS

66 Royal Hospital Rd. ☎020 7352 5646 www.chelseaphysicgarden.co.uk

The physic gardens are some of the oldest botanic gardens in Europe. Established in 1673 by a society of apothecaries, the gardens contain pharmaceutical and perfumery plant beds, tropical plant greenhouses, Europe's oldest rock garden, and a total of 5,000 different plants. The garden was also important to the establishment of the tea industry in India, but apart from that, they're simply beautiful, peaceful, and well worth a visit.

Sloane Sq. Left onto Lower Sloane St.; right onto Royal Hospital Rd. i Call ahead to arrange wheelchair-accessible visits. Free guided tours, depending on availability of guides. £8, children, students, and the unemployed £5, under 5 free. Open Apr 1-Oct 31 W-F noon-5pm, Su noon-6pm.

CHELSEA OLD CHURCH HISTORIC CHURCH

64 Cheyne Walk ☎020 7795 1019 www.chelseaoldchurch.org.uk

Though this church was bombed like so many others in 1941, the story of its rebuilding is slightly different than most; parishioners simply picked up many of the pieces of destroyed plaques and monuments and put them back together, with the cracks and rough edges serving as delicate reminders of the war. The church has also played host to several celebrity worshippers. Henry VIII is rumored to have married Jane Seymour here, while Queen Elizabeth I, "Bloody" Mary, and Lady Jane Gray, the nine-day queen, worshipped here. Henry James also frequented the church, and Thomas More prayed in the chapel that is named after him. In 1958, the church was reconsecrated and opened by the Queen Mother. This quiet, removed church isn't an obvious sight, but it rewards those willing to look closely.

Sloane Sq. Left onto Lower Sloane St., right onto Royal Hospital Rd., and right onto Cheyne Walk. i Wheelchair-accessible. Free. Open Tu-Th 2-4pm, Su open for services: Holy Communion 8am, children's service 10am, mattins 11am.

ST. LUKE'S GARDENS PARK

Sydney St.

Only one street removed from the bustle of King's Rd., St. Luke's Gardens feels a world apart. Rose gardens of pink, red, white, and yellow fragrant roses arranged in open circles flourish in the summer, lending a sweet fragrance to the whole park. A large mulberry tree in the center of the park casts a shadow over the benches arranged in a semi-circle around it. On the side of the park sits St. Luke's, a magnificent Gothic church. As it is in a quiet part of town, the park can be safely enjoyed while it's light out.

Sloane Sq. Go down King's Rd. away from the Tube. Take a right onto Sydney St. Open daily 7:30am-dusk.

NATIONAL ARMY MUSEUM MUSEUM GALLERY

Royal Hospital Rd. ☎020 7730 0717 www.nam.ac.uk

Yet another museum with far too many plaster-people for its own good, the National Army Museum answers the question on everybody's mind: what are British soldiers wearing? There are funny hats galore, and the museum is packed with information on British military conquests, even if most of it is directed toward a younger audience. The true gems of this museum are W. Siborn's expansive, 420 sq. ft., 172-year-old model of the battle of Waterloo, and the skeleton of Marengo, Napoleon's favorite horse. Of course, there's the colo(u)ring station and the guns that you can "load" and "fire," but if you want to see what a real gun is like, you might have to wrestle one off an **actual guard.**

Sloane Sq. Left onto Lower Sloane St., right onto Royal Hospital Rd. i There is also an art gallery. Free. Open daily 10am-5:30pm.

GAGLIARDI ART GALLERY

ART GALLERY

509 King's Rd. ☎020 7352 3663 www.gagliardi.org

Run by the Gagliardi family, the gallery showcases contemporary artists painting in styles that include abstract, Surrealist, figurative, and landscapes, among others. Works on display range from the late 20th century to the early 21st century. All the art is for sale and goes for about half as much as it would in the galleries on the West End.

Sloane Sq. Exit the Tube and go straight down Sloane Sq. The street slanting gently left is King's Rd. If you don't want to walk the road (it's manageable but long), the following buses service the area: 11, 19, 22, 211, 319. Open daily 1-7pm.

FLYING COLOURS

ART GALLERY

6 Burnsall St. ☎020 7351 5558 www.flyingcoloursgallery.com

When most people commemorate their trip to London, they buy Big Ben keychains, squeezable Teddy Bears that bark "Mind the gap!" and, for those Americans between 17 and 21, Svedka in the duty-free. If you want to step up your souvenir purchasing, check out Flying Colours. All the art is contemporary British, with a specialty in Scottish painting. Exhibitions change once a month. Even if you aren't going to buy, the paintings are still worth seeing.

Sloane Sq. Go down King's Rd. away from the Tube. Take a right onto Burnsall St. Open M-F 10:30am-5:30pm.

london

HOLBORN AND CLERKENWELL

THE TEMPLE

SIGHT

Between Essex St. and Temple Ave. ☎020 7427 4820 www.templechurch.com, www.middletemple.org.uk

The Temple was a complex of buildings established by the Knights Templar, catapulted into stardom by *The Da Vinci Code*. Established as the English seat for the order in 1185, the buildings were leased to lawyers after the order ended in 1307, and the site is now devoted to legal and parliamentary offices. The medieval church, gardens, and Middle Temple Hall are open to the public. The 1681 Fountain Court is a place for peaceful reflection and was featured in Dickens's *Martin Chizzlewit*. Also beautiful is Elm Court, the small garden enclosed by stone structures. Originally used as a stable for the Knights Templar, Middle Temple Hall became a bit more distinguished later when Shakespeare acted in the premiere of *Twelfth Night* there. This historic building—which survived WWII—is an excellent example of 16th- and 17th-century Elizabethan architecture with its beautiful double hammer beam roof. On the night of his return from the Spanish Indies in 1586, Sir Francis Drake came to Middle Temple Hall. Today, the temple houses a table known as the "Cup-board" made from the hatch of his ship.

Temple. Go to the Victoria Embankment, turn left and turn left at Temple Ln. i 1hr. tours T-F at 11am (but not in Aug and Sept when the church is closed); book tours ahead of time. You can book to stay for lunch if you are appropriately dressed. Church and tours free. Middle Temple Hall open M-F 10am-noon and 3-4pm, except when in use. Su service 11:15am. Hours for church vary, but are posted oustide. Organ recitals W 1:15-1:45pm. No services in Aug and Sept.

ROYAL COURTS OF JUSTICE

♿ SIGHT

Where Strand becomes Fleet St. ☎020 7947 7684

This stunning Neo-Gothic structure was designed by G.E. Street and was opened by Queen Victoria on December 4, 1882. It is home to more than 1000 rooms, and 3.5 mi. of corridor. Justice had better be pretty swift with all the walking it takes to get anywhere in this building. Supposedly, a tributary of the Fleet River, the namesake of Fleet St., runs beneath the building. It is also famous for its large and beautiful mosaic. Guests can sit in the back two rows of the court rooms and listen to the proceedings if court is in session. Order!

⊖Temple. Right onto Temple Pl., left onto Arundel st., right onto Strand. i There is a sign with wheelchair accessibility and routes in the entrance to the main building off the Strand. $ Tours (usually on 1st and 3rd Tu of every month) £10; should be booked in advance. ⏰ Open M-F 9am-4:30pm.

ST. JOHN'S SQUARE

♿ SIGHT, MUSEUM

St. John's Ln. ☎020 7324 4005 www.sja.org.uk/museum

This was originally the site of the 12th-century Priory of St. John, former seat of the Knights Hospitallers. The foundation of a round church in the Norman style, built by the Order of St. John, is marked in the square by gray cobblestones. The crypt of the original church is still intact and was probably used as a chapter hall for the early order. William Weston, the last prior, who"died of a broken heart" in the face of the dissolution, has an effigy in the crypt, near an effigy of a Spanish knight of the order who died in 1575 sculpted by famous sculptor Esteban Jordan. The crypt is one of the few surviving examples of Norman architecture in London and is well worth seeing. The fantastic gate which guards the square was originally built in 1504 as the entrance to the priory. (Shakespeare had his plays licensed by the master of the revels at the priory, and William Hogarth lived in the gate, where his father ran a Latin-only cafe.) The order of St. John bought back the gate in 1874, and the modern order of St. John has been an order of chivalry headed by Her Majesty since 1888.

⊖Farringdon. Left onto Cowcross St., left onto St. John St., left onto St. Johns Ln. $ Free. ⏰ The museum will be finished in fall 2011. Hours to be determined. Check the website. Tours will reopen in Sept.

mind the doors

In many other countries, the train doors for Underground equivalents are pushovers. If you're having a bad hair day and your sleeve is caught in the sensor, the train won't go anywhere. However, things are different in England, and the Brits' gentility is not shared by their train doors. If you try and get on a packed train as the doors are closing, you may wind up leaving your bag and half a limb behind you.

THE CHARTERHOUSE

♿ SIGHT

North on Charterhouse Sq. ☎020 7253 9503 www.thecharterhouse.org

Built by Thomas Sutton in 1611 on a burial ground for victims of the Black Death, the Charterhouse was a widely acclaimed school and home for the elderly. While the school moved elsewhere, it remains a functional senior-citizens home. In 1371, it was a Carthusian priory, but its religious functions were expunged during the Reformation. Elizabeth I stayed at the Charterhouse immediately prior to her coronation.

⊖Barbican. Left onto Carthusian St., right onto Charterhouse Sq. i Partially wheelchair-accessible. $ Tour £10; Apr-Aug W at 2:15pm; must be booked in advance. To book, send a letter with 3 dates and a check to "Charterhouse." Include a contact number and a self-addressed envelope. Send to Tour Bookings Charterhouse Sutton's Hospital, Charterhouse Sq., London EC1M 6AN.

KENSINGTON AND EARL'S COURT

VICTORIA AND ALBERT MUSEUM — GALLERY MUSEUM

Cromwell Rd. ☎020 7942 2000 www.vam.ac.uk

The V and A is one of the most bizarre and all-encompassing museums out there. Originally founded because the director, Henry Cole, wanted to promote different design ideas to the British public, the V and A has examples of styles from all around the world and is as much about the making of things as it is about the artifacts themselves. The many galleries include **Asia, Europe, The British Galleries, Modern,** and **The Fashion Gallery.** With such specific topics, who could possibly be interested in the collections? The **Asia** gallery features everything from ornate, gold Buddhist shrines to traditional suits of armor. Especially popular is the beautiful Iranian Ardabil Carpet, which is lit for 10min. every hour. The **Europe** gallery features the gorgeous Hereford Screen, which is 11m long and 10.5m high, and depicts Christ's Ascension. The British Galleries showcase the ever-popular Great Bed of Ware, which, for a bed, was a remarkably big deal back in 1596 when the first mention of it was made. The **Materials and Techniques** gallery details different techniques of art-making. The stained glass collection on the 3rd floor is not to be missed, nor are sketches by Matisse. Those looking for education on the arts or art-making can find it in the **Lecture Theatre** or the famous **National Art Library,** which houses some of Dickens's manuscripts and da Vinci's sketches (register online to see these). When you enter the main rotunda, be sure to look out for the Rotunda Chandelier by Dale Chihuly. It's pretty hard to miss.

South Kensington. Take a right onto Thurloe Pl. and turn left on Exhibition Rd. The museum is to your right across Cromwell Rd. i Wheelchair-accessible guides available at the Grand Entrance Information Desk. Exhibit on "Diaghileu and the Golden Age of the Ballets Russes 1909-1929" from Sept 25-Jan 9. Free, with the exception of the special exhibitions which are generally £6-£10. Open M-Th 10am-5:45pm, F 10am-10pm, Sa-Su 10am-5:45pm. National Art Library Tu-Th 10am-5:30pm, F 10am-6:30pm, Sa 10am-5:30pm. Free daily tours available; look at screens in entrances for times.

SCIENCE MUSEUM — MUSEUM

Exhibition Rd., South Kensington ☎087 0870 4868 www.sciencemuseum.org.uk

The Science Museum is an exciting look at the history and cutting edge of the discipline. Featuring tons of cool, interactive displays (granted, many of these are directed at children), the Science Museum has myriad valuable and historic artifacts from all areas of science; including many that you won't even realize you wanted to see until you've seen them. A Newcomen-type atmospheric engine dwarfs its surroundings in the Energy Gallery, and the space galleries remind visitors of all ages of the excitement of space travel through their history of rockets and artifacts like a V2 Engine from 1944, and things like wrist watches used on the Apollo missions. Learn about Charles Babbage English, the man responsible for mechanical calculators and shoes for walking on water (conspiracy theorists will be disappointed once reminded that he lived long after Jesus). And if you were wondering what an inventor's brain looks like (we hope this isn't on your mind), they have one in a **jar!** Charles Babbage English's, in fact. If you want to appreciate how far we've come, pay ERNIE 1 a visit. The Electronic Random Number Indicator Equipment computer is the size of most dorm rooms, and was used to generate random numbers so premium bond owners could win prizes. From brains in jars to men on the moon, the Science Museum has it all.

South Kensington. Take a right onto Thurloe Pl. and turn left onto Exhibition Rd. The museum is to your left just past the Natural History Museum. i A climate change exhibit will open in Nov. The museum also features a popular IMAX cinema. Tickets to IMAX 3D shows £8, children £6.25. Concession £6.25. Open daily 10:00am-6:0pm. Last admission at 5:30pm, but it starts closing at 5:40pm.

ST. MARY ABBOTS — CHURCH

High St. Kensington ☎020 7937 5136 www.stmaryabbotschurch.org

This gorgeous and silent church sits on a site where Christians have worshipped for 1000 years. Designed in 1873 by a famous Victorian architect, Sir George Gilbert, the church is known for its beautiful and simple stained glass by Clayton and Bell and the scorch marks of the 1944 bombing that are visible in the pews. Fridays from 1-2pm musicians from the Royal Academy of Music perform for free.

High St. Kensington. Right onto Kensington High St., left onto Kensington Church St. M 8:30am-6pm, Tu 8:30am-6pm, W-F 7:10am-6pm, Sa 9:40am-6pm, Su 8am-6pm.

church concerts

For free access to churches, be on the lookout for services and concerts. St. Paul's (p. 41) gives free organ recitals every Sunday from 4:45-5:15pm, as does St. Stephen Walbrook (p. 47) on Fridays at 12:30pm, but access to that church is already free.

NATURAL HISTORY MUSEUM — MUSEUM

Cromwell Road ☎020 7942 5011 www.nhm.ac.uk

Sure, the museum may be more directed at kids, but who doesn't love a moving T-Rex? Known as the "Cathedral of the Animals," the Natural History Museum houses exhibitions on everything from animal anatomy to histories of scientific research. The Darwin Centre has more than 20 million species in jars. Dinosaurs rule the museum, and the moving T-Rex is especially popular. Watch the parents' faces as they unwittingly lead their kids into the Human Biology section, featuring a red-lit walk-in womb (Freud would have a field day) with a terrifyingly large fetus, and aptly entitled "MORE ABOUT THE PLACENTA." The museum is pretty simple and easy to navigate, so come for a low-investment, reasonable-return trip.

South Kensington. Take a right onto Thurloe Pl. and turn left on Exhibition Rd. The museum is to your left across Cromwell Rd. i Book early for special tours of Darwin's special collections. Free. Special exhibits are around £8, and students get discounts. Open daily 10am-5:50pm. Last entry 5:30pm.

KNIGHTSBRIDGE AND BELGRAVIA

APSLEY HOUSE — HISTORICAL SIGHT, MUSEUM GALLERY

Hyde Park Corner ☎020 7499 5676 www.english-heritage.org.uk

Named for Baron Apsley, the house later known as "No.1, London" was bought in 1817 by the Duke of Wellington, whose heirs still occupy a modest suite on the top floor. The house is a stunning architectural triumph, from the gilded mirrors to the gilded oval spiral staircase. Perhaps the most fantastic of all the valuable collections in the house is Wellington's art collection, much of which he received from monarchs around Europe after the Battle of Waterloo. One of the most sought after pieces is Velazquez's beautiful *The Water-Seller of Seville,* which he painted in 1600. Throughout the house you can find various trinkets, such as a silver-gilt dessert plate bearing Napoleon's arms, the key to the city of Pamplona (granted after the Duke captured the city), the death masks of Wellington and Napoleon, and a stunning 6.7m Egyptian service set, given by Napoleon to Josephine as a divorce present. Scholars maintain that the dessert service was meant as a mean joke about Josephine's weight. It's huge.

Hyde Park Corner. i Arch is wheelchair-accessible; house is not. Complimentary audio tours. June 18th is Wellington Day, so check for special events. £6, joint ticket with Wellington Arch £7.40, concessions £5.10, concession joint with Wellington Arch £6.30; children £3, joint £3.70; family joint £18.50. Open W-Su Apr-Oct 11am-5pm; Nov-Mar 11am-4pm. Last entry 30min. before close.

SERPENTINE BOATING LAKE — LAKE BOATING

Hyde Park ☎020 7262 1330 www.theboathouselondon.co.uk

Created in memory of Queen Caroline between 1727 and 1731, the Serpentine Boating Lake is one of the most beautiful parts of Hyde Park. Rented boats drift lazily across the placid waters as fat waterfowl battle it out on the shore for pieces of bread. Boats can be rented and taken out for any amount of time. Be sure to check out the nearby Rose Garden.

Hyde Park Corner. Hyde Park. Pedal boats and row boats £7 per person per 30min., £9 per person per hr. Open daily 10am-6pm (earlier in low season). Stays open later depending on weather. Boats don't go out if it's raining. Closed in Dec.

THE WELLINGTON ARCH — HISTORICAL SIGHT

Hyde Park Corner ☎020 7930 2726

Commissioned by King George IV and built between 1828 and 1830 as a back gate to Buckingham Palace, the Wellington Arch is a famous London landmark. Visitors are treated to a history of the arch, which doesn't quite merit the cost, and then a reasonable view from the observation deck, which is more or less tree-level with Hyde Park. The arch was originally topped with a large statue of the Duke of Wellington, but he was taken down in 1883. In 1912, a new statue took its place. The current statue is Quadriga, the angel of Peace, descending on the chariot of war driven by youth. It's an interesting commentary on British society's evolution, but the exhibition and view are most worth it if you also get the well-priced joint ticket with the Apsley House.

Hyde Park Corner. Adult £3.70, joint ticket with Apsley House £7.40. Concessions £3.10, concession joint with Wellington Arch £6.30; child £1.90, joint £3.70; family joint £18.50. Open W-Su Apr-Sept 10am-5pm; Oct-Mar 10am-4pm. Last entry 30min. before close.

BROMPTON ORATORY — CHURCH

Brompton Rd. ☎020 7808 0900 www.bromptonoratory.com

Built between 1880 and 1884, the Brompton Oratory is named after its founders, the Oratorians. Its nave, wider than St. Paul's, is breathtaking. The architecture of this still-functional church is marble-packed and filled with Baroque flourishes, as well as Soviet secrets: the KGB used the oratory as a drop point for secret messages during the Cold War.

Knightsbridge. Left onto Brompton Rd. i Wheelchair-accessible at side entrance to the left of the church. Free. Open M-Su 6:30am-8pm. Services: M-F mass at 7am, 8am, 10am, 12:30pm, 6pm (Latin), Sa 7am, 8am, 10am, 6pm.

london

MARYLEBONE AND REGENT'S PARK

THE REGENT'S PARK — PARK

Regent's Park ☎020 7486 7905 www.royalparks.org.uk

In 1811, the Prince Regent commissioned the parks as private gardens, and hired **John Nash** to design them. However, in 1841, the parks were opened to the public, and the city lives all the better for it. Locals, pigeons, thirty couples of herons, and tourists alike frolic among the 10,000 wild flowers and 50 acres of pitches and courts. **Queen Mary's Garden** houses the national collection of delphiniums as well as a gorgeous collection of 30,000 roses. It is also home to an interesting strain of pink flower known as **Sexy Rexy.** The park's popular open-air theater is the setting for all kinds of shows, the screams from the more dramatic performances intermingling with those of children deprived too long of **ice cream.** The Gardens of **St. John's Lodge** are behind one of the eight villas on the park, and serve as a place for quiet meditation beneath the gorgeous latticed archways—a sort of secret garden which also affords a peek into the back of St. John's Lodge. Be aware that security's tight. Also, be sure to check if the grass is greener on his side of the fence. The **Winfield House** just off the outer circle is the home of the US ambassador.

⊖Regent's Park. i Call ☎020 7486 8117 for information on the deck chairs. Book plays through www.openairtheatre.com. $ Deck chair £1.50 per hr., £4 per 3hr., £7 per 1 day. Boats £6.50 per 1hr., £4.85 per 1½hr. Park open daily 5am-dusk. Boating lake open Mar-Oct 10:30am-7pm.

THE WALLACE COLLECTION — ♿ GALLERY

Manchester Sq. ☎030 7563 9552 www.wallacecollection.org

Housed in the palatial **Hereford House,** the Wallace Collection features an array of paintings, porcelain, and armor collected by over five generations of the Wallace family and bequeathed to the nation by **Sir Richard Wallace** in 1897. The mansion's stunning collection is rendered even more dazzling by its grand gilded setting. The ground floor's four **Armoury Galleries** boast scads of richly decorated weapons and burnished suits of armor while the **State Rooms** hold a collection of sumptuous Sèvres porcelain. The East Galleries feature 17th-century masterpieces by **Van Dyck, Rembrandt, Rubens, Ruisdael, Velazquez, Titian** and **Gainsborough** within the **Great Gallery.** One of the collection's most celebrated pieces, Frans Hals's *The Laughing Cavalier* is in here as well.

⊖Marble Arch. Left onto Oxford St., left on Duke St., right onto Manchester Sq. i Private tours W, Sa, Su 11:30am and 3pm; call for details. $ Gallery free. Suggested donation £5. Audio tours £4. Open daily 10am-5pm.

THE CITY OF LONDON

Most stereotypical "London" sights are located here and can't be missed—even if having a camera slung around your neck is practically required for entrance.

SAINT PAUL'S CATHEDRAL — ♿ CHURCH

St. Paul's Churchyard ☎020 7246 8350 www.stpauls.co.uk

Entering Saint Paul's Cathedral and not taking the Lord's name in vain is a challenge. Like many churches in the area, Saint Paul's was destroyed in the Great Fire of London. Christopher Wren's masterpiece is the fourth cathedral on the site, with the first building dating to 604 CE. From the start, Wren wanted to include the fantastic dome that is now visible throughout London, but the Church of England was hesitant to include a piece of architecture that was characteristically Roman Catholic. Ultimately, Wren won.

INTERIOR. The first thing you see upon entering the Cathedral is the nave. The baptismal font stands next to an elaborately designed wax candle in the south part of the nave. If you can pull your eyes away from the dome, which was painted by Sir James Thornhill, look out for the terrifyingly huge memorial to the **Duke of Wellington** (on your left in the north aisle as you walk through the nave) and William Holman Hunt's *The Light of the World* which can be found in the Middlesex Chapel, a chapel set aside for private prayer dedicated to the members of the Middlesex regimen of the British army. Also look out for Henry Moore's strikingly modern *Mother and Child* sculpture as well as the memorial to American and British service men in WWII.

SCALING THE HEIGHTS. We know what you're thinking—yes, you are allowed to climb to the top of the dome. After 257 short, dizzyingly tight wooden steps, guests find the Whispering Gallery, a seating area around the inner ring of the dome where, under the right conditions, you can whisper and be heard on the other side. Many people try this at the same time, which makes standing at the rim of Wren's magnificent dome feel a bit like one of the scarier whisper segments in *Lost*, but it's worth giving this acoustic novelty a try. The experience of climbing to the top is greatly enhanced if you make the journey while a choir sings in the nave; the acoustics in the Whispering Gallery are incredible. After 376 steps, visitors can climb out onto the Stone Gallery which is open-air, low-stress, and thoroughly enjoyable. Then it's another 152 steps to the Golden Gallery, an open-air, super high look out onto the city. The army used this gallery in the second World War to spot enemy planes coming from up to 10 miles

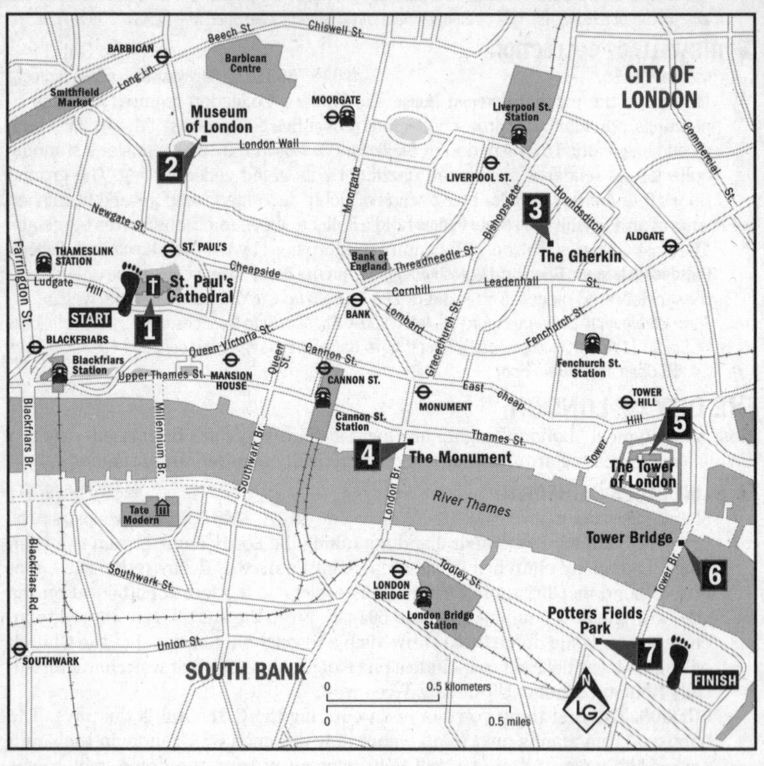

the city of london

Let's be real. London's big, and you probably can't experience the entire city in one day. But that doesn't mean you can't experience the City of London in one day. Right in the heart of town, the "Square Mile" packs a ton into one single neighborhood. Back in the Middle Ages, it actually made up the entire British capital, and though many diverse, bustling neighborhoods have come to surround it, "The City" is still the financial and historical center of London today. With its own mayor and separate jurisdiction, The City of London even has sway over the Queen, who must ask permission of the Lord Mayor before entering. Lucky for you, visitors have easier access than Lizzie does, so you can grab your camera and head over there on the Tube. The City has some of London's best sights, so a walking tour won't necessarily be quick. Still, **Let's Go** has a simple plan for you to cover the City of London in seven easy stops.

1. ST. PAUL'S CATHEDRAL. Before you begin your walk through the City of London, get off the Tube at ⊖St. Paul's and follow the signs until you reach St. Paul's Cathedral, London's grandest and most beautiful church. In order to get an early start on your day through the "Square Mile" and avoid the church-going tourist crowds, try to arrive at St. Paul's before 10am. If you really want to catch a tour, the earliest is at 10:45am. If you're not struggling too hard with jet lag, climb to the Golden Gallery atop St. Paul's for the best views of London.

2. MUSEUM OF LONDON. Head north through Paternoster Sq. onto Edward St., which becomes Montague St. Follow it until you reach the roundabout where you'll find the Museum of London. For no money, you'll get the most in-depth lesson on the history of London, from the city's pre-Roman beginnings to its present-day culture. Our walking tour may last you just a day, but a 45min. tour at this museum will take you on a journey through a milenia or two.

3. THE GHERKIN. Walk west along London Wall until it becomes Wormwood St., which then becomes Camomile St. Make a right onto St. Mary Ave. and walk south two blocks. You've arrived at 30 St. Mary Ave., most commonly known as "The Gherkin." Sure, the rounded glass skyscraper may stick out like a sore thumb in the City of London, but it stands its ground among Wren's legendary architecture. Serving as one of London's financial centers, the Gherkin itself isn't open to the public, but be sure to stop and look up at this award-winning mod monument.

4. THE MONUMENT. Continue down St. Mary Ave. and turn right onto Leaderhead St. Then make a left onto Gracechurch St. and walk south until you cross Eastcheap onto Fish St. Hill. In the middle of the street, you'll find the Monument, a 202 ft. stone column commemorating the Great Fire of London in 1666. You can climb to the top for another great view of the city, but that daunting walk up the inner staircase isn't suited to those afraid of heights, enclosed spaces, or exercise.

5. THE TOWER OF LONDON. Walk south on Fish St. Hill and make a left onto Lower Thames St. Walk east several blocks until you reach the Tower of London, right beside the Thames. Though this fortress was once a prison, the scariest thing about it today are the tourists you'll come across when you visit. If you can survive them, you should have no fear being trapped in the Tower of London as you hang out with Beefeaters for an hour or so. The last tickets are sold at 4pm during low season and 5pm during high season, so be sure to get to the tower in time.

6. TOWER BRIDGE. Follow signs to Tower Bridge, directly to the east of the Tower of London. The iconic bascule bridge crossing the River Thames opens and closes daily, but you can get onto it until 5:30 pm during high season (low season 5pm). If you'd like to learn fun facts about the iconic bascule bridge, you'll enjoy the fun and inexpensive tour.

7. POTTERS FIELDS PARK. Once you've crossed Tower Bridge going south, turn right on Tower Bridge Rd. to reach Potters Fields Park. After a long day of walking and sight-seeing, take a breather and stretch out on its peaceful greens. The park offers the best views of the City of London, so you can take one last look at the capital's capital.

WALKING TOUR

Let's Go www.letsgo.com

away. The only drawback to the view is that you can't see the grandeur of St. Paul's itself.

PLUMBING THE DEPTHS. A veritable who's who of famous Britons reside in the loins of St. Paul's. Descend beneath the cathedral to find the tombs and memorials of **Captain John Cooke, Horatio Nelson, Florence Nightingale, the Duke of Wellington** (whose massive tomb is footed by sleeping stone lions), **William Blake, Henry Moore,** and finally **Christopher Wren.** Wren's inconspicuous tomb (to the right of the OBE Chapel) is inscribed "*Lector, si monumentum requiris circumspice*" which translates to "Reader, if you seek his monument, look around." Saint Paul's Cathedral is jaw-droppingly magnificent; there could be no better monument to its visionary architect than the simple words etched on his tomb.

⇞ ⊖St. Paul's. There are signs outside the station that will lead you to the Cathedral. i Guided tours are 1.5hr., and they occur at 10:45am, 11:15am, 1:30pm, and 2pm. £3, children £1. A free multimedia tour will be provided starting mid-July-early Sept 2010. Audio tours available in 8 languages including English (adults £4). Ⓢ Adults £12.50, students £9.50, seniors £11, children £4.50; family (2 adults, 2 kids) £29.50; group rates (10+) adults £11.50, students £8.50, seniors £10.50, children £4. ⏰ M-Sa 8:30am-4:00pm (last ticket sold). Least crowded early in the day. Get in for free (though you'll have limited access) at one of the church services; 7:30am is Mattins, 8am is the Holy Communion, 12:30pm is the Holy Communion, 5pm is Evensong. Free Organ Recitals every Su from 4:45-5:15pm.

sacred sights

Many sights will self-advocate based on their superior views of the city. In our opinion, the view from the Golden Gallery atop **St. Paul's Cathedral** trumps all others. There's plenty of room, it's higher than the Monument, and more central than the Tower Bridge.

MUSEUM OF LONDON — ♿ MUSEUM

By the London Wall (London EC27 5HN) ☎020 7001 9844 www.museumoflondon.org.uk

The Museum of London is an exhaustive celebration of the city, tracing its history from the pre-Roman days, through the fall of that empire (too bad the city's no longer known as Londinium), up to the present through a series of timelines, walk-in exhibits, and artifacts. Among the fascinating pieces of history on display are a walk-in replica of a London Saxon house from the mid-1000s, a beautiful model of the original St. Paul's cathedral, a taxi from 1908, and Beatlemania paraphernalia. Relatively compact for its sheer scope, the Museum of London yields tremendous bang for your buck, especially because it's free!

⇞ ⊖St. Pauls. Go up St. Martins and Aldersgate. i 45min. tours at 11am, 12pm, 3pm, and 4pm. Ⓢ Free. ⏰ Open M-F 10am-6pm.

POTTERS FIELDS PARK — ♿ PARK

Tooley St. towards Tower Bridge ☎020 7407 4702 pottersfields.co.uk

Providing wide patches of grass for denizens of the park to stretch out on, as well as breathtaking views of Tower Bridge and the Thames, Potters Fields Park is an oasis in such a busy city. It's at the heart of London, but far removed from its bustle. City Hall sits within the park and is just as architecturally magnificent as Tower Bridge. After seeing the park, you may want to check out more of the waterfront and do some shopping in **Hay's Galleria**. Also, be sure to notice the **HMS Belfast**, which is just down the river from the park; a ticket is required to board the vessel.

⇄ ⊖London Bridge. Walk down Tooley St. towards Tower Bridge. Go through Hay's Galleria and walk along the river towards Tower Bridge. Ⓢ Free.

TOWER BRIDGE SIGHT

Tower Bridge ☎020 7403 3761 www.towerbridge.org.uk

If Fergie had gone to the Tower Bridge exhibition, she would have known that bascule bridges come down more often than London Bridge. Built between 1886 and 1894, Tower Bridge was created because London Bridge had become too crowded. It is a bascule bridge, meaning that, if you're lucky, you'll get to see it rise (and then come down). The exhibition is enjoyable, though if you're afraid of heights, it might not be for you. Hear fun facts about the bridge as well as enchanting anecdotes such as the story of a 1952 double-decker bus that accidentally jumped the bridge while it was rising—clearly the driver never heard the phrase "Mind the gap." The bridge is less of a tourist trap than the Tower of London, and just as engaging. Of course, the stunning architecture and eye-popping colors of the bridge can be enjoyed for free.

⇄ ⊖Tower Hill. Follow signs to Tower Bridge. Ⓢ £7, ages 5-15 £3, under 5 free; concessions £5; 1 adult and 2 children £11.00; 2 adults and 1 child £14; 2 adults and 2 children £16; 2 adults and 3-4 children £18. ⏰ April 1-Sept 30 open 10am-5:30pm daily; Oct 1-Mar 31 open 9:30am-5:00pm daily.

GUILDHALL ART GALLERY HISTORICAL SIGHT, ART GALLERY

Between Basinghall St. and Coleman St. ☎020 7332 3700 www.guildhall-art-gallery.org.uk

The entrance to the gallery is through fantastic **Guildhall Yard,** which feels isolated from the city. The gallery specializes in Victorian art but also has a rotating exhibit of art from all periods relating to London (they're currently running an exhibit on the Royal Post). "I'm sold!" you say. But wait. You haven't heard the best part! While constructing the gallery in 1988, archaeologists uncovered an amphitheater from Londinium (Roman London). The intact portions from the site are left as they were found beneath the gallery in an impressive exhibition. Also included in the exhibition is a display of a Roman drainage system.

⇄ ⊖Bank. Go up Princes St., take left on Gresham St. and right on Basinghall St. Guild Yard will be on your right. Ⓢ £2.50, free after 3:30pm and all day F; concessions for students, seniors, and unemployed £1. ⏰ M-Sa 10am-5pm (last entry at 4:30pm), Su noon-4pm (last entry 3:45pm).

TOWER OF LONDON SIGHT

Between Tower Hill and the Thames ☎084 4482 7777 www.hrp.org.uk/toweroflondon

In its 1,000-year history, the Tower of London has been a fortress, a royal palace, a prison, a zoo, a mint, the house of the first royal observatory, and a tourist trap. If tourists were an invading army back in the day of William the Conqueror, he would have surrendered instantly. The Tower has tours led by "Beefeaters," the men and women who guard and live within the tower.

TRAITOR'S GATE. Originally named "Watergate," Traitor's Gate was the passage from the Tower to the River Thames through which prisoners entered the tower.

SOME OF THE TOWERS. Byward Tower is part of the Tower's intriguing, if somewhat gimmicky, attempt at living history. Byward Tower currently houses many of the Tower's more than 100 residences. Wakefield Tower is near the home of the famous six ravens. The legend of the ravens claims that if they fly away the white tower will crumble and disaster will befall the monarchy.

BLOODY TOWER. The tower was built in 1225, and the most famous anecdote surrounding it is one of bizarre death (as are most stories surrounding the Tower). Prince Edward V and Richard, Duke of York, were suffocated by pillows in the tower, and their bodies weren't found until 191 years after their deaths. This tale was the inspiration for Shakespeare's *Richard III.*

THE WHITE TOWER. Built by William of Normandy in 1078 as the first structure of the Tower of London, the White Tower was once a royal palace with the top floor reserved for kings and queens, the floor below housing the servants, and the basement serving as a dungeon (and guest house!). Part of it is built on the Roman city wall of London. The White Tower currently houses the "Royal Armoury: Fit for a King" exhibit which features armor from the Normans to the Windsors, with notable sections that feature Henry VIII's personal armor. Be sure to take note of his enhanced codpiece, as well as the chuckling British and cackling Americans pointing at it, while their kids try to figure out what all the fuss is about.

JEWEL HOUSE. The Jewel House contains all of the regalia used for the coronation of British royalty and boasts jewels with enough glitter to induce an epileptic seizure. The gems are the focal point of many people's trips to the tower, so try to go earlier in the day, if possible. Inside, you'll find the sovereign's scepter highlighted by a cross with the world's largest perfect diamond in the world, the **First Star of Africa** (530.2 carats).

TOWER GREEN. The Green is a lovely grass area at the center of the tower, outside the Chapel Royal of St. Peter and Vincula. The eight friends of the monarch who were beheaded by the government had the good fortune to get their heads lopped off on the Tower Green. Whatever happened here, it did **wonders for the grass**.

OUTSIDE THE TOWER. Outside the tower lies **Tower Hill,** the primary execution site. The last execution (that of Lord Lovat) was held here in 1747. Every night for the last 700 years, the Ceremony of the Keys has been performed. To get a ticket, you must send an application with the names of everyone you hope to bring and two possible dates of attendance at least two months in advance (earlier if you're attending in the summer) inside an envelope with proper stamps (or at least 2 coupon-response international) to "Ceremony of the Keys Office, Tower of London, LONDON, EC3N 4AB, Great Britain." The Ceremony is free, but you need tickets, and groups are limited to six people max.

Tower Hill. Buy tickets at the metro stop or at the Welcome Center, as these places tend to be less crowded. £17; student, senior, and disabled £14.50; children under 5 free; family (1-2 adults and up to 6 kids) £47. Audio tours available in 9 different languages; £4.00, students £3. An individual Membership gives you unlimited, year round access to all the Royal Palaces for £41.00, with a family membership available for £80. Portions of the site wheelchair-accessible. Mar 1-Oct 31: M 10am-5:30pm, Tu-Su 9:00am-5:30pm, last ticket sold at 5pm. Nov 1-Feb 28: M-Tu and Su 10:00am-4:30pm, W-Sa 9am-5:30pm, last entry sold at 4pm. Cafe: Tu-Sa 9:30am-5pm, Su-M 10:30am-5pm. Ceremony of the Keys 9:30pm nightly.

CLOCKMAKERS' MUSEUM

MUSEUM

Inside Guildhall Library off Aldermanbury — 020 7332 1868

The 1-room Clockmakers' Museum is sort of like the interior of Doc Brown's house from *Back to the Future*, except with more clocks. Each clock, watch, sun dial, and chronometer from the 500 year history of clocks is explained either historically or technically by its accompanying pamphlet. For those less inclined to horological technology, the museum has famous watches and clocks, like the watch worn by Sir Edmund Hillary during his successful 1953 climb of Mount Everest and some of the first mass-produced watches. Worth a brief visit, if only to hear the sound of so many clocks ticking together.

St. Paul's. Go down Cheapside with your back to St. Paul's Cathedral. Turn left on King St., left on Gresham and right on Aldermanbury. Enter through the library. Free. M-Sa 9:30am-4:45pm. Closed Sa on bank holiday weekends.

SAINT MARY-LE-BOW

CHURCH

Cheapside, near Bow Ln. — 020 7248 5139 www.stmarylebow.co.uk

Though the chapel dates back to 1080 when there was first a church on the site, the church has been restored several times. First, it was burned in the Great Fire of London in 1666, but it was rebuilt by Christopher Wren. Then, it was bombed during World War II, rebuilt in its modern form, and reconsecrated in

1956. London lore says that if you're born within the sound of Bow bells (which used to ring the 9pm city curfew, signaling all the apprentices to stop working) you're a true cockney. The interior of the church is a masterpiece, filled with gorgeous gold-laced Corinthian columns.

St. Pauls. Walk down Cheapside away from St. Paul's Cathedral. Free. M-W 7am-6pm, Th 7am-6:30pm, F 7am-4pm.

THE MONUMENT SIGHT

Monument ☎020 7626 2717 www.themonument.info

Built between 1671 and 1677, the Monument stands in memory of the Great Fire of London that burned most of the city in 1666. At 202ft. tall, with an inner shaft containing 311 stairs that must be climbed in order to reach the breathtaking open-air top floor, the Monument is what your Stairmaster would look like in the pre-mechanical age. If you were to lay the tower on its side pointing in a certain direction, it would land on the spot where the fire started. It would also cause mass hysteria. It is the only non-ecclesiastical Christopher Wren building, though some scholars maintain that it was built to worship **rock hard thighs**. Enjoy the view from the top!

Monument. Get off the Tube and it will be directly in front of you as you exit the station. £3.00, children £1; concessions £2. Combined tickets are available with the Tower Bridge exhibition. Combined prices: £8, children £3.50; concessions £5.50. Open 7 days a week, 9:30am-5pm. Closed on Christmas and Boxing Day.

ST. STEPHEN WALBROOK CHURCH

39 Walbrook ☎020 7626 9000 www.ststephenwalbrook.net

You may wonder about the marshmallow-like object sitting in the center of the room, but this is merely Henry Moore's controversial idea of what an altar should look like. Rumored to have "the most perfectly proportioned interior in the world," St. Stephen Walbrook, a Saxon church built in the seventh century, is a beautiful Wren construction. The church used to be bordered by a river, and the structure fights a continuous battle against gravity as it slips downward. Visit toward the end of the day during the summer to bask in the light that floods through the glass windows.

*Mansion House. Take right onto Cannon St., then left onto Walbrook. **i** Eucharist is M at 1pm. Free. M-F 10am-4pm. Organ recitals F 12:30pm.*

ST. MARY WOOLNOTH CHURCH

Intersection of King William and Lombard St. ☎020 7626 9701

This church is seated near the center of one of the busiest intersections in the City of London, and was restored by (who else?) Christopher Wren after the Great Fire of London. John Newton (the co-composer of Amazing Grace) was also a rector here from 1779-1807. St. Mary Woolnoth's is an undiscovered piece of history in a city full of crowded gems.

*Bank. Intersection of King William and Lombard St. **i** Free meditation hr. weekly, W 6:30pm. Free. M-F 9:30am-4:30pm.*

THE SOUTH BANK

IMPERIAL WAR MUSEUM MUSEUM

Lambeth Rd. ☎020 7416 5000 www.iwm.org.uk

Housed in what used to be the infamous Bedlam insane asylum, the Imperial War Museum is mad for history. The exhibits start out right with two massive naval guns guarding the entrance to the imposing building. The first room is cluttered with enough devices of war to make any general salivate. Highlights include a **Polaris A3 Missile,** the first submarine-launched missile, a full-size **German V2 Rocket,** and the shell (not the inner mechanisms, luckily) of a **"Little Boy,"** the type of bomb detonated above Hiroshima. Luckily, the bomb is non-functional, but it gets unnerving when kids whack the casing. The third floor houses the expansive **Holocaust Exhibition.** This haunting exhibit traces the catastrophic injustice of WWII Nazi atrocities with cartographic precision and deep feeling, with miles of film exploring everything from the rhetoric of the Nazi party to a history of anti-Semitism. Of course, many visitors may feel like a visit to a museum would be unbalanced with only such light subject matter, and they'll take solace in the **Crimes Against Humanity** exhibition one floor down.

Art nuts will enjoy **"Breakthrough,"** the museum's fantastic art collection. The first floor houses the exciting, if sensational, "Secret War" exhibit of WWII spy gadgetry, providing a brief history of MI5 and the Special Operations Executive. The popular **Blitz Experience** and **Trench Experience** exhibits recreate the experience of hiding during an air raid and living in the trenches respectively.

⊖Elephant and Castle. Turn right onto Elephant and Castle (roundabout), right onto St. George's Rd., and then left onto Lambeth Rd. Ⓢ Free. Special exhibits £5, students £4. Multimedia guides available in English £3.50. Open daily 10am-6pm. The Blitz Experience daily schedule is downstairs. It lasts around 10min.

TATE MODERN

FAMOUS GALLERY, MODERN

53 Bankside ☎020 7887 8008 www.tate.org.uk

Located in George Gilbert Scott's Brutalist old Bankside Power Station, Tate Modern defies traditional organizational methods, opting out of the chronological in favor of thematic organization. The permanent collection rotates through two floors. Those desperate to see one work in particular should check out the computers on the fifth floor, which enable users to scan through the entire collection.

Level 3 houses the **Material Gestures** gallery, which focuses mainly on postwar European and American art and showcases works by Monet, Francis Bacon and **Anish Kapoor.** Sculptures by Giacometti can also be found here. **Poetry and Dream,** an area centering on Surrealism and its associated themes, displays the work of **Dali** and **Picasso** among others.

On Level 5, **Energy and Process** looks at Arte Povera, the movement from the 1970s that used everyday materials and natural laws to create art. **States of Flux** focuses on cubism and futurism among other important modern movements, displaying the works of **Roy Lichtenstein, Robert Frank, Warhol,** and **Duchamp,** among others.

⊖Southwark. Left onto Blackfriars Rd. Right onto Southwark St., left onto Sumner, left onto Holland St. Ⓢ Free. Multimedia guide available in English, £3.50, concessions £3. Open M-Th 10am-6pm, F-Sa 10am-10pm, Su 10am-6pm. Free 10min. talks are given around the various galleries. Check schedule signs for details.

THE HAYWARD GALLERY

GALLERY

South Bank Centre ☎084 4847 9910 www.haywardgallery.org.uk

The Hayward Gallery was opened in 1968 and designed by a group of Brutalist architects. The Gallery has been showing cutting edge modern art in its galleries for years. Two to three shows run at once. Check online to see how the space is currently being used.

⊖Waterloo. Head toward York Rd., turn right onto York Rd. and left onto Waterloo Rd. The gallery's left of the bridge and the signage in the center will help you find it. i Mostly wheelchair-accessible. Ⓢ £11, seniors £10, concessions £8, ages 12-18 £6.50, under 12 free. Open M-Su 10am-6pm, F 10am-10pm.

DESIGN MUSEUM

GALLERY

Shad Thames ☎020 7940 8790 www.designmuseum.org

Though the museum has no permanent collection, it is consistently fascinating. Featuring a range of installations from architecture to illustration, fashion, product design, and occasional retrospectives and competitions, the Design Museum is an excellent place to come think about the aesthetics of everyday life and to see those of the future.

Tower Hill. Cross Tower Bridge. Left onto Queen Elizabeth St., left onto Shad Thames. £8,50, students £5, concessions £6.50. Open M-Su 10am-5:45pm. Last entry 30min. before close.

THE LONDON EYE — SIGHT

Minister Court ☎087 0990 8881 www.londoneye.com

Also known as the **Millenium Wheel,** the **London Eye** is one of the most popular tourist attractions in London. The massive Ferris wheel takes visitors on a 30min. ride, giving them unparalleled arial views of London. An exciting 4D movie experience opens the entire trip which, while gimmicky, is worth it.

Westminster. Cross the bridge heading toward the Eye. £17.95, ages 4-15 £9.50, under 4 free, seniors and disabled £14.30. Savings of 10% if you book online. Hours vary. Call or check the website. In general, Oct-Mar 10am-8pm; Apr 10am-9pm; May-July M-Th 10am-9pm; F-Sa 10am-9:30pm; Su 10am-9pm; July-Aug 10am-9:30pm; Sept 10am-9pm.

SHAKESPEARE'S GLOBE — EXHIBITION, HISTORICAL SITE

21 New Globe Walk ☎020 7902 1500 www.shakespeares-globe.org

A recreation of the original **Globe Theatre** which burnt down during a performance of *Henry VIII* in 1613—who's idea was it to fire a real cannon toward a thatched roof?—Shakespeare's Globe does a pretty accurate job of recreating the unique, open-air theater, with numerous exhibits and a tour on the history of Shakespeare and area theater. Though short on actual artifacts, the historical overview offered by the exhibit is fascinating and well-designed. Special booths allow visitors to speak lines with automated casts, and other booths enable visitors to hear iconic Shakespearean monologues read by famous actors.

Southwark. Left onto Blackfriars Rd., right onto Southwark St., left onto Great Guildford, right onto Park St., left onto Emerson St. *i For information on productions, see* **Arts and Culture,** *p. 85.* *Exhibition and tour £10.50, just exhibition £5. Exhibition and bankside tour £7.50, students £6.50, ages 5-15 £4.50, under 5 free. Exhibition open M-Su 9am-5pm. Exhibition and bankside tours T-Sa 1-5pm, Su noon-5pm. Tours stop around 12:30pm, when there's a matinee performance.*

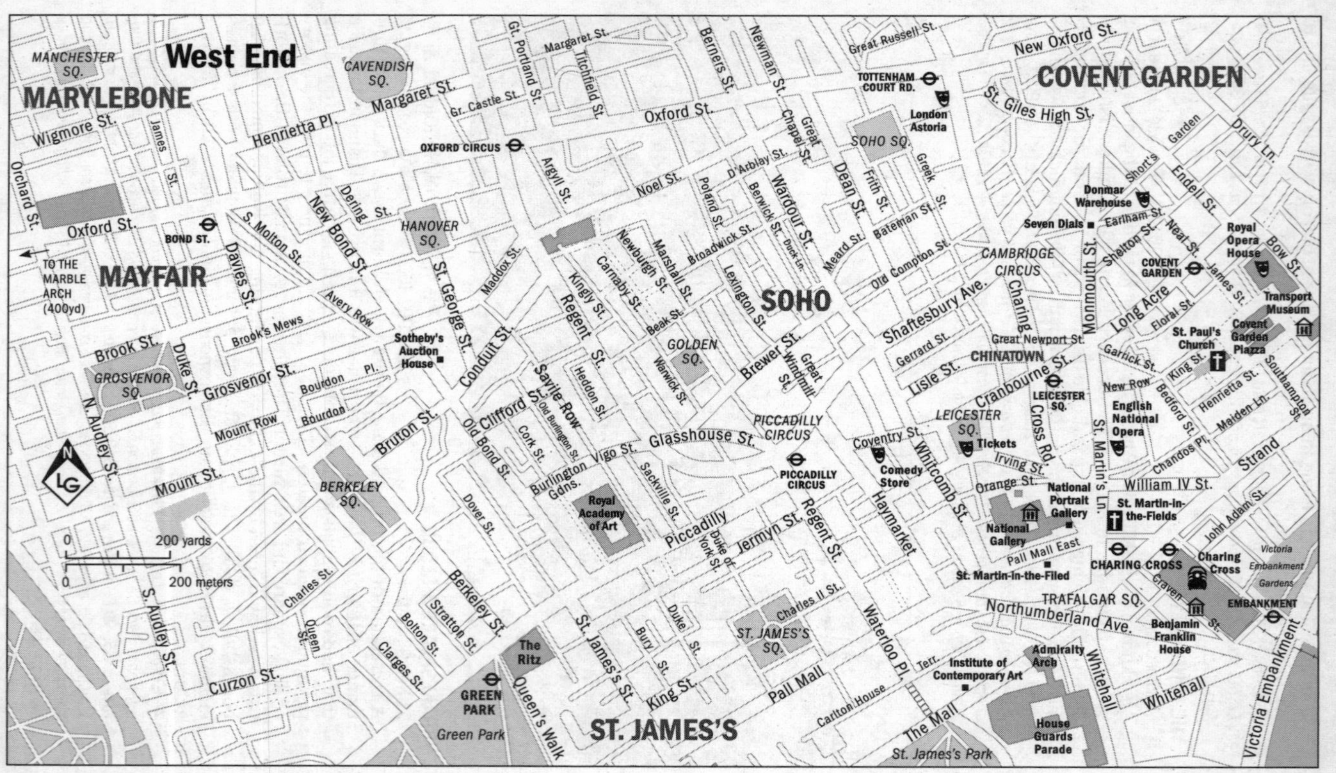
West End
MARYLEBONE
MAYFAIR
SOHO
COVENT GARDEN
ST. JAMES'S
MANCHESTER SQ.
CAVENDISH SQ.
HANOVER SQ.
GROSVENOR SQ.
BERKELEY SQ.
SOHO SQ.
GOLDEN SQ.
LEICESTER SQ.
ST. JAMES'S SQ.
TRAFALGAR SQ.
PICCADILLY CIRCUS
CAMBRIDGE CIRCUS
CHINATOWN
OXFORD CIRCUS
BOND ST.
TOTTENHAM COURT RD.
PICCADILLY CIRCUS
LEICESTER SQ.
COVENT GARDEN
CHARING CROSS
EMBANKMENT
GREEN PARK
Green Park
St. James's Park
TO THE MARBLE ARCH (400yd)
200 yards
200 meters
Wigmore St.
James St.
Orchard St.
Oxford St.
Henrietta Pl.
Margaret St.
Gr. Castle St.
Gt. Portland St.
Margaret St.
Titchfield St.
Berners St.
Newman St.
Great Russell St.
New Oxford St.
St. Giles High St.
Drury Ln.
Short's Gardens
Endell St.
Earlham St.
Neal St.
Shelton St.
Monmouth St.
Long Acre
Floral St.
James St.
Bow St.
Southampton St.
Henrietta St.
Maiden Ln.
King St.
Garrick St.
New Row
Bedford St.
Chandos Pl.
Strand
William IV St.
John Adam St.
Craven St.
Victoria Embankment
Northumberland Ave.
Whitehall
St. Martin's Ln.
Charing Cross Rd.
Great Newport St.
Cranbourne St.
Irving St.
Orange St.
Pall Mall East
Whitcomb St.
Lisle St.
Gerrard St.
Shaftesbury Ave.
Old Compton St.
Greek St.
Frith St.
Bateman St.
Dean St.
Meard St.
Great Chapel St.
Wardour St.
Duck Ln.
Berwick St.
D'Arblay St.
Poland St.
Broadwick St.
Lexington St.
Great Windmill St.
Brewer St.
Marshall St.
Newburgh St.
Beak St.
Warwick St.
Carnaby St.
Kingly St.
Noel St.
Argyll St.
Regent St.
Heddon St.
Glasshouse St.
Coventry St.
Haymarket
Waterloo Pl.
Charles II St.
Pall Mall
Carlton House Terr.
The Mall
Jermyn St.
Duke of York St.
Piccadilly
Sackville St.
Vigo St.
Savile Row
Old Burlington St.
Burlington Gdns.
Cork St.
Clifford St.
Old Bond St.
Dover St.
Duke St.
Bury St.
King St.
St. James's St.
Queen's Walk
Berkeley St.
Stratton St.
Bolton St.
Clarges St.
Charles St.
Queen St.
Curzon St.
S. Audley St.
N. Audley St.
Mount St.
Mount Row
Grosvenor St.
Brook St.
Duke St.
Davies St.
Brook's Mews
Bourdon Pl.
Bourdon
Bruton St.
Conduit St.
St. George St.
Maddox St.
Avery Row
New Bond St.
S. Molton St.
Dering St.
Sotheby's Auction House
The Ritz
Royal Academy of Art
Comedy Store
Tickets
National Gallery
National Portrait Gallery
St. Martin-in-the-Filed
St. Martin-in-the-Fields
English National Opera
Charing Cross
Benjamin Franklin House
Admiralty Arch
Horse Guards Parade
Institute of Contemporary Art
London Astoria
Donmar Warehouse
Seven Dials
St. Paul's Church
Royal Opera House
Covent Garden Plazza
Transport Museum
Victoria Embankment Gardens

THE NATIONAL GALLERY

GALLERY

Trafalgar Sq. ☎020 7747 2885 www.nationalgallery.org.uk

The National Gallery presides over **Trafalgar Square** and is nearly as impressive as the Square itself. Founded in 1824 and moved to its current location in 1838, the gallery encompasses all the major traditions of Western European art. The more recent **Sainsbury Wing** was opened in 1991, and it encompasses the 13th through 15th centuries. Often, visitors are in such a hurry to see the master works, that they traverse the main steps without looking at the floor. They are ignoring one of the most impressive artworks in the gallery, Boris Anrep's mosaics. The first landing depicts the awakening of the muses, the top landing depicts the modern virtues such as compassion, humor, open-mindedness, pursuit, wonder, and curiosity, all of which will be evoked in a thorough viewing of the gallery. The **West Vestibule** ponders art, astronomy, commerce, music and sacred love among others, for a start, while the **East** celebrates the pleasures of life (Christmas pudding, conversation, cricket, mud pie, profane love, speed). Ask for the pamphlet on the mosaics at the front desk for more details! The gallery is all-encompassing, but here are the highlights from a few rooms:

Room 4. Are there many German fans of *Let's Go*? If so, this is for you: **Room 4** has some works by Hans Holbein, one of Germany's best known partners.

Room 6, 7 and 8 showcase works by **Michelangelo** and **Raphael.** If you really want to piss people off, ask them where they're keeping the **Donatellos. Room 18** was donated by **Yves St. Laurent. Room 23** features **Rembrandt.**

Room 30. Focused mainly on religious painting, Room 30 has several famous Velázquez's including *Rokeby Venus*, and *La Tela Real*, which depicts Philip IV hunting wild boar. It is also a must-see for any aspiring mustache-growers, see Velazquez's 1656 *Philip IV of Spain* for curl, and the nearby Juan Bautista del Mazo's *Don Adrián Pulido Pareja* for volume and under-lip work.

Room 32 explores the introduction of naturalism to more traditional styles of painting through works such as Caravaggio's *Boy Bitten by a Lizard*, and Guercino's famous *The Incredulity of Saint Thomas* which shows St. Thomas touching a post-resurrection Christ's wounds out of doubt.

Room 34 is best seen while *Rule Brittania* blares loudly in the background, but the gallery assistants who are posted at each room probably wouldn't take very kindly to that. Showcasing art from Great Britain between 1750 and 1850, Room 34 concerns itself mainly with heroic acts, huge ships and bold, grand landscapes. Especially of note are the several paintings from **Turner.**

Room 43 is a heavy-hitter. **Manet** and **Monet:** so much more distinct than their one-letter difference might lead you to believe. This is the home of some of Monet's **water lilies** paintings and his beautiful *The Grand Canal, Venice* with its soft-hewn domes and gentle brush strokes. *The Gare St-Lazare* from 1877 may rekindle the romance of train stations for tired travelers. As if all this weren't enough, one of **Van Gogh's** famous *Sun Flowers* is also on display in this room.

Room 44 is for people interested in pointillism and impressionism, featuring **Pissarro** and still lifes from **Gauguin** as well as **Renoir's** famous *The Umbrellas*. Many people have heard that the best way to view an impressionist work is by squinting and backing away from it. We share this not to advise you, but rather to explain why three people just backed into you. **Room 46** will make fans of **Degas** happy.

The Sainsbury Wing. Fans of **Botticelli, Van Eyck** and **Bellini** would be well-served to pay the wing a visit. Many of the paintings are taken from religious structures, so the canvases are often interestingly designed or shaped like arches.

⊖Charing Cross. Ⓢ Free. Audio tours in English £3.50, students £2.50. Maps £1 and are well-worth the purchase as the gallery is huge. Special exhibits cost around £10 on average. Open M-Th 10am-6pm, F 10am-9pm, Sa-Su 10am-6pm.

TRAFALGAR SQUARE ♿ HISTORICAL SIGHT

Trafalgar Square

People flock to Trafalgar Square like pigeons in Hyde Park to bread, and if you're homesick for your native tongue, you'll likely hear it here (yes, American English counts). Designed by Sir Charles Barry, who also designed the Houses of Parliament, Trafalgar Square commemorates Admiral **Horatio Viscount Nelson's** heroic naval victory at the Battle of Trafalgar. The Square serves as a gathering point and has hosted national celebrations and rallies of all sorts. The square is bordered by institutions from many different countries such as the New Zealand House, Uganda House, Canada House, and South Africa House. The National Gallery is north of the Square. Every Christmas, a tree is erected in Trafalgar Square. Norway has given the tree annually since 1947 as thanks for British aid during WWII.

A statue of Nelson tops **Nelson's column,** which is the central point of the square. The four panels surrounding its base celebrate his naval victories at St. Vincent in 1797, the Nile in 1798, Copenhagen in 1801 and Trafalgar in 1805 (the panel for this victory says "England expects every man will do his duty"). A bronze lion rests on each of the four corners of the block supporting the column, and on any given day, you can see children climbing all over them, and occasionally dangling from their mouths.

The Fountains. There are two beautiful fountains in the square, each with teal statues of strange merpeople holding fish. To call them strange merpeople may seem redundant, but the two tails will make you double-take. The water in the fountains is so blue that it makes the Thames look black, instead of sickly green. ⊖*Charing Cross.*

NATIONAL PORTRAIT GALLERY ♿ GALLERY

St. Martin's Pl. ☎020 7306 0055 www.npg.org.uk

In London, it's easy to get lost in history. You have to remember names of monarchs, gossip stars, the insanely wealthy, the star-crossed lovers—and we haven't even talked about those outside of the royal family. The National Portrait Gallery is less about the art of the portraits themselves than it is about the people behind the portraits and what they meant for England. In fact, the gallery presents excellent short histories of the subjects and organizes them by room in such a way as to trace British history through its greatest asset—its people. Highlights:

Room 2 displays Queen Elizabeth I circa 1600, and the famous "Ditchley Portrait" in which Her Majesty is depicted standing on a globe.

Room 12 shows greats of the 18th century, such as **Samuel Johnson** and **Johann Christian Bach.**

Room 14 deals with the rise of the British Empire, including a brief mention of the American Revolution in the form of a replica of a **Gilbert Stuart** portrait of **George Washington.** It also has the dramatic *Death of the Earl of Chatham*, who is portrayed mid-collapse after trying to persuade the British government to go easy on America.

Room 16 documents the sordid tale of Lady Jane Grey, the "nine-day queen."

Room 18 has portraits of **John Keats, William Wordsworth** and **Thomas Paine** as well as a rather romantic depiction of **Byron** who looks like a mixture of **Jake Gyllenhaal** in the *Prince of Persia* and **Captain Jack Sparrow.**

Room 27 features **Charles Darwin** in cartoon and portrait form (in one of them he has the body of an ape) as well as *Lost* star **Michael Faraday,** who discovered electro-magnetic induction. The question remains, could he discover what the hell was going on with that damn island?

Room 31 has got all your **Winston Churchill.** Also worth noting is the exhibition dedicated to **D. H. Lawrence,** and its history of *Lady Chatterley's Lover.* A priceless photograph of three men on the Tube shows the two men flanking the central figure (who's reading *Lady Chatterley's Lover*) gazing over his shoulder at its "obscene" pages.

Artists and Sitters has modern portraits such as the extra-large portrait of **Paul McCartney.**

The **Ground Floor** features contemporary portraits like Julian Opie's Blur portraits (fans of the band will recognize the images from the cover of the Greatest Hits collection) and his animated self-portrait.

Room 38 houses Marc Quinn's *Self.* The room is set up in such a way that you enter and notice the reddish bust of a man's head sitting in a refrigerated case. Then you read the plaque and realize its made out of the artist's own frozen blood.

⊖Charing Cross. Walk down Strand to Trafalgar Square and turn right along the square. Tickets for small special exhibits £5, tickets for large exhibitions £10. Audio tour in English £3. Open M-W 10am-6pm, Th-F 10am-9pm, Sa-Su 10am-6pm. Guided tours Tu at 3:00pm, Th at 1:15pm, Sa-Su at 3pm (departing from main room). Certain scheduled nights open until 10pm.

ST. MARTIN-IN-THE-FIELDS — CHURCH

Trafalgar Sq. ☎020 7766 1100 www.smitf.org

The beautiful church is notable for its sculptures that sit outside; for its strange, contemporary "East Window"; for its status as the Royal Parish Church which has been frequented by the queen; and for its massive organ. But St. Martin-in-the-Fields is most well-known for its long musical history. Every Monday, Tuesday and Friday at 1pm, they have a 45min. "lunch-time concert," which is a classical recital from students at the musical academies and colleges. In the evening, more renowned artists perform in the beautiful space. Additionally, St. Martin is a charitable organization, feeding and sheltering around 3000 homeless people annually. Famous for tourists is the brass rubbing downstairs which allows you to make your own rubbing of the massive bronze tiles. Known as the "Church of the ever-open door" because of its use as a place of refuge for soldiers en-route to France in WWI, St. Martin-in-the-Fields is a must see for any music lover.

*⊖Charing Cross. It's to the east of Trafalgar Square. **i** Audio tour available in English. Brass rubbing £4.50, reserved ticket for jazz £9, unreserved ticket for jazz £5.50. Church open daily 8am-5pm at least, but it stays open later on off-concert days. Shop open M-W 10am-7pm, Th-Sa 10am-9pm, Su 11:30am-6pm. W 8pm is Jazz night.*

COVENT GARDEN PIAZZA — HISTORICAL SITE, SHOPPING

Located between a market filled with tasty food and St. Paul's Church, where there is sometimes summer theater, Covent Garden Piazza is instantly recognizable from films such as Hitchcock's *Frenzy* and *My Fair Lady.* The site of the first Punch and Judy performance in 1662, the Piazza still sees many talented street performers. Once host to Mike Myers and Neil Morrissey, Covent Garden Piazza is worth a visit for its history and its entertainment.

⊖Covent Garden. Turn right down James St.

INSTITUTE OF CONTEMPORARY ART — GALLERY

The Mall ☎020 7930 3647 www.ica.org.uk

The Institute of Contemporary Art is a typically British study in contrast. Located just down the road from Buckingham Palace, the ICA puts on some of the most cutting edge, modern work out there. The cinema shows independent and world cinema and has director Q and As, and has gigs with the likes of Devendra Banhart, Joanna Newsom, Amy Winehouse, and M.I.A. The ICA has no permanent collection, so check the website to see what's on.

*⊖Charing Cross. Turn left down Strand, under the arch and down the mall. The ICA is on your right. **i** Partially wheelchair-accessible. Exhibits rotate out every 6-7 weeks. Free. Cinema £9, concessions £8. Hours are likely to change, so check, but they are W noon-7pm, Th noon-9pm, F-Su noon-7pm. Film screenings 6:15pm, 7:30pm and 8:30pm.*

SEVEN DIALS ♿ HISTORICAL SITE

At the intersection of Mercer, Monmouth, and Earlham St.

Referring to the intersection of seven streets at the column, Seven Dials is an architectural marvel. Thomas Neale owned the land in the area and wanted to generate a profit. To maximize that, he laid out the streets so he could have the seven converge at that point, maximizing space and allowing for more shops and residences. The sundial, known as the Sundial Pillar, at the center was built in 1694, removed in 1773, and replaced in 1989 at an unveiling by the queen of the Netherlands.

Leicester Square. Turn right onto Long Acre and left down Monmouth.

WESTMINSTER

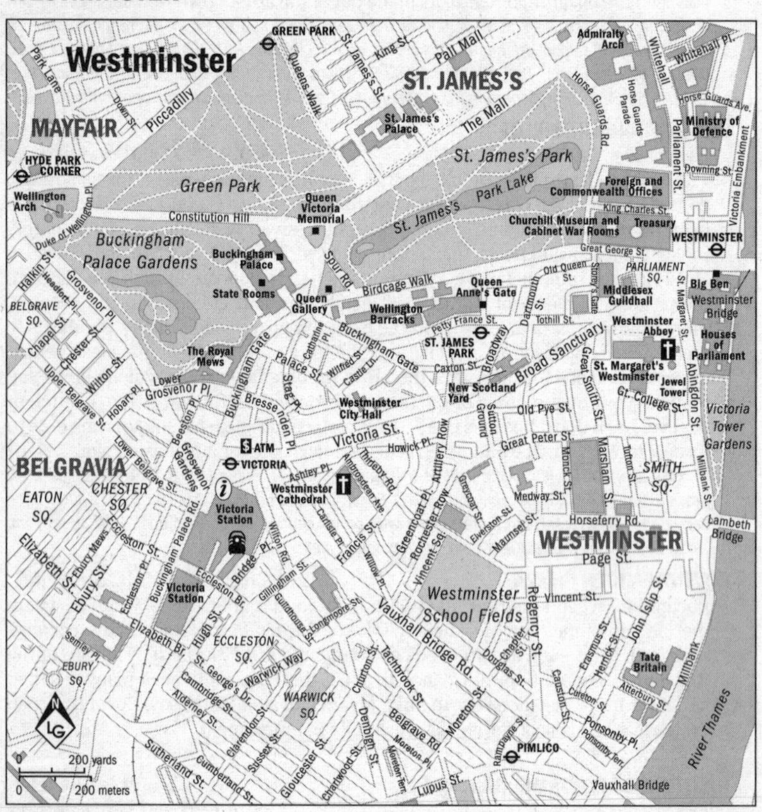

WESTMINSTER ABBEY ♿ ABBEY, HISTORICAL SITE

Off Parliament Sq. ☎020 7222 5152 www.westminster-abbey.org

Founded in 960CE, Westminster Abbey became the royals' church after the crowning of William the Conqueror in 1066. Nearly every monarch since William has been crowned here. Henry III built the modern abbey, but Edward the Confessor built the first church on the site. Inside the abbey, you can see the high altar where kings and queens are crowned and where coffins are displayed during funerals. The chapels interspersed throughout the church house gloriously sculpted monuments. Especially impressive is the statue of Lord and Lady

Norris in the north chapel. Sunlight floods the Lady Chapel during the day, and it's a sight worth seeing. In the Poets' Corner rests the tomb of Chaucer as well as monuments to W.H. Auden, George Eliot, Dylan Thomas, D. H. Lawrence, Lord Byron, Alfred Lord Tennyson, Lewis Carroll, Jane Austen, Charles Dickens, William Shakespeare, and Laurence Olivier. Also buried in the church are Sir Isaac Newton and Charles Darwin. At the end of the audio tour, you'll come across the Tomb of the Unknown Soldier, as well as the Chapter House, where monks signed the abbey over to the king. Nearby is Britain's oldest door, built around 1050. Outside the main building lies St. Margaret's Church, the "parish church of the House of Commons." This church was built by the abbey because the monks didn't want their worship to be disturbed by the masses of commoners coming to worship there. Sir Walter Raleigh was buried in St. Margaret's in 1618.

*Westminster. Walk down Westminster Bridge away from the water on the side of the Westminster Tube stop. Parliament Square and the abbey will be on your left. **i** Audio tours in 11 languages, including English. Definitely take advantage of this free tour (narrated by Jeremy Irons in true Troy Mclure fashion), as there aren't many signs around the abbey. £15, students and seniors £12, ages 11-18 £6, under 11 (accompanied by adult) free, family ticket (2 adults and 1 child) £30 plus £6 for each additional child. Open M-Tu 9:30am-3:30pm, W 9:30am-6:00pm, Th-Sa 9:30am-3:30pm. Abbey Museum 10:30am-4pm daily.*

CHURCHILL MUSEUM AND CABINET WAR ROOMS MUSEUM, HISTORICAL SITE

Clive Steps, King Charles St. ☎020 7930 6961 www.iwm.org.uk/cabinet

The War Rooms opened in 1938, a week before WWII broke out. They were used as a shelter for important government officers, and Winston Churchill spent almost every day of the war in the windowless, airless subterranean rooms, recreated here and opened for public access. The rooms are tense with wartime anxiety, and the map room, with lights that were not turned off for six years during the war, still burns bright. Connected to the Cabinet War Rooms is the Churchill museum. Visitors can step on the sensors to hear excerpts from some of his most famous speeches and watch videos detailing the highs and lows of his career. Also on display are his alcohol habits, which included drinks with breakfast, lunch, and dinner daily, and his patented "romper," better known as a onesie. The interactive, touch-screen "lifeline" is phenomenally detailed; be sure to touch his 90th birthday and August 6th, 1945, but be prepared to draw stares from the other patrons of the museum. It should be noted that, while a lock of his childhood hair is on display, the heavy security surrounding it makes it impossible to use a voodoo doll or potion to bring the great man back to life.

*Westminster or St. James's Park. From Westminster, take a right down Parliament St. and a left onto King Charles St. **i** Free sound guide available in English, French, German, Italian, Spanish, Hebrew, Dutch and Mandarin. £14.95, students and seniors £12, disabled £9, under 16 free. Special rates available for groups, so call ahead. Open daily 9:30am-6pm (last admission 1hr. before close). Call about scheduling a 2hr. tour.*

ST. JAMES'S PARK PARK

The Mall.

Despite its proximity to the crowds of Buckingham Palace, St. James's Park is a true haven. Established in 1531, St. James's is more natural than its more popular, well-tended cousin, Hyde Park. It features a wildlife reserve area reminiscent of a scene from Bambi. The park lake is placid and beautiful, and pelicans feed on the rocks. In fact, the lake and the grassy area surrounding it are an official waterfowl preserve.

St. James's Park. Take a left off Tothill St. onto Broadway. Follow it until you hit the park. Open daily 5am-midnight.

BUCKINGHAM PALACE

George III bought Buckingham House—which wasn't originally built for the royals—in 1761 for his wife, Queen Charlotte. Charlotte proceeded to give birth to 14 out of her 15 children at Buckingham Palace. The house was expanded by George IV, who commissioned John Nash to transform the existing building into a palace. In 1837, Queen Victoria moved into Buckingham Palace, and it has remained a royal residence since then.

Every day at 11:30am from April to late July, and every other day the rest of the year, the **Changing of the Guard** takes place. The "Changing of the Guard" is the exchange of guard duty between different regiments. Forget the dumb American movies where an obnoxious tourist tries in every immature way possible to make the unflinching guards at Buckingham Palace move; the guards are far enough away so that tourists can do no more than whistle every time they move 3 ft. and salute. The entire spectacle lasts 40min. To see it, you should show up well before 11:30am and stand in front of the palace in view of the morning guards. The middle of the week is the least crowded time to watch.

THE STATE ROOMS

At the end of the Mall. ☎020 7766 7300 www.royalcollection.org.uk

The Palace opens to visitors every August and September while the royals are off sunning themselves. Visitors are granted limited access and are only allowed in the State Rooms which are used for formal occasions. As a result, these rooms are sumptuous and as royal as you could hope them to be. As you tour them, look for the secret door concealed in one of the White Drawing Room's mirrors, through which royals entered the state apartments. Also not to be missed are the Throne Room and the glittering Music Room. The Galleries display master works from the royal collections, and the gardens display birds that are marginally prettier than the birds you'd see outside.

Victoria. Turn right onto Buckingham Palace Rd. and follow it onto Buckingham Gate. i Audio guide provided. Wheelchair users should book by calling ☎020 7766 7324. £17, students and seniors £15.50, under 17 £9.75, under 5 free, family (2 adults and 3 children under 17) £45. Open daily late July-Oct, 9:45am-4pm (last admission 45min. before close) daily.

THE ROYAL MEWS

MUSEUM, CARRIAGE HOUSE

At the end of the Mall. ☎020 7766 7300 www.royalcollection.org.uk

The Royal Mews functions as a museum, stable, riding school, and a working carriage house. The carriages are fantastic—especially the "Glass Coach," which is used to carry royal brides to their weddings, and the four-ton Gold State Coach which is not, as the name would suggest, a coach dedicated to California. Unfortunately, the magic pumpkin carriage that the royals use to escape evil step-royals is only visible until midnight, but if you're in the Royal Mews past midnight, you have other problems.

Victoria. Turn right onto Buckingham Palace Rd. and follow it onto Buckingham Gate. Entrance to the Mews and Gallery will be on your left. i Wheelchair-accessible. £7.75, students and seniors £7, under 17 £5, under 5 free, family (2 adults and 3 children under 17) £20.50. Open Mar 20-Oct 31 11am-4pm (last admission 45 min. before close) M-Th, Sa-Su; Nov 1-Dec 23 M-F 11am-4pm (last admission 45min. before close).

QUEEN'S GALLERY

GALLERY

At the end of the Mall. ☎020 7766 7300 www.royalcollection.org.uk

The Queen's Gallery is dedicated to temporary exhibitions of jaw-droppingly valuable items from the Royal Collection. Five rooms, designed to look like the interior of the palace are filled with glorious artifacts that applaud the sovereign. Once purchased, passes can be registered online for 12 months of unlimited access.

Victoria. Turn right onto Buckingham Palace Rd. and follow it onto Buckingham Gate.

Entrance to the Mews and Gallery will be on your left. ***i*** *Wheelchair-accessible.* ⏰ *Open daily 10am-5:30pm (last admission 1hr. before close), July 27-Oct 1 9:30am-5:30pm (last admission 1hr. before close). Closed Nov 1-Apr 14, 2011.*

NORTH LONDON

HAMPSTEAD HEATH ♿ PARK

Hampstead ☎020 7332 3030

Hampstead Heath was initially much smaller than its present 800 acres. After Sir Thomas Maryon Wilson tried to develop and sell off the Heath in the early 19th century, the public began to fight for the Heath, culminating in an Act of Parliament in 1872 that declared the Heath open to the public forever. Now it sprawls gloriously in the heart of Hampstead. The **Hill Gardens** are in the southwest corner of the Heath just off North End Avenue. The Hill House was owned by Lord Leverhulme (of Lever Soap), and he modified the surrounding landscapes to create the beautiful, tamer Hill Gardens. A pergola presides over the gardens, its lattice work is entwined with roses, and painters often station themselves around the gardens and pergola. The view through its Georgian columns is best enjoyed around sunset. **Parliament Hill** is one of the higher points in London, offering those willing to climb its deceptively steep sides a glorious reminder that they aren't in the middle of rural England, but are, in fact, only four miles from London proper. Parliament Hill likely derives its name from its use as a point of defense for Parliament loyalists during the English Civil War, but legend has it that Guy Fawkes watched Parliament from the hill as he waited for it to explode. A surfeit of benches strangle the opening that yields the view, but if you stand on one you can keep everyone irritated and your picture intact. Locals say that "gangs of teenagers" roam the Heath at night, so it's best to visit during the day.

Bus #210 will drop you at the north of the Heath, from which you can access Kenwood House and work your way southeast towards Parliament Hill. Alternatively, you can get off at ⊖Hampstead and turn right onto Heath St., up North End Way, left onto Inverforth Close and left onto a path will take you to the hill gardens. Bus #214 allows easy access to Parliament Hill. ⏰ *Heath open 24hr. Hill Garden open daily May 24-Aug 1 8:30am-8:30pm; Aug 2-May 23 8:30am-1hr. before sunset.*

KENWOOD HOUSE ♿ GALLERY

Hampstead Ln. ☎020 8348 1286 www.english-heritage.org.uk

The Kenwood House was the primary residence of Lord Iveagh, a Barrister and Lord Chief Justice who lived in the house during the 18th century. It currently houses his fabulous art collection, and stands as a representation of an upper-class house from that era. Each room is equipped with laminated sheets explaining the function, decor, and art of the space. The Iveagh Bequest fills the house with paintings that are essentially odes to London of yore. Views of the city from the Heath, like Crone's "*View of London from Highgate*," and an early Turner depicting, per usual, a nautical subject touch upon themes common to the bequest—typical British life. Many come to see Rembrandt's "*Portrait of the Artist*" and Vermeer's "*The Guitar Player.*" The Suffolk Collection, composed mainly of portraits, is on semi-permanent exhibition on the first floor (second floor, for American readers).

Bus #210 will stop on Hampstead Ln. ***i*** *Only ground floor is wheelchair-accessible.* Ⓢ *Free. Booklets £4.* ⏰ *Open daily M-Su 11:30am-4pm. Last entry 3:50pm.*

KEATS'S HOUSE ♿ HISTORICAL SITE

Keats Grove ☎020 7332 3868 www.cityoflondon.gov.uk/keatshousehampstead

John Keats lived with his friend Charles Brown in the house from 1818-1820, right before his death. It is also where he fell in love with Fanny Browne, and

where he composed some of his famous poems such as "Ode to a Nightingale." Meant more for die-hard fans, the museum doesn't offer much beyond a few sheets in each room, some of which feature angst-ridden love letters, famous poems and explanations of the history of the house and the functions of the rooms. This museum has recreated the rooms in all their Regency-inspired glory, though, so the site is as much about the building as it is the writing. Still, if you want to be a writer, and you believe in osmosis, this is the place for you.
Hampstead Heath. Left onto South End Rd., follow it until it hits Keats Grove. Only ground floor is wheelchair-accessible. English audio tour free. £5, concessions £3, under 16 free. Free room guide. Open Apr 6-Oct 31 T-Su 1-5pm; Nov 1-Easter F-Su 1-5pm.

matching colors

Some Tube tracks run multiple lines. To be sure you're on the correct line, just look at the color of the poles in the train; they'll match the color of the line.

EAST LONDON

WHITECHAPEL GALLERY — CONTEMPORARY ART

77-82 Whitechapel High St. ☎020 7522 7888 www.whitechapelgallery.org

This edgy gallery has been showing important contemporary art since it opened in 1901. Originally an effort of hoity-toity uppity-ups to bring art to the culturally decrepit inhabitants of the East End, the gallery's mission has changed, though its commitment to excellence hasn't. Gallery 7 is dedicated to collections that change four times a year. Gallery 2 features year-long commissioned works, and the rest of the gallery deals with contemporary art and occasional mid-career retrospectives. Art films can be seen running on loop in the cinema space.
Aldgate East. Left on Whitechapel High St. Free. Special exhibits normally under £10, with £2 off for students. Open Tu-Su 11am-6pm, first Th of every month 11am-9pm.

NATIONAL MARITIME MUSEUM — MUSEUM

Romney Rd. ☎020 8312 6608 www.nmm.ac.uk

Housed in the formal training center for boys who dreamt of naval careers, the National Maritime Museum provides a history of the organization that gave credence to the claim that Britannia **rules the waves.** This museum has something for all British naval history fanatics. Exhibits include a recreation of the **Starvation Cove,** where Sir John Franklin froze to death, complete with a **frozen arm** hanging over the ship edge, and the uniform in which Horatio Nelson was shot, including blood-soaked stockings and the fatal bullet wound, the museum has something for all fanatics of British naval history. Especially of note are the stained glass windows from the Baltic Exchange which include the intact half-dome which was recreated after it was destroyed in a terrorist attack. The Bridge Simulator allows visitors to take control of a full-size (simulated) ship.
Greenwich. Left on Kay Way, right down Straightsmouth to Greenwich High Rd., right onto Stockwell St., left onto Nevada St., left onto King William Walk. Right onto Romney Rd. Free. Open M-Su 10am-5pm. Last entry 30min. before close. Last entry to the Bridge Simulator M-F 4:35pm, Sa-Su 4:30pm.

THE ROYAL OBSERVATORY — HISTORIC SITE, MUSEUM

Blackheath Ave. ☎020 8312 6608 www.nnn.ac.uk

Charles II founded the Royal Observatory in 1675 to "advance navigation and astronomy." Translation: to stop British ships from sinking so frequently. Greenwich now serves as a marker of hemispheres, with its Prime Meridian, or longitude 0° 0'0" lying in the courtyard of the Royal Observatory. Visitors to the observatory can take pictures in two hemispheres simultaneously by straddling the red LED strip and taking pictures of the floor. After seeing the intersection of the hemispheres, visitors choose one of two routes. The **Meridian route** explores the history of time, with most of the exhibition in the Flamsteed House, former home and workspace of John Flamsteed, the first Astronomer Royal. This route features the original Harrison timekeeper intended to solve the longitude problem and more telescopes than should ever be necessary. The **Meridian Building** features a clever "Time Stood Still For Me When..." exhibit which allows visitors to write about moments when, well, time stood still for them. A true tear-jerker reads, "time stood still for me when I came home to see my pet hamster had died. (His name was Lucky, but in the end he was not)." The **Astronomy route** will give you the opportunity to touch a 4.5-billion-year-old piece of the Gibeon meteorite and also provides access to the popular planetarium.

Greenwich. Left on Kay Way, right down Straightsmouth to Greenwich High Rd., right onto Stockwell St., left onto Nevada St., left onto King William Walk. Right onto Romney Rd., up the hill. ***i*** *Guided tours are free at different times and languages depending on the day. Check online under events. Handicapped tourists should know that, while there is parking on top of the hill, the hill itself is very steep.* *Free. Planetarium £6.50, concessions £4.50. Audio guides available in English, £3.50.* *Open daily in summer M-Su 10am-7pm; in winter 10am-5pm.*

food

British food doesn't have a great reputation. Yes, it is bad for you and no, it doesn't have complex flavors, but it is so intrinsically a part of British life that to forego it would be a grave error for any visitor to England. **Fish** and **chips, bangers** and **mash, tikka masala** (a British invention), and, of course, **warm ale** are all different names for the same thing: comfort food. Neighborhoods like Bloomsbury and Shoreditch serve up wide varieties of ethnic food (read: Indian), but "pub grub" and British food are inescapable. There's a reason that old war propaganda line, "Keep Calm and Carry On," is plastered all over the place; there's a reason the Queen still rolls down the Mall every June 12th; there's a reason the Brits always think England will win the Cup; and there's a reason fair Albion still has the pound; and for that same reason, British food is what it is. Now eat your mushy peas—the cod's getting cold.

BAYSWATER

Shocking though it may be, most travelers like to take a break from bubble and squeak and bangers and mash. When you get itchin' for a little something from an ethnic kitchen, give Bayswater a shot. A wide range of affordable Middle Eastern and Indian restaurants abound in this neighborhood.

LA BOTTEGA DEL GELATO — GELATO ❸

127 Bayswater Rd. ☎020 7243 2443

Simply put, this gelato, made in-store, is divine. La Bottega Del Gelato fills the hole in the London ice cream scene with a variety of delicious flavors. Enjoy it outside on Bayswater Rd. in their seating area; even in the heart of the city, this gelato will make you feel like you're on a quiet street in Roma. The Ferrero Rocher is especially good.

Bayswater. Right onto Queensway, follow it until you hit Bayswater Rd. *1 scoop £2, 2 scoops £3.50, 3 scoops £4.50; milkshakes £3.50.* *Hours change depending on weather, but the store opens daily 10:30am.*

APHRODITE TAVERNA — GREEK ❷

15 Hereford Rd. ☎020 7229 2206 www.aphroditerestaurant.co.uk

Decorated with statues of Aphrodite and a few inexplicable pineapples, Aphrodite Taverna serves up fantastic Greek food at prices that even recession-era Greece can't beat! Too soon? Let's hope not. Come and enjoy a meal of chicken kofta with rice *(£5.90)* or homemade pita *(£4.50)*, and relax as power pop pipes through the store speakers.

Bayswater. Left onto Queensway, left onto Moscow Rd., right onto Hereford toward Westbourne Grove. Entrees £5.50-6.80. M-Su 8am-5pm.

DURBAR RESTAURANT INDIAN 3

24 Hereford Rd. ☎020 7727 1947 www.durbartandoori.co.uk

An authentically Indian interior complements the warm smells from the kitchen of Durbar, where the same family has served p Indian specialties for the last 54 years. A popular Indian restaurant before Indian restaurants were popular, it has the history and accolades to back it. The menu ranges across India with a collection of favorites and some unexpected dishes. Be sure to try one of the 13 varieties of bread baked fresh daily.

Bayswater. Left onto Queensway, left onto Moscow Rd., right onto Hereford toward Westbourne Grove. Tikka £6.95. M-Su noon-2:30pm (closed F lunch), 5:30-11:30pm.

KHAN'S RESTAURANT INDIAN 2

13-15 Westbourne Grove ☎020 7727 5420 www.khansrestaurant.com

Dine among the faux palm trees at this affordable Indian restaurant. Nearly 35 years old, this family-run joint serves the traditional tandoori specialties *(chicken tikka £5.80)* as well as other popular Indian dishes.

Bayswater. Left onto Queensway until you hit Westbourne Grove. Entrees around £4.50-5.80. Open M-Th noon-2:45pm and 6pm-11:45pm, F-Su noon-11:45pm.

THE BATHURST DELI DELI 2

3 Bathurst St. ☎020 7262 1888

Despite its outrageous orange and green exterior, the Bathurst Deli still manages an authentic deli experience. With a friendly staff serving up lasagna, quiches, cannoli, and toasted sandwiches, you can get a good, affordable down-to-earth meal at this eatery.

Lancaster Gate. Take a left onto Westbourne St. and a right onto Banhurst St. Lasagna, quiche, and cannoli £2.20, toasted sandwiches £4-5. Open M-Sa 7am-11pm, Su 8am-11pm.

BLOOMSBURY

Riddled with cheap student eats, Bloomsbury is an exciting and accessible culinary neighborhood. Here are some of the true gems.

NEWMAN ARMS BRITISH PIES 3

23 Rathbone St. ☎020 7636 1127 www.newmanarms.co.uk

Established in 1730, the Newman Arms has been serving succulent British pies about as long as the Queen's relatives have been on the throne. The menu reads like an ode to comfort food, with pies like beef and Guinness, steak and kidney, and lamb and rosemary. The warm upstairs dining room fills up fast, so be sure to reserve a table one day in advance during the summer and much further in advance during the winter (sometimes even months). This food will warm your heart without shrinking your wallet.

Goodge St. Turn left onto Tottenham Court Rd., left onto Tottenham St., left onto Charlotte St., and right onto Rathbone St. i Enter through the corridor next to the entrance to the pub. Pies £10. Puddings £11. Open M-F noon-2:30pm and 6-9:30pm.

NAVARRO'S TAPAS BAR TAPAS 3

67 Charlotte St. ☎020 7637 7713 www.navarros.co.uk

It would make sense if, upon entering this restaurant, you began patting yourself for your passport and looking for the customs agent who won't take "I've nothing to declare" as a personal challenge. Bathed in candlelight and strains of

Flamenco music, Navarro's boasts an excellent selection of regional wines that will convince you you're on your way to Spain. The waitresses wear black and red traditional outfits, and the food lives up to the hype. Tapas are small plates of food, and most people order two or three, with three being a typical meal. Don't forget your castanets.

Goodge St. Turn left onto Tottenham Court Rd., turn left onto Tottenham St. and left onto Charlotte St. i Nicer dress is preferable, as is booking in advance. Mainly vegetarian dishes £4.85-4.95, fish and shellfish £5.75-6.10. Open M-F noon-3pm and 6-10pm, Sa 6-10pm.

i want candy

What could be more British than a bar of Cadbury chocolate? Well, in early 2010, Cadbury, the famed UK confectioner that started up in 1824, unfortunately fell victim to a hostile takeover by the US based international conglomerate Kraft Foods. However, any Cadbury chocolate you buy in the UK is still made from a different recipe than its American counterpart, and is generally thought to be far more delicious—according to the British, at any rate. In addition to making the classic Dairy Milk bar, Cadbury enables chocoholics with their Curly Wurly, Crunchie, and Flake bars. The last of these is often added to the top of soft-serve vanilla icecream to create a British summertime staple known as the "99." While there is debate as to where the name comes from, it is universally agreed that a Flake bar and ice cream is a scrumptious dessert. Visitors to the UK should also sample the Cadbury Crème Egg (not to be confused with a Scotch egg—the latter is an actual hard-boiled egg coated in ground sausage, herbs, and breadcrumbs and then deep-fried).

In the realm of candy, the word "Smarties" may induce unpleasant memories of chalky, pastel colored tablets, but never fear—in Britain, Nestlé Smarties, originally known as "Chocolate Beans," are reminiscent of MandMs. Those looking for a non-chocolate candy treat can channel their inner Edmund Pevensie from C.S. Lewis's *The Lion, the Witch, and the Wardrobe* and try Turkish Delight. This sugary, gelatinous treat, often flavored with rosewater and rolled in powdered sugar, tends to be rather divisive—people either love it or hate it. Since it is widely available throughout the UK, you can decide for yourself whether Turkish Delight is delectable or disgusting. Be sure to keep in mind that while rosewater is one of the most common flavors, it's also something of an acquired taste; a safer choice might be lemon or mint.

NORTH SEA FISH RESTAURANT — FISH AND CHIPS ❸

7-8 Leigh St. ☎020 7387 5892 www.northseafishrestaurant.co.uk

In a country where you'd think "chips" were a natural part of the fish, North Sea Fish takes the British staple one step further with a wide-ranging menu encompassing dishes such as the Seafood Platter (fried goujons of cod, haddock, plaice, pieces of scotch scampi, squid, and sardines). Basically, most of the menu is fish and chips, and the fact that this is still a good restaurant speaks volumes.

Russell Sq. Go down Colonnade with your back to Russell Sq. Turn left on Grenville St. Follow it onto Hunter St., which will become Judd St. Turn left at Leigh St. i Cheap takeaway available next door to the restaurant. Entrees £14-15. Open M-Sa noon-2:30pm and 5:30-10:30pm.

SAVOIR FAIRE BISTRO ❷

42 New Oxford St. ☎020 7436 0707 www.savoir.co.uk

This place looks a little bit like a New Orleans whorehouse, and we mean that in the best way possible. Handwritten notes on the ceiling advise customers to "make love to every woman you meet." If you get 5% on your outlays, it's a "good investment," while a mural of dancing, drinking French women covers the wall. The ceiling is also partially filled with notes from friends, emphasizing the community feel of the restaurant. What Savoir Faire knows how to make is immediately obvious and is explained by their slogan: "affordable gourmet food." Omelettes are served with fresh baked bread, and sandwiches come on fresh baguettes.

Tottenham Court Road. Turn onto New Oxford St. so that Tottenham Court Rd. is on your left and Charing Cross Rd. is on your right. Omelettes £5-6, sandwiches £4.50. Open M-Sa noon-11pm, Su noon-10:30pm.

ANDREAS GREEK AND MEDITERRANEAN ❺

40 Charlotte St. ☎020 7580 8971 www.andreas-restaurant.com

Andreas is expensive, but some say that Mediterranean cuisine is the healthiest for you; so if you want to live long in poverty, eat here often. Offering well-made Greek and Mediterranean food at correspondingly high prices, Andreas hits all of the classics. The menu features dishes like moussaka, dolmades, and garlic poussin that are chic and upscale, yet accessible.

Goodge St. Turn left onto Tottenham Court Rd., turn left onto Tottenham St. and left onto Charlotte St. Entrees £13-15. Open M-F 11:30am-3:30pm and 5:30-11pm, Sa 5:30-11pm.

CHELSEA

BUONA SERA ITALIAN ❸

289a King's Rd ☎020 7352 8827

People haven't eaten like this since our ancestors moved out of the trees and onto the ground. The small restaurant manages to fit 14 tables into its tight space by stacking the booths one atop the other. It's sort of like a game of Tetris, except involving delicious and affordable Italian food. Plants on the upper level make the experience feel like it's taking place in the canopy of a tree, but the food will remind you of the pleasures of civilization.

Sloane Sq. Exit the Tube and go straight down Sloane Sq. The street slanting gently left is King's Rd. If you don't want to walk the road (it's manageable but long), the following buses service the area: 11, 19, 22, 211, 319 Salads £4.50-5.70, lunch entrees £7.90-8.50. Pasta and risotto £8.60-9.80. Meat and fish entrees £14.50-14.80. Pizza £3.80, plus £1.50 per topping set (tuna and onions, ham and mushrooms, etc.). Open M 6pm-midnight, Tu-F noon-3pm, 6pm-midnight, Sa-Su noon-midnight.

GORDON RAMSAY CELEBRITY, FRENCH ❺

68 Royal Hospital Rd. ☎020 7352 4441 www.gordonramsay.com

Owned by celebrity chef Gordon Ramsay, this haven for those with cash to drop hides behind a simple black and white facade on a quiet stretch of Royal Hospital Rd. On the curb by the restaurant, you may see the sleeping drivers of the Masters of the Universe who dine within. You can join their charges for dinner only if you book exactly three months in advance. With a prix fixe menu *(£90)* offering three delicious courses of exquisite French food, Gordon Ramsay may be the splurge you're looking for.

*Sloane Sq. Straight onto Sloane Sq., left onto Lower Sloane St., right onto Royal Hospital Rd. **i** See website for dress code. Jeans, T-shirts or sportswear not accepted. Reservations for lunch do not need to be made as far in advance. Open M-F noon-2:30pm and 6:30-11pm.*

LA BOTTEGA ITALIAN COFFEE ❷

65 Lower Sloane St. ☎020 7730 8844 www.labottega65.co.uk

Some London cappuccino connoisseurs insist that there's no better cappuccino than the one at La Bottega. Made with Illy Coffee, their cappuccino transcends the health food kick and is always made with creamy whole milk. In addition to fantastic coffee, La Bottega offers handmade breadsticks, Italian favorites like meat lasagna and eggplant parmesan. Most of the ingredients are imported weekly from Italy, and a shelf opposite the counter houses select vinegars and olive oils straight from the culinary king of countries.

Sloane Square. Left onto Lower Sloane St. Entrees from £4.90. Open M-F 8am-8pm, Sa 9am-7pm, Su 10am-5pm.

THE CITY OF LONDON

Many of the culinary offerings in the City of London are geared toward businessmen (expensive) and tourists (expensive, but not very good). Fortunately, there are a few promising options for the budget traveler.

SPIANATA ITALIAN, SANDWICH, PIZZA ❶

73a Watling St. ☎020 7236 3666 www.spianata.com

Enjoy the delicious taste of Italy in every sandwich served on Spianata's freshly baked bread. The businessmen in the city know that some of the best sandwiches and pizzas in the city are served at this authentically Italian shop, so arrive before the peak lunch hour.

St. Paul's. Go down Cheapside away from St. Paul's Cathedral; turn right at Bread St. and left at Watling St. Sandwiches £3.25-4; pizza £1.60 cold, £1.90 hot. M-F 7:30am-3:30pm.

YE OLDE CHESHIRE CHEESE PUB ❸

145 Fleet St., down Wine Office Court

The current Cheese was built in 1667, but a pub has been in its current location since 1538. **Charles Dickens** and **Samuel Johnson,** author of the first dictionary (a copy is upstairs), frequented the pub. Despite its history, Ye Olde Cheshire Cheese remains a personable, old-timey watering hole, serving traditional English "fayre" alongside their phenomenally cheap and excellent Samuel Smith brews from Yorkshire. If you explore the downstairs dining room, be wary of the sign that says "mind your head." They mean it.

St. Paul's. Take a right on New Change, a right onto Cannon St. which becomes St. Paul's Churchyard, Ludgate Hill and then Fleet St. Entrees £9.95-11.95; bangers and mash £3.50. Shots £1.89-2.20; 1/2 pint of lager £1.14; pint of lager £2.27; 1/2 pint of ale £1.00; pint of ale 1.99. M-Sa 11am-11pm, Su 11am-6pm.

CAFE BELOW CAFE ❸

Underneath St. Mary-Le-Bow, in Crypt. ☎020 7329 0789 www.cafebelow.co.uk

Cafe Below gives those of us alive and kickin' reason to visit the crypt. The cafe serves up delicious, wholesome breakfast, lunch and dinner to visitors and non-visitors alike. With a beautiful dining room that takes full advantage of the church's fantastic architecture, Cafe Below provides food that's uniquely home-made at reasonable prices.

St. Paul. Go down Cheapside with your back to St. Paul's Cathedral. Breakfast, £4.50-50, lunch £7.50-8.50, dinner £10.50. Take-away tends to be roughly 1.00 less. M-F 7:30am-9pm.

S AND M BRITISH FOOD ❷

28 Leadenhall Mkt. ☎020 7626 6646 www.sandmcafe.co.uk

S and M will give you serious pleasure. We're both talking about sausage and mash, right? Dedicated to the preservation of British cuisine, S and M serves authentic British breakfasts in addition to their various varieties of sausage and mash. It gets crowded at lunch, so if you're going to do S and M, come early.

Bank. Walk down Cornhill towards Leaden Hall St. Breakfast from £3.25, SandM dishes £8.50-8.95, entrees £8.95-9.50. Open M-T 8am-3pm, W-Th 8am-9pm, F 8am-3pm.

HOLBORN AND CLERKENWELL

Holborn offers standard fare plus a few high-class restaurants and bistros mixed in with typical take-away sandwich joints. Clerkenwell has a lot more in the vein of hip, light, and interesting restaurants.

THE CLERKENWELL KITCHEN — HEALTHY, BRITISH, SEASONAL ❸

31 Clerkenwell Close — ☎020 7101 9959 www.theclerkenwellkitchen.co.uk

Normally when a restaurant advertises "soft drinks," they mean cola and root beer. At the Clerkenwell Kitchen, a "soft drink" means a taste-bud-exploding concoction like their elderflower cordial *(£2)*. The closest they come to Coke is their organic cola. Cooking with locally grown ingredients and organic, free-range meat, the Clerkenwell Kitchen welcomes guests to the lighter side of British fare. In the summer months, bask in the light that fills their terrace; in the winter, enjoy dishes like slow-roast pork belly with braised lentils, chard, and quince aioli. The menu changes daily based entirely on which fresh and local ingredients they receive, but if one thing is consistent, it's the high quality of this hidden restaurant.

Farringdon. Right onto Cowcross St., right onto Farringdon, right onto Pear Tree Ct., right onto Clerkenwell Close. Walk straight as if still on Pear Tree Ct. If you see the church, backtrack. Entrees £9-10. Teas and coffees £1.50-1.85. Open M-F 8am-5pm and noon-3pm.

DANS LE NOIR — FRENCH ❺

30-31 Clerkenwell Green — ☎020 7253 1100 www.danslenoir.com/london

Remember that Halloween game you played when you were a kid? Someone's mom would bring out a bowl of spaghetti and you would put your hands in it and squirm at the thought that you were touching real human intestines. Dans le Noir recreates that experience, only this time, once you're done sticking your hand in your plate, you eat the intestines. Served by blind waiters, patrons of the restaurant dine in a pitch black dining room, getting served a surprise meal of meat, fish, vegetarian, or "surprise" varieties. It may be expensive, but you're paying for a full sensory experience as well as the fantastic food.

Farringdon. Left onto Cowcross St., left onto Turnmill St., and a right at the Vine St. Bridge. It's across the green. Surprise 2-course meal £39, surprise 3-course menu is £44. You can book for a 6:30-9pm meal or a 9pm-whenever your meal ends (by midnight) meal.

BLEEDING HEART TAVERN FRENCH, TAVERN ❸

Entrance to Bleeding Heart Yard ☎020 7242 2056 www.bleedingheart.co.uk/tavern

Bleeding Heart Tavern takes the challenge of reinventing pub food and succeeds. While holding onto its status as an excellent tavern that'll get you "drunk for a penny, and dead drunk for two pence," the Bleeding Heart Tavern also produces mouth-watering pub food, like its salt beef sandwich served on delectable home-made bread with a side of delicious coleslaw. From homemade pork sausages to spinach and three cheeses roulade, Bleeding Heart Tavern does it all with a French twist, and they do it well.

Farringdon. Take a right onto Cowcross St., and continue onto Greville St. Open M-F noon-2:30pm and 6-10:30pm; Sa noon-3pm and 6-11pm.

BLEEDING HEART BISTRO FRENCH BISTRO ❹

Bleeding Heart Yard www.bleedingheart.co.uk/bistro

A classic and classy bistro experience, the Bleeding Heart Bistro takes excellent tavern fare (mentioned above) to the next level. With an adventurous menu featuring more than 450 wines, the Bleeding Heart Bistro offers an atmosphere that, despite the anti-smoking laws in the UK, manages to seem romantically smoke-filled at all times.

Farringdon. Take a right onto Cowcross St. and continue onto Greville St. Entrees £10.95-11.95. Open M-F noon-2:30pm and 6-10:30pm, Sa noon-3pm and 6-11pm.

MARYLEBONE AND REGENT'S PARK

THE GOLDEN HIND FISH AND CHIPS ❷

73 Marylebone Ln. ☎020 7486 3644

The Golden Hind might just have the best fish and chips in London. With a wide selection of fish and a selection of classic sides, the menu will challenge you in ways you never thought fish and chips could.

Bond St. Left onto Davies St., right onto Oxford St., left onto Marylebone Ln. Fish (fried or steamed) £4.70-5.70. Chips £1.50. Peas £1. Open M-F noon-3pm and 6-10pm, Sa 6-10pm.

PATOGH PERSIAN ❷

8 Crawford Pl ☎020 7262 4015

Patogh is the definition of hole-in-the-wall. Small and crowded but nicely decorated and exquisitely scented, Patogh provides traditional Persian food like minced lamb and huge servings of sesame flatbread in a highly atmospheric setting.

Edgward Rd. Right onto Chapel St., left onto Edgware Rd., left onto Crawford Pl. Entrees £8-9. Open daily noon-11pm.

LE RELAIS DE VENISE L'ENTRECOTE STEAK FRÎTES ❹

120 Marylebone Ln. ☎020 7486 0878 www.relaisdevenise.com

Amid the warm decor and wall-size paintings of canals that decorate this restaurant, hungry diners just in from a queue that typically stretches around the block feast on one thing and one thing only: L'entrecote's fantastic *steak frîtes.*

Bond St. Left onto Davies St., right onto Oxford St., left onto Marylebone Ln. Open M-Th noon-2:30pm and 6pm-10:45pm. F noon-2:45pm and 6pm-10:45pm, Sa 12:30pm-3:30pm and 6:30-10:45pm, Su 12:30pm-3:30pm and 6:30-10:30pm.

ROYAL CHINA DIM SUM ❸

24-26 Baker St. ☎020 7487 4688 www.royalchinagroup.co.uk

This micro chain is a good place to find Dim Sum if you're craving it. Though the decor walks the fine line between elegant and cheesy, the restaurant is quiet and pleasant, and the selection is expansive.

Baker Street. Left Baker St. Most dim sum items £2.65-3.15. Noodles £7.50-8. Entrees £8.50-9.20. Set meals for 2+ people £30 per person. Open M-Sa noon-11pm. M-Sa Dim Sum noon-5pm, Su 11am-5pm.

THE WEST END

MÔ CAFÉ
CAFE, TEA, NORTH AFRICAN ❷

23-25 Heddon St. ☎020 7434 4040 www.momoresto.com

When juxtaposed with the absurd decadence of nearby Absolut Icebar (yes, that is a bar...made of ice), the Mo Cafe's own absurd conceit feels a little less ridiculous. With waiters wearing bright red shirts and black pants, chandeliers that are draped in tassels and strings and bronze table tops surrounded by low chairs, the Mo Cafe looks like it's trying too hard. However, try the hummus or the mint tea (made with tea imported from Morocco, obviously), and you'll feel your skull tingle where your fez once was. The restaurant is a true experience, especially when the other patrons are enjoying £18 hookah in your general vicinity. That's right, hookah. Only in Soho would that just as easily be a mispronunciation of another commonly purchased service.

Piccadilly Circus. Turn left onto Regent St. and left onto Heddon St. Cold mezze £4.50-4.75. Hot mezze £5.50-5.80. M-Sa noon-1am, Su noon-11pm.

FERNANDEZ AND WELLS CAFE
CAFE, SANDWICHES ❸

73 Beak St. ☎020 7287 8124 www.fernandezandwells.com

Yuppified to the max, Fernandez and Wells knows its crowd and it serves them well. A bright space with simple wood and thin counters for eating, the restaurant prides itself on its coffee and gives out a map to all the good coffee spots in London, serving the yuppy desire to be "cool" and "in-the-know." Providing ready-made, delicious sandwiches with well-prepared ingredients, Fernandez and Wells is a good spot for a fast and easy lunch.

Piccadilly Circus. Turn right down Shaftesbury Ave. and left onto Lexington St., left onto Beak St. Croissaints £1.65-1.80. Chelsea bun £2.45. Coffee £2.20-2.50. Sandwiches £4.25-5.50. Open M-F 7:30am-6pm, Sa 9am-6pm, Su 9am-5pm.

KOYA
JAPANESE ❸

49 Frith St. ☎020 7434 4463 www.koya.co.uk

Unlike many Japanese restaurants, where Chinese or British cooks pretend to make authentic Japanese dishes, Koya is the real deal. Through the cloth that guards the front door lies a dining room where only the most authentic and delicious *hiya-atsu* and *atsu-atsu* (cold and hot udon) is served. This place is good, and Soho knows it, so try and come sometime other than 6:30pm, as they don't take reservations, it gets crowded, and the starving people you'll stand outside with may or may not be very pleasant.

Tottenham Court Rd. Turn down Oxford St. with your back to Tottenham Court Rd and then left onto Soho St. Go around Soho Sq to the left and turn left onto Frith. Udon is around £8.50-9. Open M-Sa noon-3pm and 5:30pm-10:30pm.

BAR ITALIA
COFFEE BAR ❸

22 Frith St. ☎020 7437 4520 baritaliasoho.co.uk

Bar Italia is about as close as you'll get to what would've happened if Ed Hopper had painted the *Nighthawks* in Soho. Its simple, unassuming decor is as authentic as the coffee is strong, and photos of its storied past (replete with coffee drinkers of yore) line the walls. On a nice day, many sit outside and watch the parade of altered life that is Soho. The clientele runs the gamut—hip or unhip, it matters not: they belly up to the same counter for Bar Italia's classic coffee.

Tottenham Court Rd. Turn down Oxford St. with your back to Tottenham Court Rd and then left onto Soho St. Go around Soho Sq to the left and turn left onto Frith. Espresso £2.50-3.80. Cappuccino is £2.80-3.80. Caffe latte £3-4. Pizzas around £11.50. Panini £6.20-6.80.

SOFRA MEDITERRANEAN ❹

18 Shepherd St. ☎020 7493 3320 www.sofra.co.uk

Sofra has a brightly lit, wide open dining room that somehow feels like it's sitting on the edge of a Mediterranean beach where men in three-button-undone shirts seduce women in red dresses. Is that just us? Well, either way, this pleasant dining space provides fairly high-priced Mediterranean classics like Lamb Tagine, kebabs and salmon stew.

Hyde Park Corner. Go down Piccadilly Arcade staying to the left of the Wellington Arch with your back to Hyde Park. Turn left onto White Horse St. Entrees around £11.95, but there's a wide range. Open daily 8am-11pm.

NORTH LONDON

LA CRÊPERIE DE HAMPSTEAD CRÊPES, STREET STAND ❶

Around 77 Hampstead High St. www.hampsteadcreperie.com

Walking down Hampstead High St. from the underground station, a traveler may notice several people lining the bus stop benches, ravenously eating crêpes out of small conical cups. Walk a bit further down, and you'll see La Crêperie de Hampstead. Serving the community since 1929, the creperie is not the average street vendor's booth. The crêpes are expertly crafted—a perfect balance of light and doughy—and the ingredients, sweet or savory, are well-blended to create crêpes that burst with flavor.

Hampstead. Left onto Hampstead Heath St. i No seating available, but check the nearby benches. Savories £4.30-4.65. Sweets £3.40-3.90. Open M-Th 11:45am-11pm, F-Su 11:45am-11:30pm.

MANGO ROOM CARIBBEAN ❸

10-12 Kentish Town Rd. ☎020 7482 5065 www.mangoroom.co.uk

Located near bustling Camden Town, the Mango Room is the perfect place to escape the excitement. The cool room decorated with bright paintings that nicely complement the food is perfect for anyone who regrets choosing rainy London over the sunny Caribbean for a vacation. Serving Caribbean dishes like ackee and saltfish with scallions and sweet peppers *(£11)*, the Mango Room is about as escapist and pleasant as the name suggests.

Camden High St. Left onto Camden High St., left onto Camden Rd., Left onto Kentish Town Rd. i Minimum £10. Dinner entrees £10.50-11. Lunch entrees £7-8.50. Mixed drinks £4 during happy hour. Open daily noon-11pm. Bar open until 1am F-Sa. Happy hour 6-8pm.

CARMELLI BAKERY KOSHER BAKERY ❶

128 Golders Green Rd. ☎020 8455 2074 www.carmelli.co.uk

Carmelli Bakery is overfilling with delicious kosher foods—everything from fresh made bagels to delicious chollas and chocolate eclairs. While there's no seating in the store, the nearby bus stop has a bench.

Golders Green. Cross Finchley Rd. to Golders Green Rd. Bagels £2-2.20 closed, £1.40-1.50 open (with toppings like cream cheese, chopped herring, salmon and cream cheese). Eclairs £.85. Chocolate mousse £.90. Open daily 6am-1am.

MARINE ICES GELATO ❷

8 Haverstock Hill ☎020 7482 9003 www.marineices.co.uk

Though it looks like someone decided to move part of the Jersey Shore to London, Marine Ices serves some of the finest quality Italian ice in London at affordable prices. They make it all in-house and then serve it in hearty portions to regular patrons and local restaurants alike. While there isn't much else to do at Chalk Farm, Marine Ices is right near the Tube and, if you're in the area, might just be worth a stop.

Chalk Farm. i Credit card £5 min. Wheelchair-accessible through the window (where they serve ice cream on nice days), not through restaurant. 1 scoop £1.90, 2 scoops £3.50, £4.90 3 scoops. Each topping £.60. Open Tu-Su noon-11pm, window is open in the window as well.

EAST LONDON

Most of East London's culinary offerings are packed into the unbeatable **Brick Lane.** If you're looking for curry, you'd have to be blind and smell-challenged not to find it. However, if you want to partake in the Shoreditch scene but can't handle the pressure of choosing just one curry restaurant, here are a few good alternatives.

NUDE ESPRESSO — CAFE ❸

26 Hanbury St. ☎078 0422 3590 www.nudeespresso.com

Most good cafes pride themselves on buying exotic coffee beans, but Nude Espresso takes their gimmick a step further, actually roasting the coffee beans themselves. Serving up some of the best coffee in London, the hip Nude Espresso is a welcome break from the myriad curry restaurants hawking their wares on Brick Ln. With its aluminum cups and stylish interior, Nude Espresso gets the aesthetic right while never forgetting what its clients came for: damn good coffee.

Aldgate East. Left onto Whitechapel Rd., left onto Osborn St., continue onto Brick Ln.; left onto Hanbury. i Min. £6 purchase with credit card. Wi-Fi available, but they don't allow plugins. $ Breakfast and lunch entrees £6-£7.50. Espresso £2-£2.50. Specialty coffee drinks around £3.60. Open M-F 7:30am-6pm, Sa-Su 10am-6pm.

CAFE 1001 — CAFE ❷

91 Brick Ln. ☎020 7247 9679 www.cafe1001.co.uk

Under the overhang connecting Cafe 1001 to the Truman Ale factory, hip East Enders bask in the British sun's occasional appearances and share in the good coffee served from the cafe's year-round outdoor cart. Inside the cafe, numerous patrons listen to music from the likes of Caetano Veloso and kick back in the warehouse-like space. At night, the salad bar turns into a real bar, and the back room becomes a venue for up-and-coming bands and DJs, and sometimes it even serves as a classroom for aspiring swing dancers. Basically, this cafe is as close as a cafe comes to being a cultural center. Incidentally, Jack the Ripper killed someone out behind the back room, so prostitutes might want to take their business elsewhere. Bloc Party also filmed their video for "The Prayer" here. "East London is a vampire," as the boys would say.

Aldgate East. Left onto Whitechapel Rd., left onto Osborn St., continue onto Brick Ln. i Credit card min. £4 purchase. F, Sa, Su are club nights from 7pm-midnight, with DJs playing in the back room. Live bands every Tu (rock) and W (folk and jazz). Swing dancing classes Th 11am-5pm. $ Coffee £1.20-1.70 for a small, £.40-£2 for a large. Cover charge £3-5 after midnight. Free Wi-Fi. Open daily 7am-midnight, sometimes no closing F-Su (as in, it stays open continuously).

BEIGEL BAKE — BAGELS ❶

159 Brick Ln. ☎020 7729 0616

This sparse-looking bakery may not seem appealing to the casual observer, but once the sweet and heavy perfume of their classic, fresh-made bagels has enveloped you, you'll have a harder time passing it by.

Aldgate East. Left on Whitechapel Rd, left on Osborn St., continue onto Brick Ln. $ Filled bagels £.80-1.50. Open daily 24hr.

OTHER NEIGHBORHOODS

POILÂNE — BAKERY ❸

46 Elizabeth St. ☎020 7808 4910 www.poilane.com

Poilâne is one of the most famous bakeries from Paris, which means that, by London standards, it's ungodly good. The commitment to excellence at Poilâne is unparalleled. Many of the bakers live above the shop, baking the bread all through the night to ensure that it's fresh for the morning crowd. They use only the oldest, most time-honored traditions and techniques when creating their sourdough masterpieces, and the *pain au chocolat* is to die for. Also worth noting is the fact that they bake in wood-fired ovens of the type that started the Great Fire of London—but don't worry, Poilâne is both safe *and* delicious.

Victoria. Left onto Buckingham Palace Rd., right onto Elizabeth St. Custard tart £16. Walnut bread £4. Pain au chocolat £1.20. Sourdough bread £4.40. Open M-F 7:30am-7pm. Sa 7:30am-6pm.

DA SCALZO — ITALIAN ❸

2 Eccleston Pl. ☎020 7730 5498 www.dascalzo.com

You should really be wary of Italian restaurants, especially ones in close proximity to train and bus stations, like da Scalzo, but da Scalzo defies all odds. The food is well-priced and fantastically portioned, making for a real Italian feast to be savored. Their pastas and pizzas are especially delish, but they do amazing things with the preparation of other dishes that'll make you double take when you see the bill (which, for food of this caliber, is strikingly low). More important than all of this, however, is the atmosphere at da Scalzo. The waiters and waitresses pal around with each other, putting on informal shows with pizza dough, and they have the incredible ability to make you feel that, though you may have just gotten off the plane, you've been dining at da Scalzo for your whole life.

Victoria. Left onto Buckingham Palace Rd., right onto Elizabeth St. Pasta and risotto £6-7. Stone baked pizza £8.50-9. Meat £12.50-14. Fish £12.50. Open M-Sa 8am-11pm, Su 8am-8pm.

BAKER AND SPICE — NEW EUROPEAN PASTRIES ❸

54-56 Elizabeth St. ☎020 7730 3033 www.bakerandspice.uk.com

Baker and Spice is the *part deux* of the one-two pastry punch on Elizabeth St. The street boasts Poîlane, and, less than a block away, the equally good Baker and Spice. Serving freshly made pastries, strong, delicious coffee and a wide variety of ready-made meals and salads, Baker and Spice is gourmet on the go. Ideal for takeaway, but delicious enough to be savored slowly in the al fresco dining areas, Baker and Space does it all with ample style and grace.

Victoria. Left onto Buckingham Palace Rd., right onto Elizabeth St. Open M-Sa 7am-7pm, Su 8am-5pm.

THE KENSINGTON CRÊPERIE — CRÊPES ❸

2-6 Exhibition Rd. ☎020 7589 8947 www.kensingtoncreperie.com

Close to the museums off Exhibition Rd., the Kensington Creperie serves fantastic and affordable crepes and less affordable, equally fantastic ice cream sundaes. With delicious crepes like the garlic, spinach, and cream cheese option, the Kensington Creperie produces ice cream sundae masterpieces such as the Stone Age. (hazelnuts, walnuts, peanuts, coconuts, flaked almond, two scoops of ice cream, sauce of choice, honey, and walnuts). With alfresco dining on Exhibition Rd., each delicious savory and sweet crepe only tastes better.

South Kensington. Turn right onto Thurloe St., left onto Exhibition Rd. Crepes £7.75-8.30. Sundaes £5.95. Open M-Su 8am-11pm.

THE GATE — VEGETARIAN, VEGAN, GLUTEN FREE ❹

51 Queen Caroline St., 2nd floor. ☎020 8748 6932 www.thegate.tv

Tucked away down Queen Caroline St. in the lofty, sunlit studio of a former puppet-maker, the Gate has been serving a menu composed almost entirely of vegetarian, vegan, or gluten-free dishes for the last twenty years. Everything is made from seasonal ingredients, and the massive window that illuminates the dining room is bordered by sunflowers. If you like what you eat, you can buy their own cookbook, too.

Hammersmith. Take the south exit from the Hammersmith shopping center toward the London Apollo and follow Queen Caroline St. Reservations recommended 3 days in advance. Entrees £12.50-13.50. Open M-F noon-2:30pm and 6-10pm, Sa 6-11pm.

PATIO POLISH, ENGLISH ❷

5 Goldhawk Rd. ☎020 8743 5194

Patio is literally buried in the numerous accolades and press given to the restaurant over its 24-year career. Owned by a former Polish opera singer, Patio is filled with warm carpets and stuffed upholstered chairs, meant to create a casual but pleasant dining experience. Diners enjoy traditional English and Polish fare (the menu is filled with veal), and selections from the Polish menu come with complimentary Polish vodka. There's also a dusty-sounding piano which any guest can play. Come and enjoy and then catch a show nearby.

Shepherd's Bush. Cross Uxbridge Rd. and turn right onto Shepherd's Bush Green. Follow it until it becomes Goldhawk Rd. Entrees £8.50-11. Seafood £8.50-9.50. Open M-F noon-3pm and 5-11pm, Sa-Su 6-11:30pm.

JENNY LO'S TEAHOUSE ASIAN TEA ❷

14 Eccleston St. ☎020 7259 0399 www.jennylo.co.uk

Thought you'd never hear about J. Lo again? This unassuming teahouse serves delicious Asian classics like Vietnamese-style vermicelli rice noodles, Thai-style lamb in green curry, and wok noodles—it's a wok to remember. They have their own herbalist (Dr. Xu) and a terrific selection of delicious teas. Come here for a quick, quiet, and delicious meal.

Victoria. i Min. £5 per person. Takeaway available. Entrees £7.50-8.50. Therapeutic teas £2. Mint tea £3.50. Chinese teas £2. Open M-F noon-3pm and 6-10pm.

CHARLIE'S PORTOBELLO RD. CAFE BRITISH CAFE ❸

59A Portobello Rd. ☎020 7221 2422 www.charliesportobelloroadcafe.co.uk

Tucked away in a small alcove off busy Portobello Rd., Charlie's Portobello Road Cafe is a hidden gem in one London's most over-exposed areas. Light streams into the spacious, authentically worn dining space through the huge French windows which are thrown open to a plant-lined patio. An atmospheric restaurant, Charlie's is a great place for a good, old-fashioned English breakfast.

Notting Hill Gate. Take a right onto Pembridge Rd. and then left onto Portobello Rd. i Free Wi-Fi. Full English breakfast £9.50. Open M-Sa 9am-5pm, Su noon-2:30pm.

THE HUMMINGBIRD BAKERY PASTRY ❸

133 Portobello Rd. ☎020 7229 6446 www.hummingbirdbakery.com

Priding themselves on bold, simple, American-style baked goods, the Hummingbird Bakery serves up their popular cupcakes and cakes in a simple space decorated by paintings of (surprise!) hummingbirds.

Notting Hill Gate. Take right onto Pembridge Rd. and then left onto Portobello Rd. i Credit cards £5 min. Takeaway cheaper than eat-in. Cupcakes £1.75-2. Open M-F 10am-6pm, Sa 10am-6pm, Su 11am-5pm.

BON GUSTO SANDWICHES, ITALIAN ❶

75-77 Buckingham Gate ☎020 7222 7185

London, and Westminster especially, is teeming with touristy, budget restaurants that advertise themselves as *"Ristorante Italiano,"* but serve up the most British Italian food ever. Bon Gusto advertises as such, but anyone passing the front door will find it hard to turn away. The restaurant unleashes a gust of hearty Italian smells on any passerby, and the toasted sandwiches on ciabatta and focaccia are delicious at unbeatable prices.

Victoria. Right on Victoria St., left onto Buckingham Gate. Sandwiches £3.85-3.90. Open M-Sa 7am-10pm, Su 7am-3pm.

nightlife

If you seek the club scene of say, Barcelona, go to Barcelona. The elitist impulse often rears its head in British club life—this is especially evident in Kensington and Chelsea where many clubs are "members only," meaning they'll make you ask to have your name put on a guest list. That doesn't mean that there's no nightlife. Visitors can find evening kicks in bars that serve some exciting drinks (check out Soho for lessons in **mixology**). Music venues like the **Troubadour** in Kensington provide killer atmospheres and young crowds late at night.

Still, pubs are the fabric of British life. Most are open daily 11am-11pm with some variation in regards to the weekend. Pubs are where Brits come to eat and drink too much. At lunchtime, the pubs in Westminster and the City of London fill with men in matching suits. The best are the ones that claim residence in the oldest drinking locations in London, meaning that people have been drunk there since the dawn of time. Be wary of the "George Orwell drank here" or the "Dylan Thomas drank here" line—you will see those names everywhere, because not only were they fantastic drunks, they were also prolific walkers. Parliament even passed the **Defense of the Realm Act** during WWI to limit pub hours in order to keep the munitions workers sober. This law was in effect until 1988, and many pubs still retain the early hours. Always bring cab fare or plan your **night bus** route home as the **Tube** closes early.

BLOOMSBURY

VATS WINE BAR — WINE BAR

51 Lambs' Conduit St. — 020 7242 8963 — www.vatswinebar.com

The epitome of a warm, British restaurant, Vats imports much of its wine while keeping the feel of the place properly British. With a menu boasting around 160 vintages from all over, Vats is an upscale and pleasant evening experience. Upscale pub food like venison sausages with creamed mash, broccoli florets, belotte beans, bacon sauce, and a garnish of cranberries are par for the course. Dine downstairs or outside between the two latticework fences that shield the restaurant's facade. The food is hearty and delicious, and the wine flows freely.

Russell Square. Left onto Colonnade, right onto Grenville St., left onto Guilford St. and right onto Lambs' Conduit St. Sides £3.75. Entrees £13-15. Open M-F noon-2:30pm and 6-9:30pm.

THE FITZROY TAVERN — FAMOUS TAVERN

16A Charlotte St. — 020 7580 3714

Many pubs try to ensnare tourists by claiming they are the oldest pub in England or telling bizarre perversions of famous stories ("and that penny that **Dickens** gave to the little boy was spent on whiskey in our pub...") that lend a historical grandeur to what is actually just a decrepit pub with bad ales. The Fitzroy Tavern actually has a published book about its history, and artifacts from that history coat the walls. Famous for the charitable program instated by the tavern to send kids on outings to the country and for the authors who frequented the pub, most notably **Dylan Thomas** and **George Orwell,** The Fitzroy Tavern is the real deal. Pints are cheap, the history's free, and there's a comedy night too.

Goodge St. left on Tottenham Ct. Rd., left on Tottenham St., left on to Charlotte St. i With credit cards, £10 min. and 1.5% surcharge. Most pints under £3.15; £2.50 is the average. Open M-Sa noon-11pm, Su noon-10:30pm. Comedy night W 8:30pm.

THE COURT — PUB

108a Tottenham Court Rd. — 020 7387 0183

A true-blue student pub for a student neighborhood, The Court boasts loud music, cheap beers, juke boxes, and a hip crowd. In the upstairs area, there's a pool table, but most of the pubgoers sit outside or inside the brightly-lit pub area, under hanging strings of lights. Burgers cheap and tantalizing.

Warren St. Left on Warren St., right on Tottenham Court Rd. Pints £3. Burgers £4.95-5.95. With student discount (you qualify if you buy the yellow student discount card at the pub), the pints are around £2.50. Open M-W 11am-midnight, Th-Sa 11am-1am. Food served until 9pm.

PRINCESS LOUISE PUB

208 High Holborn ☎020 7405 8816

A student-packed local hang, the Princess Louise has a classic interior filled with elaborately-designed fogged glass, worn leather seats, and various other pieces of ornate decor. Perhaps the most beautiful things in the pub are the (figurative) price tags on the beers, which are much cheaper than what you'll find in most pubs in the area. A fun atmosphere with a young crowd, the Princess Louise is a neighborhood favorite.

Holborn. Left onto High Holborn. Pint of bitters £1.99. Pint of lager £2.27. Open M-F 11:30am-11pm, Sa-Su noon-11pm.

THE OLD CROWN PUBLIC HOUSE PUB

33 New Oxford St. ☎020 7836 9121 www.theoldcrownpublichouse.com

Old Crown meets young crowd. The pub is filled with old, beat-up wood tables and worn leather-backed chairs. The pipes from an ancient organ appear distorted through the bottles of hard alcohol behind the bar, and nicely framed, goofy pictures line the walls. In addition to the pub, there's a function room with another bar and space for dancing.

Holborn. Left onto High Holborn right onto New Oxford St. Pint £3.80. Open M-W noon-midnight, Th-Sa noon-3am, Su noon-midnight. DJs F-Sa 9pm-3am.

QUEENS LARDER PUB

1 Queen Sq. ☎020 7837 5627 www.queenslarder.co.uk

Queen Charlotte, the wife of George III, stored special treats for her hubby in th cellar beneath this pub. Now, the larders are stocked with other sorts of special treats perfect for today's student-aged Englishmen, and you won't find Queen Charlotte hanging here anymore. The pub is bustling, with outdoor seating and a pleasant upstairs lounge.

Russell Square, right onto Colonnade, left onto Herbrand St. right onto Guilford St., left onto Russell Sq., continue onto Southampton Row left onto Cosmo Pl. Pint £3.55. Open M-Sa 11am-10:30pm. Lunch served noon-3pm.

CHELSEA

Chelsea is now one of the more exclusive and pretentious places to find nightlife in London. Many clubs advertise as members-only private establishments, but for many, you only have to call to get on the guest list. There are a few excellent pubs and many clubs, but if you're looking for an easily accessible, young scene, look elsewhere.

THE CHELSEA RAM PUB

32 Burnaby St. ☎020 7351 4008

A classy neighborhood pub that's more of a quiet hang than it is a rowdy party, the Chelsea Ram specializes in cultivating a pleasant atmosphere. With loads of regulars congregating under the pub's high, bright ceilings, the pub provides friendly staff, good books, fun board games, and interesting art that's for sale (if you tend to buy art when drunk, beware). Any pub with the love poetry of John Donne is a good pub. It's near the rougher section of King's Rd. though, so it may be best to enjoy it earlier or take a cab home.

Sloane Square. Exit the Tube and go straight down Sloane Sq. The street slanting gently left is King's Rd. If you don't want to walk the road (it's manageable but long), the following buses and night buses service the area: 11, 19, 22, 211, 319, N11, N19, N22. Left on Lots Rd., left Burnaby St. Pint £4. Entrees £11.50-12.95. Open M-Sa noon-11pm. Su noon-7pm. Lunch served M-Sa noon-3pm and 6-10pm.

HENRY J. BEAN'S BAR AND GRILL PUB

195-197 King's Rd. ☎020 7352 9255 www.henryjbeans.co.uk/chelsea

Henry J. Bean's attitude toward nightlife is very much embodied in its license-plate map of the states: really cool but a little mixed-up (why is Delaware in the Midwest?) Henry J. Bean's is jam-packed with a super loud young crowd grooving to a wide range of blaring music. Booths provide seating for food, TVs show sporting events, and taps pour beer. The good times await.

Sloane Square. Exit the Tube and go straight down Sloane Sq. The street slanting gently left is King's Rd. If you don't want to walk the road (it's manageable but long), the following buses and night buses service the area: 11, 19, 22, 211, 319, N11, N19, N22. Pints £3.80. Open M-W 11am-11pm, Th-Su 11am-midnight.

THE CADOGAN ARMS PUB

298 King's Rd. ☎020 7352 6500 www.thecadoganarmschelsea.com

At the bottom of the Cadogan Arms' fantastic menu, there's a little note that many diners unfortunately miss: "Please note that game dishes may contain shot." In summary: The Cadogan Arms is classy, but it's still a pub. With more horns on the wall than there are known horned animals, the Cadogan Arms is high on atmosphere. Meals best enjoyed with excellent company and conversation, drinks best shared with friends.

Sloane Square. Exit the Tube and go straight down Sloane Sq. The street slanting gently left is King's Rd. If you don't want to walk the road (it's manageable but long), the following buses and night buses service the area: 11, 19, 22, 211, 319, N11, N19, N22. Entrees £15-17. Open M-F noon-3:30pm, 6-10:30pm, Sa noon-10:30pm, Su noon-9pm.

EMBARGO 59 CLUB

533b King's Rd. ☎020 7351 5038 www.embargo59.com

Climbing the steel steps to Embargo (when referring to it, you drop the 59), it's hard to know what to expect. Suddenly, guests enter the pink backlit reception area from the cold staircase. Then, the main room has a long bar, a lengthy cushion-backed bench with small tables and a dance floor composed of panels that change light. There is also a gorgeous smoking terrace with its own cocktail bar, and a roof made of string lights that look like especially bright stars. Though the club caters to a 20-something professional crowd, like most clubs in Chelsea, W nights, intended for students, feature cheaper drinks.

Sloane Square. Exit the Tube and go straight down Sloane Square. The street slanting gently left is King's Rd. If you don't want to walk the road (it's manageable but long), the following buses and nightbuses service the area: 11, 19, N11, N22. Turn left onto Lots Rd. ***i*** *Cash only for the cover, MC/Visa at the bar. Cover W-Th £5-10, F-Sa £10-15. Bottles of beer W-Th around £2.50, F-Sa £3-4. Mixed drinks W-Th £5, F-Sa £6.95-8.95. Open W-Th 10pm-2am, F-Sa 10pm-3am.*

THE ANTELOPE PUB

22-24 Eaton Terr. ☎020 7824 8512

Established in 1827, The Antelope enjoyed a brief stint as a celebrity pub in the'60s, hosting such rising stars as Roman Polanski. More recently, Prince William came in to drink, but these days The Antelope is otherwise a quiet, small, and cozy neighborhood bar with a Scrabble set, and a worn couch that sits by a lamp and under a bookshelf.

Sloane Sq. Take a right onto Sloane Sq. and another right onto Eaton Gate. Take a left onto Eaton Terr. ***i*** *Free Wi-Fi. AmEx/MC/Visa for purchases over £10.00. Pints £3.50. Open M-Sa noon-11pm.*

THE CROSS KEYS PUB

1 Lawrence St. ☎020 7349 9111 www.thexkeys.co.uk

Tucked away among Chelsea's beautiful residences. The Cross Keys is recognizable thanks to the gigantic, crossed gold keys which are embedded in the perfectly circular hedge on the building's facade. There has been a pub on the site since

1708, when the river ran right up to its wall. The dining room is James Bond meets Vermont ski lodge, with a sliding roof and uniquely-cut rustic wood tables. Beautiful art lines the walls, stained mirrors decorate the ground floor, and a graceful, billowing chandelier dangles from the top floor to illuminate your pint *(£3.40).*

Sloane Square. Exit the Tube and go straight down Sloane Sq. The street slanting gently left is King's Rd. If you don't want to walk the road (it's manageable but long), the following buses and night buses service the area: 11, 19, 22, 211, 319, N11, N19, N22. Turn left onto Glebe Pl. and then right onto Lawrence St. Pints £3.40. Open M-Sa noon-midnight, Su noon-11:30pm. Food served M-F noon-3pm, and 6-10:30pm, Sa-Su.

THE PHOENIX

PUB

23 Smith St. ☎020 7730 9182 www.geronimo-inns.co.uk

The Phoenix is a case study in the power of understatement. Down a quiet street off of King's Rd., The Phoenix sits behind a quiet exterior, calmly offering reasonably-priced drinks (for Chelsea anyway) and fine food. It caters to a definitively local crowd, and most of the patrons are over 30. Chalkboards around the bar offer words of wisdom from famous drunkards.

Sloane Square. Exit the Tube and go straight down Sloane Sq. The street slanting gently left is King's Rd. Left at Smith St. Pints £3.30-3.75. Entrees £12-14 Open M-Sa 11am-11pm, Su noon-10:30pm.

151 CLUB

CLUB

151 King's Rd. ☎020 7351 6826

Right in the middle of posh King's Rd., the 151 Club offers a fairly standard and pleasant club space to a wide variety of people six nights a week. The club is decorated with oversized bottles, and leather chairs abound. The ceiling above the dance floor has tiny white lights that shift in intensity, creating a mesmeric effect. Expect to hear top-of-the-chart songs and cheesy club classics.

*Sloane Square. Exit the Tube and go straight down Sloane Sq. The street slanting gently left is King's Rd. If you don't want to walk the road (it's manageable but long), the following buses and night buses service the area: 11, 19, 22, 211, 319, N11, N19, N22. **i** Most crowded W-Sa. Drink deals M-W. 5% charge on all card payments. Cover Th £5, F-Sa £10. Beer £4.50, M-W £2.50. Open M-Sa 11pm-3am.*

QUEEN'S HEAD PUB

GLBT PUB

25-27 Tryon St. ☎020 7589 0262 www.the1440.co.uk

Over a 100 years old, The Queen's Head (make of that what you will) is one of the oldest gay pubs in London. A friendly and convivial watering hole with an older clientele of both gay and straight patrons. Bingo once a month, karaoke every other week, and quiz night weekly.

Sloane Square. Exit the Tube and go straight down Sloane Sq. The street slanting gently left is King's Rd. If you don't want to walk the road (it's manageable but long), the following buses and night buses service the area: 11, 19, 22, 211, 319, N11, N19, N22. Turn right onto Tryon St. Pint of lager £3-4.50. Bitters £3.15+. Pub grub £6.95-7.25, all-day breakfast £6.95. Open M-Th noon-11:00pm, F-Sa noon-midnight, Su noon-10:30pm.

MARVEL LONDON

CLUB

196-198 Fulham Rd. ☎020 7351 1711 www.marvellondon.com

A cool, chilled-out club, Marvel caters to 25-35 year-old Chelseans. The back room has a bean bag, striped pillows, and, of course, glass cases with killer robot toys. Pretty relaxed, but nothing that exciting. Week nights feature quiet couples' PDA on the sofa near the bar.

*Sloane Square. Exit the Tube and go straight down Sloane Square. The street slanting gently left is King's Rd. If you don't want to walk the road (it's manageable but long), the following buses and night buses service King's Rd: 11, 19, 22, 211, 319, N11, N19, N22. Turn right onto Park Walk and then left onto Fulham Rd. **i** Credit card for purchases over £10. Be warned, sometimes when it gets busy, a 21+ rule is instated. White wine 175ml £4.50-39. Classic mixed drinks £7.50-8, martinis £7.50-8.50. Open M-Su 11am-1am, DJ on F and Sa from 9pm on. Live music Sa 2-5pm and 9-11pm.*

CHELSEA POTTER PUB

119 King's Rd. ☎020 7352 9479

Though serving a slightly older crowd, Chelsea Potter provides a comfy, open space in which to drink with friends. Comfortable benches sit outside the pub, providing an excellent angle for people-watching, and few roads could provide better subject matter.

Sloane Square. Exit the Tube and go straight down Sloane Sq. The street slanting gently left is King's Rd. If you don't want to walk the road (it's manageable but long), the following buses and nightbuses service the area: 11, 19, 22, 211, 319, N11, N19, N22. Pint £3.50, different guest ale every few weeks. Entrees £7.45-8.25. Sandwiches £4.75-4.95. Open M-Th 11am-11pm, F-Sa 11am-midnight, Su noon-10:30pm.

HOLBORN AND CLERKENWELL

Holborn is a pub town, and Clerkenwell is on the up-and-up. Look out for a mix of pleasant, old pubs and hip clubs, most of which can be found on Charterhouse St.

THE THREE KINGS PUB

7 Clerkenwell Close ☎020 7253 0483

On warm evenings, patrons of The Three Kings line the curbs outside and drink their pints *(£3.30-3.50)* of Timothy Taylor, Staropramer, and Beck's. Inside, customers sit in the arm chairs under the watchful gazes of luminaries like Woody Allen, Hunter S. Thompson, Smokey Robinson, and that fake rhino the pub has on the wall. Strings of colored lights swoop down over a sign that says "Stop Bush," and sausage sandwiches are made on ciabatta bread with basil oil *(£4.50)*. This is a bar with character, grace, and an easy-going vibe. Classic rock, soul, and jazz pipe out of the speaker system, originating in the pub's trusty record player which sits atop a vast record collection. Weekly music quizzes Monday at 9pm; poetry night first Tuesday of every month at 8:00pm.

Farringdon. Right onto Cowcross St., right onto Farringdon, right onto Pear Tree Ct., right onto Clerkenwell Close. Open M-F noon-11pm, Sa. 5pm-11pm.

YE OLDE MITRE PUB

Ely Court ☎020 7405 4751

You're only going to get to Ye Olde Mitre if you're looking for it. It's a pub with history (it was established in 1546 and sits to the side of an ancient church), but it doesn't equate "historic" with run-down. The downstairs and upstairs areas are bright, clean, and pleasant. While it caters to an older audience, it has an easy-going atmosphere and a good selection of relatively cheap beers and what they refer to as "English Tapas," including toasted sandwiches *(£2)*. Also, *Snatch* with Brad Pitt was filmed here—proof that good-looking people drink in this pub, too. While the pub seems safe, it's down a small, removed alley, so women especially may not want to travel here alone.

Farringdon. Right onto Cowcross St., left onto Farringdon Rd. right onto Charterhouse St., right onto Ely Pl. Most pints £3.20. Pints of lager £3.30. Open M-F 11am-11pm; closed on bank holidays.

THE 3 TUNS STUDENT PUB

Houghton St. ☎020 7955 7156

While this place is not rich in the atmosphere department, the 3 Tuns customers are rich in the money department, thanks to this pub's dirt-cheap pints. This London School of Economics pub is frequented by (you guessed it) LSE students and is a good place to come if you want to meet university-aged people or play a game of pool in a sparsely furnished room where people drink beer from plastic cups.

Temple. Right onto Temple Pl., left onto Surrey St., cross the Strand. Continue onto Melbourne Pl., left onto Aldwych, right on Houghton St. Pints £2.10. Term-time hours: M, Tu and Th 10am-11pm, W 10am-midnight, F 10am-2am, Sa 9pm-3am. During school holidays, call for hours.

THE JERUSALEM TAVERN PUB

55 Britton St. ☎020 7490 4281 www.stpetersbrewery.co.uk

A truly ancient tavern, the Jerusalem Tavern was originally in St. John's Gate before it was reopened at its present location on Britton St. The tavern is homey and warm and—more importantly—the only tavern in London to offer all of the St. Peter's ales. These fantastic and specialized ales have brands like "Golden Ale," "Ruby Red Ale" "Honey Porter," and "Cream Stout." All of them are worth trying, but we're not saying you should try all of them at once...that would be irresponsible and would probably lead to the **craziest night ever.**

Farringdon. Left onto Cowcross St., left onto Turnmill St., right onto Benjamin St., left onto Britton St. Pints around £3.10, 1/2 pints £1.55. Open M-F 11am-11pm, lunch served noon-3pm.

FABRIC CLUB

77a Charterhouse St. ☎020 7336 8898 www.fabriclondon.com

Do you go to dances and stand to the side clutching your drink? Do you frequently call the police at parties to report a mass epidemic of seizures? Do you not find "September" by Earth, Wind, and Fire irresistibly funky? Worry not! Fabric has the cure to this fatal disease. The club, which inhabits an abandoned meat packing warehouse, boasts Europe's premier "bodysonic dancefloor," a floor which, because of the subwoofers that line its rubbery surface, vibrates in time with the music. Yes, the floor does it for you. Try it Friday between 10pm and 6am or Saturday from 11pm-8am. The club is a true phenomenon, and its three dance floors are sure to be packed with 20-somethings. The queue starts getting really long around 11pm, and the peak hour is 2am.

Farringdon. Left onto Cowcross St. Continue until you hit Charterhouse St. £15, students £11. After 3am discount £6. Bottle of Stella £4. Open F 10pm-6am, Sa 11pm-8am.

FULLER'S ALE AND PIE HOUSE PUB

194 Fleet St. ☎020 7430 2255

Fuller's Ale and Pie House traces English history: once a tavern, then a bank, now a pub. Make of that what you will. The pub plays up the grandeur of the old Bank of England. Though more upscale than a traditional pub, Fuller's has an exciting atmosphere, and any drink there feels unique. Additionally, it sits between Sweeney Todd's barber shop on Fleet St. and his girlfriend's pie shop, so be sure to try one of their pies if you're feeling adventurous.

Temple. Right onto Temple Pl., left onto Arundel St., right on Strand, continue onto Fleet. Pints £3.45-3.65. Shots £2-3. Open M-F 11am-11pm.

KENSINGTON AND EARL'S COURT

JANET'S BAR BAR

30 Old Brompton Rd. ☎020 7581 3160 janetsbar@yahoo.com

Janet's Bar is all about spirits, in both senses of the word. Run by Janet herself, who knows most of the people in the bar and has organized something of a lively ex-pat community around the place, Janet's Bar is a well-formed but instantly welcoming community. All-encompassing memorabilia, photos of club regulars, and the Red Sox and Yankees pennants that are closer than most fans would like. If the atmosphere doesn't make you feel welcome, the Beatles sing-alongs will.

South Kensington. As you exit, Old Brompton Rd. will be across from you. i Though not wheelchair-accessible, a ramp can be arranged if you call in advance. £3 min. on credit cards. Bottle of beer around £4.50. Pint £5.95. Shots around £5. Mixed drinks £6.50-8.50 Mixed drinks around £9.50. Bottle of wine from £18.50. M-W 11:45am-1:00am, Th 11:45am-1:30am, F 11:45pm-2:30am, Sa noon-2:30am, Su 2pm-1am. Live music Tu-Su after 9:30pm.

PIANO PIANO BAR

106 Kensington High Street ☎020 7938 4664 www.pianokensington.com

If you ever dreamed of lying atop a piano in a dimly lit room while someone played sultry jazz, blues, rock and sing-along music, Piano will do you one better: you can eat on the piano, and there's a different pianist every night of the week. Piano is a classy joint loaded with pictures of **Old Blue Eyes** (Frank Sinatra) and New York, as well as photos from shoots that have happened in the bar, such as the one with Estelle and John Legend or the one with an ex Sugar Babe.

High Street Kensington. Turn right on Kensington High Street. i £5 min. on credit cards. Most entrees £6.50-7. Bottle of beer £4.50. Glass of house red or white £4.50. Tu-Sa 11am-midnight, Su 4:30pm-11:30. Music starts at 6pm T-F, 8pm on Sa and the jazz trio goes on Su 8pm.

THE DRAYTON ARMS PUB

153 Old Brompton Rd. ☎020 7835 2301 www.thedraytonarmssw5.co.uk

The Drayton Arms is a comfortable, well-kept pub with high ceilings and white string lights that amble up the tree trunk and soft red lights that border the ceiling. Enjoy affordable beers around the fire place, and then go see a film or play in the black box theater on the second floor. Check the site for theater, sporting and film events in the upstairs theater.

Gloucester Rd. Turn right onto Gloucester Rd., turn right onto Old Brompton Rd. Average pint £3.20. Burgers £7-8.25. Sandwiches £4.25. Entrees £7.50-8.25. Open M-F 11am-midnight, Sa-Su 10m-midnight.

THE PEMBROKE PUB

261 Old Brompton Rd. ☎020 7373 8337 www.thepembroke5.co.uk

Spacious and easy-going, The Pembroke is a solid neighborhood pub in the typical Kensington style: lofty ceilings and clean decoration. Chandeliers dangle from the ceiling on the second floor and people stand on the terrace when it's nice out. There are DJs at the pub *(F-Sa from 8:30pm on).*

West Brompton. Turn right onto Old Brompton Rd. Average pint £3.80. Open M-Sa noon-midnight, Su noon-11pm.

THE SCARSDALE TAVERN PUB

23a Edwardes Sq. ☎020 7937 1811

Bottles upon bottles line the window sills and ceiling trimmings, and old, tasseled and worn curtains drape beside large windows. Edwardes Sq. was initially meant as a living space for the French officers who would arrive when Napoleon invaded, and the Scarsdale cheerfully revises history with its warm French style.

High Street Kensington. Turn left onto Kensington High St., left onto Edwardes Sq. Entrees £9-11. Average pint £3.30-3.50. Open M-Sa noon-11pm, Su noon-10:30pm.

MARYLEBONE AND REGENT'S PARK

THE GOLDEN EAGLE PUB, MUSIC

59 Marylebone Ln. ☎020 7935 3228

The Golden Eagle is one of the most special pubs in London. Though aesthetically basic, it has some of the friendliest patrons and staff that can be found around town. Three nights a week, the bespectacled Tony "Fingers" Pearson rolls out an old stand-up piano and proceeds to hammer out classics like "La Vie En Rose," "Tenderly," "I'm Confessing I Love You" and "Just One of Those Things." There's no better way to feel welcome in the country than by catching a rousing, boozy chorus of "Consider Yourself." Between the alcohol-induced golden haze, the music, and the unbelievably friendly company, the Pub is a living Capra film, and in no way is that a bad thing.

Bond St. Right onto Oxford St., left onto Marylebone Ln. Average pint £3.50. Open M-Th 11am-11pm, F-Sa 11am-midnight, Su noon-7pm. Music Tu, Th, and F 8:30pm.

london

THE SOCIAL

CLUB, BAR

5 Little Portland St. ☎020 7636 4992 www.thesocial.com

Though the upstairs looks like a typical hip bar with its exposed light bulbs and bare wood floor (though there are DJs on the first floor most nights), the downstairs space at The Social is where the action is. Here is where the ragingly popular hip-hop karaoke night happens every other Th as well as other events like club nights and live performances. Many nights have no cover charge. Check online to see what's happening at this popular and exciting hang.

Oxford Circus. Right onto Regent St., right on Little Portland St. Credit card min. £10. Pints around £3.70. Mixed drinks around £7. Cover £5-7 on club night. Student cards will get you discounts on most covered nights. Open M 5pm-midnight, Tu-W noon-midnight, Th-F noon-1am, Sa 7pm-1am.

THE COCK

PUB

27 Great Portland St. ☎020 7631 5002

Crowds of students gather beneath the red patterned ceiling, crowding the bar for some of the cheapest pints in London. Traditional decor rounds out the great deals at this pub—and there's nothing obscene about it.

Oxford Circus. right on Oxford St., left on Great Portland St.. Min. £5.00 and small surcharge with credit card. Bitter £2. Pint of lager around £2.27-3.10. Open M-Sa noon-11pm, Su noon-10:30pm.

THE COACH MAKERS OF MARYLEBONE

PUB

88 Marylebone Ln. ☎020 7224 4022 www.thecoachmakers.com

The Coach Makers of Marylebone, unsurprisingly, used to be the offices of coach makers...in Marylebone. Now the place is an upscale pub, featuring music on weekends *(from 7pm)*, old gilded mirrors, and deep leather couches that rest beside a fireplace. Simple and elegant, the Coach Makers is a pleasant pub.

Bond St. Right onto Oxford St., left onto Marylebone Ln. Pints £3.70. Entrees £11.50-12.50. Open M-Th noon-11:30pm, F-Sa noon-midnight, Su noon-10:30pm.

NOTTING HILL

Notting Hill is not an ideal neighborhood for nightlife. The pubs thrive on daytime tourists, and many of the locals are young professionals who tend to frequent other spots. The neighborhood can feel deserted at night, and while it's a safe area, the emptiness isn't conducive to late-night revelry.

PORTOBELLO STAR

BAR

171 Portobello Rd. ☎020 7229 8016 www.portobellostarbar.co.uk

If cafes could have superhero alter egos, the Portobello Star would be Superman. By day, it's a pleasant cafe with internet access; by night, it's a bustling bar... with internet access. It's popular but not too crazy, sophisticated but with fun drinks *("Rock the Kasbah," Grey Goose vodka with lemon juice, mint tea syrup, orange flower water and egg white, £10)*. You'll hear your favorite classic rock, soft rock, R and B, soul, and hip-hop from the bar or the leather couches in the calmer chill-out room on the second floor of the building. The crowd is in their early 20s to early 30s, and the place is hopping.

Notting Hill Gate. Take right onto Pembridge Rd. and then left onto Portobello Rd. Mixed drinks £7.50-8. Su-Th 10am-midnight, F-Sa 10am-1am.

RUBY AND SEQUOIA

BAR

6-8 All Saints Rd. ☎020 7243 6363 www.ruby.uk.com/sequoia

Upscale, chic, bright, and with a painting of firefighting nuns (clearly the highlight here), Ruby and Sequoia is a pub filled with many local, young professionals enjoying hearty meals and lengthy drinks. Dress up a bit, but nothing too fancy. Just prime yourself for a relatively glamorous yet relaxed night on the town. There's a lounge downstairs with a DJ starting at 9pm. Bring friends to sit with, as people tend to come in groups. The street leading to the bar isn't that well lit, and the area is a bit deserted. Regardless, the warmth of the bar keeps the dark from the street at bay.

Notting Hill Gate. Take right onto Pembridge Rd. and then left onto Portobello Rd.; take right on Westbourne Park Rd. and then left on All Saints Rd. Mixed drinks £8-8.50. Shots £4-5. Large glasses of wine £6. M-Th 6pm-12:30am, F 6pm-2am, Sa 10am-2am, Su 10am-12:30am.

SUN IN SPLENDOUR PUB

7 Portobello Rd. ☎020 7792 0914 www.suninsplendourpub.co.uk

A fun, typical pub with a young crowd (20s-30s). The major draw is the fantastic beer garden in the back. The garden has benches and wood tables, lattices with ivy and primrose, lanterns, and heaters. It closes at 9:30pm, so try and get out there early. Food is served noon-10pm every weekday but is limited on Sa and Su.

Notting Hill Gate. Take right onto Pembridge Rd. and then left onto Portobello Rd. Small glass of white wine £3.95-4.25; small glass of red wine £3.85-4.10; pint of draught £3.15-3.95. M-Th noon-11pm, F noon-midnight, Sa 9am-12am, Su 9am-10:30pm.

PRINCE ALBERT PUB

11 Pembridge Rd. ☎020 7727 7362 www.the-prince-albert.co.uk

Prince Albert pub blares rowdy, retro indie music and serves veggie plates with olive, falafel, tomato, hummus, crudites, mozzarella, cherry tomato salad, garlic flatbread, and chips *(£10).* Fun, young, and crowded (but its size accommodates).

Notting Hill Gate. Take right onto Pembridge Rd. 8 oz burgers £8-9. Sandwiches £4.50. Entrees £7-8. M-F 10am-noon, Sa-Su 10:30am-12pm.

PORTOBELLO GOLD PUB

95 Portobello Rd. ☎020 7229 8528 www.portobellogold.com

An old-fashioned pub with a crowd that will sing along to the classic rock that's playing. The clientele represents the whole age spectrum—from students to 70-something locals. The pub is endearingly ragged, bright, and just what you'd think an English pub should look like. There's a full service restaurant with pub grub in the back. The peak hours on Sa are after 11pm.

*Notting Hill Gate. Take right onto Pembridge Rd. and then left onto Portobello Rd. **i** Live music Su 6:30-10pm. Half-pints £1.90-2.60; full pints £3.60-4.10; bottles £3.60-4.80; glass of red wine £4.20-4.60; glass of white wine £3.80-5.60; Cuban cigars £10.50. M-Th 10am-noon, F-Sa 10am-12:30am, Su 10am-11:30pm.*

MAU MAU BAR

265 Portobello Rd. ☎020 7229 8528 www.maumaubar.com

Mau Mau rests at the bottom of Portobello Rd., and though on Notting Hill's main drag, it feels totally removed from the touristy bustle of the street outside. The cool reds and greens of the walls reflect the smooth tones of the music, which is mainly jazz, trip-hop, and soul. If you're into pool, there's a table, but look out for a long queue by 10:30pm, the bar's peak hour. Clientele tends to be 40-something locals.

*Notting Hill Gate. Take right onto Pembridge Rd. and then a left onto Portobello Rd. **i** Live Music Th 8:30-10:30pm and Su 8:30-10pm. Shots £3.50-5; half-pint £1.75; full pint £3.30; bottles £3. M-Th noon-10:30pm, F-Sa noon-midnight, Su 1-10:30pm.*

THE WEST END

ABSOLUT ICEBAR BAR

31-33 Heddon St. ☎020 7478 8910 www.absoluticebarlondon.com

This bar is absurd in the best way possible—the way where everything is made out of ice imported from the Torne River in Sweden. Located in the former wine vault for the monarchy, Absolut Icebar is the perfect place to escape all that British...er, cold. Before entering the hip, "cool" bar, visitors are given designer thermal wear. Each stay is 40 minutes, during which time you drink as much as possible so you don't feel your face as it slowly freezes off. All drinks are served in glasses made of ice. Chipping ice off the wall and into your drink is frowned upon. Highly.

Piccadilly Circus. Turn left onto Regent St. and left onto Heddon St. i Tickets include first vodka cocktail. Refills £6. Reserve for weekends around 2 weeks in advance. Reservations are taken up to 28 days in advance. Ⓢ M-W is £13.50 (£12.50 if booked in advance), Th until 6:30pm £13.50 (£12.50 if booked in advance), Th night-Sa £15, Th-Sa all day £16 without reservation, Su £13.50 (£12.50 if booked in advance). M 3:30pm-11:00pm, Tu 3:30pm-11pm, W 3:30pm-11pm, Th 3:30pm-11:45pm, F noonpm-1:15am, Sa 12:30pm-1:15am, Su 3:30pm-11pm, last entry is 45min. before close. DJs on F and Sa start around 8pm.

GORDON'S WINE BAR — WINE BAR

47 Villiers St. ☎020 7930 1408 www.gordonswinebar.com

Once down the narrow staircase visitors come upon what looks like a cave. Bottles draped in melted wax and rough, irregularly sloping walls lit by flickering candles fill the space between people sharing bottles of wine from around the world. Out on Watergate Walk, winos sip the fine wines of London's oldest wine bar if the weather permits.

Charing Cross. Upon exiting, turn 180 degrees and go down Villiers. Ⓢ Wine £16-17 per bottle, around £4.50 per glass. Hot meals £9-11, items from the grill are around £6.65. Open M-Sa 10am-11pm, Su noon-10pm.

FREUD — BAR

198 Shaftesbury ☎020 7240 9933 www.freudliving.com

You wouldn't find Freud unless you were looking for it. With original art decorating the otherwise spare space, Freud is a study in successful understatement. The young and hip come to Freud and get a seat wherever they can, enjoying the reasonably priced drinks.

Piccadilly Circus. Exit with Haymarket on your right and Regent to your left. turn right around the triangular intersection and right at Shaftesbury. i Credit card min. £10. Ⓢ Beer £3.15-3.65. Mixed drinks £5.55-6.50 on average. Open M-Sa 11am-11pm, Su noon-10:30pm.

KU — GLBT

25 Frith St. ☎020 7287 7986 www.ku-bar.com

A more relaxed alternative to some of the more pulsing gay clubs on the Soho scene, Ku serves up well-priced drinks with a friendly staff. Located above the bar is the gay tourist office *(open from noon-6:00pm M-Su)*, providing tips for gay travelers. A comfortable and fun bar (and accompanying club downstairs) with a good heart, Ku is the place to be.

Tottenham Court Road. Turn left onto Oxford St., turn left onto Soho St., left around Soho Sq., left onto Frith St. Free Wi-Fi. Single+mixer is £3.50. Double shot+mixer is £6.00. Pints £3.50. Bar open daily noon-midnight. Nightclub open daily 7pm-midnight.

CAFE PACIFICA MEXICAN BAR TEQUILA

5 Langley St. 020 7379 7728 www.cafepacifico-laperla.com

Though at first glance Cafe Pacifica may seem a typical Mexican restaurant, its 130 varieties of tequila beg to differ. Though you have to order food to drink, the atmosphere is pleasant, with light Latin music piping through the speakers and classic Mexican entrees like enchiladas. If you're feeling like a real taste in exorbitant spending, pick up a shot of the Cuervo Collecion *(£125)*. If you buy it, you'll get your name on a board in the restaurant, and also possibly on the IRS's auditing list.

Covent Garden. Left on Long Acre, right on Langley. Shots of tequila £3-15. Enchiladas around £9.50. Open M-Sa noon-11:45pm, Su noon-10:45pm.

LAB BAR

12 Old Compton 020 7437 7820 www.labbaruk.com

LAB, which is short for the London Academy of Bartenders, is known for its bartenders, who compete as drink makers, sometimes internationally. When off the circuit, they serve up affordable cocktails that fill up thirty-two pages of a menu. With drinks ranging from the Aviation *(Plymouth gin, maraschino liqueur shaken hard with freshly squeezed lemon juice, served straight up with a cherry, £7)* to the Hemmingway Daiquiri, death in the afternoon and the playful Satan's Whiskers, Lab does it all in a pleasant, retro 70s bar space.

Tottenham Court Road. Turn right down Charing Cross Rd. and turn right on Old Compton St. Most cocktails £7-7.50. Open M-Sa 4pm-midnight, Su 4-10:30pm. Table service downstairs Th, F, and Sa. DJs W-Sa 8pm-midnight.

THE EDGE GLBT, MIXED

11 Soho Sq. 020 7439 1313 www.edgesoho.co.uk

With four floors, The Edge is a full clubbing experience. Disco balls and a crazy light-changing chandelier that looks like an exploding atom decorate the space. The first floor has a lounge bar which is quieter filled with couches. The second floor is the al fresco lounge, serving up massages every night where the recipient pays however much he or she feels it's worth. The third floor has fake trees with climbing blue lights and a dance floor with tiles that change color.

Tottenham Court Road. Turn left onto Oxford St., turn left onto Soho St., Edge is on your right. Pint £3. Open M-Sa noon-1am, Su noon-10:30pm. Dance floor open F-Sa 8pm.

THIRST BAR

53 Greek St. 020 7437 1977 www.thirstbar.com

A hip, spare space where the music's always funky and it's always either "Stupid" hour, where the drinks are almost half price, or happy hour (the two never coincide, so ignorance is never bliss). Thirst is stylish with its candles, spray-painted signs and stainless steel tables. Ask for a student discount. Dancing is downstairs whenever your feet start to move uncontrollably.

Tottenham Court Road. Turn left onto Oxford St., turn left onto Soho St., left around Soho Sq., left onto Greek St. To pay with credit card, min. £10 purchase. "Stupid" prices are £4.25-4.50, "happy" are around £6, "normal" £8. Open M-Su 5pm-3am. Stupid hour (almost 1/2 price cocktails) 5pm-7:30pm daily. Happy hour is M-W 7:30pm-3am, Th-Su 7:30pm-10:30pm. Downstairs bar is open Th, F, and Sa, as well as busy nights.

SOHO VILLAGE MIXED CLUB, BAR

81 Wardour St. 020 7434 2124 www.village-soho.co.uk

Walking down Wardour St., it's hard to miss Soho Village, even if you aren't looking for it. A typical night has crowds of giggling spectators of all sexual orientations whose faces are lit by occasional flashes of light in time to pulsing music. Inside, "Gogo Boys" *(Th, F, Sa from 8pm)* might be dancing on platforms, and hot and sweaty dancers abound. Down the steel staircase is another dance floor, bordered by cool blue-lit booths, where people of all sexual orientations come to have a good time. Though the club is primarily gay, it is definitely straight-friendly.

Tottenham Court Road. Turn down Oxford St. with your back to Tottenham Court Road, turn left onto Wardour St. Open M-Sa 4pm-1am, Su 4-11:30pm.

PROFILE GLBT BAR

84-86 Wardour St. ☎020 7734 3444 www.profilesoho.com

With one of the brightest yellow interiors in Soho, Profile practically screams good time. Serving up American diner food and providing events like Bingo at 6pm on Sundays and psychic Sundays on off-bingo weeks (get your fortune read!), Profile is a great GLBT bar. Downstairs is the cleverly-titled Low Profile, the bar's corresponding nightclub.

Tottenham Court Road. Turn down Oxford St. with your back to Tottenham Court Road, turn left onto Wardour St. Mixed drinks £6-7. Beer £3.50. Profile M-Sa 11am-11pm, Su 11am-10:30pm. Low Profile F-Sa 10:30pm-4am (drinking stops at 3am), Thursday 10:30pm-2am. DJs upstairs F 7pm, Sa 8pm. Happy hour at Profile daily 5-7pm.

BAR RUMBA CLUB

36 Shaftesbury Ave. ☎020 7287 6933 www.barrumbadisco.co.uk

Boasting a very young crowd, Bar Rumba is one of the more popular clubs in the area. In a spare space with low ceilings, booths and tables, the dance floor is where all the action takes place among the flashing lights and young crowd. Watch out for the long queue, though! Themed Saturdays advertised on the website, and if you dress in theme you get in free. Check the website for details.

Piccadilly Circus. Turn left onto Great Windmill St. and follow it to Shaftesbury Ave. i Credit card £10 min. Up until 10:30pm guys get in for £5, girls get in free. 10:30pm-11:30pm, guys pay £10, girls pay £5. After 11:30pm, everyone pays £10. Cash only for cover. M-Su 8:30pm-3am.

22 BELOW BAR

22 Great Marlborough ☎020 7437 4106 www.22below.co.uk

A simple bar in every way, 22 below is, appropriately, in the basement of the 22nd building on Great Marlborough St. Seasonal themes dominate the decoration, but the space is small, bright and relaxed. The drinks menu includes award winning recipes, and many of the drinks are associated with authors. The Thai Sorbet *(£8.50)* nearly won the Bacardi Capital Cocktail Competition, so drink it slow.

Oxford Circus. Turn left onto Regent St., left onto Great Marlborough St. Cocktails £7.50-8.50. Open M-F 5pm-midnight, Sa 7pm-midnight.

G-A-Y BAR GLBT BAR

30 Old Compton St. ☎020 7494 2756 www.g-a-y.co.uk

Bringing in an eccentric and eclectic clientele, G-A-Y Bar serves up cheap drinks and loud chart music throughout the whole space. Decked out with tons of TVs embedded in the walls, pink walls and just the right number of flashing lights, G-A-Y is a solid bar.

Tottenham Court Road. Turn right down Charing Cross Rd. and turn right on Old Compton St. Some drinks available for £1.59 noon-8pm M-F. Su-Th noon-midnight house, red, or white wine is £1.60.. Open daily noon-midnight.

ALPHABET BAR

61-63 Beak St. ☎020 7439 2190 alphabet@a3bars.com

Alphabet is the kind of pub that can mix soul, funk, top forty and Frank Sinatra without it seeming incongruous. Between the stylish decor, the sharing boards of meat and cheese, and the graffiti-covered walls, Alphabet covers "stylish" from several different angles, and its customers are all the better for it. The downstairs area is spacious and replete with leather couches and stools. As you descend, heed the wall's warning to "Mind yer bloody head!!"

Oxford Circus. Left down Regent St., left onto Beak St. Credit card min. £5. Mixed drinks £6.50. Entrees £8-8.20. Shooters £3.60. Pints £4. Open M-Sa noon-11pm. Kitchen open noon-9pm.

MADAME JOJO'S LIVE ENTERTAINMENT VENUE

8-10 Brewer St. 020 7734 3040 www.madamejojos.com

Built on the cabaret and live entertainment traditions of yore, Madame Jojo's is not your average club. Every night begins with some form of entertainment before the cabaret tables disappear and the dance floor gets hopping. Dress is smart casual, music is smoking and, when the curtain goes down, the dancing begins.

Piccadilly Circus. Go down Shaftesbury and turn left on Wardour St., turn left on Brewer St. Sometimes cover is cash only. Tu is indie night (which is also pretty much a student night). Show finishes around 9:30, and then club night begins with DJs. F is northern soul and funk. Sa is 1950s rockabilly and drive. Su is Latin, house, and bebop. W is Trannyshack night, aimed at the transgender community. Tickets £10-52.50 depending on event, so check website. Single measure spirits+mixer, bottles of beer and glasses of the house red or white £4.50. Open daily 7pm-3am. 7-9pm is live music, burlesque, comedy, magic or variety show.

CANDY BAR GLBT

4 Carlisle St. 020 7287 5041 www.candybarsoho.co.uk

Though open only to women and their male friends, Candy Bar is otherwise a pretty standard bar. There are occasional student nights featuring a student DJ and a female pole dancer every other week on Friday or Saturday around 10pm (check online). Karaoke happens on Tuesdays and open mikes will be on Thursdays.

Tottenham Court Road. Turn onto Oxford St. with your back to Tottenham Court Rd, turn left onto Dean St. Credit card min. £5. Su-Th 20% off everything: mixed drinks become £5. Pints £3.30. Mixed drinks average £7. Open daily noon-3am.

ESCAPE DANCE BAR GLBT BAR

10a Brewer St. 020 7734 2626 www.escapesoho.co.uk

This stylish gay bar has a wide open dance floor with flashing lights and wallpaper with horses on them. Speakers with excellent quality sound thump out hits from the charts, and, on Wednesdays and Saturdays, karaoke reinterpretations of said tunes.

Piccadilly Circus. Go down Shaftesbury and turn left on Wardour St., turn left on Brewer St. £.50. for paying with credit card. Pint of Stella £2. Other pints around £3.80. Open M-Sa 5pm-3am. Karaoke W 8pm-midnight, Sa 5-8pm.

THE CHANDOS PUB

60 Chandos Pl. 020 7836 1401

A classic, Sam Smith's pub near Trafalgar Square, the Chandos is a welcome change from the bar and club culture of the West End. Welcoming guests graciously into its open space, The Chandos has booths that are very secluded, and which keep visitors bathed in colored light from the stained glass that looks out onto the street. It also boasts some of the cheapest pints in town.

Charing Cross. Turn left onto Strand, right onto St. Martin's Ln. and right onto William IV St. Credit card min. £5. Pints £2.00. Burgers £4.50-5. Entrees £6-6.30. Open M-Sa 11am-11:30pm, Su noon-10:30pm. Kitchen closes 7pm.

BOX CAFE BAR GAY-FRIENDLY MIXED

32-34 Monmouth St. 020 7240 5828 www.boxbar.com

This gay-friendly bar has a very mixed crowd. Decorated with glittering paintings of stars such as Marilyn Monroe and lit by orange, blue and green hanging lights, The Box Cafe Bar is an exciting and friendly place to drink. They have a different promotion every day, so check ahead to find out how you an save!

Covent Garden. Turn left onto James St., left on Long Acre. Turn right onto Upper Mercer St. and then left onto Monmouth. Free Wi-Fi with purchase. Average pint £3.50-3.80. Open M-Th noon-11pm. F-Sa noon-midnight, Su noon-11pm.

DOGAND DUCK PUB

18 Bateman St. ☎020 7494 0697

Formerly one of George Orwell's favorite pubs, the Dog and Duck is a standard pub in the middle of Soho's otherwise off-the-wall nightlife scene. The interior is decorated with elaborate mirrors, and every Thursday night from 5-10pm is Sausage night, with sausage and mash and a beer *(£8)*.

Tottenham Court Road. Turn down Oxford St. with your back to Tottenham Court Road, turn left onto Soho St., right around Soho Sq. and right onto Frith St. and right onto Bateman St. Pints £3-3.50. Open M-Th 10am-11pm, F-Sa 10am-11:30pm, Su noon-10:30pm.

WESTMINSTER

Westminster isn't an ideal location for nightlife, pubs, or clubs. Enjoy it during the day, and then take the party elsewhere, old sport.

THE BUCKINGHAM ARMS PUB

62 Petty France ☎020 7222 3386 www.buckinghamarms.com

When the lawmen and -women who keep order in this country need to unwind, they can come here: it is right down the street from the Ministry of Justice. Partially lit by a cool skylight, the pub has comfy armchairs and large windows, so homey charm abounds. It is also worth noting that the Ministry of Justice is on a street named "Petty France." Coincidence? We think not.

Victoria. Right onto Grosvenor Pl. Continue onto Victoria St., left onto Buckingham Gate, right on Petty France. Pint of Youngs £3. Open M-F 11am-11pm, Sa-Su noon-6pm.

THE CASK AND GLASS PUB

39 Palace St. ☎020 7834 7630 www.shepherd-neame.co.uk

A small pub hidden in the concrete and brick facades of Westminster, the Cask and Glass imports a bit of that old 1698, the year of the brewery's founding, charm to which pubs in other parts of town aspire. The beer is good but a bit expensive in this pleasant, neighborhood joint.

Victoria. Right onto Grosvenor Pl. Continue onto Victoria St. Left on Palace St. Pint £3.35-3.85. M-F 11am-11pm, Sa noon-8pm.

THE PHOENIX PUB

14 Palace St. ☎020 7828 8136 www.geronimo-inns.co.uk

A basic, slightly posh pub, The Phoenix is well located and filled with 30-something professionals. Enjoy the relaxed beer garden or a dinner of upscale pub grub served in the Yalumba room upstairs. Even if you're bored by this pub, you'll be able to say you're eating in the *Yalumba* room. Try saying Yalumba 10 times fast.

Victoria. Right onto Grosvenor Pl. Continue onto Victoria St. Left on Palace St. Pint £3.55-3.85. Ales £3.25. M-F 11am-11pm, Sa 11am-11pm, Su noon-10:30pm.

arts and culture

You might wonder if the city that brought the world Shakespeare and Harold Pinter has lost its theatrical edge. Not to fear, however—the London theater scene is as vital as ever. From the perennial hard-hitters at the Royal Court to daring musical fare like *Enron: The Musical*, the London stage remains packed with the dramatic flare that put it on the map in the first place.

For those weary of Coldplay, who fear that the country that brought you the

Rolling Stones, The Sex Pistols and The Clash hit a roadblock, turn your ears from the arenas and put them to the ground—underground, in fact—to city hotspots where young bands committed to their fans are not interested in seeing their names in gaudy lights. There's that famed British wit making audiences chuckle from the gut in basements everywhere. And one can't neglect the elegant ballet that graces the stage of the Royal Opera House.

CINEMA

London is teeming with traditional cinemas, the most dominant of which are **Cineworld** and **Odeon,** but the best way to enjoy a film is in one of the hip repertory or luxury cinemas. *Time Out* publishes show times, as does **www.viewlondon.co.uk.** Americans will find the cinema in London to be particularly illuminating, as most films are about a certain kind of American—namely, the stupid, stereotypical kind that would make Europeans hate Americans.

BFI SOUTHBANK

THE SOUTH BANK

Belvedere Rd. ☎020 7928 3232 www.bfi.org.uk

Hidden under Waterloo Bridge, the BFI Southbank is one of the most exciting repertory cinemas in London. Showcasing everything from art to foreign, British to classic, the BFI provides a range of styles to keep all cinema lovers happy. It runs in seasons, with a different theme each month featuring different elements of film. (For example, a season could be on a director or cinematographer or actor.) The **Mediatech** is free for anyone and allows people to privately view films from the archives.

Waterloo. i Call ☎020 7815 1329 for details on Mediatech hours. Evenings M-F £9, concessions £6.65, under 16 £5. Tu £5. Mediatech open T-Su noon-8pm .

ELECTRIC CINEMA

NOTTING HILL

191 Portobello Rd. ☎020 7908 9696 www.electriccinema.co.uk

This 100-year-old theater is the epitome of a luxury viewing experience. With a bar inside the auditorium and luxury leather arm chairs that come equipped with a table, a footstool and a wine cooler, it almost doesn't matter what films are showing. The Electric shows some vintage films but sticks mainly to big, new releases.

Notting Hill Gate. Turn right onto Pembroke Rd., then left onto Portobello Rd. i Tickets must be booked at least 2 weeks in advance, but some shows sell out faster than that. Discounts for children. £7.50-14.50. Appetizers £4.50. Pints £3.75. Wine £4.25-7. Open M-Sa 9am-8:30pm, Su 10am-8:30pm.

RIVERSIDE STUDIOS

WEST LONDON

Crisp Rd. ☎020 8237 1111 www.riversidestudios.co.uk

Riverside Studios derives its name from its close proximity to the Thames. Frequently showing films in old-school double-bill packages, Riverside Studios specializes in foreign films, art house flicks, and old gems. The building itself is a hotbed for culture, featuring an exhibition space and occasional live theater performances.

Hammersmith. Take south exit and pass the Hammersmith Apollo. Continue to follow Queen Caroline St. and turn left onto Crisp Rd. i Handicapped people should book in advance. Ethernet in cafe. Tickets £7.50, concessions £6.50. Pints £3.70. Open daily noon-9pm. Shows are normally M-F 6:30pm and 8:30pm, Sa-Su 1:30pm, 3:30pm, 6:30pm, 8:30pm. Bar open noon-11pm M-Sa and 11am-10:30pm on Su.

COMEDY

The English are famous for their occasionally dry, sophisticated wit and often ridiculous ("We are the knights who say Ni!") sense of humor. This humor continues to thrive in the standup and sketch comedy clubs throughout the city. Check *Time Out* for listings, but be warned that the city virtually empties of comedians come August when it's festival time in Edinburgh.

COMEDY STORE — THE WEST END

1a Oxendon St. ☎0844 847 1728 www.thecomedystore.co.uk

This comedy venue offers everything from stand-up to the Cutting Edge, a show every Tuesday that does up-to-date topical humor.

Piccadilly Circus. Turn left onto Coventry, then right onto Oxendon. Tickets £14-20. Box office open M-Th 6:30-9:30pm, F-Sa 6:30pm-1:15am, Su 6:30-9:30pm. Doors open daily 6:30pm. Bar and diner open daily 6:30pm.

DANCE

As with everything else artistic in London, the dance scene here is diverse, innovative, and first-rate. Come for the famous ballets at older venues like the Royal Opera House or stop by one of the smaller companies for some contemporary dance.

SADLER'S WELLS — CLERKENWELL

Rosebery Ave. ☎0844 412 4300 www.sadlerswells.com

Encapsulating all forms of dance, Sadler's Wells puts its belief in the power of dance to good use in wide-ranging and always exciting presentations. The site holds 300 years of dance history.

Angel. Left onto Upper St., then right onto Rosebery Ave. i Some shows offer student discounts. Tickets £10-£55. Open M-Sa 9am-8:30pm. By phone M-Sa 9am-8:30pm.

ROYAL OPERA HOUSE — THE WEST END

Bow St. ☎020 7304 4000 www.roh.org.uk

The Royal Opera House (ROH) may be opera-oriented in name, but in repertoire, it's split between opera and ballet. Though no student discounts are offered, students can try and get standby tickets by going online and selecting "student standby" from the website. Top-price seats are available for £10 if you get lucky.

Covent Garden. Right onto Long Acre, right onto Bow St. Tickets £5-150. Booking office open M-Sa 10am-8pm.

MUSIC

Clubs are expensive, and pubs close at 11pm. Especially during the current recession, fewer young people are willing to shell out the £10-15 it takes to get into a club, especially since beers cost £4-5 on top of that. Much of the London nightlife scene thus lies beyond pub-and club-hopping in the darkened basements of bars everywhere and the glaringly bright, seismically loud music clubs. With a musical history including **The Beatles, Radiohead,** and **The Clash,** all of the bands from the infamous "British Invasion," and most of the best bands from '90s anthemic pop, London has always had a fantastic music scene. Frequently, English musicians respond to American tropes and take them to the next level: where America had the blues, England had **Eric Clapton** and the **Stones,** and when America learned rock, England fired off **The Clash** and **The Sex Pistols.** The London music scene is very much intact, and makes for both a great night out and an excellent way to forge lasting travel friendships. The London music scene is not to be missed.

Classical

There are several large organizations that supply the city with some of the most renowned classical performances in the world. For free chamber and classical music, check out some of London's churches, where students from famous music schools often give free, professional-quality recitals.

ROYAL OPERA HOUSE — THE WEST END

Bow St. ☎020 7304 4000 www.roh.org.uk

Though the glorious glass facade of the Royal Opera House makes it look more like a train station than a theater, patrons of the opera enjoy all of the great works of opera and some of the more contemporary pieces too. Though no discounts are offered, students can try and get standby tickets by going online and selecting "student standby" from the website. Top price seats are available for £10 if you get lucky. Booking opens around two months before each performance, so try and book early. The ROH also sponsors free outdoor film screenings, so look out for those on their website.

Covent Garden. Right onto Long Acre, then right onto Bow St. Tickets £5-150. Booking office open M-Sa 10am-8pm.

PERFORMANCES AT ST. MARTIN-IN-THE-FIELDS — WESTMINSTER

Trafalgar Sq. ☎020 7766 1100 www.smitf.org

Every Monday, Tuesday, and Friday at 1pm, they have a 45min. **"lunch-time concert"** in which conservatory students perform classical recitals. In the evening, more renowned artists perform in the space. Known as the "Church of the Ever-Open Door" because of its use as a place of refuge for soldiers en route to France in WWI, St. Martin-in-the-Fields is a must-see for any music lover.

Charing Cross. To the east of Trafalgar Square. i W 8pm is jazz night. Reserved jazz ticket £9, unreserved jazz tickets £5.50. Open daily 8am-5pm, but it stays open later on off-concert days. Gift shop open M-W 10am-7pm, Th-Sa 10am-9pm, Su 11:30am-6pm.

ROYAL ALBERT HALL — KENSINGTON

Kensington Gore ☎0845 401 5045 for box office www.royalalberthall.com

Deep in the heart of South Kensington, the Royal Albert Hall was commissioned by Prince Albert in order to promote the arts, and has been in continuous operation since 1871. Offering some of the biggest concerts in London, the famous **BBC Proms** classical festival (see p. 94), and a range of other phenomenal musical events, the hall is an experience in history and culture that's not to be missed.

Knightsbridge. Turn left onto Knightsbridge and continue onto Kensington Rd. From £10. Open daily 9am-9pm.

THE LONDON COLISEUM — WESTMINSTER

33 Saint Martin's Ln. ☎087 1472 0600 www.eno.org

Home of the English National Opera, The London Coliseum shows opera in English translation. Showcasing mostly new, cutting-edge ballet and opera, the Coliseum is a must for anyone who's ever wondered what exactly the fat lady is singing when she closes out the show.

Charing Cross. Go along the east side of Trafalgar Square up Charing Cross Rd., turn right onto Chandos Pl., and left onto Saint Martin's Lane. i Sometimes students and other concessions can get discounted tickets 3hr. before the performance. Tickets £15-90. Open M-Sa 10am-8pm on performance days, 10am-6pm on non-performance days.

SOUTHBANK CENTRE — THE SOUTH BANK

Belvedere Rd. ☎084 4847 9915 www.southbankcentre.co.uk/classical

The gorgeous classical music played at the riverside Southbank Centre may clash with its Brutalist design, but that's no reason to skip it. Queen Elizabeth and Purcell rooms provide much more intimate spaces, while the Royal Festival Hall aims for a grander, classically classical experience.

Waterloo. Right onto York Rd. and left onto Waterloo Rd. i Call ☎084 4847 9910 for disabled access. Tickets £9-45. Students can get 50% off all sorts of tickets to some concerts. Available by phone daily 9am-8pm. Royal Festival Hall Ticket office open daily 10am-8pm.

Jazz

RONNIE SCOTT'S — SOHO

47 Frith St. ☎020 7439 0747 www.ronniescotts.co.uk

Ronnie Scott's has been defining "hip" in Soho for the last 51 years. It's hosted everyone from **Tony Bennett** to **Van Morrison,** and **Chick Corea** to the **Funk Brothers.** The venue is all flickering candlelight and dulcet reds and blues. Pictures of jazz greats line the walls in black and white, and a diverse crowd imbibes such creations as Jazz Medicine, Jagermeister, sloe gin, Dubonnet, fresh black berries, angostia bitters *(£8)*. The venue's cool, but the jazz is hot. Stop by if the Soho scene gets overwhelming.

Tottenham Court Rd. Turn down Oxford St. with your back to Tottenham Court Rd. and turn left on Soho St. turn right onto the square and then right onto Frith St. £10 cover, more for big acts. Champagne £8-10. White wine £4.80-5.30. Red wine bottles £22-26. Mixed drinks £8.50-9. Open M-Th 7:15pm-late, F-Sa 6pm-1:30am, Su noon-4pm and 6-10:30pm. Box office open M-F 10am-6pm, Sa noon-5pm.

THE 606 CLUB KNIGHTSBRIDGE

90 Lots Rd. 020 7352 5953 www.606club.co.uk

On quiet Lots Rd., opposite what appears to be a rather foreboding abandoned factory, the 606 Club has been quietly hosting the best of the UK music scene since 1969. Properly underground (it's in a basement), the club itself is candlelit and dim. The musicians play on a marked patch of floor that serves in place of the stage as the diners, frequently musicians who are sitting in on the jams, surround them at tables. Musical styles run the gamut from jazz, Latin, soul, gospel, R and B, and rock, and while the artists may be relatively unknown, they're worth hearing. And be sure to satisfy your stomach, as well as your ears: entrees served range from linguine *(£9.40)* to Cajun-style roast chicken breast *(£14)*. Note that the area around the club is residential and fairly abandoned at night, so it might be safest to take a cab there and back.

*Sloane Square. Exit the Tube and go straight down Sloane Sq. **i** Non-members have to eat in order to drink. Check website for special Su afternoon lunch and show. Cover M £10, Tu-W £8, Th £10, F-Sa £12, Su £10. Entrees £9-18. Bottled beers from £3.45. Open M 7:30pm-midnight, Tu-Th 7pm-midnight, F-Sa 8pm-1:30am, Su 7-11pm.*

JAZZ CAFÉ NORTH LONDON

5 Parkway 020 7688 8899 www.jazzcafe.co.uk

One of the most well-known jazz venues in London, the Jazz Café often surprises people with the expansiveness of its repertoire. It has hosted De La Soul and GZA as well as jazz luminaries, and every Saturday night starting at 10:30pm they have DJs playing'80s hits, followed by'90s nights on Fridays and karaoke hairbrush nights on the third Friday of every month (they're songs you would sing into your hairbrush.) While no student discount is offered by the club, some of the outside promoters who hire it out occasionally offer student discounts.

*Camden Town. Left onto Camden High St., and right onto Parkway. **i** With credit card, £1 charge for purchases under £12. Tickets £5-40. Average £25 at door and £17.50 in advance. Pints around £3.80. Drink deals on club nights £2 for vodka, mixer, Carlsberg pint. Box office open 10:30am-5:30pm. Shows generally start at 7pm. Some nights are double-bills with the late show starting at 11pm.*

Pop and Rock

THE TROUBADOUR CAFE KENSINGTON

263-267 Old Brompton Rd. 020 7370 1434 www.troubadour.co.uk

Many famous acts have graced the Troubadour's small stage since its founding in 1954. Its hanging string lights and stage lights illuminated **Bob Dylan, Jimi Hendrix,** and **Joni Mitchell,** and pictures of some of these artists are plastered into the tops of the tables. To this day, The Troubadour is a community of aspiring and acclaimed artists bound by great music, good drinks and the intoxicating atmosphere of artistic promise. Come here to see some of the city's most exciting acts before they break.

*Gloucester Rd. Turn right onto Gloucester Rd., then turn right onto Old Brompton Rd. **i** Most nights feature several bands. Every other M poetry night. Cover is cash only. Open M-W 8pm-midnight, Th-Sa 8pm-2am, Su 8pm-midnight. Happy hour Tu-Su 8-9pm.*

KOKO NORTH LONDON

1a Camden High St. ☎087 0432 5527 www.koko.uk.com

Koko's lodgings are not typical of a rock n' roll venue. Originally a theater, then a cinema, then one of the first BBC radio broadcasting locations, and then the famous Camden Palace Nightclub, Koko holds all its 110 years of history within its beautiful red walls and its gilded, curved wrought-iron fences guarding the balconies from which music-lovers can look down to the stage. Bringing in mostly big-name indie acts, but also some big names in pop and rock (they've had everyone from Madonna to the Hold Steady and Andre Bird; James Blunt, Kanye West and Usher to Devendra Banhart and Justice), Koko is one of the premier venues in London.

Mornington Crescent. Right onto Hampstead Rd. It's to your right. *i* *Cash only for in-person purchases. Tickets sold through various outlets online. Indie night (indie music and dancing) F 9:30pm-4am. Credit card at £10 min.* *Concert tickets £10-30. Beer £3.50-4. Mixed drinks £4. For indie night, the first 100 people get in free. Cover: students £5 up to midnight, students £7 after midnight, non-students £7 all night.* *Box office open noon-5pm on gig days.*

BORDERLINE SOHO

Orange Yd. 16 Manette St. ☎084 4847 2465 www.venues.meanfiddler.com/borderline

A simple venue that, despite its lack of the outlandish Art Deco, theatrical trappings of other similar London concert halls, oozes the spirit of rock and roll from every beer-soaked wall and ear-blowing speaker. Often, big name artists will play the Borderline when starting solo careers. Townes Van Zandt played his last show at the Borderline, Eddie Vedder, Jeff Buckley, and Rilo Kiley have played there, and **Spinal Tap** played the Borderline right after the movie came out. The amps go to eleven, the music's piping hot, and the location is prime.

Tottenham Court Road. Right on Charing Cross. *i* *Club nights W-Sa 11pm-3am.* *Tickets £6-20. Pints £3.40.* *Doors open for shows daily 7pm. Tickets available at the Jazz Cafe box office M-Sa 10:30am-5:30pm.*

HMV APOLLO WEST LONDON

15 Queen Caroline St. ☎020 8563 3800 www.hmvapollo.com

Like many of the big, architecturally stunning venues in London, the Art Deco HMV Apollo was originally a cinema. It was formerly known as the Hammersmith Odeon and hosted **Bruce Springsteen** in his 1975 Hammersmith Odeon film (he would go on to play there four times). It has hosted big name acts like Oasis,

R.E.M, Elton John, the Rolling Stones, and even The Beatles once.

Hammersmith. Opposite the Broadway Shopping Centre. Call in advance about wheelchair accessibility. Call 084 4844 4748 for tickets. Tickets depend on the event, check online. Box office open 4pm-start of the show on performance days.

02 ACADEMY BRIXTON SOUTH LONDON

211 Stockwell Rd. 020 7771 3000

Home to Europe's largest fixed stage, the 02 Academy Brixton's set list is rife with the big names of our generation. Past acts include MGMT, Echo and the Bunnymen, Plan B, Pavement, LCD Soundsystem, and the Gaslight Anthem. They also occasionally have club nights (which aren't on a fixed schedule, so check the website).

Brixton. Right onto Brixton Rd., then left onto Stockwell Rd. The area can be a bit rough, so you may want to take a cab. Bars are cash only. Call in advance for wheelchair accessibility. Ticket prices vary, most £20-35. Pints £4. Venue box office opens 2hr. before doors on gig nights.

HMV FORUM NORTH LONDON

9-17 Highgate Rd. 020 7428 4099 www.kentishtownforum.com

One of the big-name venues in London, the HMV Forum gets some of the most famous acts to come to town. The 75-year-old theater has hosted N.E.R.D., Slayer, Limp Bizkit, Wolf Parade, and the Decemberists on its massive stage. The hall holds 2350, and is just right for a big show.

Kentish Town. Right onto Kentish Town Rd., then left onto Highgate Rd. Cash machine. Gigs are 14+. Tickets £10-60. Pints £4. Box office open on show days 5-9pm. Doors open 7pm.

02 EMPIRE WEST LONDON

Shepherd's Bush Green 020 8354 3300 www.02shepherdsbushempire.co.uk

A popular space hosting large rock acts, the 02 Empire is one of the big names on the London music scene. With a classic feel greatly augmented by the bold stonework and old-fashioned hand-placed letters on the awning out front, the Empire hearkens to the heyday of rock and roll.

Shepherd's Bush. Right onto Uxbridge Rd. then left at the end of Shepherd's Bush Green. Call 084 4477 2000 for tickets. Box office open 4-6pm and 6:30-9:30pm on show days.

HAMMERSMITH IRISH CULTURAL CENTRE WEST LONDON

Blacks Rd. 020 8563 8232 www.irishculturalcentre.co.uk

Located on a quiet, unassuming street in Hammersmith, the Irish Cultural Centre is shockingly full of life within. Families—both Irish and otherwise—congregate in the main room before consulting reception and going to different parts of the building to participate in such varied events as clog lessons, concerts from Irish folk artists, book readings, free jams (participation encouraged), film screenings, and storytelling. Check the website for details on prices and events, but come prepared with a love for the Emerald Isle.

Hammersmith. Black's Rd. is just off of Queen Caroline St. near where it intersects with Beadon Rd. Monthly movie screening £1.50. "The Session" (Irish jam) Th 6-8pm. Movies are shown the first Th of every month. Hours vary. Box office open M-F 9am-1pm. If something is happening in the afternoon, box office is open 1-3pm.

THEATER

Ah, "theatre" in London. While in London, many people choose to see a show because the city is renowned for its cheap theater. Tickets for big musicals on the **West End** go for as cheap as £25 the day of, which is pittance compared to the $100 tickets sold on Broadway, the American equivalent. On the West End, the main theater district, you'll find the bigger musicals that are produced in only one theater. For instance, *Phantom of the Opera* is entering its 25th year at Her Majesty's Theatre. Other theaters in the area and throughout London put on more cutting-edge or intellectual plays. Many pubs have live performance spaces in the back where theater groups rehearse and perform for an audience that, thanks to a few pints, always finds the second act more confusing than the first. Also, many churches, such as St. Paul's in Covent Garden, put on summer theater, and there are ways to get your culture for free. Always check discount prices against the theater itself. Only buy discounted tickets from booths with a circle and check mark symbol that says **STAR** on it. This stands for the Society of Tickets Agents and Retailers, and it vouches for the legitimacy of a discount booth.

ROYAL COURT THEATRE — KNIGHTSBRIDGE

Sloane Sq. ☎020 7565 5000 www.royalcourttheatre.com

Famous for pushing the theater envelope, the Royal Court is the antidote to all the orchestral swoons and faux-opera sweeping through the West End. The Royal Court's 1956 production of John Osborne's *Look Back in Anger* (not to be confused with the Oasis song of a similar title) was largely credited with launching Modern British drama. Royal is known as a writers' theater, purveying high-minded works of great drama for audiences that will appreciate them.

Sloane Square. Tickets M £10, Tu-Sa £12.18-£25. Student discounts available on day of performance, preview and Sa matinees. Open M-F 10am-6pm or until the doors open, Sa 10am-curtain up on performance days.

THE NATIONAL THEATRE — THE SOUTH BANK

Belvedere Rd. ☎020 7452 3400 www.nationaltheatre.org.uk

Opened in 1976 by appointment of the monarchy, the National Theatre shows great new and classic British drama on its three stages, of which the Olivier is largest. It also revives lost classics from around the world. Special Travelex shows mean half the seats are available for £10 only.

Waterloo. Right onto York Rd. then left onto Waterloo Rd. Tickets £10-44. Box office open M-Sa 9:30am-8pm, Su noon-6pm.

THE OLD VIC — SOUTH LONDON

The Cut ☎084 4871 7628 www.oldvictheatre.com

This famous theater was built in 1818 and has hosted the likes of **Laurence Olivier.** Though dealing in a huge range of styles, the Old Vic is predominantly a traditional theater showing the classics. Fans of Kevin Spacey will want to visit now, since he is the theater's current artistic director.

Southwark. Right onto The Cut. Tickets £10-47. Open M-Sa 10am-7pm on non-show days, 10am-6pm on show days.

THE YOUNG VIC — SOUTH LONDON

66 The Cut ☎020 7922 2922 www.youngvic.org

Formerly the studio space for the Old Vic, the Young Vic puts on a variety of shows, most of which are edgier, more exciting, and newer than the more traditional Old Vic down the road. They frequently do reinterpretations of classic works as well as newer stuff. The three spaces in the theater allow for great versatility, with one main house and two studio spaces.

Southwark. Right onto the Cut. Tickets £10-22. Open M-Sa 10am-6pm.

DONMAR WAREHOUSE — THE WEST END

41 Earlham St. ☎084 4871 7624 www.donmarwarehouse.com

The warehouse puts on everything from Shakespeare to contemporary works, occasionally by little known artists. Though it is a mainstream theater, it rotates in new plays once every two months. The space has a studio feel, with cushioned red benches facing the stage.

Covent Garden. Turn right onto Long Acre, left on Endell St., left onto Shelton St., right onto Neal St., and then left on Earlham St. Tickets £15-29, students £12 tickets ½hr. before the show if it's not sold out. Ticket office open M-Sa 10am-showtime.

SHAKESPEARE'S GLOBE — SOUTH LONDON

21 New Globe Walk ☎020 7401 9919 www.shakespeares-globe.org

Though the original Globe theater burnt down in 1613 during a performance of *Henry VIII*, this accurate reconstruction was opened in 1997. Much like the original Globe, it has an open roof and standing area for the "groundlings." Steeped in historical and artistic tradition, the theater stages Shakespeare as well as two new plays a year.

Southwark. Left onto Blackfriars Rd., right onto Southwark St., left onto Great Guildford, right onto Park St., left onto Emerson St. Standing £5, seats £35. Box office open M-Sa 10am-8pm, Su 10am-7pm. Telephone open M-Sa 10am-6pm, Su 10am-5pm.

BATTERSEA ART CENTER SOUTH LONDON

176 Lavender Hill, Old Town Hall 020 7223 2223 www.bac.org.uk

Located in the old Clapham Town Hall, the Battersea Art Center is automatically a strange theater experience. Throw in the BAC's reputation for hosting young producers, new companies, and some of the most cutting-edge and bizarre theater when deemed too young to be "on the scene," and you have a night of some wild shows ahead of you. The BAC boasts 72 rooms that host everything from closets to more traditional spaces. In a famous performance at the BAC, an Italian theater company put on a show where the audience had to pretend to be dogs. This resulted in audience members rolling around on wheel trays with oven mitts on their hands and eating scraps off a table while tennis balls were thrown at them. One of the best parts about the BAC is the SCRATCH program, in which artists show a work in development and get feedback from the audience. This famous program only cements the BAC's status as a hip, young, unconventional theater.

Clapham Common. Take bus #345 from just outside headed toward South Kensington and it will let you out nearby on Lavender Hill. Min. £10 at the bar. i Under 26-ers should also note that the BAC is part of "A Night Less Ordinary." Ticket prices vary. Pints £3.20. Check the website for details, and look out for the occasional "pay what you can Tuesday!" Box office open M-F 10am-6pm, Sa 3-6pm.

THE BUSH THEATRE WEST LONDON

Shepherd's Bush Green 020 8743 5050 www.bushtheatre.co.uk

Located on the edge of Shepherd's Bush Green in an old building, The Bush Theatre's repertoire is in stark contrast to its old London surroundings. Presenting new writing in its unique, intimate theater space, which rarely looks the same between two shows, The Bush is the place to come for some of the most forward-thinking theater in London.

Shepherd's Bush. turn right down Shepherd's Bush Green. Tickets £20, concessions are £10. Matinees £15; concessions £7.50. The Bush is part of A Night Less Ordinary. Box office open M-Sa 10am-6pm except for show days, in which case noon-8pm. Shows are normally M-Sa 7:30pm depending on the run. Sa matinees 2:30pm.

HACKNEY EMPIRE EAST LONDON

291 Mare St. 020 8985 2424 www.hackneyempire.co.uk

With great, bold sandstone letters announcing its presence on an otherwise normal block, the Hackney Empire looks just as an old variety theater that once showcased the likes of **Charlie Chaplin** and **Harry Houdini** should. All faded grandeur and vaudeville-esque decor, the Hackney puts on everything from comedy gigs to productions from the Royal Shakespeare Company.

Take the overline to Hackney Central (in East London). Left onto Graham Rd., right onto Mare St. Tickets £10-22.50, student discount £2 off. Box office open M-Sa 10am-6pm, showdays M-Su 10am-9:30pm.

OPEN-AIR THEATRE REGENT'S PARK

Regent's Park 084 4826 4242 www.openairtheatre.com

Housed inside the beautiful Regent's Park, the Open-Air Theatre puts on a variety of shows best enjoyed in the warm summer months. After the show, take a stroll around the park and enjoy observing the less-dramatic lives of the herons who reside therein.

Regent's Park. Tickets M-Th evening £10-43, F-Sa £19-46. Standby £15 for best available. Telephone box office open M-Sa 10am-6pm.

rail penalty

On many of the stations used in the National Rail and DLR system, the stations are not guarded by gates, and passengers are forced to remember to touch in and out at small stands. Don't forget to do this—it's easy to get on the train, but it's not easy to pay the penalty. And they do check.

FESTIVALS

BBC PROMS KNIGHTSBRIDGE

Kensington Gore ☎0845 401 5045 www.bbc.co.uk/proms

BBC Proms is a world famous classical music festival put on by the BBC in the Royal Albert Hall. What in the world is a "Prom," you ask? "Prom" stands for "Promenade Concert"—a performance at which some of the audience stands on a promenade in the arena. During the proms, there is at least one daily performance in London's Royal Albert Hall, in addition 70-odd events and discussions. Note that performances are broadcast for free.

Knightsbridge. Turn left onto Knightsbridge, continue onto Kensington Rd. ***i*** *Check website for specific wheelchair-accessibility information. From £10. July-Sept.*

GLASTONBURY FESTIVAL SOMERSET

Pilton, England Festival Office ☎01458 834 596 www.glastonburyfestivals.co.uk

One of the most famous rock festivals in the world, the Glastonbury Festival explodes onto the scene every June. Possibly as close as you will ever get to going to Woodstock, it's essentially a bunch of festivals jam-packed into one, distributed through the Dance Village, Green Field, Circus and Theatre fields and the Park.

Festival office: 28 Northload Street, Glastonbury, Somerset BA6 9JJ. ***i*** *National Express has routes to Glastonbury. Bristol and Glastonbury town shuttles provide transportation to the festival. Disabled patrons must register in order to use the festival's accessible facilities; to get a registration form, request a disabled access packet, which includes information on the site's accessible facilities. Standard ticket £185 + £5 booking fee per ticket + £5 P and P per booking. June. Performance dates and times vary.*

BLAZE THE CITY OF LONDON

Barbican Centre, Silk Street London, EC2Y 8DS ☎020 7638 8891 www.barbican.org.uk/blaze

An annual festival that features major international artists in the Barbican and open-air performance spaces throughout London. Blaze makes for a full-immersion arts experience, as audience participation is encouraged.

Barbican. ***i*** *The main entrance to the venue is wheelchair-accessible, and all venues have seating for wheelchair users. The Barbican Centre requests that patrons inform them of access requirements upon booking their tickets. Annual membership £20. Event prices vary. June-July.*

LONDON LITERARY FESTIVAL THE SOUTH BANK

Southbank Centre Belvedere Road, SE1 8XX ☎0844 847 9939 www.londonlitfest.com

Some of the world's hottest thinkers and writers assemble at the South Bank Centre every July. This literary extravaganza has featured poets, novelists, musicians, and scientists. Visit the website to download podcasts of the events.

Waterloo; Embankment. ***i*** *For complete wheelchair-accessibility details, see "Access Information" on website. Check website for ticket prices. Online booking transaction fee £1.45. Telephone booking transaction fee £2.50. Call between 9am-8pm daily. Book through Royal Festival Hall Ticket Office 10am-8pm daily.*

shopping

London is known as one of the shopping capitals of the world. With its famous department stores (**Harrods** and **Harvey Nichol's**) keeping the old flame of shopping as spectacle alive over in Knightsbridge, London has kept some of its old shopping class and the prices that come with it. Vintage stores and hip, independent record stores fill Soho, and the East End has lots of fun boutiques. Notting Hill is famous for Portobello Market, but even in off-market days, the road has a host of cute boutique shopping options. Chelsea is for those with a bit more money and a serious commitment to shopping. For you literary junkies, **John Sandoe's** is our favorite bookstore in the city. Shopping is a significant part of tourism in London, so if you aren't broke and have some extra room in your backpack, window shop the day away.

WESTMINSTER

Westminster is filled with chains. The area is worth seeing for the sights, but die-hard shoppers might be best served by looking elsewhere.

WESTMINSTER BOOKSHOP

BOOKSTORE

8 Artillery Row ☎020 7802 0018 www.westminsterbookshop.co.uk

The last independent bookstore in Westminster, this little shop is fighting the chains with an excellent and specialized selection. In case experiencing London first-hand isn't enough for you, you can utilize the store's impressive British history, British politics, biography, political thought, and London sections for a full English intellectual experience. Just be sure to swing by the classics for some Austen, Dickens, or Woolf (among many, many others) on your way out. If you're looking to pick up the 5000th Bourne book that you saw advertised on the subway, this is not the store for you

Liverpool St. Take a right onto Liverpool St., a left onto Bishopsgate, right onto Artillery Lane, and then right onto Artillery Rw. M-F 9:30am-5:30pm, Sa 11am-4pm.

HOTEL CHOCOLAT

CHOCOLATE

133 Victoria St. ☎020 7821 0473 www.hotelchocolat.co.uk

One of a chain, Hotel Chocolat is one of the more exciting chains in Westminster. The inside is sleek, like a more efficient version of Willy Wonka's Chocolate Factory. Seventy percent of the chocolate here is made in Britain, and it's packaged into ridiculous items like framed chocolate portraits and chocolate dipping sets, all for sale. For anyone who's ever felt that a chocolate "slab" is preferable to a chocolate bar, you have found your store.

Victoria. Take right onto Grosvenor Pl and follow it onto Victoria St. Open M-F 8:30am-7pm, Sa 9:30am-6pm, Su 11am-5pm.

MARYLEBONE AND REGENT'S PARK

IT'S ONLY ROCK 'N' ROLL

ROCK PARAPHERNALIA

230 Baker St. ☎020 7224 0277 www.itsonlyrocknrolllondon.co.uk

London is known for its rich musical history, and It's Only Rock 'N' Roll exploits that fact as much as possible. Filled with paraphernalia both gimmicky and original, like gold and platinum records, binoculars from the Stones' Bridges to Babylon Tour, Pink Floyd shower slippers, a Coldplay calendar, and a signed vinyl cover of the Who's *Rock Opera Quadrophenia*, It's Only Rock'N Roll is a must for any visiting rock fan.

⊖Baker St. Right on Baker St. Open daily 10am-6:30pm.

BAYSWATER

Bayswater is full of quirky little shops, though it's not a major shopping center like Notting Hill.

BAYSWATER MARKET ♿ MARKET

Bayswater Rd.

Every Sunday, local artists of all media and skill levels decorate the Hyde Park Fence with their wares, making it look like an art gallery with commitment issues. It's open all afternoon, so join the crowds as they move from touristy London pictures to more original works from rising stars in the London art scene. Art is for sale at all prices, so come with an open mind and be ready to dig a sizeable hole in your wallet.

⊖Lancaster Gate. Open Su late morning through the afternoon.

CHELSEA

Shopping in Chelsea runs the gamut, with stores from the neighborhoods punk-rock salad days to a stifling amount of kitchen and home shops. Still, if you want to trick out your hostel room, we've seen some lovely linoleum.

JOHN SANDOE BOOKS ♿ BOOKSTORE

10 Blacklands Terr. ☎020 7589 9473 www.johnsandoe.com

While taking the stairs to the fiction section on the second floor, one remembers the joy of independent bookstores. There's barely space for peoples' feet as half of each stair is taken up by a pile of carefully selected books. On the crammed second floor, a cracked leather chair presides over shelves so packed with masterworks and little known gems that they are layered with moving shelves. There are books everywhere in this store, and the knowledgeable staff is personable and ready to hand with excellent suggestions. Book lovers beware: it would be easy to spend the day in this shop.

⊖Sloane Sq. Exit the Tube and go straight down Sloane Sq. The street slanting gently left is King's Rd. Go straight onto it and turn right at Blacklands Terr. Open M-Sa 9:30am-5:30pm, Su noon-6pm.

TASCHEN ♿ ART BOOKSTORE

12 Duke of York Sq. ☎020 7881 0795 www.taschen.com

If you've ever heard of Taschen, or the art-book-publishing company, you'll want to see this store. Packed with high quality, well-written, high-culture art books about everything from Impressionism to logo design and some low-culture books such as those pertaining to big butts, breasts, penises, and, of course, architecture. Taschen's got everything a self-respecting art aficionado could want...except the originals.

⊖Sloane Square. Exit the Tube and go straight down Sloane Sq. The street slanting gently left is King's Rd. go onto it and turn left onto Duke of York Square (it's the one by the Saatchi Art Gallery). Prices vary, but the books can be surprisingly inexpensive. Open M-Tu 10am-6pm, W 10am-7pm, Th-F 10am-6pm, Sa 10am-7pm, Su noon-6pm.

AD HOC ♿ WOMEN'S CLOTHING, SEX TRINKETS

153 King's Rd ☎020 7376 8829 www.adhoclondon.co.uk

If you have an inescapable yet reasonably innocuous fascination with breasts and penises (and really, who doesn't), then Ad Hoc might be the shopping experience you've been missing. There are tassels, flashing breast lights, grow your-own willies, inflatable boobs, bouncing boobs, and glow-in-the-dark cock straws. There are also shirts, hats, adventurous tights, and sunglasses. Randomly, Fllann's tattoo parlor is a part of the shop. Sex and tattoos, what more convincing do you need?

⊖Sloane Square. Exit the Tube and go straight down Sloane Sq. The street slanting gently left is King's Rd. Open M-Su 10am-6pm. W 10am-7pm.

KENSINGTON AND EARL'S COURT

BOOKTHRIFT ♿ BOOKS

22 Thurloe St. ☎020 7589 2916

Advertising "Quality books at Bargain Prices," Bookthrift buys overstock books off publishers, meaning they can sell new books at used prices. Featuring a wide selection of Art Books, History and Fiction, Bookthrift has fun deals like 3 books for the price of 2 in Military History or the 3 for £2 on £2.99 paperback fiction. The selection isn't as good as it is in other bookstores, but if you look closely, you're likely to find a good read at a great price.

South Kensington. Take a right down Thurloe St. Open M-F 10am-8pm, Sa 11am-7pm, Su 12pm-7pm.

TRINITY HOSPICE BOOKSHOP BARGAIN BOOKS MUSIC DVDs EQUIPMENT

31 Kensington Church St. ☎020 7376 1098

With all proceeds going to charity, the Trinity Hospice Bookshop is a good place for any socially conscious traveler who wants a book that's cheap enough to abuse guilt-free. All the products are donated, and since the store gets them for free, they sell them at next to nothing. Paperbacks are £2.00, hardbacks are £3.00, CDs are £2.00, all vinyls (with the exception of rare jazz records) are £1.00. The selection ranges wildly, so set aside some time for digging and you just might find a cheap, vintage gem.

High Street Kensington. Turn right onto Kensington High St. and left onto Kensington Church St. Open M-Sa 10:30-6pm, Su 11am-5pm.

WHOLE FOODS GROCERY STORE

63-97 Kensington High St. ☎020 7368 4500 www.wholefoodsmarket.com

For those living nearby who have the hankering for some health-food cookin', look no further than this centrally located Whole Foods location. Also a good antidote to homesickness for those coming from the States and Canada.

High Street Kensington. Turn right onto Kensington High St. Open M-Sa 8am-10pm, Su sales: 12pm-6pm, restaurant open 8am-9:45 M-Sa, 10am-5:45pm Su.

KNIGHTSBRIDGE AND BELGRAVIA

Mostly posh shops and chains, Knightsbridge isn't the most friendly place for shopping, price-wise. However, the spectacle of its famous department stores make browsing enjoyable.

HARRODS DEPARTMENT STORE

87-135 Brompton Rd. ☎020 7730 1234 www.harrods.com

An ode to the shopping experience, Harrods is probably the most famous department store on the planet. Packed with faux-hieroglyphs, rooms named "Room of Luxury" or its sequel, "Room of Luxury II," Harrods is just as much a sight to see as it is a place to shop. Especially entertaining are the prices and the people who pay them. Be sure to check out the toy section—it's hard to not rediscover your inner child. Also worth seeing is the candy section of the food court, which is where they sell chocolate shoes *(£84 for a pair)*. On the bottom floor, they sell "Personalised Classics" which enable you to insert names in place of the ones already in a given book. Who needs "Romeo and Juliet" when you could have "Fred and Agnes?" "Fred, Fred, wherefore art thou Fred?" The answer: In shopping heaven.

Knightsbride. Take the Harrods Exit. Open M-Sa 10am-8pm, Su 11:30am-6pm.

PANDORA CONSIGNMENT DRESSES

16-22 Cheval Pl. ☎020 7589 5289 www.pandoradressagency.com

If you get tired of the prices at the more expensive department stores, come to Pandora and see the same designer clothes second-hand at a lower price! Clothe yourself in Chanel, Dior, Yves St. Lauren, and Gucci and be sure to save money for accessorizing.

Knightsbridge. Turn left onto Brompton Rd., right onto Montpelier St. and left onto Cheval Pl. Open M-Sa 10am-7pm, Su noon-6pm.

HARVEY NICHOLS DEPARTMENT STORE

109-125 Knightsbridge ☎020 7235 5000 www.harveynichols.com

Whoever was looking for the Fountain of Youth clearly never checked out the ground floor of Harvey Nichols. The entire level is packed with women arming themselves for the battle against age. In fact, four floors of the great department store are taken up by fashion, cosmetics, beauty, and accessories. After that, there's menswear and food and hospitality. Most high-end designers are sold here. Foreigners can shop tax-free if they go to the fourth-floor customer services and fill out a form. The store is upscale, densely populated with women, and a little less of a scene than nearby Harrods.

⊖Knightsbridge. Open M-Sa 10am-9pm, Su 11:30am-6pm (browsing only 11:30am-noon).

london

NOTTING HILL

Like we said, Portobello Rd. is truly where it's at. Otherwise, shopping options in Notting Hill consist mainly of antique stores, souvenir sellers and high-end clothing shops.

MUSIC AND VIDEO EXCHANGE MUSIC

42 Notting Hill Gate www.mveshops.co.uk

Though part of a chain, this Music and Video Exchange will entertain any audiophile endlessly. The staff engage in Hornby-esque conversations oozing with musical knowledge, while customers browse through the vinyls, CDs, and cassettes in the bargain area. Upstairs in the rarities section, you can find anything from a 12£ original vinyl of the Rolling Stones' *Get Yer Ya-Ya's Out!* to the original German sleeve for the Beatles' final record, *Let it Be.* Customers can trade in their own stuff in exchange for cash or—in a move betraying MVE's cold-hearted understanding of a music lover's brain—twice the cash amount in store vouchers.

⊖Notting Hill Gate. Walk out the south entrance and go down Notting Hill Gate. Daily 10am-8pm.

THE TRAVEL BOOKSHOP BOOKS

13-15 Blenheim Crescent ☎020 7229 5260 www.thetravelbookshop.com

You may be tempted to disregard this bookstore as soon as you figure out why Americans are taking their pictures in front of it, but that would be a mistake. The inspiration for the "Travel Book Company" in the film *Notting Hill*, the shop has all the charm the filmmakers thought it had. The shelves are piled high with

travel literature, travel guides, and maps. You can even find stylish postcards, children's books, and historical literature. We're sure you're perfectly content with the travel book you're currently using, but the shop's worth a browse.
Notting Hill Gate. Exit the station from the north exit. Turn right onto Pembridge Rd. and then left onto Portobello Rd. Follow Portobello down and turn left on Blenheim Crescent. Open M-Sa 10am-6pm, Su noon-5pm.

THE SOUTH BANK

MARCUS CAMPBELL ART BOOKS — ART BOOKS

43 Holland St. ☎020 7261 0111 www.marcuscampbell.co.uk

Close enough both in theme and proximity to the **Tate Modern** (p. 48) to be its unofficial bookstore, Marcus Campbell Art Books sells a wide variety of what you might expect. Cheap catalogues are on sale *(£1 and £2)*, and rare and expensive books run the gamut, with some coming in at over £3000. A fun store for browsing and shopping alike.
Southwark. Left onto Blackfriars Rd. Right onto Southwark St., left onto Sumner, left onto Holland St. Open M-Sa 10:30am-6:30pm, Su noon-6pm.

SOUTHBANK PRINTMAKERS — ART SHOP

Unit 12 Gabriels Wharf, 56 Upper Ground ☎020 7928 8184 www.southbank-printmakers.com

Every five minutes, someone in London is sold a cheap work of bad, tourist-trap art. Southbank Printmakers have a chance to put a stop to this grave injustice. This artist cooperative has been around for 10 years, producing quality lino cuts, wood cuts, etchings, and monoprints at affordable prices. Many of the prints are London-themed, making them perfect, original, and affordable souvenirs.
Southwark. Left onto Blackfriars Rd., left onto Stamford St., right onto Duchy St. Open in summer M-F 11:30am-6:30pm, Sa-Su 10am-8pm, in winter M-F 11:30am-5:30pm, Sa-Su 10am-7pm.

TATE MODERN BOOKSHOP — ART BOOKS

53 Bankside ☎020 7401 5167 www.tate.org.uk/shop

Located just off Turbine Hall in the fabulous Tate Modern, the Tate Modern Bookshop has everything for the art lover. Sketch pads, high-art postcards, art theory books, kids' books, books on films, and films are all sold in this comprehensive bookshop which lies close to its inspiration.
Southwark. Left onto Blackfriars Rd. Right onto Southwark St., left onto Sumner, left onto Holland St. Open M-Th 10am-6pm, F-Sa 10am-10pm, Su 10am-6pm.

THE WEST END

Shopping in the West End is more student-oriented than most areas in London. Filled with cool independent stores, most of them selling books, CDs, vinyls and more vintage clothes than the Motown stars ever wore, the West End is a fun shopping district that tends to emphasize the cheap. Break out the chucks, Ray-Bans and tight black jeans—your wallet must lighten.

SISTER RAY — INDEPENDENT RECORDS AND CDS

34-35 Berwick St. ☎020 7734 3297 www.sisterray.co.uk

An old school record shop of the best kind, Sister Ray has every sort of genre, from constant chart-toppers to one-hit wonders. The stellar staff is adept at creating musical matches-made-in-Heaven, directing listeners to artists. Hip, cheap books about music line the check-out counter, and listening stations are throughout the store.
Tottenham Court Rd., left on Oxford St. left on Wardour St., left on Berwick St. Wheelchair access at the top of the store, ramp available on request. Open M-Sa 10am-8pm, Su noon-6pm.

THE SCHOTT MUSIC SHOP — SHEET MUSIC, PRACTICE ROOMS

48 Great Marlborough St. ☎020 7292 6090 www.schottmusic.co.uk

This quiet and spacious shop is one of the oldest sheet music shops in London. Open since 1857, The Schott Music Shop sells everything from the Beatles to

Bartok and Muse to Mendelssohn. Especially of note to musical travelers are the three **practice rooms** beneath the shop which are available for 1hr rehearsal times. There you'll find two baby grand Boston pianos and one Steinway, all of which are tuned every two months. They also hold recitals in the performance space of young musicians for admittance *(£8-10)*.

Oxford Circus. Left on Regent St., left on Great Marlborough St. i Students get 10% discount on print music. Only upstairs is wheelchair accessible, not the practice rooms. £10 per hr. before noon, £12 per hr. noon-6pm, £15per hr. after 6pm. Open M-F 10am-6:30pm, Sa 10am-6pm.

BM SOHO MUSIC DJ RECORD STORE

25 D'Arblay St. ☎020 7437 0478 www.bm-soho.com

A favorite for many local DJs, BM (known to those in the know as **Black Market**) has all things House and drum and bass. Most striking is just how many sub-genres of house there are. DJ gear like slip mats and cases for records are on sale in the back, and regular customers get discounts *(£1-3)*, but you have to ask for it. Check the website for the occasional in-store appearance of a famous DJ who'll jam out while patrons enjoy free cider.

Tottenham Court Rd., left on Oxford St. left on Wardour St., left on Berwick St., right on D'Arblay. i You have to ask a clerk to take records down for you. Most records £5-10. Open M-W, Sa 11am-7pm, Th-F 11am-8pm, Su noon-6pm.

a sohovian conversation

I was in Soho (yes, there is a Soho in London, too) the other day when I noticed a high number of rickshaws circling the area. Thinking it would make good fodder for a tip, I approached one of the drivers. The following conversation ensued:

Me: Excuse me, I was wondering what your rates are.

Rick: Get in.

Me: No, that's alright, I just wanted to know how much you charge per block or so.

Rick: You want to go where?

Me: I don't want to go anywhere, but if I were to take your rickshaw, how much would it cost me to get to the other side of Soho Square?

Rick: I'll give you a ride, sure.

Me: How much?

Rick: Alright, let's go.

Me: No thanks, I'll just walk.

Rick: So you want go to a strip club then?

Ah, Soho.

Benjamin Naddaff-Hafrey

PRACTICALITIES

- **TOURS: Big Bus Company** *(48 Buckingham Palace Rd. Victoria. 020 7233 9533 www.bigbustours.com Buses leave every 15min. 8:30am-6pm.)* offers a **Red Tour** (history) which stops at the Green Park Underground, Hyde Park Corner, Trafalgar Square, Whitehall, Westminster Bridge, London Eye, Tower of London, Buckingham Palace and Victoria. **Original London Walks** *(020 7624 9255 £8, 65+ and students £6)* has themed walks like "Jack the Ripper Walk" and "Alfred Hitchcock's London." Check the website for schedules. **Britain Visitor Centres** *(1 Regent St. Piccadilly Circus. www.visitbritain.com Open M 9:30am-6:30pm, Tu-F 9am-6pm, Sa 9am-5pm, Su and Bank Holidays 10am-4pm.)* **London Information Centre** *(Leicester Sq. Leicester Sq. 020 7292 2333 M-Su 8am-midnight.)*
- **US EMBASSY:** *(24 Grosvenor Sq. Bond Street. 020 7499 9000 www.usembassy.org.uk.).*
- **CREDIT CARD SERVICES: American Express** *(www.amextravelresources.com)* locations at *(78 Brompton Rd. Knightsbridge. 084 4406 0046 Open M-T 9am-5:30pm, W 9:30am-5:30pm, Th-F 9am-5:30pm, Sa 9am-4:00pm)* and *(30-31 Haymarket. Piccadilly Circus. 084 4406 0044 Open M-F 9:00am-5:30pm.)*
- **GLBT RESOURCES: Boyz** *(www.boyz.co.uk)* lists gay events in London as well as an online version of its magazine. **Gingerbeer** *(www.gingerbeer.co.uk)* is a guide for lesbian and bisexual women with events listings.
- **POST OFFICE: Trafalgar Square Post Office.** *(24-28 William IV St., Westminster. Charing Cross. 0207 484 9305 Open M 8:30am-6:30pm, Tu 9:15am-6:30pm, W-F 8:30am-6:30pm, Sa 9am-5:30pm.)*

EMERGENCY!

- **POLICE:** Call **City of London Police** *(020 7601 2000)* or **Metropolitan Police** *(030 0123 1212).*
- **HOSPITAL: St. Thomas' Hospital.** *(Westminster Bridge Rd. Westminster. 020 7188 7188.)* **Royal Free Hospital.** *(Pond St. Hampstead Heath. 020 7794 0500.)* **Charing Cross Hospital.** *(Fulham Palace Rd. Hammersmith. 020 3311 1234.)* **University College Hospital.** *(235 Euston Rd. Warren Street. 0845 155 5000.)*
- **PHARMACY: Boots** *(www.boots.com)* and **Superdrug** *(www.superdrug.com),* the most popular drugstores in London, are scattered throughout the city. **Zafash Pharmacy.** *(233-235 Old Brompton Rd. Earl's Court. 020 7373 2798 www.zafash.com.)* **Bliss Pharmacy.** *(107-109 Gloucester Rd. Gloucester Rd. 020 7373 4445.)*

GETTING THERE

By Plane

The main airport in London is **Heathrow** *(084 4335 1801 www.heathrowairport.com).* There are five terminals at Heathrow, which is commonly regarded as one of the busiest international airports in the world. Terminal 2 is closed, and there are exceptions to the rules concerning the location of airlines. The best way to find your terminal is through the **"Which terminal?"** function on the Heathrow website.

This tool enables you to search via airline and destination as well as specific flight number.

The cheapest way to get from London Heathrow to Central London is on the Tube. The two Tube stations servicing the four terminals of Heathrow form a distressing looking loop at the end of the **⊖Piccadilly** line which runs between Central London and the Heathrow terminals *(⏰ 1hr. every 5min. M-Sa 5am-11:54pm, Su 5:46am-10:37pm.)*

Heathrow Express *(☎084 5600 1515 💻www.heathrowexpress.com)* runs between Heathrow and Paddington four times an hour. The trip is significantly shorter than many of the alternatives, clocking in at around 15-20min. *(⏰ M-Sa 1st train from terminals 1, 2 and 3 5:12am; Su 5:08am. M-Su first train from Terminal 5 5:07am)*, but the £16.50 *(when purchased online; £18 from station; £23 on board)* makes it a little less enticing. The **Heathrow Connect** also runs to Paddington but is both cheaper and longer because it stops at five places on the way to and from Heathrow. There are two trains per hour, and the trip takes about 25min.

The **National Express** bus runs between Victoria Coach Station and Heathrow three times an hour. Though cheap and often simpler than convoluted Underground trips, the buses are subject to that great parasite of the Queen's country: traffic. There are naysayers roaming the halls of Heathrow moaning terrifying tales about people spending vacations on buses, but if you're looking for a cheap thrill and you're from anywhere with normal driving laws, you can look forward to that first time when they pull onto the highway and your travel-addled mind instructs you to wrench the steering wheel from the driver's mad hands. *(☎08717 818 178 💻www.nationalexpress.com)*. Posing a similar traffic threat, **taxis** from the airport to Victoria cost around £60 and take around 45min. In short, they aren't worth it.

Getting to **Gatwick Airport** *(☎084 4335 1802 💻www.gatwickairport.com)* takes around 30min., making it less convenient than Heathrow but less hectic too. The swift and affordable train services that connect Gatwick to the city make the trip a little easier. The **Gatwick Express** train *(☎084 5850 1530 💻www.gatwickexpress.com ⓢ 1-way £15.20; 2-way £25.80 and valid for a month)* runs non-stop service to Victoria station *(⏰35min., every 15min., 5:50-12:35am)*. Buy tickets in terminals, at the station, or on the train itself.

National Express runs services from the North and South terminals of Gatwick to London. The National Express bus *(☎08717 818 178 💻www.nationalexpress.com)* takes approximately 85min., and buses depart for London Victoria hourly. Taxis take about 1hr. to reach central London. **easyBus** *(☎084 4800 4411 💻www.easybus.co.uk)* runs every 15min. from North and South terminals to Earls Court and West Brompton *(ⓢ Tickets from £20. ⏰ 65min., every 15min.)*

The Europeans are far ahead of Americans in terms of train travel, and London offers several ways to easily reach other European destinations. **Eurolines** *(☎08717 818 181 💻www.eurolines.co.uk ⏰ Open 8am-8pm)* is Europe's largest coach network, providing service to 500 destinations throughout Europe. Many buses leave from **Victoria Coach Station,** which is at the mouth of Elizabeth St. just off of Buckingham Palace Road. Many coach companies, including **National Express, Eurolines,** and **Megabus** operate from Victoria Coach. National Express *(☎087 1781 8178 💻www.nationalexpress.com)* is the only scheduled coach network in Britain and can be used for most intercity travel and for travel to and from various airports. It can also be used to reach Scotland and Wales. **Greenline** *(☎087 1200 2233 💻www.greenline.co.uk)* provides services throughout London. One of its stops is by **Eccleston Bridge,** right next to Victoria, but it also reaches such convenient areas as **Hyde Park Corner** and **Baker Street.**

GETTING AROUND

Though there are daily interruptions to service in the Tube (that's right, not the metro, not the subway, but the Tube, or Underground), the controlling network, **Transport of London** does a good job of keeping travelers aware of these disruptions to service. Each station will have posters listing interruptions to service, and you can check service online at **www.tfl.gov.uk** or the 24hr. travel information service at ☎0843 222 1234. Most stations also have ticket booths and informed TFL employees who can help you and guide you to the proper pamphlets.

Though many people in the city stay out past midnight, the Tube doesn't have the same sort of stamina. When it closes around midnight, night owls have two choices: a cab or **nightbuses.** Most nightbus lines are prefixed with an **N,** (N13, for instance) and some stops even have 24hr. buses.

Travel Passes

Travel Passes are almost guaranteed to save you money. The passes are priced based on the number of zones they serve (the more zones, the more expensive), but zone 1 encompasses central London and you will not likely need to get past zone 2. If someone offers you a secondhand ticket, don't take it. There's no real way to verify whether it's valid—plus, it's illegal. Those under 16 get free travel on buses and trams. Children under 5 rule the public transportation system, getting free travel on the Tube, trams, **Docklands Lights Railway (DLR),** overground, and **National Rail** services (though they must be accompanied by someone with a valid pass). Passengers ages 11-15 enjoy reduced fares on the Tube with an Oyster photocard. Students eighteen and older must study full-time *(at least 15hr. per week over 14 weeks)* in London to qualify for the Student Photocard, which enables users to save 30% on adult travel cards and bus and tram passes. You can apply for one online but you need a passport-sized digital photo and an enrollment ID from your school. It's worth it if you're staying for an extended period of time. (Study abroad kids, we're looking at you...)

Oyster Cards store everything you need and enable you to pay in a variety of ways. Fares come in peak *(M-F 4:30am-9:29am)* and off-peak *(any other time)* varieties and are, again, distinguished by zone. In addition to letting you add Travelcards, Oysters enable users to "pay as you go," meaning that you can store credit on an as-needed basis. The cards have price capping that will allow you to travel as much as you want, while ensuring that you don't pay above the cost of the day Travelcard you would otherwise have purchased. Register your card, especially if you put a lot of money on it. That way, you can **recover everything if it's lost.**

Season Tickets. Weekly, monthly, and annual Travelcards can be purchased at any time from Tube stations. They yield unlimited *(within zone)* use for their duration *(\$ Weekly rates for zones 1-2 £25.80. Monthly £99.10. Day off-peak £5.60. Day anytime is £7.20.)*

By Underground

Most stations have **Tube maps** on the walls as well as free pocket maps. Please note that the Tube map barely reflects an above-ground scale, and should not be used for even the roughest of walking directions. Platforms are organized by line, and will have the **colors** of the lines serviced and their names on the wall. The colors of the poles inside the trains correspond with the line, and trains will often have their end destination displayed on the front. This is an essential service when your line splits. Many platforms will have a digital panel indicating ETAs for the trains and sometimes type and final destination. When transferring in stations, just follow the clearly marked routes. Yellow **"WAY OUT"** signs point toward exits.

The Tube runs Monday to Saturday from approximately **5:30am** (though it depends on which station and line) to around **midnight.** If you're taking a train within 30min. of these times (before or after), you'll want to check the signs in the ticket hall for times of the first and last train. The Tube runs less frequently on Sunday, with many lines starting service after 6am. Around 6pm on weekdays, many of the trains running out of central London become packed with the after-work crowd. It's best to avoid the service at this time.

You can buy **tickets** from ticket counters (though these often have lines at bigger stations) or at machines in the stations. You need a ticket to swipe in at the beginning of the journey, and also to exit the Tube. If your train is randomly selected, you will need to present a valid ticket to avoid the £50 penalty fee, which is reduced to £25 if you pay in under 21 days.

By Bus

While slower than the Tube for long journeys (traffic and more frequent stops), **buses** can be useful for traveling short distances covered by a few stops (and several transfers) on the Tube. For one-stop distances, your best bet may be walking.

Bus stops frequently have lists of buses servicing the stop as well as route maps and maps of the area indicating nearby stops. Buses display route numbers.

Every route and stop is different, but buses generally run every 5-15min. beginning around **5:30am** and ending around **midnight.** After day bus routes have closed, **Night Buses** take over. These routes are typically prefixed with an N and operate similar routes to their daytime equivalents. Some buses run 24 hour services. If you're staying out past the Tube closing time, you should plan your nightbus route or bring cab fare.

Singles for adults and students cost £2; fare is only £1.20 with Oyster pay-as-you-go. Sixteen and up Oyster Photocard users get £.60 rates on pay-as-you-go. 11-15 year olds are free with Oyster Photocards. Under 11s are free regardless of Oyster photocard.

OXFORD

Oxford has **prestige** written all over it. The renowned university has educated some of the most influential players in Western civilization, serving as a home to intellectual royalty, royal royalty, and at least a dozen saints. Students from all around Britain and the world aspire to join the ranks of **Adam Smith, Oscar Wilde,** and **Bill Clinton**...but if you can't join 'em, visit 'em. Swarms of tourists descend on Oxford throughout the year, so don't expect everybody you see to be a local (or a genius). The town is rich in history, and it's not very cheap either. Accommodations are notoriously pricey, and a visit to most of the colleges will even cost you. Still, from the university lore to the town pubs, there's something for everybody on the breathtaking grounds of Oxford. Make room in your budget for some extra-credit **college knowledge.**

greatest hits

- **GO ASK ALICE.** At Christ Church College (p. 113) wander the winding walkways where Lewis Carroll first met the Alice.
- **BIRDY BONES.** Head to the Oxford Museum of Natural History (p. 120) for your first ever encounter with dodo bones.
- **VEGGIES AT VAULTS.** Snack on organic vegetables while overlooking a world-famous university at Vaults and Garden (p. 122).
- **BOOKS AND BOOZE.** Stop by the Eagle and Child (p. 124) to find that some of England's greatest writers were also some of its greatest boozers.

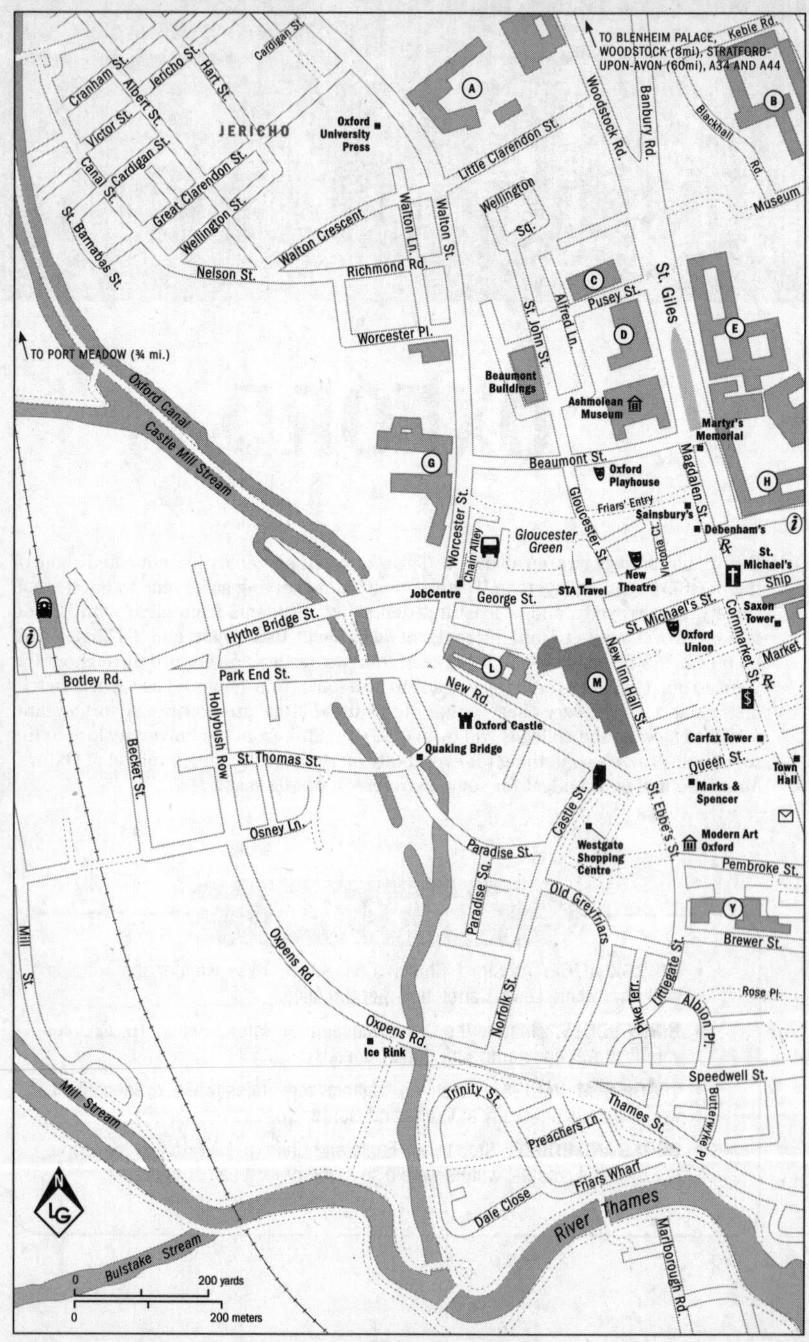

TO BLENHEIM PALACE, WOODSTOCK (8mi), STRATFORD-UPON-AVON (60mi), A34 AND A44
JERICHO
Oxford University Press
Cranham St.
Albert St.
Jericho St.
Hart St.
Cardigan St.
Victor St.
Canal St.
Great Clarendon St.
Wellington St.
St. Barnabas St.
Walton Crescent
Walton Ln.
Walton St.
Little Clarendon St.
Woodstock Rd.
Banbury Rd.
Keble Rd.
Blackhall Rd.
Museum
Wellington Sq.
Nelson St.
Richmond Rd.
Worcester Pl.
St. Giles
Pusey St.
Alfred Ln.
St. John St.
TO PORT MEADOW (¾ mi.)
Oxford Canal
Castle Mill Stream
Beaumont Buildings
Ashmolean Museum
Martyr's Memorial
Beaumont St.
Oxford Playhouse
Friars' Entry
Magdalen St.
Sainsbury's
Debenham's
Gloucester St.
Gloucester Green
Worcester St.
Chain Alley
Victoria Ct.
St. Michael's
Ship
JobCentre
George St.
STA Travel
New Theatre
Hythe Bridge St.
St. Michael's St.
Saxon Tower
Oxford Union
Cornmarket St.
Market
Botley Rd.
Park End St.
New Rd.
New Inn Hall St.
Hollybush Row
Becket St.
Oxford Castle
Quaking Bridge
Carfax Tower
St. Thomas St.
Queen St.
Town Hall
Marks & Spencer
Castle St.
St. Ebbe's St.
Osney Ln.
Paradise St.
Westgate Shopping Centre
Modern Art Oxford
Pembroke St.
Paradise Sq.
Old Greyfriars
Mill St.
Oxpens Rd.
Brewer St.
Norfolk St.
Pike Terr.
Littlegate St.
Rose Pl.
Albion Pl.
Ice Rink
Speedwell St.
Trinity St.
Mill Stream
Thames St.
Preachers Ln.
Butterwyke Pl.
Friars Wharf
Dale Close
River Thames
Marlborough Rd.
Bulstake Stream
0
200 yards
0
200 meters
N
LG
A
B
C
D
E
G
H
L
M
Y

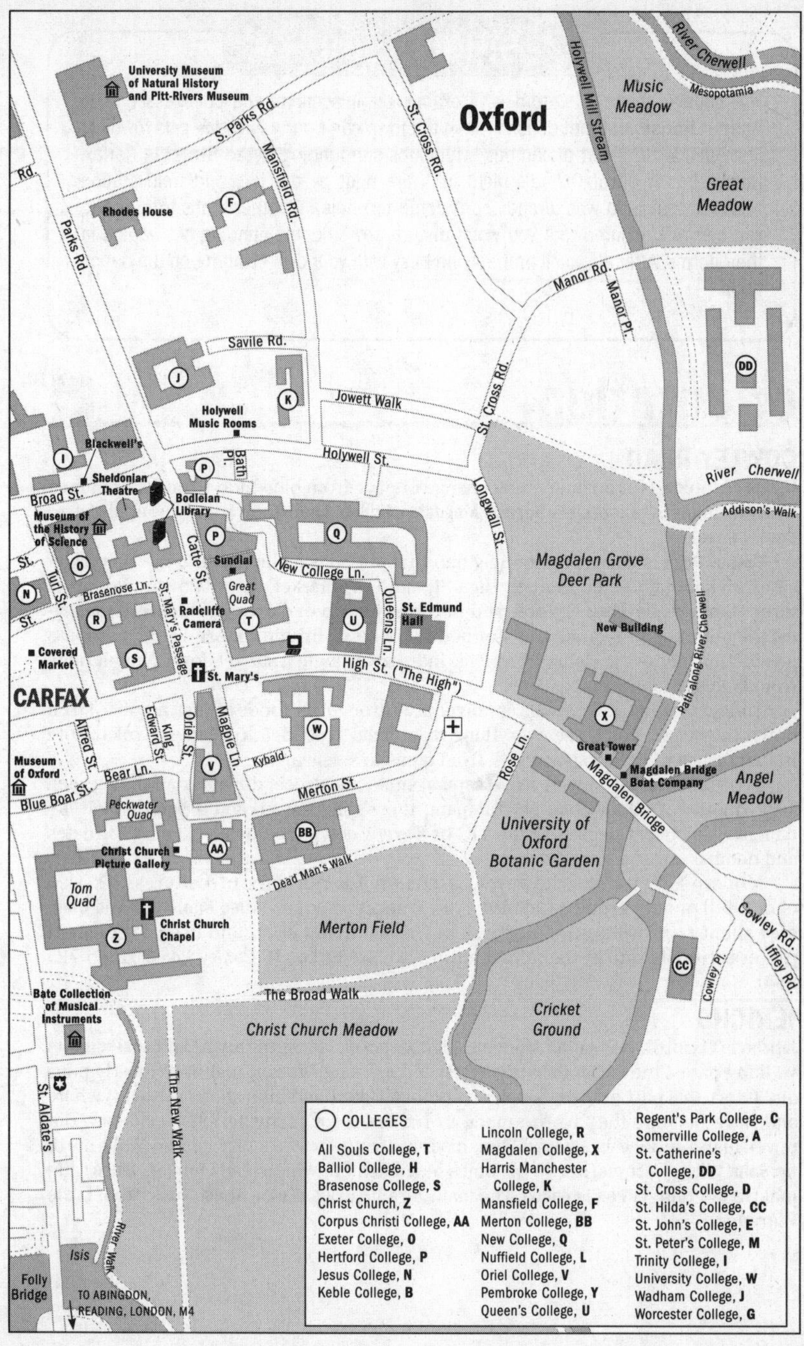
Oxford
University Museum of Natural History and Pitt-Rivers Museum
S. Parks Rd.
Mansfield Rd.
St. Cross Rd.
Holywell Mill Stream
River Cherwell
Mesopotamia
Music Meadow
Great Meadow
Rhodes House
Parks Rd.
Manor Rd.
Manor Pl.
Savile Rd.
Jowett Walk
Holywell Music Rooms
Holywell St.
Bath Pl.
Blackwell's
Sheldonian Theatre
Broad St.
Bodleian Library
Museum of the History of Science
Catte St.
Sundial
Great Quad
New College Ln.
Queens Ln.
St. Edmund Hall
Longwall St.
Magdalen Grove Deer Park
New Building
Addison's Walk
Path along River Cherwell
Turl St.
Brasenose Ln.
St. Mary's Passage
Radcliffe Camera
Covered Market
St. Mary's
High St. ("The High")
CARFAX
Alfred St.
King Edward St.
Oriel St.
Magpie Ln.
Kybald
Rose Ln.
Great Tower
Magdalen Bridge Boat Company
Magdalen Bridge
Angel Meadow
Museum of Oxford
Bear Ln.
Blue Boar St.
Merton St.
Peckwater Quad
Christ Church Picture Gallery
Dead Man's Walk
University of Oxford Botanic Garden
Tom Quad
Christ Church Chapel
Merton Field
Cowley Rd.
Iffley Rd.
Cowley Pl.
Bate Collection of Musical Instruments
The Broad Walk
Christ Church Meadow
Cricket Ground
St. Aldate's
The New Walk
River Walk
Isis
Folly Bridge
TO ABINGDON, READING, LONDON, M4
COLLEGES
All Souls College, T
Balliol College, H
Brasenose College, S
Christ Church, Z
Corpus Christi College, AA
Exeter College, O
Hertford College, P
Jesus College, N
Keble College, B
Lincoln College, R
Magdalen College, X
Harris Manchester College, K
Mansfield College, F
Merton College, BB
New College, Q
Nuffield College, L
Oriel College, V
Pembroke College, Y
Queen's College, U
Regent's Park College, C
Somerville College, A
St. Catherine's College, DD
St. Cross College, D
St. Hilda's College, CC
St. John's College, E
St. Peter's College, M
Trinity College, I
University College, W
Wadham College, J
Worcester College, G

oxford

student life

The college scene at Oxford isn't exactly reminiscent of the college scene in **Animal House,** but that doesn't mean the town can't party. Nightlife gets rowdiest just outside the heart of campus, with clubs surrounding **Hythe Street** in Carfax. Rumor has it all of Oxford's nightclubs are right by the bus and train station because that area was already considered too noisy. Whether that's true or not, you can rest assured that you won't disturb any students grinding out papers in their dorms. After all, you'll probably be busy with your own **grinding** on the dance floor.

orientation

COWLEY ROAD

If you're looking for an interesting change of pace from blue-blood, tourist-crammed Oxford, take an excursion across **Magdalen Bridge,** then follow the roundabout to **Cowley Road.**

Cowley Road is Oxford's shopping hub that provides a glimpse into the rich diversity thriving outside the touristy High St. and Cornmarket shops. Cowley Rd. leads through inner-city East Oxford, and into the suburb of Cowley, which **William Morris,** the automobile tycoon, transformed into one of Britain's most significant mass production plants à la Henry Ford. This industry brought a steady flow of immigrants from Wales from the early 1900s.

Today, Cowley Rd. reveals its diversity through its food: in just a quick stroll down the street, you'll see everything from halal groceries to Chinese woks, from Italian dishes to Polish specialties, from tapas to shishas.

A vibrant annual Cowley Rd. **carnival** shuts the streets down for a full day each July. Booths of ethnic food are rampant, there's live music and a parade, and debauchery ensues. Check with the TIC or www.cowleyroadfestival.co.uk for dates and details.

Modern Cowley Rd., however, is not only a rich mix of cultures; it's also chock-full of natives and students. For example, current **Prime Minister David Cameron** spent part of his student years at Oxford living here, and used to frequent the notoriously quirky Jamaican eating house, **Hi Lo** *(70 Cowley Rd. ☎01865 725 984).*

JERICHO

Jericho is Oxford's bohemian student neighborhood. Home to the **Oxford Canal** with its walking paths, the **Oxford University Press,** and a young, vibrant nightlife (mostly pubs and bars), this part of town is up-and-coming. Bikes, and bike shops are everywhere and have become the favorite mode of transport for many Jericho residents. But never fear—Jericho is easy walking distance from Oxford's city center. Walk north up **Saint Giles** (Cornmarket St. becomes Magdalen St., which leads into St. Giles) and make a left onto **Little Clarendon.** The main Jericho drag, **Walton Street,** runs off of Little Clarendon.

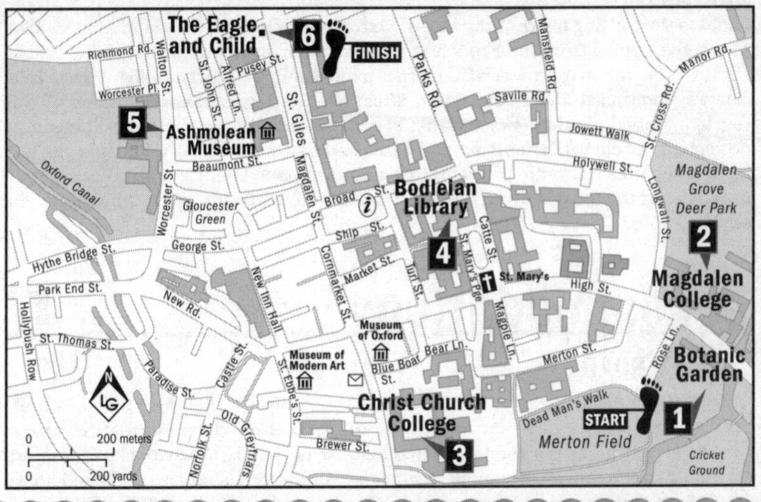

oxford

Oxford may not be as large or imposing as London, but don't take that the wrong way; it's still full of gems you won't want to miss. In case you're crunched for time and need to experience the city in just a single day, **Let's Go** has consolidated some of Oxford's highlights into a six-step plan. So tie up your laces and let's get going!

1. UNIVERSITY OF OXFORD BOTANIC GARDEN. Start off with a whiff of the oldest botanic garden in Britain, located on High Street in the eastern part of campus.

2. MAGDALEN COLLEGE. Once you're sufficiently high on nature, simply cross High St. to get to Magdalen College. Arguably the sexiest of Oxford's colleges, Magdalen has churned out such superstars as Cardinal Wolsey, Oscar Wilde, and Seamus Heaney.

3. CHRIST CHURCH COLLEGE. From Magdalen, make your merry way along High St. in an westward direction for a few blocks, before turning left onto Aldate St., where Christ Church College is located. Maybe you'll be lucky enough to hear the world-famous cathedral choir sing a little ditty.

4. BODLEIAN LIBRARY. Next, head north onto St. Aldate St., which will become Cornmarket St. Turn right onto Market St., left onto Turf St., and right onto Broad St., where you'll find the famed Bodleian Library—but probably no talking caterpillars or a Queen of Hearts.

5. ASHMOLEAN MUSEUM. Walk eastward along Broad St. before turning right onto Magdalen St. E. Use caution, as these streets are busy and may be missing walkways. Turn left at Beaumont St., where the Ashmolean Museum is located. Guy Fawkes' lantern is among its treasures.

6. THE EAGLE AND CHILD. Travel north along St. Giles St. (again, exercising caution) and finish your day off right at the 17th-century Eagle and Child. After a few pints, you may either feel like you've sprouted wings or reverted to infancy.

WALKING TOUR

Let's Go
www.letsgo.com

CARFAX

Carfax is the pulsing heart of the city of Oxford, with both ancient and modern ties. The name comes from the French word *carrefour*, meaning "crossroads." Today, Carfax is at the crossroads of Oxford's main shopping district: **High Street, Saint Aldate's, Cornmarket Street,** and **Queen Street** are the busiest thoroughfares of this tourist-mobbed district. (Cornmarket is pedestrian only, but that doesn't mean its not equally packed.) **Carfax Tower** and **Saxon Tower,** two ancient structures in the city center, serve as convenient orientation points. Meanwhile, the magnificent looming spires of the most centrally-located colleges hover over Carfax, dominating the skyline.

accommodations

COWLEY ROAD

HEATHER HOUSE

BED AND BREAKFAST ❹

192 Iffley Rd. ☎01865 249 757 www.heatherhouse.plus.com

This cozy home is a good value in otherwise pricey Oxford, with clean, comfortable rooms and a welcoming guest living room, with a homey couch and books about Britain and Oxford, plus the free advice of a local host. Heather House is located on a residential main street about a 10min. walk from the colleges. Tea lovers will be pleased that there's a wide selection of herbal teas included with breakfast.

10-15min. walk from the Magdalen College, but a good 30min. from the train station. Walking: cross the Magdalen Bridge and bear right at the roundabout onto Iffley Rd. From train station, take bus # 4 (A, B, or C) from New Rd. bus stop. Get off opposite the Greyfriars Church bus stop. i Includes full English breakfast. Free internet use on a communal computer. Longer stays are cheaper per night. Ⓢ Singles with private bath £38-£48; ensuite twins £68-80; doubles £70-80. Open 24hr.

ACORN GUEST HOUSE

BED AND BREAKFAST ❹

260 Iffley Rd. ☎ 01865 247 998 www.oxford-acorn.co.uk

Comfy, family-run guest house with selection of singles, twins, doubles, and family rooms, with windows and a sunny ambiance. Singles are shared bath, but with wash basins in the room. Full breakfast and free Wi-Fi help justify the price jump.

Walking: cross the Magdalen Bridge and bear right at the roundabout onto Iffley Rd. By bus: Take bus # 4 (A, B, or C) from New Rd. bus stop. Get off at Iffley Rd. adjacent Magdalent Rd. i Breakfast included. TVs and tea and coffee in all rooms. Discounts for longer stays. Ⓢ Singles shared bath £35; twins (with private or shared baths) from £63; doubles £70-75; triples £90. Open 24hr.

THE ISIS

BED AND BREAKFAST ❹

45-53 Iffley Rd. ☎01865 613 700 www.isisguesthouse.com

Owned and operated by St. Edmund's Hall, one of Oxford's colleges, the guest house is only open in July, August, and September. Less than a 5min. walk from the colleges and 10min. to downtown shopping, with nearby cafes and bars on Cowley Rd., this large Victorian house offers simple basic rooms, some with bathrooms and some without.

Walking: cross the Magdalen Bridge and bear right at the roundabout onto Iffley Rd. By bus: take bus # 4 (A, B, or C) from New Rd. bus stop. Get off at The Plain, on Iffley Rd. i Breakfast included. Laundry facilities included. TVs in all rooms. Ⓢ Basic singles £37; ensuite singles £45; basic double/twin £74; ensuite £80; family basic £37 per person, ensuite £40 per person. Open July-Sept. Reception 24hr.

CARFAX

CENTRAL BACKPACKERS

HOSTEL ❷

13 Park End St. ☎01865 24 22 88 www.centralbackpackers.co.uk

The relaxed rooftop garden with couches and a big screen is the perfect place to kick back and watch a game while throwin' back a pint. The only drawback to a prime downtown location are the sounds of Beyoncé from nearby clubs at 10pm every night. Think of it as motivation, though—shouldn't you be out enjoying Oxford? For those who don't agree, the hostel handily provides free earplugs.

Short walk from Train station; Botley Rd. becomes Park End St. i Continental breakfast included. Free luggage storage. Free lockers. Self-catering kitchen. Laundry £3.50. Beers on the terrace £1. $ 4-bed dorms £21, 8-bed £19, 6-bed female £20, 12-bed £18. £1 per debit/credit transaction. Reception open 8am-11pm.

YHA OXFORD

HOSTEL ❷

2A Botley Rd. ☎01865 727 275 www.yha.org

Don't let the less-than-stylish exterior deceive you: YHA Oxford is recently renovated, with modern facilities and spotlessly clean rooms. Special amenities include an intimate library perfect for cozying up to a good book, a "Boathouse" restaurant, an outdoor seating area, and snacks for sale at reception. Like at many YHAs, however, the guest list is made up of significant numbers of schoolkids and other large groups, so you might not find people kicking back and relaxing. If you're lonely, try debating philosophy with the famous Oxfordians in picture frames on the walls. Still and lifeless as they are, they'll give you a run for your money.

Next to train station. i Breakfast not included, £4.95 for full English breakfast. Self-catering kitchen. Internet £1 per 15min. Wi-Fi £5 per day. Library and TV lounge. All rooms ensuite, plus extra bathrooms in hallyways. $ Dorms £16-22; singles £28; doubles/twins £45-55. £3 charge for non-YHA members. Reception open 24hr.

OXFORD BACKPACKERS

HOSTEL ❷

9a Hythe Bridge St. ☎01865 721 761 www.hostels.co.uk

The self-proclaimed "Funky Backpackers" hostel has brightly colored walls, and you'll have a colorful experience there. The big-screen projector in the lounge makes for a lively communal space for its international crowd. The dorms, though adequately clean, are less than spacious.

Hythe Bridge St., down the road from the bus station. i Small continental breakfast included. Free lockers, but bring your own padlocks. Luggage storage £1 per item for guests. Laundry £2.50. Wi-Fi £2 per day or £5 per week. Ethernet cables free for use in common area. Self-catering kitchen. $ Dorms £15-19.50; £75 per week. Discounts online. Reception open 8am-11:30pm.

WESTGATE HOTEL

HOTEL ❹

1 Botley Rd. ☎01865 726 721 www.westgatehoteloxford.co.uk

Simple hotel, right next to train station, is nothing luxurious, but has all the basic amenities you'd need. The decor is a little old-fashioned, but rooms are clean and fairly large, with mostly ensuite bathrooms. Come prepared for noise at night: trains abide by no curfew, and the nearby clubs mean that people are out and about at night.

2min. walk from train station down Botley Rd. i Full breakfast included. Free Wi-Fi in main building, not in annex. $ Singles £48-58; doubles/twins £82-86, family (ensuite, sleeps 3-4) £88-£120. Possible discounts in off-season. Reception open 7am-11pm.

UNIVERSITY ACCOMMODATIONS

The University of Oxford's conferencing website, **www.conference-oxford.com** lists some individual email contacts for B and B accommodations at the colleges. The process can be a hassle, but worth it if you'd like to stay in the medieval digs of one of Oxford's prestigious colleges.

In addition, **www.universityrooms.co.uk** has a simple online booking service for the nine colleges that offer B and B options for individual travelers: **Balliol College, Keble College, Lady Margaret Hall, Mansfield College, The Queen's College, St. Hugh's College, Trinity College, University College,** and **Wadham College.** Book in advance, as all of these usually fill up quickly. Prices vary and follow the rules of Balliol College attendee Adam Smith: price is determined by supply and demand, and therefore the prices at the more historic colleges generally run higher. You'll also pay some extra quid for ensuite rooms.

LINCOLN HALL BED AND BREAKFAST DORMS, BED AND BREAKFAST ❸

Museum Rd. beckie@internal.linc.ox.ac.uk

Lincoln College offers up to 60 single ensuite rooms with shared kitchens in historic, brightly-colored Victorian townhouses. Centrally located to university sites, like the **Bodleian Library** (p. 118) and **Pitt Rivers Museum.**

Near the University science area. ***i*** *Continental breakfast included. Must pay in full before stay. £10 key deposit. Internet access via Ethernet port.* *Ensuite singles £40.* *Open July-Aug. Reception 24hr.*

accepted

It happens sometimes in my travels that I'm mistaken for a student.

Well, after all, I am one. I walk around town, too-cool-for-school in my sunglasses, with a simple tote bag, sometimes a computer, sometimes a notebook, on a mission, looking like I know where I'm going. Some days I'm a bit grungier than I should be, but I think that's pretty normal too.

Yesterday afternoon was my first day in Oxford, and within three hours, I had already been asked four times for directions to various university buildings and sights. Let me clarify. I've discovered that I've actually come to Oxford at the perfect time. The University is hosting a huge annual program for potential applicants, across all the colleges.

Witnessing the whole scene made me realize how very glad I am to be past that stage of life. I thought it was only American parents that were ridiculously intense and overbearing about the college process. I thought wrong. These British parents were just as bad, if not worse, peppering every possible student they saw with a rapid stream of questions—"Which A-Levels did you take?" "What kind of school did you come from?" "How many other people do you think you were competing with for your engineering spot at Trinity in your year?"

But I digress. The reason this whole "Open Days" program is great for me is that I could breeze through the doors of any college I wanted, free of charge, free of hassle. Not only that, but there were loads of student guides around in bright colored T-shirts, giving tours, offering to show us the bedrooms and the dining halls and libraries and all those other things that you normally need a swipe card to access. I went college-hopping and tour-hopping, switching between guides when I would spot something interesting and leaving when they would start talking too much. I amused myself with the various courses I was interested in studying when asked, starting off with closest-to-the-truth, P.P.E. (Politics, Philosophy and Economics) and then getting more adventurous with law, chemistry, and Russian.

I wound up with a free lunch at Somerville College via a voucher, a good pub recommendation, and my own collection of informational pamphlets. It had been a productive day. Now, time to be 20 again.

Rachel Lipson

COLLEGES

Oxford's extensive **college system** (distributing its 20,000 students among 38 official colleges and 6 permanent private halls of the university—each with its own structure and rules—means that there are plenty of beautiful grounds to stroll year-round. We've picked out a few of the most frequented to save you the purchase of a guide—well, *another* guide. Full books, however, are published on just single colleges. For information on others, pick up one of the many guides found at the Tourist Information Center or the paperback books found in souvenir shops all over town.

The **Tourist Information Centre** on **Broad Street** sells the *Oxford What to See and Do Guide* for £.60, which lists all of the colleges' visiting hours and prices and has a handy map. Hours can also be accessed online at **www.ox.ac.uk.** Note that hours and the list of sites open to tourists can be changed at any given time without explanation or notice. Some colleges charge admission, while others are accessible only through the official blue badge tours, booked at the TIC (see **Practicalities,** p. 130), and a few are generally off-limits. Take this as warning that it's not worth trying to sneak into Christ Church outside open hours. College bouncers in bowler hats, affectionately known as "bulldogs," will squint their eyes and promptly kick you out.

One of the best ways to get into the colleges for free (and also to witness a beautiful, historic ritual) is to check out one of the church services in the college chapels during term-time, for "Evensong" in particular. Usually, this takes place at around 6pm. Show up 15min. before it starts and tell the people at the gate that you'd like to attend the service; they generally let you in for free.

CHRIST CHURCH

COLLEGE

St. Aldates ☎01865 276 492 www.chch.ox.ac.uk/college

Oxford's most famous college has the university's grandest quad and some of its most distinguished alumni, including 13 saints and past prime ministers. During the English Civil War, "The House" was also the home to **Charles I** and the royal family, who used the Royalist-friendly university as a retreat during Cromwell's advance, and escaped Oxford dressed as servants when the city came under threat. The college is also notable as the place where Lewis Carroll first met **Alice,** the young daughter of the college dean, before she headed to Wonderland. In other cultural references, the dining hall and central quad serve as shooting locations for many *Harry Potter* films (tourists mob to see the site of Hogwarts' dining hall). In the early summer months, don't judge the students if they seem somewhat moody as they navigate their way through the crowds of visitors: while you're snapping pictures, they're taking exams.

Through an archway to your left as you face the cathedral is **Peckwater Quad.** The chalk markings on the wall are the standings for rowing competitions among the colleges, and certain corners will honor past Christ College teams that have finished the season with success. Also look out for Christ Church's library—perhaps the most elegant Palladian building in all of Oxford. Though it's closed to visitors, its exterior is impressive in itself.

Perhaps the most peaceful part of the college grounds is **Christ Church Meadow,** which stretches east and south from the main entrance. This attempt to compensate for Oxford's lack of "backs" (the riverside gardens in Cambridge) seems pretty successful to us: not only are the meadows beautiful, with flower-adorned views of the college, but they are also free, so those guarding their wallets can still enjoy a piece of the Christ Church atmosphere.

Down St. Aldates from Carfax. Admission £6.30, concessions £4.80, family ticket £12. Open M-Sa 9am-5:30pm, Su 1-5:30pm.

CHRIST CHURCH CHAPEL — CHAPEL

St Aldates ☎01865 276 492 www.chch.ox.ac.uk/cathedral

Christ Church Chapel is the only church in all of England to serve as both a cathedral (for the archdiocese of Oxford) and college chapel. The church was founded in AD 730 by Oxford's patron saint, **St. Fridesweide,** who built a nunnery here in honor of two miracles: the blinding of her persistent suitor and his subsequent recovery. A stained-glass window, c. 1320, depicts **Thomas Becket** kneeling moments before his death in Canterbury Cathedral.

Down St. Aldates from Carfax. Admission £6.30, concessions £4.80, family ticket £12. Hall and cathedral open M-F 10:15am-11:45am, 2:15pm-4:30pm, Sa-Su 2:30-4:30pm only. Last admission 4:30pm. Chapel services M-F 6pm; Su 8am, 10am, 11:15am, and 6pm.

TOM QUAD — QUAD

Tom Quad adjoins the chapel grounds, but more importantly, it is the site of undergraduate lily-pond dunking. The quad takes its name from **Great Tom,** the seven-ton bell that rings **101 times** (the original number of students) at 9:05pm, the original undergraduate curfew, every evening since 1682. The bell rings specifically at 9:05pm because, technically, Oxford should be 5min. past Greenwich Mean Time. Christ Church keeps this time within its gates. Nearby, the college hall displays portraits of some of Christ Church's famous alums—**Sir Philip Sidney, William Penn, John Ruskin, John Locke,** and a bored-looking **W.H. Auden** in a corner by the kitchen.

CHRIST CHURCH PICTURE GALLERY — GALLERY

Canterbury Quad ☎01865 276 172 www.chch.ox.ac.uk

Architecture and gardens aren't the only source of visual beauty in Oxford. At this picture gallery, generous alumni gifts have allowed for a small but noteworthy collection of works by **Tintoretto, Vermeer,** and **da Vinci,** among others.

Entrances on Oriel Sq. and at Canterbury Gate; visitors to the gallery should enter through Canterbury Gate. Admission £3, concessions £2. Open Apr-Sept M-Sa 10:30am-1pm and 2-5:30pm, Su 2-5pm; Oct-Mar M-Sa 10:30am-1pm and 2-4:30pm, Su 2-4:30pm.

ALL SOULS COLLEGE — COLLEGE

Corner of High and Catte St. ☎01865 279 379 www.all-souls.ox.ac.uk.

All Souls College (founded in 1438) is so exclusive that admission is solely offered on an invitation-only basis: the graduate fellows who live here are engaged in intense academic research, and are rumored to rarely leave their rooms because of it. You might notice that the **Great Quad,** with its carefully manicured lawn and two spires, is also one of the quietest, with hardly a living soul passing over. Check out the unusual **sundial** designed by **Christopher Wren,** moved here from the Front Quad in 1877.

Rumor has it that All Souls currently serves as a think-tank of sorts for the British Department of Defense. How does one join this premier group of scholars? Candidates who survive the admission exams to All Souls are invited to a dinner, where the dons repeatedly confirm that they are "well-born, well-bred, and only moderately learned." As further reward for admission, All Souls is also reported to have the best wine cellar in the city. Once every century, a bizarre torchlight procession takes place here with the **"Mallard Society."** During the ceremony, the Mallard Song is sung and a "Lord Mallard" is hoisted high in an ancient chair. No one really knows how the Mallard came to be affiliated with All Souls, but the song is sung frequently at college **gaudies,** or feasts, and the ritual on the Quad has been going strong for centuries.

i The next processions will happen on January 14th, 2011. Ⓢ Admission Free. ⏰ Open Sept-July M-F 2-4pm.

BALLIOL COLLEGE COLLEGE

Broad St. ☎01865 277 777 www.balliol.ox.ac.uk

Along with Merton and University, **Balliol** has a legitimate claim to being the oldest college in Oxford, founded in approximately 1263. According to tradition, the story of Balliol begins with the story of a lord and a princess: John Balliol married Dervorguilla, a Scottish princess. Shortly thereafter, a land dispute with the Bishop of Durham compelled Balliol, father of John Balliol, future and short-lived King of Scotland, to rent out a house just outside of the Oxford town walls for 16 poor scholars to live in as penance. When he died, his wife made the community permanent. Matthew Arnold, Gerard Manley Hopkins, Aldous Huxley, Adam Smith, three British prime ministers, and **six members of the Obama administration** were products of Balliol's mismatched spires.

Ⓢ Admission £2, students £1, under 18 free. ⏰ Open daily 10am-5pm or dusk.

MAGDALEN COLLEGE COLLEGE

High St. ☎01865 276 000 www.magd.ox.ac.uk

Many consider Magdalen (MAUD-lin), with its winding riverbanks, flower-filled quads, and 100 acres of grounds, to be Oxford's best-looking college. Magdalen boys have also been traditionally quite a catch: they've produced seven Nobel Prizes, Dudley Moore, and **Oscar Wilde.** The college has a **deer park,** where deer have grazed aimlessly for centuries (the first written record of the deer is from 1705) in front of students playing (also aimlessly?) croquet. The path following the river brings you back around to the college's **New Building,** where, "New" means 1733, when this building was erected.

The college skyline is ruled by the 144 ft. **Great Tower,** built by **Cardinal Wolsey,** a former bursar of the college, and used as a vantage point during the English Civil War. Since the days of Henry VII, each year on May Day at 6am, the choir members from Magdalen and its sister school meet on the roof of the tower to sing together, culminating with "Te Deum patrem colimus." This a well-known and popular Oxford tradition that consistently brings throngs of crowds and is followed by much revelry, including champagne breakfasts and Morris dancing.

Admission £4.50, concessions £3.50. Open daily Oct-June 1-6pm or dusk; July-Sept noon-6pm.

MERTON COLLEGE COLLEGE

Merton St. ☎01865 276 310 www.merton.ox.ac.uk

Though Balliol and University were endowed before it, **Merton** has the earliest formal college statutes (1274), so it can boast of being the oldest college in its own right. Merton's library houses the first printed Welsh Bible. **JRR Tolkien** was the Merton Professor of English, inventing the **Elven** language and writing some minor trilogy in his spare time. The college's 14th-century **Mob Quad** is Oxford's oldest and one of its least impressive—the "little" quadrangle was where the junior members of the college were housed after the grander Fellows' Quadrangle was built in 1610—but nearby St. Alban's Quad has some of the university's best gargoyles.

Grounds admission free. Library tours £2. Open M-F 2-4pm, Sa-Su 10am-4pm.

NEW COLLEGE COLLEGE

New College Ln. ☎01865 279 555 www.new.ox.ac.uk

Apparently, New College is said to have been the model that **Henry VI** had in mind when he founded King's College, Cambridge. The college was set up to replace all the ministering men who died of the **Black Death** in the 14th century, when the country was in desperate need of new clergy. New College boasts **Kate Beckinsale** and **Hugh Grant** as attractive alums. The college's cloisters were used in **Harry Potter.**

i Easter to mid-Oct enter via New College Lane; mid-Oct to Easter enter via Holywell St. Gates. Admission £2, students and children £1, seniors £1.50. Open daily from Easter to mid-Oct 11am-5pm; mid-Oct to Easter 2-4pm.

QUEEN'S COLLEGE COLLEGE

High St. ☎01865 279 120 www.queens.ox.ac.uk

Though the college was founded 1341, Queen's was rebuilt in the 17th and 18th centuries in the distinctive Queen Anne style. Queen's College has a strange Christmastime tradition of ushering in a boar's head. The ceremony apparently pays homage to the time when a Queen's student, with his head stuck in a book of Aristotle on a country walk, ran into a savage wild boar and saved himself by ramming the philosopher's book down the boar's throat. Meanwhile, in a dinnertime ritual here, students are called to all formal dinners by the sounds of a trumpet. How melodious.

i Open to blue-badge tours only.

the most curious thing i ever saw

Today was Alice Day in Oxford.

That means little girls dressed up like Alice in Wonderland, a few not-so-little girls dressed up like the Queen of Hearts, and everyone enjoying picnics, plays, and all the fanfare that comes with celebrating Lewis Carroll's most famous heroine in her, and his, old stomping grounds of Oxford. The real Alice, Alice Liddell, was the daughter of a former dean of Christ Church College and Carroll (real name: Charles Dodgson) used to tell her stories about turtles and ducks and the Jabberwocky out on the Thames River while he was a Professor of Mathematics here at the college.

Unlike my grandfather, who can recite lines of Alice's Adventures in Wonderland from memory, I don't think I ever quite finished the book. (I hate that I'm one of those people who have seen the movie, but never read the book. Terrible.)

Still, I was curious to see what all the fuss was about. First, I tried to talk to the costumed characters standing outside of Blackwell's bookstore but they had run out of leaflets and weren't sure where the next event was taking place. Then, I followed a family of face-painted children and wound up at the National History Museum. Outside there was a man with a guitar singing Alice verses to mobs of clapping and giggling toddlers. I was just about to head out and give up on Alice shenanigans completely when I saw a sign for the lecture hall. (You know you've been out of school for too long when you start gravitating towards the mention of lectures.)

The room was packed to the brim with Alice fans of all (well, 16+) ages, everyone there to listen to the president of the Lewis Carroll Society (yes, there is such a thing) give a free lecture on "Carroll and Surrealism." I plopped down in one of the few empty chairs and eagerly pulled out my notebook.

The lecturer read off his notes for about a half-hour, and the climax of the presentation (aka the final slides of the PowerPoint) was supposed to be Salvador Dali's famous surrealist paintings of Alice in Wonderland. Just as he's about to switch over to the slide, though, the projector freezes and then turns blue. The man fiddled for a few seconds with the computer, but with no luck. I felt bad for whomever the tech guys working in the museum were: as the Queen of Hearts would say, "Off with their heads!"

Rachel Lipson

TRINITY COLLEGE COLLEGE

Broad St. ☎01865 279 900 www.trinity.ox.ac.uk

Trinity was the home of some of Oxford's most eccentric college presidents. One of them, Ralph Kettell, elected in 1599, would allegedly come to dinner with a pair of scissors to chop off anyone's hair that he deemed too long. To keep them out of trouble in town, he made it his duty to ensure that Trinity had some of the best beer in Oxford at its table, keeping the students at home and comparatively sober. Check out the hall named after him in the front quadrangle. Kettell was also known for great achievements in fostering a sense of community and making architectural improvements and expanding the college.

Founded in 1555, the college itself has a Baroque chapel with a limewood altarpiece, cedar latticework, cherubim-spotted pediments, four large quads, a spacious lawn and gardens, and a small area of woodland. It was founded by **Sir Thomas Pope,** a devout Catholic who, with no surviving children, wanted to find a way ensure that someone would still remember and pray for him and his family. Why not start a college at Oxford?

Admission £2, concessions £1. Open M-F 10am-noon and 2-4pm, Sa-Su 2-4pm.

UNIVERSITY COLLEGE

COLLEGE

High St. ☎01865 276 602 www.univ.ox.ac.uk

Built in 1249, this soot-blackened college is known by many as **"Uni"** and is where **Bill Clinton** spent his Rhodes Scholar days. Other notable students and fellows include **Bob Hawke,** a former prime minister of Australia who set the Guinness world record for downing a yard of beer during his Oxford days, **CS Lewis, Stephen Hawking,** and Prince Felix Yusupov, the assassin of **Rasputin.** The famed Romantic poet **Percy Bysshe Shelley** came here in 1810, but he was expelled a year later after the dissemination of a pamphlet he had written entitled **"The Necessity of Atheism."** Today, though, the college honors him with a prominent statue that you can see on your right as you enter.

i Entry for groups by prior arrangement with the domestic bursar. Entry for individuals and families at the discretion of the lodge porter, and to blue badge tours only.

MUSEUMS

ASHMOLEAN MUSEUM

MUSEUM

Beaumont St. ☎01865 278 000 www.ashmolean.org

Oxford University's Museum of Art and Archeology is newly reopened after a multi-million-dollar renovation that added 39 new galleries and doubled its display space. The Ashmolean collection (named for 17th-century English antiquary, politician, and wealthy collector Elias Ashmole) is the oldest public museum in Europe, with seriously world-class exhibits from every region of the world. In addition to beautiful exhibits that shed light on how world cultures developed through contact with one another, Oxford's only rooftop restaurant lies upstairs. Though the restaurant is pricey, it has excellent views of the city. Pick up a free Ashmolean *What's On* booklet to find out about upcoming lectures and special exhibitions.

Opposite the Randolph Hotel. i Free lunchtime gallery talks for first 12 interested Tu-F 1:15-2pm. Pick up tokens from the information desk. Free. Open Tu-Su 10am-6pm.

BODLEIAN LIBRARY

LIBRARY

Broad St. ☎01865 277 178 www.bodleian.ox.ac.uk

As you enter through the Great Gate into the Old Schools Quadrangle, you'll be in good company—in spirit, anyway. Five kings, 40 Nobel Prize winners, 28 British prime ministers, and writers like Oscar Wilde, CS Lewis, and JRR Tolkien also entered this gate at some point. Included in the large complex is Oxford's Divinity School, the oldest teaching room in the university, completed in 1488 and seen as a masterpiece of English Gothic architecture with its elaborate fan-vaulted ceiling. The standard and mini guided tours include stops here and in Duke Humfrey's medieval library. The 1hr. tour also enters the 17th-century Convocation House and Court, where Parliament was held during the Civil War. Extended tours include entry to the Radcliffe Camera, the first rotunda library built in Britain, and the underground tunnels and passages leading to the book stacks where millions of volumes of the Oxford collection are stored.

Entrances on Broad St., Cattle St. and Radcliffe St. i Extended tour includes visit to underground mechanical book conveyor, tunnel, and the Radcliffe Camera. Ⓢ *Entrance to the courtyard free. 30min. tour of Library and Divinity Hall £4.50, standard 1hr. tour £6.50, extended tour £13.50. Audio tour £2.50. Entrance to Divinity Hall £1.* ⏰ *Open M-F 9am-5pm, Sa 9am-4:30pm, Su 11am-5pm.*

OTHER SIGHTS

OXFORD CASTLE

CASTLE

44-46 Oxford Castle ☎01865 260 666 www.oxfordcastleunlocked.co.uk

As you wander around the serious students and mobs of tourists, it's easy to forget that Oxford had a history that involved people and things a little more scandalous than philosophers, books, and elegant churches. Oxford Castle reminds one of Oxford's darker past: stories of escapes, betrayal, and romance are told within the walls of the city's 11th-century castle and prison. Tours include a climb up Saxon St. George's tower and a trip down to a 900-year-old underground crypt.

Off New Rd. Ⓢ *Admission £7.75, concessions £6.50.* ⏰ *Tours daily 10am-4:20pm.*

CARFAX TOWER

TOWER

Junction of St. Aldates/Cornmarket St. and High St./Queen St. ☎01865 792 633

This was the site of the former City Church of Oxford (St. Martin's Church). However, in 1896, university leaders decided that the church needed to be demolished to widen the roads and make room for more traffic in the downtown area. Still, the tower was left untouched. Look for the church clock on the east side of the facade: it is adorned by two "quarter boys," who hit the bells every 15min.

Ⓢ *Admission £2.20, under 16 £1.10.* ⏰ *Open daily Apr-Sept 10am-5:30pm; Oct 10am-4:30pm; Nov-Mar 10am-3:30pm.*

SAXON TOWER

TOWER

St. Michael's Church, North Gate ☎01865 240 940 www.smng.org.uk

Out of all of Oxford's ancient and medieval spires, this is actually the city's oldest building, dating back to the Late Saxon period, or about 1040. Later on, this same tower was attached on the west side to the Bocardo Prison, where the famous Oxford Martyrs, **Bishops Latimer, Ridley,** and **Cranmer** were burnt at the stake by Queen Mary for refusing to convert to Catholicism. Though the North Gate, where the prison was located, was later demolished because of congestion concerns, the door to their former cell is still inside the tower.

Ⓢ *Church free, Tower £2 concessions £1.50.* ⏰ *Open daily Apr-Oct 10:30am-5pm; Nov-Mar 10:30am-4pm.*

UNIVERSITY OF OXFORD BOTANIC GARDEN

GARDEN

Rose Lane ☎01865 286 690 www.botanic-garden.ox.ac.uk

Back in the day (meaning, of course, the 1600s), this garden, though created to enhance the glory of God and the learning of man, actually had a practical purpose as well: they sold fruit grown in the garden to pay for its upkeep. Today, the garden has another useful purpose: a peaceful haven to resort to if you get overwhelmed by the mobs of tourists on High St. Stay for at least an hour to justify paying to see flowers. The oldest botanic garden in the UK, it lies outside of the city walls, and it happens to be on top of an ancient Jewish cemetery.

Off High St. Ⓢ *Admission £3.50, concessions £3. Year-long season ticket £12, students £10.* ⏰ *Open Nov-Feb 9am-4:30pm; Sept-Oct and Mar-Apr 9am-5pm; May-Aug 9am-6pm. Glasshouses open at 10am.*

OXFORD MUSEUM OF NATURAL HISTORY ♿ MUSEUM

Parks Rd. ☎01865 272 950 www.oum.ox.ac.uk

Animal-bone lovers will rejoice at this 150-year-old museum: the collections of zoological, entomological, and geological specimens include dinosaur bones found in the Oxford area, **Charles Darwin's** crustaceans, and the most complete remains of a **dodo** found in the world. A famous debate on evolution that took place inside the building in 1860 between Thomas Huxley and Bishop Sam Wilberforce. The building itself is pretty memorable, with admired Neo-Gothic architecture and statues of famous figures like **Aristotle, Bacon,** and **Darwin.** Attached is the **Pitt-Rivers Museum** (Archeology and Anthropology), also worth a visit for its collection of lifestyle objects from across the globe—and for its shrunken heads *(☎01865 270 927 www.prm.ox.ac.uk).*

Off Broad St. Free. Open daily 10am-5pm. Pitt-Rivers Museum open M noon-4:30pm, Tu-Su 10am-4:30pm.

food

Here's one major perk of living in a student town: **kebab trucks** line High St., Queen St., and Broad St. (we recommend **Hassan's,** on Broad St.) and stay open until 3am during the week and 4 or 4:30am on weekends to fulfill late-night cravings. People think kids here have better things to do, like study? Please.

COWLEY

KAZBAR
♿ TAPAS ❷

25-27 Cowley Rd. ☎01865 202 920 www.kazbar.co.uk

They say this is where southern Spain meets Northern Africa. Granted, Cowley Rd. is very ethnically diverse...but we think their geography might be a little off. Still, the authentic atmosphere almost makes us forget it. Meat, fish, cheese, and vegetable tapas are enjoyed on Moorish-style cushioned benches, with burning incense, colorful tiles, patterned rugs, and an open ceiling. On nice summer days, hip people sip glasses of wine *(£3.25-4.50)* outside in the sun.

Across from Magdalen Bridge. ***i*** *½-price tapas M-F 4-7pm, Sa-Su noon-4pm. Tapas £3.10-4.60. Open M-Th 4pm-midnight, F 4pm-12:30am, Sa noon-12:30am, Su noon-midnight.*

ATOMIC BURGER
♿ BURGERS ❷

96 Cowley Rd. ☎01865 790 855 www.atomicburger.co.uk

A "far-out" selection of homemade beef, chicken, and veggie burgers *(£6.50-8.75),* including a "burger of the week," in a funky outer-space-themed restaurant. If the hanging figurines and comic-book-covered walls don't get you in a cosmic mood, maybe a milkshake with "spacedust" sprinkled on it will do the trick *(£3.50).*

i *All burgers come with free side order. 10% discount on takeaway. Weekend breakfast options, including waffles, muffins, pancakes, and huevos rancheros. Gluten-free options. Entrees £4.50-10.50. Double your burger and choose 2 side orders, for £5 more. Open M-F noon-2:30pm and 5-10:30pm, Sa-Su 9:30am-10:30pm.*

GRAND CAFE
♿ BURGERS ❷

84 High St. ☎01865 204 463 www.thegrandcafe.co.uk

Grand Cafe contends with across-the-street neighbor Queens Lane Coffee Shop for claim to the site of the first coffee house in England (according to Samuel Pepys' diary, 1650). No matter, the cafe has much else to boast about, especially when it comes to tea. Afternoon teas are available 2-5pm, ranging from a simple leaf tea in a pot *(£2.50 per person)* to a cream tea, which comes with scones, butter, jam, and clotted cream *(£7.50)*, to the grand high tea, which includes smoked salmon with cream cheese and egg mayonnaise sandwiches, scones with jam and clotted cream, handmade chocolate truffles, and a glass of champagne *(£16.50)*. The classy decor of marble pillars and gold borders, gives your tea time an authentic Victorian feel. And if you've enjoyed your tea so much that you'd like to recreate the experience, teacups and saucers are available for purchase.

At intersection of High St. and Queen's Ln. Open M-Sa 9am-11pm, Su 9am-7pm. Kitchen open 9am-6pm.

JERICHO

G AND D'S — CAFE ❷

55 Little Clarendon St. ☎01865 516 652 www.gdcafe.com
94 St. Aldate's ☎01865 245 952
104 Cowley Rd. ☎01865 727 111

G and D's is a favorite Oxford haunt, with a Ben-and-Jerry's-caliber obsession with cows. Known for their bagel combinations and their natural, homemade ice cream. Bagels and ice cream—what better combination is there?

Three locations. i Lunchtime meal deal M-F noon-2pm: Bagels £3.50. Greek/Caesar salad, regular filter coffee, tea, and pack of chips or piece of fruit. Cow night Tu 7pm-midnight. Get 20% off with anything cow-related. $ Bagels £2-5. Ice cream from £2. Open daily 8am-midnight.

FREUD — PIZZA, COCKTAILS ❷

119 Walton St. ☎01865 311 171 www.freud.eu

Beneath the vaulted ceilings of a 19th-century Greek Revival church sits a local club/bar/cafe/art gallery. The disco ball may seem out of place (and a little unholy) among stained glass windows, and you sit on old pew benches while eating your whole-wheat pizzas with marinated olives *(£3.25)* or hummus with pita *(£3.85)*, but on nights when there's live jazz, they say the music can make the church's old ghosts come alive.

Next to Radcliffe Infirmary. i Vegetarian options. Organically grown food. Express lunch: pizza slice of day with side salad £5.25. $ Mains £5.55-£10. Cocktails £5 and up. Open M-Th 5-11pm, F 5pm-2am, Sa 10am-2am, Su 10am-11pm. Kitchen open until 10pm.

JERICHO CAFE — CAFE ❷

112 Walton St. ☎01865 310 840 www.thejerichocafe.co.uk

This cozy neighborhood cafe is a staple of Walton St. Offers breakfast, salads *(£7-£8.55)*, melts *(£5.25)*, and filling entrees, many of them fish dishes (like fish pie with salmon, haddock, and prawns) or eggplant parmesan. Free newspapers and yummy pastries. If you're new to Oxford and looking for things to do, check out the wall next to the staircase: it's blanketed with fliers advertising various musical and other cultural events.

Next to Radcliffe Infirmary. i Vegetarian options. Takeaway available. $ Entrees £7-12. Open M-W 8am-9:30am, Th-Sa 8am-10pm, Su 9am-8pm.

THE STANDARD TANDOORI — INDIAN ❷

117 Walton St. ☎01865 553 557

The decor might look a little dated, but the Indian food is fresh, and the service is friendly. Students say they make one of the best curries in all of Oxford. Many items are £2 cheaper to take out than to eat in, so if you're looking to save a few quid, you might want to call in, stroll over, and pick up.

Next to Radcliffe Infirmary. i Vegetarian options. Takeaway available. $ Mains £3.65-12. Open daily noon-2:30pm and 6-11:30pm.

GREEN'S CAFE CAFE ❶

50 St. Giles ☎01865 316 878 www.greenscafeoxford.co.uk

This student-friendly coffee shop has a relaxed upstairs seating area filled with friends having a drink or breakfast and individuals with their laptops Facebook-stalking...or, rather, studying. There's a a selection of British newspapers available if you're looking for some reading material.

Next to the Eagle and Child.

CARFAX

THE VAULTS AND GARDEN CAFE ❷

St. Mary's Church, Radcliffe Sq. ☎01865 279112 www.vaultsandgarden.com

In the summertime, this is possibly the best setting in Oxford for lunch. Based out of the University Church of St. Mary the Virgin, the large garden eating area offers picturesque views of the Bodleian Library, Radcliffe Camera, and nearby colleges. There are even picnic blankets on the grass to stretch out and sunbathe with your coffee, meal, and book. The menu changes daily, with buffet-style serving and fresh salads, sandwiches, and soups, along with coffees, yogurt, and pastries. All vegetables come from nearby organic garden.

Turn up St. Mary's Passage off Queens St. or High St. ***i*** *Menu changes daily for breakfast and lunch. 10% student discount.* *Lunch entrees £4.50-9.* *Open daily 8:30am-6:30pm.*

BEN'S COOKIES COOKIES ❶

108-109 Covered Market ☎ 01865 247 407 www.benscookies.com

Yes, you might have seen a few of these quaint little cookie stands in London, but this was the original, around for over 25 years in Oxford's 18th-century covered market. This tiny little stall sells what are most definitely the best cookies in town. They come in 10 delicious flavors, like white chocolate chip and triple chocolate chunk, and are served basically fresh out of the oven, nice and gooey.

By High St. *Cookies £1 and up. Sold by weight. Tins of 3 £5.50, tins of 8 £11.50.* *Open M-Sa 9:15am-5:30pm, Su 11am-4pm.*

CHIANG MAI KITCHEN THAI ❷

130A High St., Kemp Hall Passage ☎ 01865 202 233 www.chianmaikitchen.co.uk

It might seem a bit incongruous inside a classic 16th-century English building, but the herbs and spices flown in weekly from **Bangkok** give the food a deliciously tangy flavor and pack this two-story restaurant with hungry people every night. Wash down your chicken, beef, pork, or veggies with the authentic Thai iced tea *(£3.50).*

Hidden in an alley to the right of the Starbucks at 127 High St. Look for signs pointing you back behind the street. *Mains £6.30-11.50* *Open M-Sa noon-2:30pm and 6-10:30pm, Su 6-10:30pm.*

QUEEN'S LANE COFFEE HOUSE MEDITERRANEAN ❷

40 High St. ☎01865 240 082 www.queenslanecoffeehouse.co.uk

On this spot in 1654, Cirques Jobson is said to have started selling a revolutionary new drink called coffee; thus, Queen's Lane Coffee House claims itself to be the oldest coffeehouse in Europe (though Grand Cafe across the street seems to reserve the honor for itself). Meanwhile, its prime location also made it a supposed favorite retreat for 17th-century scholars who debated issues of the day. Today, though, the large, laid-back restaurant is a good place for a solo traveler to eat a meal without feeling self-conscious. Full breakfasts *(£3.50-£7.45),* pastries *(£1.50),* lasagna, Turkish pizza *(lahmacun),* Kiev, moussaka, spicy Turkish sausage on ciabatta *(£5.45).* Typical coffee house fixtures, mixed with Mediterranean and Turkish specialties.

High St. begins right after Magdalen Bridge. Restaurant on the right coming from the direction of Magdalen College. i Credit card min. £5. Entrees £6.45-9. Open M-Sa 8am-9pm, Su 9am-9pm.

THE KING'S ARMS

PUB ❷

40 Holywell St. ☎01865 242 369

For at least 350 years, this was a gents-only pub. By 1973, this was the last male-only pub in Oxford, and after a fire that conspiracy theorists say was started by radical feminists, they re-opened with the doors clear for the ladies as well. Today this is one of the popular spots for students in the nearby colleges, with large cozy wooden tables for patrons, a rotating selection of Young's cask ales, and classic pub fare. The King's Arms is especially known for its **Pimms** and late-night snacks. After the kitchen closes you can still grab yummy bar snacks like olives, popcorn, and candy bars up until closing. If you're more ambitious, come earlier while the kitchen's still running and try the traditional faggots, braised in red onion gravy.

Intersection with Broad St. Holywell St. is parallel with High St. Longwall St. connects the 2. Open daily 10:30am-midnight. Kitchen open 11:30am-9:30pm.

GEORGINA'S COFFEE SHOP

CAFE ❶

Ave. 3, Covered Market ☎01865 249 527

This bohemian coffee shop is one of the only places in town where any self-respecting hippie can feel safely hidden from the prepsters and mobs of tourists. With old-school movie posters on the ceilings, charmingly shabby tables and chairs, yummy vegetarian wraps and pastries, and peaceful alternative background music, this is a place worth checking out.

Above Brothers in the Covered Market. i Takeaway available. Entrees £5-6. Open M-Sa 8:30am-4:30pm.

THE NOSEBAG

ORGANIC CAFE ❸

6-8 St. Michaels St., 2nd fl. ☎01865 721 033 www.nosebagoxford.co.uk

Piping-hot home-cooked dishes in a cozy and relaxed, but informal, setting (don't expect elegance, but rather economical service). The second-floor location in a 15th-century building means nice views of the quaint street below. Healthy organic options, along with vegetarian alternatives. Pastries and wine top off the casseroles, pies, salads, and fish. Menu changes daily.

i Vegetarian options available. Entrees £8-£10. Open M-Th 9:30am-10pm, F-Sa 9:30am-10:30pm, Su 9:30am-9pm. Last orders taken 30min. before close.

EDAMAME

JAPANESE ❷

15 Holywell St. ☎01865 246 916 www.edamame.co.uk

This tiny, hip Japanese restaurant is one of the hottest spots in town, beloved by students and 20-somethings. Thursday sushi nights are particularly popular; arrive on the early side to avoid waiting in lines. Other favored menu times include ramen *(£7-8)*, sake *(£3.50-6)*, and of course, some of those weirdly addictive green baby soy beans for which the restaurant is named *(£2)*.

Holywell St. is parallel with High St. Longwall St. connects the two. i Vegetarian options available. Lunch cash only. Dinner credit card min. £10. Lunch entrees £5-9. Evening entrees £3-8. Sushi nights sets £6-9. Open W 11:30am-2pm, Th-Sa 11:30am-2pm and 5-8:30pm, Su noon-3:30pm.

The main clubbing area in Oxford is near the train station, on **Park End Street** and **Hythe Bridge Street.** Maybe they figured that there was enough noise already with the trains going by, so a little bit of blasting music couldn't hurt. Both of these streets split off from **Botley Road** (the train station's home). From the center of town, George St. turns into Hythe Bridge St. as you head eastward, and New Rd. likewise becomes Park End.

CARFAX

THE BRIDGE — CLUB

6-9 Hythe Bridge St. ☎01865 242 526 www.bridgeoxford.co.uk

This mainstream club is very popular with Oxford's crowds of students, English or foreign, especially for their frequent student nights *(Student nights on M and Th; international student night W)*. The modern art on the walls may seem out of place at this pretty conventional venue, or it might be welcomed as a nice alternative touch. Either way, come prepared for R and B and the biggest pop hits of the month. If you're not into that mass-produced..."stuff," this might not be your cup of tea.

Down the road from the bus station. No shorts, no hats, no ripped jeans, no white sneakers. Cover £3-8. Open M 10pm-2am, W 10pm-2am, Th-Sa 10pm-3am.

THIRST — BAR, CLUB

7-8 Park End St. ☎01865 242 044 www.thirstbar.com

This lounge bar is hopping all nights of the week because of its blasting DJs, free cover on weeknights, and spacious outdoor garden, where those who are so inclined can share a hookah (better known as shisha here) to complement their cocktails. Not classy, but not trashy either.

Down the road from the bus station. Cover Th-Su £3. Open M-W 7:30pm-2am, Th-Sa 7:30pm-3am, Su 7:30pm-2am.

LAVA AND IGNITE — CLUB

Cantay House, Park End St. ☎01865 250 181 www.lavaignite.com/oxford

Perhaps the most popular club in Oxford, the space is newly refurbished and packed with partying packs of patrons. There are three separate and distinct dance floors, plus a separate "chill-out" space for sitting, drinking and talking (three plus one equals four bars), so if you get tired of the scenery, feel free to rotate. Call ahead to be put on the guest list and skip the lines on weekends.

Across the street from Thirst and Central Backpackers. Student nights M and W. Covers £3-8. Open W 9:30pm-2am, Th-Sa 10pm-3am.

JERICHO

THE EAGLE AND CHILD — PUB

49 St. Giles ☎01865 302 925

This brick-and-wood pub might be a stop on Oxford's literary trail, but that doesn't mean it shouldn't be on your pub crawl as well. Around as a public house since 1650, this was a former playhouse for Royalist soldiers during the English Civil War and then, four centuries later, a favorite watering hole of **JRR Tolkien, C.S. Lewis** and the group of writers who dubbed themselves the "Inklings." Have a drink in what used to be the back room (before the garden area was incorporated into the pub), the **Rabbit Room,** where the group had what Lewis referred to as "golden sessions" with drinks in hand and philosophy and literary genius spilling from mouths. There's a letter hung up by the bar bearing witness to the writers' presence, with their signatures and a statement that the men have drunk to the landlord's health.

Down St. Giles, north of the Ashmolean Museum. Mains £6.45-10. Open M-Th 11am-11pm, F-Sa 11am-11:30pm, Su midnight-10:30pm.

livin' the pub life

I have to admit that one of my favorite things about the UK is the pub culture.

Cliché as it might be, I've rarely felt as distinctly British as when I sit down in a 16th-century pub in the middle of the afternoon with a pint of cider. On cloudy days, I sit inside and admire the fine woodwork and the idiosyncratic wall decorations. On sunny days, I like sitting out in the beer garden and basking in the summer sunshine with whatever ale the bartender has recommended. This kind of relaxed, communal space is something that we Americans are seriously lacking (along with an appropriate legal drinking age).

Oxford has some of the best pubs I've seen so far. Not only are they old, and oozing with character, but they all have great stories behind them.

Last night a friend and I tried out the King's Arms. Until 1973, this was the last male-only pub remaining in Oxford. The bartender was proud to tell me that Hugh Grant (Oxford alum) had stopped by just last week. Right nearby was the Turf Tavern, where former Australian Prime Minister Bob Hawke set a Guinness World Record for finishing off a yard glass of ale in just 11 seconds. As local legend has it, this was also the site where a young Bill Clinton, during his days as a Rhodes Scholar, purportedly "didn't inhale."

Today I stopped by The Eagle and the Child. Here, C.S. Lewis, J.R.R. Tolkien and other members of the "Inklings," a little club of writers, used to meet weekly to drink, discuss and debate the issues of the day. They say that the Chronicles of Narnia and The Hobbit were first read aloud in the back "Rabbit Room."

Rachel Lipson

JERICHO TAVERN TAVERN

56 Walton St. ☎01865 311 775 www.thejerichooxford.co.uk

Radiohead first made its debut here back in 1984; since then, it has been sold and bought, remodeled, rebranded, but thankfully the Jericho Tavern remains a good place to find live music in Oxford. The heated outdoor beer garden is also a plus—especially if you get a Fruli Strawberry Beer *(£3.50)* to enjoy out there—the spacious inside is good for big groups of friends, and there are board games for your entertainment on nights without music. Live acoustic on Sunday nights from 8pm. Check out the music listings on the tavern's website.

Near the Phoenix cinema. Entrees £6.50-11. Open daily noon-midnight. Kitchen open noon-10pm.

THEATER

NEW THEATRE

CARFAX

George St. ☎01865 320 760, 0844 847 1588 for booking www.newtheatreoxford.org.uk

It's showtime. Formerly known as the **Apollo Theater,** this is the main commercial theater in Oxford. The Art Deco building is home to many visiting concerts, musicals, and dramas.

From the bus station, follow Hythe Bridge St. to Worcester St. Make a right and follow down George St. Ⓢ Tickets £17.50-42.50. Concessions sometimes for weekday showings. Occasionally £11 student standbys on day of performance. Inquire at box office. Box office open M-W 10am-5pm, Th 10am-5:30pm, F non-performance days 10am-6pm, performance days 10am-3min. before curtain, Sa 10am-5pm.

OXFORD PLAYHOUSE

CARFAX

11-12 Beaumont St. ☎01865 305 305 www.oxfordplayhouse.com

Oxford's independent theater, better known to locals as simply "The Playhouse," puts on British and international drama, family shows, contemporary dance and music, student and amateur shows, comedy, lectures, and poetry. The Playhouse also produces and tours its own shows and hosts Artists in Residence.

Down Beaumont St. from the Ashmolean Musem. Ⓢ Advance concessions £2 off ticket prices. Student standbys available day of show at box office for £9.50. Box office open M-Sa 10am-6pm or until 30min. before curtain. Su performance days 2hr. before curtain. Cafe open 10am-11pm or until 5:30pm on non-performance nights.

MUSIC

One of the most popular outlets for music lovers visiting Oxford are the university colleges' **choirs.** These choirs are professional quality—many of them go on international tours, (hopefully) a clear marker of success, and also have CDs that are available for purchase. Many tourists take full advantage of the opportunity to hear them in their natural environment at **Evensong.** Better yet, Evensong is always free. Generally during term time at Oxford *(Oct-Dec, Jan-Mar, and Apr-June),* the college choirs are present at daily evening services, usually held at 6pm *(show up about 15min. beforehand and tell the porter or security that you've come for Evensong).* However, confirm the choir performance information on the college website or with the porters' lodge during the day before showing up for the service.

OXFORD COFFEE CONCERTS

CARFAX

Holywell Music Room ☎01865 305 305 www.coffeeconcerts.com; www.ticketsoxford.com

This is one of the premier chamber music series in the country. Concerts held weekly on Sunday mornings feature string quartets, ensembles, and other classical duos and trios. Though you can't actually bring coffee inside, it's served beforehand at the nearby Turf Tavern, Vaults and Garden Cafe, and King's Arms. The concerts take place in the historic 1748 Holywell Music Hall, the oldest purpose-built concert hall in Europe.

Located on Holywell St., past the King's Arms and before Mansfield Rd. Ⓢ Tickets £11, concessions £10. Season tickets £96, concessions £84. Tickets can be purchased online or in person at the Oxford Playhouse Box Office, Beaumont St. Oxford Playhouse Box Offce open M-Sa 10am-6pm or until 30min. before curtain. Tickets can also be bought in person at the door on the day of the performance starting at 9:45am. All concerts start at 11:15am.

OXFORD PHILOMUSICA CARFAX

Various Venues ☎020 8450 1060 www.oxfordphil.com

Oxford's professional symphony orchestra is the first-ever orchestra in residence at the University of Oxford. It has established itself as a top-rate orchestra in the region.

i Held at Christ Church Cathedral, Chipping Norton Theatre (2 Spring St.), Holywell Music Room (Holywell St.), Jacqueline du Pre Music Building (St. Hilda's College, Cowley Pl.), Oxford Town Hall (St. Aldate's), Sheldonian Theatre (Broad St.), University Church of St. Mary (High St.), and Wyvern Theatre (Theatre Sq.). Tickets available through www.ticketsoxford.com or at Oxford Playhouse, Beaumont St. Tickets £10-37, students £5, under 18 half off. Oxford Playhouse Box Offce open M-Sa 10am-6pm or until 30min. before curtain. Box Office at each venue opens for door sales and ticket collection 2hr. before each concert.

DANCE

BURTON TAYLOR STUDIO CARFAX

11 Beaumont St. ☎01865 305 305 www.oxfordtickets.com

The Burton Taylor Studio or BT Studio puts on occasional dance performances in its theater space, hosting visiting companies of contemporary dance. Ask at the box office of the Oxford Playhouse (above).

Across from Ashmolean Museum. Open M-Sa 10am-6pm or until 30min. before curtain. Su performance days from 2hr. before curtain.

the race

Started in 1829, the annual Boat Race between Oxford and Cambridge has become a worldwide spectacle. Each year, the universities' rowing teams dash down the Thames from Putney to Mortlake, as tens of thousands of spectators line the banks. As of now, Cambridge reigns supreme with 79 victories, while Oxford follows closely behind with 75 wins. This competition has become serious, high-stakes business. As one Oxford oarsman so aptly put at the 2007 race, "You have to put everything on the end of the oar."

shopping

Cornmarket St. is Oxford's chain-happy heaven, turning into Magdalen St. You will find many of the department stores in this area. Jericho has more alternative shopping, while High St. and St. Aldates, with their historic-looking decor, are generally aimed at tourist shopping (i.e. souvenir-hunting). High St. begins directly off Magdalen Bridge, passing colleges and meeting up with Cornmarket St. and St. Aldates to the East before becoming Queen St.

CLOTHING

JACK WILLS CARFAX

125 High St. ☎01865 794 302 www.jackwills.com

The "University Outfitters" pride themselves on being "fabulously British." While you won't be able to afford a new wardrobe, it's worth a quick peek inside the store on ritzy High St., if only to pat yourself on the back and leave satisfied that there do exist the people who fit that stereotype you had of Oxford before arriving. Check out the old memorabilia from Oxford-Cambridge matches, then outfit yourself in British attire of choice. You'll never feel more British.

From Carfax Tower, walk down High St. Open M-Sa 9:30am-6pm, Su 11am-5pm.

DEBENHAMS JERICHO

Magdalen St. ☎0844 561 6161 www.debenhams.com

Department stores are always a convenient one-stop shop for all the essentials you've forgotten to bring. Though not always the most affordable, there are some deals to be had. Debenhams is a typical British department store: massive size, attempt at grandeur, lots of cooking supplies and home furnishings, and then the clothing. There's a restaurant and bus information on the upper floors.

Magdalen St. begins where Beaumont St. and Saint Giles St. meet, not by Magdalen College or Bridge. Open M-W 9:30am-6pm, Th 9:30am-8pm, F 9:30am-7pm, Sa 9am-7pm, Su 11am-5pm.

HABIBI JERICHO

21 Little Clarendon St. ☎01865 558 077

This small, independent shop features a mishmash of accessories, including jewelry, scarves, handbags, and earrings. There are also plenty of mirrors—for sale—but also good for checking out whether those sunglasses look cute or not.

Down the road from St. Johns College. Open M-Sa 10am-5.30pm, Su 11am-4pm.

UNCLE SAMS JERICHO

25 Little Clarendon St. ☎01865 510 759

It's not surprising that Oxford's funkiest neighborhood has its own vintage clothing shop to serve all its hippies, past and present. What is a little more unexpected, though, is that the outlet features all American-themed items. That might seem to imply that American shoppers should feel right at home, but a lot of the merchandise consists of velvet and jean vests from the'60's and'70's—so it might be a little before your time. If you're into that sort of thing, though, it's perfect.

Down the road from St. Johns College. Open M-Sa 10am-5:30pm, Su noon-4pm.

HOBBIES AND GAMES

ALICE'S SHOP CARFAX

83 St. Aldates ☎01865 723 793 www.aliceinwonderlandshop.co.uk

Alice's Shop, located across the road from Lewis Carroll's old stomping grounds (he was a professor at Christ Church College and first dreamed up the story there), is in the spot where the real Alice, Alice Liddell the Dean's daughter, used to buy her sweets back in Carroll's day. There's even a drawing of the shop in the original Alice book. Like Wonderland, the store is "full of all manner of curious things," with Alice in Wonderland Christmas ornaments, chess sets, teacups, Mad Hatter key racks, and Cheshire Cat tea cozies.

Open July-Aug daily 9:30am-6:30pm; Sept-June daily 10:30am-5pm.

HOYLES CARFAX

72 High St. ☎01865 203 344 www.hoylesonline.com

An endearing specialty shop for all kinds of nifty games, puzzles, juggling, and magic accessories. Pick up one of over 50 different kinds of chess sets, **Monopoly the Oxford Edition,** or Stonehenge playing cards. Tired of studying and need a toy to distract yourself with? Scrabble, Disney version? Oh yeah.

Open in summer open daily 9:30am-6pm; in winter M-Sa 9:30am-6pm.

BOOKS

THE ALBION BEATNIK JERICHO

34 Walton St. ☎01865 511 345 www.albionbeatnik.co.uk

In this independent bookstore, almost half of the space is dedicated to an impressive collection of Beat poets and music books and general things related to the "Beat" lifestyle. Open up the coolly decorated cupboard in the back corner: inside you'll find hundreds of jazz CDs. There's also a cafe of sorts inside, so you can enjoy a cup of tea *(£1.50)* in an armchair with your book while Dylan and Coltrane play on in the background.

North on St. Giles Rd.; left into Little Clarendon St. At the end turn right. New and second-hand books from £1. Open M-W noon-7pm, Th-Sa 1-11pm, Su 3-5:30pm.

OXFORD UNIVERSITY PRESS

CARFAX

116-117 High St. ☎01865 242 913 wwww.oup.com/uk/bookshop

The OUP Bookshop is the official retailer for the largest university publisher in the world. The prestigious Oxford University Press is actually a department of the University of Oxford, and it printed its first book way back in 1478. The shop, though, has only been around on the High St. site since 1872—so practically yesterday in Oxford time. There are five levels, but the most unique section is the dictionary area, obviously. The Oxford English Dictionary is sold here in sizes ranging from 20 volumes to "shorter" to "concise" to "compact" to "pocket" to "little," and to, finally, "mini." Meanwhile, you can find Oxford Dictionaries of Quotations, Proverbs, British Place Names, and Dentistry, among others. There's such a selection, we're at a loss for words. Any suggestions?

i Ask about 10% student discount. Catalogs free. Open M-Sa 9:30am-6pm, Su 11am-5pm.

BLACKWELL'S

CARFAX

48-51 Broad St. ☎01865 792 792 www.blackwell.co.uk

Blackwell is a popular British chain bookstore, but its roots are firmly staked in Oxford. The flagship store at 48-51 Broad St. was started back in 1879. Originally, the Broad St. shop at number 50 was only 12 sq. ft., but the store quickly grew to incorporate the upstairs, cellars, and next door storefronts. Many famous writers saw their first books sold at Blackwell's. One such literary is **JRR Tolkien,** who in 1915 saw his first poem, "Goblin's Feet," published here. Today, the shop includes a coffeeshop if you'd like to nosh while you read, and the **Norrington Room,** built beneath the quad of Trinity College. This room, with 3 mi. of shelving, holds the Guinness Book of World Records award for housing the largest display of books for sale in one room anywhere in the world. Check the posters on the walls for listings of author visits, literary walking tours (see **Practicalities,** p. 130), and signings. Art fans and music aficionados should definitely check out the nearby sister Blackwell shops on Broad St.: Blackwell Art and Poster shop *(27 Broad St. ☎01865 333 641)* featuring a wide selection of prints, art books, photography, and Blackwell Music *(23-25 Broad St. ☎01865 333 580)* with its vast collection of sheet music, classical CDs, and musical literature.

Holywell St. becomes Broad St. Open M 9am-6:30pm, Tu 9:30am-6:30pm, W-Sa 9am-6:30pm. Su 11am-5pm

THE LAST BOOKSHOP

JERICHO

126 Walton St.

It's a tiny little place, with a correspondingly small and random collection; there's also little room to move around, and certainly no room for sitting. However, you don't need to sit, just buy: all books are £2!

Open M-Sa 9am-5:45pm.

LIQUOR STORES

THE WHISKY SHOP

CARFAX

7 Turl St. ☎01865 202279 www.whiskyshop.com

Come here for your fix of Jack Daniel's...and so much more. The wooden shelves are stuffed to the ceilings with the finest whiskeys in the worlds, plus old malts, single malts, Bailey's, and Captain Morgan. If you're admittedly clueless when it comes to whiskey, that's OK too: there are tiny sample 50mL bottles for experimentation *(from £3.20)*, Jack Daniel's fudge for the faint-hearted, and even little reviews from the the *Whisky Bible* and *Malt Whisky Companion* taped above the bottles to help you make your decision.

Behind Covered Market. Open Tu-Sa 10am-5:30pm.

essentials *i*

PRACTICALITIES

- **TOURIST OFFICE:** The Tourist Information Centre is crowded with mobs of tourists during the summer. Ask for a free *In Oxford What's On* guide and free restaurant and accommodation guides. Also sells discounted tickets to local attractions. Books rooms for free with a 10% deposit. *(15-16 Broad St. ☎01852 252 200 www.visitoxford.org Open M-Sa 9:30am-5pm, Su 10am-4pm.)*
- **STUDENT TRAVEL: STA Travel.** *(Threeways House, 36 George St. ☎0871 702 9839 www.statravel.co.uk Open M-Th 10am-7pm, F-Sa 10am-6pm, Su 11am-5pm.)*
- **TOURS:** The 2hr. official **Oxford University Walking Tour** leaves from the TIC and provides access to some colleges otherwise closed to visitors. The 2hr. tours allow only up to 19 people and are booked on a first come, first served basis, so get tickets early in the day at the TIC, by phone, or online 48hr. in advance. *(☎726 871,☎252 200 to book tickets. visitoxford.org In summer daily 10:45 and 11am, 1 and 2pm; in winter daily 10:45am and 2pm. $ £7, children £3.75.)* Themed tours, like the CS Lewis and JRR Tolkien Tour and Garden run on a varied schedule. *($ £7.50, children £4.)* Check with the TIC or pick up an Official Guided Walking Tours Brochure. **Blackwell's Walking Tours** *(☎01852 333 606)* run from April through October and leave from Canterbury Gate at Christ Church. The company runs a number of walking tours throughout the university town, including the General Literary University and City Tour *(Tu 2pm, Th 11am. $ £7, concessions £6.50)*, the Literary Tour of Oxford *(Tu 2pm, Th 11am)*, the "Inklings" Tour about CS Lewis, JRR Tolkien, and cohorts *(W 11:45am. $ £7, concessions £6.50.)*, and the Chapels, Churches, and Cathedral Tour. *(F 2pm. $ £9, concessions £8.)* **Oxford Walking Tours** runs 90min. walks through the colleges, leaving from Trinity College Gates. *(☎07790 734 387. www.oxfordwalkingtours.com Apr-Oct M-F 11am, 1, 3pm, Sa-Su every hr. 11am-4pm; Nov-Mar M-F noon, 2pm, Sa-Su every hr. 11am-3pm. $ £7.50, concessions £7.)* They also offer Ghost Tours. *(Apr-Oct 7:30pm; Nov-Mar 4, 7pm. $ £7.)* **Bill Spectre's Ghost Tours** leave every F-Sa evenings from Oxford Castle Unlocked at 6:30pm for 1¾hr. tour or from the TIC at 7pm for a 1¼hr. tour. *(☎07941 041 811 www.ghosttrail.org $£6, children £3.)* **City Sightseeing** offers hop-on, hop-off bus tours of the city with 19 stops, running every 10-15min. *(Starting at Bay 14 of the bus station. Pick up tickets from bus drivers or stands around the city. ☎01852 790 522 $ £12.50, students £10.50, children £6.)*
- **CURRENCY EXCHANGE:** Banks line **Cornmarket Street. Marks and Spencer** has a bureau de change with no commission. *(13-18 Queen St. ☎01852 248 075 Open M-W 8:30am-6:30pm, Th 8:30am-7:30pm, F 8:30am-6:30pm, Sa 8:30am-6:30pm, Su 11am-4:30pm.)* There is also a bureau of change attached to (but not affiliated with) the TIC, with no commission.

- **INTERNET:** Free at **Oxford Central Library**; however there is often a wait during prime hours; some stations are open to pre-booking if you know exactly when you'd like to use it. *(Westgate. Open M-Th 9am-7pm, F-Sa 9am-5:30pm.)* **C-Work Cyber Cafe.** *(1st fl. of Nash Bailey's House, New Inn Hall St. ☎722 044 £1 for 50min. Open M-Sa 9am-9pm, Su 9am-7pm.)*
- **POST OFFICE:** *(102-104 St. Aldates. ☎08457 223 344 Bureau de change inside. Open M 9am-5:30pm, Tu 9:30am-5:30pm, W-Sa 9am-5:30pm.)*
- **POSTAL CODE:** OX1 1ZZ.

EMERGENCY!

- **POLICE:** *(St. Aldates and Speedwell St. ☎505 505.)*
- **HOSPITAL:** **John Radcliffe Hospital.** (Headley Way. *Take bus #13 or 14. ☎741 166.)*

GETTING THERE

By Train

Botley Road Station *(Botley Rd., down Park End. ☎01865 484 950 Ticket office open M-F 5:45am-8pm, Sa 7:30am-8pm, Su 7:15am-8pm.)* offers trains to **Birmingham** *(£27. 1hr. 10min., every 30min.)*, **Glasgow** *(£98.50. 5-7hr., every hr.)*, **London Paddington** *(£20. 1hr., 2-4 per hr.)*, and **Manchester** *(£61. 3hr., 2 per hr.)*

By Bus

Gloucester Green Station has **Stagecoach** buses *(☎01865 772 250 www.stagecoach-bus.com)* running to **London Buckingham Road** *(£14, students £11. 1¼hr., 5 per hr.)* and **Cambridge.** *(£10.90. 3hr., 2 per hr.)* Buy tickets on the bus and enjoy free Wi-Fi.

The Oxford Bus Company *(☎01865 785 400 www.oxfordbus.co.uk)* runs the **Oxford Express** *(i Free Wi-Fi. £13, students £10. 100min., every 15-30min.)* and the **X70 Airline** services to **Heathrow.** *(i Free Wi-Fi. £20. 1½hr., every 30min.)* Also runs the **X80** service to **Gatwick's** north and south terminals. *(i Free Wi-Fi. £25. 2½hr., every hr.)* All leave from **Gloucester Green.** Tickets can be bought on the bus or at the **National Express** office *(£1 booking fee)*. However, the only way to secure a spot in advance on a particular bus is on the website.

National Express Bus 737 *(☎08717 818 178 www.nationalexpress.com Ticket office open M-Sa 8:30am-6pm, Su 8:30am-5:30pm)* goes to **London Stansted,** *(£19.30. 3½hr., 8 per day.)*, **Birmingham,** *(£13.40. 2½hr., 1 per day.)*, and **Bath.** *(£9.50. 2hr., 1 per day.)*

GETTING AROUND

Public Transport

Oxford Bus Company *(☎01865 785 400 www.oxfordbus.co.uk)* provides many services within the city. Fares vary depending on distance traveled. *(DayPass £3.70, weekly pass £13.)* Week passes can be purchased at the Oxford Bus Company office. *(3rd fl. of Debenham's department store on corner of George and Magdalen St. Open M-W and F 9:30am-6pm, Th 9:30-8pm, Sa 9am-6pm.)* **Stagecoach** *(☎01865 772 250 www.stagecoachbus.com)* also runs buses in the city and to some surrounding villages. One-way-tickets within the city usually cost £1.80. Be careful when buying Day Passes because they don't apply to both companies (if you buy an Oxford Bus DayPass, it only works on Oxford Bus Company buses). For real-time information on buses in Oxford, use www.oxontime.com, which can also text to your cell phone.

By Taxi

Call **Radio Taxis** *(☎01865 242 424)* or **ABC** *(☎01865 770 077)* for taxis. There are taxi ranks at **Oxford Station, Saint Giles, Gloucester Green** and **Carfax** in the evening. Taxis (like London black cabs) can be hailed in the street.

By Bike

Bike Rental: Cycloanalysts *(150 Cowley Rd. ☎01865 424 444 www.cycloanalysts.com £17 for 24hr., £25 for 2 days, £50 for 1 week. Includes locks. Open M-Sa 9am-6pm, Su 10am-4pm.)*

By Boat

Magdalen Bridge Boat House *(Cross bridge from city center and turn left; down by the banks. ☎01865 202 643 www.oxfordpunting.co.uk Open daily 9:30am-dusk.)* Rents punts *(£20 per hr., up to 5 people)* and offers chauffeured punts. *(£23 for 30min. for up to 4 people.)*

CAMBRIDGE

One of the more student-oriented cities in England, Cambridge is packed with pubs, clubs and intimate cafes. Winding lanes twist and turn between the age-old colleges of the university, each one a path through the town's fascinating history. It was here that **Watson** and **Crick** discovered the double helix, **Newton** discovered gravity, **Byron** and **Milton** wrote their famous poetry and **Winnie the Pooh** was born. If you're looking for a simplified Cambridge experience, the "P and P" formula is perhaps best: Punting and Pimm's (in other words, boating and boozing, although the two together could be a disaster waiting to happen). In the summer, multitudes of foreign exchange students come to Cambridge to learn English, making for a congested, multilingual street scene.

greatest hits

- **SWIM AND BARE IT.** Visit the fountain at Trinity College (p. 136) where Lord Byron used to skinny-dip.
- **WHIMSICAL WINDOWS.** Meditate in Kings College Chapel (p. 137), perhaps the only place on campus with both dragons and unicorns.
- **A HEADLINING PUB.** Extra! Extra! Drink all about it!...at the Free Press pub (p. 144).
- **ROLLIN' DOWN THE RIVER.** Rent a punt from Scudamore's (p. 147) and cruise down the Cam.
- **GO FOR JOE.** For cheap coffee and lively debates, head to Indigo Coffee House, a favorite among "uni" students (p. 141).

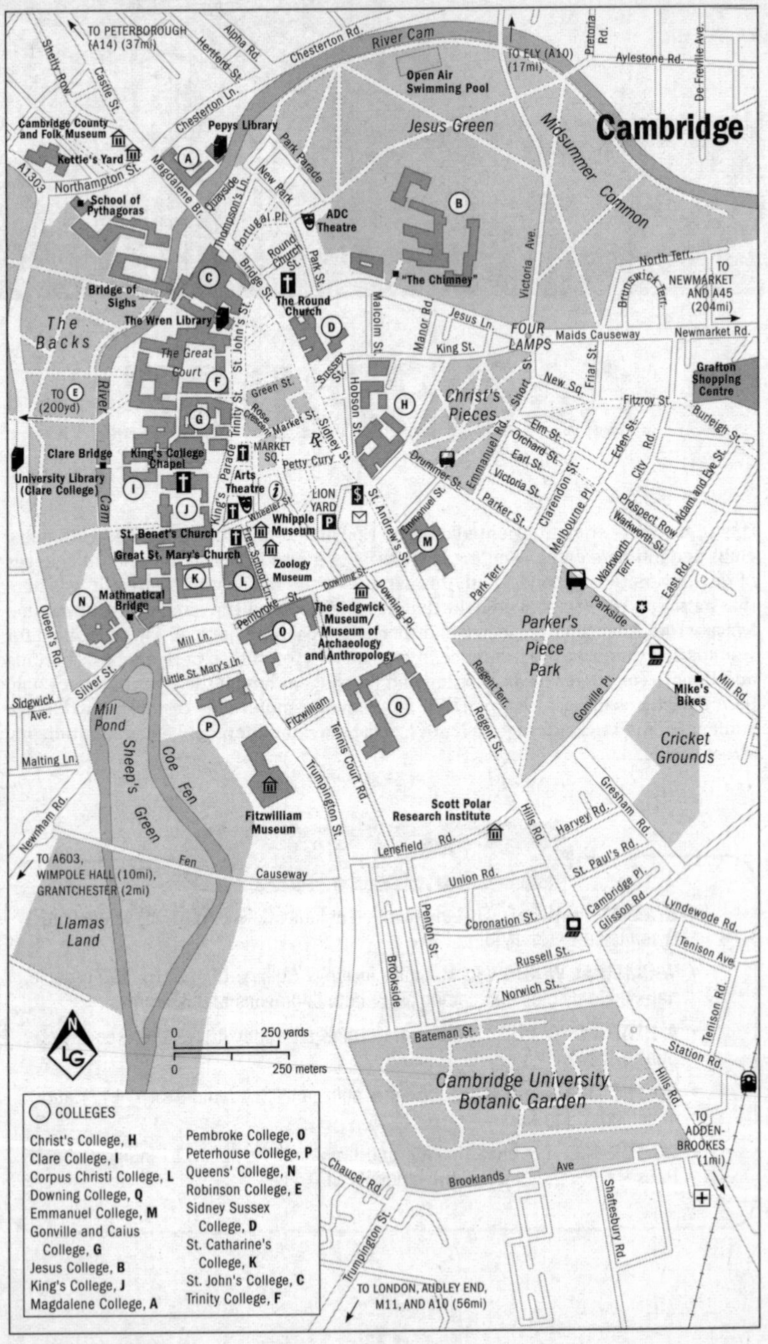
Cambridge
TO PETERBOROUGH (A14) (37mi)
TO ELY (A10) (17mi)
TO NEWMARKET AND A45 (204mi)
TO A603, WIMPOLE HALL (10mi), GRANTCHESTER (2mi)
TO LONDON, AUDLEY END, M11, AND A10 (56mi)
TO ADDEN-BROOKES (1mi)
TO E (200yd)
River Cam
Open Air Swimming Pool
Jesus Green
Midsummer Common
Cambridge County and Folk Museum
Kettle's Yard
Pepys Library
School of Pythagoras
ADC Theatre
"The Chimney"
Bridge of Sighs
The Wren Library
The Round Church
The Backs
The Great Court
FOUR LAMPS
Christ's Pieces
Grafton Shopping Centre
Clare Bridge
University Library (Clare College)
King's College Chapel
MARKET SQ.
Arts Theatre
LION YARD
Whipple Museum
Zoology Museum
St. Benet's Church
Great St. Mary's Church
Mathmatical Bridge
The Sedgwick Museum/ Museum of Archaeology and Anthropology
Parker's Piece
Park
Mike's Bikes
Cricket Grounds
Mill Pond
Sheep's Green
Coe Fen
Fitzwilliam Museum
Scott Polar Research Institute
Llamas Land
Cambridge University Botanic Garden
Shelly Row
Castle St.
Hertford St.
Alpha Rd.
Chesterton Rd.
Chesterton Ln.
Pretoria Rd.
Aylestone Rd.
De Freville Ave.
A1303
Northampton St.
Magdalene St.
Quayside
Thompson's Ln.
Park Parade
New Park
Portugal Pl.
Round Church St.
Park St.
Bridge St.
St. John's St.
Trinity St.
Green St.
Rose Crescent
Market St.
Sidney St.
Sussex St.
Hobson St.
Malcolm St.
Manor Rd.
Jesus Ln.
King St.
Victoria Ave.
North Terr.
Brunswick Terr.
Maids Causeway
Newmarket Rd.
Short St.
New Sq.
Friar St.
Fitzroy St.
Burleigh St.
Eden St.
City Rd.
Adam and Eve St.
Elm St.
Orchard St.
Earl St.
Emmanuel Rd.
Drummer St.
Victoria St.
Parker St.
Clarendon St.
Melbourne Pl.
Prospect Row
Warkworth St.
Warkworth Terr.
East Rd.
Park Terr.
Parkside
Mill Rd.
Petty Cury
St. Andrew's St.
Emmanuel St.
Wheeler St.
King's Parade
Free School Ln.
Downing St.
Downing Pl.
Pembroke St.
Mill Ln.
Little St. Mary's Ln.
Silver St.
Queen's Rd.
Sidgwick Ave.
Malting Ln.
Newnham Rd.
Fitzwilliam
Tennis Court Rd.
Trumpington St.
Regent Terr.
Regent St.
Gonville Pl.
Hills Rd.
Gresham Rd.
Harvey Rd.
Lensfield Rd.
St. Paul's Rd.
Cambridge Pl.
Glisson Rd.
Lyndewode Rd.
Tenison Ave.
Tenison Rd.
Union Rd.
Coronation St.
Penton St.
Russell St.
Norwich St.
Brookside
Bateman St.
Station Rd.
Fen Causeway
Chaucer Rd.
Brooklands Ave
Shaftesbury Rd.
Trumpington St.
0 250 yards
0 250 meters
LG
COLLEGES
Christ's College, H
Clare College, I
Corpus Christi College, L
Downing College, Q
Emmanuel College, M
Gonville and Caius College, G
Jesus College, B
King's College, J
Magdalene College, A
Pembroke College, O
Peterhouse College, P
Queens' College, N
Robinson College, E
Sidney Sussex College, D
St. Catharine's College, K
St. John's College, C
Trinity College, F

student life

There's no cooler place to be a young intellectual than Cambridge. After all, the pub where Watson and Crick announced their discovery of **DNA** is still a popular spot for cheap pints and stimulating debates. In the warmer months, though, you're more likely to find young people in the **parks** than the pubs. The beautiful gardens behind the colleges are perfect for reading a book, hanging out with students, and avoiding the tourist rush in the center of town. If you're really craving some nightlife after sunset, celebrate youth at the **Fountain Inn** or climb the **Soul Tree,** a popular three-story club with graffiti-covered walls. You're more likely to discover a hangover than the double helix, but hey, we won't judge.

orientation

Cambridge has two central avenues: the main shopping street starts at **Magdalene Bridge** north of the River Cam and becomes Bridge Street, Sidney Street, Saint Andrew's Street, Regent Street, and Hills Road. The other main thoroughfare begins as **Saint John's Street** (just off Bridge St.), becoming Trinity Street, King's Parade, and Trumpington Street. To get into town from the Drummer St. bus station, take **Emmanuel Rd.** This leads to **St. Andrew's St.**, and a bank-heavy block with loads of cash machines. To get to the center of town from the train station, follow **Station Rd.** and turn right onto **Hills Rd.** Then follow it straight until it becomes St. Andrew's St. and turn left on Downing St. and follow to Pembroke St. and turn right onto King's Parade, which will take you past King's College and onto Trinity St. by Trinity College.

accommodations

The Cambridge lodging scene is notoriously bad. There are few affordable rooms anywhere near the town center, and an excess of overpriced, occasionally sketchy bed and breakfasts fill the north and south of town. Bed and breakfasts cluster on **Arbury Road** and **Chesterton Road** to the north. Several can be found closer to town on **Tenison Road.**

WARKWORTH HOUSE — BED AND BREAKFAST ❹

Warkworth Terr. ☎01223 363 682 www.warkworthhouse.co.uk

Warkworth House is truly a cozy bed and breakfast. It's been owned by the same people for 33 years, and the beautiful rooms are all well furnished. Breakfast is not included....psych! Of course it is.

*Walk down Parkside away from town center and turn left onto Warkworth Terrace. **i** Breakfast included. $ Singles from £60; doubles from £80; family room from £100.*

TENISON TOWERS — BED AND BREAKFAST ❸

148 Tenison Rd. ☎01223 363 924 www.cambridgecitytenisontowers.com

With more affordable prices than most bed and breakfasts, Tenison Towers offers small, bright, and clean rooms as well as delicious homemade muffins and jams with the complimentary hot breakfast.

*From the station, go down Station Rd. and turn right onto Tenison Rd. **i** Breakfast included. $ Singles £40; doubles £64.*

YHA CAMBRIDGE — HOSTEL ❶

97 Tenison Rd. ☎0845 371 9728

Though rather worn, the YHA Cambridge is unbeatable for the prices it offers.

It's one of the few truly budget accommodations in Cambridge.

From the station, head down Station Rd. and turn right onto Tenison Rd. Internet £1 per 20min., £5 per 24hr., £12 per 3 days, £15 per 7 days. Reservations taken daily 7am-11pm. Dorms £14-20. Reception 24hr.

A. AND B. GUESTHOUSE BED AND BREAKFAST ❸

124 Tenison Rd. ☎01223 315 702 www.aandbguesthouse.co.uk

A pleasant, relatively centrally located B and B with clean and bright rooms. A and B has a full English breakfast, but can also satisfy vegetarian and gluten-intolerant customers upon request.

From the station, walk down Station Rd. and turn right onto Tenison Rd. Breakfast included. Singles £50, doubles £70, family £90. Reception 7am-noon and 6pm-midnight; self check-in after midnight.

LYNWOOD HOUSE BED AND BREAKFAST ❸

217 Chesterton Rd. ☎01223 500 776 www.lynwood-house.co.uk

The Lynwood House offers home-style comfort in an affordably priced B and B. Though Chesterton Rd. is outside the city center, it's not unbearably far.

Walk up Victoria Ave. away from town center and turn right onto Chesterton Rd. Breakfast included. Doubles ensuite. Singles from £40; doubles from £75; twin ensuite from £75.

THE CASTLE BED AND BREAKFAST ❹

37 St. Andrew's St. ☎01223 307 477 www.thecastlecambridge.co.uk

Just above the stylish bar of the same name, the Castle may not be exactly what you'd expect from a place called "The Castle." It's also not quite what you'd expect from a guest house above a bar, though the noise is noticeable some nights. It is, however, hard to get closer to the center of town, especially for the rates offered here.

Head north on Regent St. until it becomes St. Andrew's St. Breakfast included. Shared bathrooms. Doubles £68, but prices vary. Reception daily 8am-11pm.

ACORN GUEST HOUSE BED AND BREAKFAST ❸

154 Chesterton Rd. ☎01223 353 888 www.acornguesthouse.co.uk

This small guest house provides relatively affordable housing. Visitors can take buses into town.

Head up Victoria Ave away from town center and turn right onto Chesterton Rd. Breakfast included. Singles £50-75; doubles £70-95.

ASHLEY HOTEL HOTEL ❹

74 Chesterton Rd. ☎01223 350 059 www.arundelhousehotels.co.uk

The Ashley is the more affordable sister hotel to the Arundel, which is a little further up Chesterton Rd. The rooms are simple and clean, and stained-glass windows cast color on the bright entry hall.

Head up Victoria Ave away from town center, turn right onto Chesterton Rd. Breakfast included. Singles £65; doubles £75; twin room £75; family room £95. Reception open 7am-2pm, 5-10pm.

ARUNDEL HOUSE HOTEL HOTEL ❺

Chesterton Rd. ☎01223 367 701 www.arundelhousehotels.co.uk

More upscale than most of the B and Bs that line Chesterton, the Arundel House Hotel has the luxuries of a standard hotel and a restaurant.

Head up Magdalene St. from Sidney St. and turn right onto Chesterton Ln., which becomes Chesterton Rd. Singles £75-95; doubles £95-140. Reception 24hr.

sights

TRINITY COLLEGE COLLEGE

Trinity Ln. ☎01223 338 400

Trinity is perhaps the most popular of the colleges, drawing phenomenal numbers of tourists. **Henry VIII** intended for Trinity College to be the largest and richest in Cambridge, and with the modern-day college holding its own as third largest

cambridge

landowner in Britain (after the Queen and the Church of England), his wish has clearly been fulfilled. Trinity is famous for its illustrious alumni, including literati Dryden, Byron, Tennyson, and Nabokov; atom-splitter Ernest Rutherford; philosopher Ludwig Wittgenstein; and Indian statesman Jawaharlal Nehru. Perhaps most famously, **Sir Isaac Newton** lived there for 30 years. **The Great Court** in the center of the college is the world's largest enclosed courtyard. Visitors enter the courtyard through the Great Gate, which is guarded by a statue of Henry VIII clutching a wooden chair leg—a substitute for the oft-stolen original scepter. The apple tree near the gate is supposedly a descendant of the tree that inspired Newton's theory of gravity; in the north cloister of Neville's court, Newton calculated the speed of sound by stamping his foot and timing the echo. Lord Byron used to bathe **nude** in the college's fountain. Byron also kept a **pet bear** because college rules forbade cats and dogs. **The Wren Library** is home to alumnus A.A. Milne's handwritten copies of **Winnie the Pooh** and Newton's personal copy of his **Principia.**

Turn left onto Trinity Ln. off of Trinity St. Ⓢ Admission £3, children £1.50. Courtyard open daily 9:30am-4:30pm, Wren Library M-F noon-2pm; Hall 3-5pm.

KING'S COLLEGE

♿ COLLEGE

King's Parade ☎01223 331 100 www.kings.cam.ac.uk

Founded by **Henry VI** in 1441, King's College was originally a partner school to **Eton** until it slackened its admission policy in 1873 to accept students from other public schools. These days, King's reputation is significantly changed, and it is one of the more socially liberal of the Cambridge colleges, drawing more of its students from state schools than any other. Many visitors come for the Gothic **King's College Chapel,** where the spidering arches and stunning stained glass will stun even the most church-weary tourist. Inside the chapel, the period when Henry's mason left off and the Tudors began building is marked by a change in color of the stone. Note the roses, **dragons,** and unicorns repeated throughout the church's interior, even on its ceiling. These were the symbols of the **Tudors,** and it's a good thing for the church's decor that their coats of arms weren't all skulls, cross-bones, and vampire bats. King's alumni include: **John Maynard Keynes, EM Forster,** and **Salman Rushdie.**

Trumpington becomes King's Parade. Ⓢ Admission £5, concessions and children 12-18 £3.50, under 12 free. During term time open M-F 9:30am-3:30pm, Sa 9:30am-3:15pm. Outside of term time open M-Sa 9:30am-4:30pm, Su 10am-5pm. Chapel during term-time M-Sa 5:30pm evensong (enter through the front gate at 5:15pm). Su Eucharist 10:30am, Evensong 3:30pm.

SCOTT POLAR RESEARCH INSTITUTE

♿ MUSEUM

Lensfield Rd. ☎01223 336 540 www.spri.cam.ac.uk/museum

Founded in 1920 to memorialize **Captain Robert Falcon Scott** and his crew after they died on a return trip from the South Pole in 1912, The Polar Museum has reopened in a sleek, modern renovation packed with memorabilia from various polar expeditions, such as the barrel organ from an 1819 winter trip to the Arctic (it has 40 tunes spread across a five-barrel system) and John Ross's memoirs and narratives which are written in absurdly fine print. Especially of note is the fantastic gallery of Inuit art at the back.

Head down Regent St. away from the city center and turn right onto Lensfield Rd. Ⓢ Free. Open T-Sa 10am-4pm.

THE FITZWILLIAM MUSEUM

♿ GALLERY

Trumpington St. ☎01223 332 900 www.fitzmuseum.cam.ac.uk

Named after Richard Fitzwilliam, this beautiful museum was opened in 1848. Through the Corinthian landings of the main hall, visitors will find a variety of paintings, antiquities and applied arts. Among the numerous highlights are paintings by Monet, Pissaro and Renoir, and sculptures by Rodin. There is also a beautiful **John Constable** painting of the Heath upstairs. The museum features Impressionist artwork, Turkish pottery, and objects from everyday Egyptian life on the ground floor.

Trumpington is one of the main roads. Off Pembroke if coming from the east and Silver St. if from the West. Free. Audio Guides £3, students £2. Guided tours £4. Open T-Sa 10am-5pm, Su noon-5pm. Guided tours depart Sa at 2:30pm from the courtyard entrance.

CLARE COLLEGE

COLLEGE

Trinity Ln. ☎01223 333 200 www.clare.cam.ac.uk

Though initially founded by the **Chancellor of England,** it was refounded by **Lady Elizabeth de Clare** when the chancellor ran out of money. The thrice-widowed, 29-year-old Elizabeth's pain is bluntly referenced in the Clare coat of arms which features golden teardrops ringing a black border. The college has lush gardens of dangling ivy and weeping willows, and you can regularly hear the sound of punts hitting the riverbed. The elegant **Clare Bridge** dates from 1638 and is the oldest surviving college bridge. In wandering through Christopher Wren's Old Court, one can see the **University Library,** where **150mi.** of shelving house **eight million volumes.**

Turn left onto Senate House Passage off of Trinity St. (a continuation of King's Parade). £2.50, under 12 free. Open daily 10:45am-4:30pm.

MAGDALENE COLLEGE

COLLEGE

Magdalene St. ☎01223 332 100

Magdalene (pronounced MAUD-lin) College is housed in a fifteenth-century hostel for Benedictine monks that was, in all probability, nicer than most of the hostels you've been staying in. It's famous for the **Pepys Library,** which holds several diaries by **C.S. Lewis** who, despite his status as an Oxford man, lived in Magdalene occasionally.

Bridge St. becomes Magdalene St. i Wheelchair access in courtyard but not library. Open daily until 6pm. Library open daily Oct 6-Dec 5 2:30pm-3:30pm; Jan 12-Mar 13 2:30pm-3:30pm; Apr 20-Aug 31 11:30am-12:30pm and 2:30pm-3:30pm.

CHRIST'S COLLEGE

COLLEGE

St. Andrews St. ☎01223 334 900 www.christs.cam.ac.uk

When it was in its original location, **Christ's College** was known as "God's-house," but it moved in 1448 to the current site where it was known as "Jesus College." Either way, it's holy. The Hall pays homage to two of the most famous residents of the college—**John Milton** and **Charles Darwin**—in the form of a bust and portrait respectively. New Court is a modern concrete building constructed in 1970.

St. Andrew's St. is a continuation of Regent St. i Wheelchair access in the church but not tower. Free. Open daily 9:30am-noon.

JESUS COLLEGE

COLLEGE

Jesus Ln. ☎01223 339 339 www.jesus.cam.ac.uk

Visitors walk down a pathway known as "The Chimney" to get to the college. The arms of Bishop Alcock, the man who founded the College on the grounds of an abandoned Benedictine nunnery, are of a cock standing on an orb, a rather regal-looking visual pun. Stroll through the gardens and courts thronged by roses and enjoy the 25-acre grounds.

Go north on Sidney St. and turn right onto Jesus Ln. i Wheelchair access in the church but not the tower. Open daily 8am-dusk. Daylight hours, normally after 8am.

ST. JOHN'S COLLEGE

COLLEGE

St. John's St. ☎01223 338 600 www.joh.cam.ac.uk

Through the green arches of the entrance lies the paved plaza of St. John's college, founded in 1511 by Lady Margaret Beaufort, the mother of Henry VII. Take note of the **Bridge of Sighs,** which is designed on the same pattern as a Venetian bridge of the same name. The **School of Pythagoras** dates to the 12th century and is thought to be the oldest complete building in Cambridge. **The Fellows' Room** in Second Court, which spans an impressive 93 ft.—making it the longest room in the town—was the site of some D-Day planning.

Head north on Sidney St. Turn left off of Bridge St. onto St. John's St. i Purchase must be over

£5 for credit cards. Ⓢ Admission £3.20, students £2, children 12-16 £2, seniors £2. ⏰ Open daily Mar-Oct 10am-5pm, Nov-Feb 10am-3:30pm.

QUEENS' COLLEGE — COLLEGE

Off Silver St. ☎01223 335 537 www.queens.cam.ac.uk

Queens' College derives its name from its two founders: Queen Margaret of Anjou in 1448 and Elizabeth Woodville (the queen consort of Edward VI) in 1465. Though it's notable for having the only unaltered Tudor courtyard in Cambridge, the main attraction of the college is the **Mathematical Bridge** which is both the only bridge in Cambridge and supposedly the most perfectly structured bridge. We can't tell why, but it was designed by William Etheridge in 1749 and put in place in 1905.

Silver St. is off Trumpington St. i Partially wheelchair-accessible. Ⓢ Admission £2.50. ⏰ Open daily Mar-Oct 10am-4:30pm.

WHIPPLE MUSEUM OF THE HISTORY OF SCIENCE — MUSEUM

Free School Ln. ☎01223 330 906 www.hps.cam.ac.uk/whipple

This university museum is named after Robert Whipple, who donated a collection of roughly 1000 scientific devices to the university, many of which are on display here, such as the *Gömböc* (a strangely shaped object that, despite its homogeneous consistency, will return to the same resting position no matter where you place it), and **Fred,** a 19th-century anatomical model whose parts have been mercilessly scattered across the museum. Several intriguing planetariums, microscopes, telescopes and a wealth of pocket calculators round out the fantastic collection.

Turn left off of St. Andrew's St. onto Downing St., follow it until it becomes Pembroke and make a right onto Free School Ln. i Call ahead for wheelchair access. Ⓢ Free. ⏰ Open M-F 12:30-4:30pm.

MUSEUM OF ZOOLOGY — MUSEUM

Downing St. ☎01223 336 650 www.museum.zoo.cam.ac.uk

This museum is packed to the gills with fantastic animals (dead, of course). Come for the giant spider crab, and stay for the birds. Some of these guys are enough to make you believe in creationism. Consider the Gorgeted Bird of Paradise: was the Don King hair style necessary for flight? How did the Raggi's Bird of Paradise fly with wings that look like he got in a fight with a Hoover? These are important questions to ask, best followed by a visit downstairs where there's a little history of the fateful 1831 voyage of the HMS Beagle.

Turn left off of St. Andrew's St. onto Downing St. Ⓢ Free. ⏰ Open M-F 10am-4:45pm, Sa 11am-4pm.

THE SEDGWICK MUSEUM — MUSEUM

Downing St. ☎01223 333 456 www.sedgwickmuseum.org

Adam Sedgwick was a famous geologist who believed firmly in creationism, once writing to his pupil, Charles Darwin, that he read **Origin of Species** with "more pain than pleasure." The museum houses one of the world's leading collections of paleontology. The Whewell gallery is named after Professor Whewell, coiner of the term "scientist" and collector beautiful minerals. A collection of rocks collected by Darwin on the HMS Beagle journey is also on display.

Turn left off of St. Andrew's St. onto Downing St. Ⓢ Free. ⏰ Open M-F 10am-1pm and 2-5pm.

MUSEUM OF ARCHAEOLOGY AND ANTHROPOLOGY — MUSEUM

Downing St. ☎01223 333 516 www.maa.cam.ac.uk

The MAA is one of the eight university museums, and it features art and artifacts from various indigenous populations across the world. The archaeological displays trace the beginnings of humanity through Roman and medieval Britain, and the fantastic, towering **Haida Totem Pole** from British Columbia blows just about everything else away.

Turn left off of St. Andrew's St. onto Downing St. Ⓢ Free. ⏰ Open Tu-Sa 10:30am-4:30pm. Closed for renovations from Sept 2010-Feb 2011. Check the website when planning your visit.

CAMBRIDGE UNIVERSITY BOTANIC GARDEN GARDENS

1 Brookside ☎01223 336 265 www.botanic.cam.ac.uk

The rolling 40 acres of these lush gardens contain over 10,000 plants. Perfect for anyone with a green thumb, or those who want to bask in the sun or sit by a pond that induces poetic contemplation, the Botanic Gardens are well worth a visit. The scented garden is, unsurprisingly, fantastically fragrant.

Go down Trumpington Rd. away from town and turn right onto Bateman St. Admission £4, concessions £3.50, under 16 free. Open daily Apr-Sept 10am-6pm; Oct 10am-5pm; Nov-Feb 10am-4pm; Mar 10am-5pm.

THE ROUND CHURCH CHURCH

Bridge St. ☎01223 311 602

The simple round church, founded circa 1130 CE, is the second oldest building in Cambridge and is one of four surviving circular churches in England. Its intriguing Norman architecture is based on the Holy Sepulchre in Jerusalem.

A continuation of Sidney St. closest to the River. Admission £2. Open Tu-Sa 10am-5pm, Su 1-5pm.

KETTLE'S YARD GALLERY

Castle St. ☎01223 748 100 www.kettlesyard.co.uk

Kettle's Yard is composed of two parts: the house and gallery. The gallery rotates through innovative exhibitions while the house, which was the former home of gallery-founder and Tate Curator Jim Ede, contains early 20th-century art and sculpture.

Take Magdalene St. over the river until it becomes Castle St. at the intersection with Chesterton Ln. ***i*** *House is partially wheelchair-accessible. Free. Open Apr-Sept T-Su 1:30-4:30pm; Sept-Apr T-Su 2-4pm.*

CAMBRIDGE COUNTY AND FOLK MUSEUM MUSEUM

2-3 Castle St. ☎01223 355 159 www.folkmuseum.org.uk

Housed in the old White Horse Inn, the Cambridge County and Folk Museum provides a social history of Cambridge. Themed exhibits every few months range from Dickens-themed to '60s-themed, but generally explore Cambridge through unique lenses. Note the stunning collection of pipes, many of which are bone-white and in the suspicious shape of skulls.

Take Magdalene St. over the river until it becomes Castle St. at the intersection with Chesterton Ln. £3.50, concessions £2, children £1. Open Tu-Sa 10:30am-5pm, Su and Bank holidays 2-5pm (last admission 4:30pm). Last entry 30min. before close.

ST. BENET'S CHURCH CHURCH

Benet St. ☎01223 355 146

St. Benet's Church has been a site of worship for almost 1000 years (founded circa 1020). It's even older than the Round Church.

Turn right off of King's Parade when heading north on it from Trumpington St. Free. Open daily 7:30am-6:30pm.

GREAT ST. MARY'S CHURCH CHURCH

King's Parade ☎01223 741 716 www.gsm.cam.ac.uk

The tower of the university church of Cambridge is the highest point in town, providing views of most of the glorious colleges. Make use of the church below to pray the bells don't start clanging madly as you gingerly make your way up the 123 steps.

King's Parade. Church free. Tower £3, students £2.40. Church open M-Sa 9:30am-4pm, Su 12:30-4pm. Tower opens M 10:30am. Tower closes earlier than the rest of the church. Try to come before 3:30pm.

food

Though a student town, Cambridge has a lot of upscale dining. The cafes are nestled in its nooks and crannies and often provide delicious, cheap food and excellent coffee. Cambridge is also something of an ice cream town, so look out for the homemade ice cream and gelato that abound. Late-night food is available in the **Market Square** area.

INDIGO COFFEE HOUSE
CAFE ❷

8 St. Edward's Passage ☎01223 295 688

A student favorite, the Indigo Coffee House has two tiny floors that are sociable out of necessity. With its popular, inexpensive coffee and sandwiches, the cafe is host to a thousand eager, undergraduate debates.

Head toward Trinity on King's Parade and turn right onto St. Edward's Passage. Bagels with toppings £1.75-4. Small coffees £1.40-1.85. Large coffees £2.65. Sandwiches on ciabatta £4.80 to eat in, £3 to take away. Open M-F 10am-6pm, Sa 9am-6pm, Su 10am-5pm.

CB1
CAFE ❶

32 Mill Rd. ☎01223 576 306

Claiming to be the "oldest internet cafe in U.K.," CB1 has modern convenience with pre-inflation charm and prices. The sandwiches are delicious and unbelievably cheap, and the creaky wooden bookshelves are bursting with classic novels. Alcohol served with food.

Go southeast on Parkside until it becomes Mill Rd. Sandwiches £2.80. Toasted ciabattas £3.50. Milkshakes £2.60-2.70. Open M-Th 8:30am-8pm, F 8:30am-9pm, Sa 9:30am-8pm, Su 10:30am-8pm.

CLOWNS CAFÉ
ITALIAN CAFE ❷

54 King St. ☎01223 355 711

This cafe feels like a scene out of an old Italian movie. The effervescent staff playfully jeer at familiar customers and tell regulars they can swing by later to pay the rest of their cash-only bill, while tons of students sit around sipping coffee and tucking into Mediterranean food. There's outdoor seating on the small but pleasant roof terrace.

Turn right off Sidney St. onto Jesus Ln.; turn right onto Malcolm St. and you'll hit King St. Entrees £4-6.50. Full English breakfast £6. W 5-10pm penne carbonara with wine £8.50. Open daily 8am-11pm.

BENET'S
ICE CREAM ❸

20 King's Parade ☎01223 329 068

With the soul music blaring, the students chatting, and the homemade ice cream slowly melting in the summer heat, Benet's is a Cambridge summer staple. Their milkshakes are especially delicious.

*King's Parade. **i** Credit card min. £5. 1 scoop £2.20, 2 scoops £3.50, 3 scoops £4.40. milkshakes £3.50. Open daily 8am-9pm.*

MICHAEL HOUSE CAFÉ
CAFE ❸

Trinity St. ☎01223 309 147 www.michaelhousecafe.co.uk

Meals in the Michael House Café are truly transcendent experiences. Between the light that streams through the stained glass and the hearty mains like slow-roasted lamb shoulder with Merguez spices served with oil olive bread, the only thing keeping you from floating with happiness will be the essentially unchanged weight of your wallet.

Go up King's Parade until it becomes Trinity St. Bread £7-9. Open M-Sa 8am-5pm.

DOJO'S NOODLE BAR
NOODLES ASIAN ❷

1-2 Millers Yd. (off Mill Ln.) ☎01223 363 471

Dojo's boasts noodle dishes from all sorts of Asian cuisines, including Japanese, Chinese, Thai, and Malaysian. The quick service, large portions, and low prices make this a popular student haunt.

Turn left onto Mill Ln. off of Trumpington St. and then left onto Millers Yard. Fried entrees £6.45-6.50. Rice dishes £7.15-7.20. Soup entrees £7.20-7.50. Open M-F noon-2:30pm and 5:30-11pm, Sa-Su noon-11pm.

RAINBOW CAFÉ VEGETARIAN, VEGAN, GLUTEN-FREE ❸

9A Kings Parade ☎01223 321 551 www.rainbowcafe.co.uk

Down a small, white-walled alley and under the rainbow arch, vegetarians find their pot of gold: an affordable, exciting, and fast restaurant. Forego the veggie burgers in favor of Libyan Couscous with spinach, chick-peas, zucchini, onion, garlic, green beans and carrot *(£8.95)* or explore a wealth of vegan and gluten-free dishes. Rainbow Café is a true blessing for any vegetarian roaming the meaty wilderness of British cuisine.

King's Parade. Entrees £9-16. Open M 10am-4pm, Tu-Sa 10am-10pm, Su 10am-4pm.

CAMBRIDGE CRÊPES CRÊPES ❶

Corner of Sidney and Market St. www.cambridgecrepes.co.uk

This popular crepe stand is packed throughout the day during the summer. With delicious classic sweet crepes and more inventive fare throughout the menu, Cambridge Crêpes is a solid dining option. Note the finesse with which they make a Nutella crepe: they don't just lather on the stuff, but fling it on until it looks like a Jackson Pollock and tastes 5,000 times better. Trust us.

Sidney St. Sweet crêpes £2.50; savory crêpes £3.50-3.80. Open Tu-Su 11am-5pm.

MASSARO'S ITALIAN GELATO, SMOOTHIES ❸

85 Regent St. ☎01223 314 236

Massaro's specializes in delicious sandwiches that almost live up to the impossible hype created by their exotic ingredients lists. Between the great sandwiches, the homemade gelato, and the delicious iced drinks (iced coffee with vanilla gelato shaken, not blended), we're sold.

Regent St. Sandwiches: in-store £7-7.50, take-away £5-5.50. Iced coffee £1.20-1.50. Open M-F 8am-6pm, Sa-Su 10am-6pm.

FUDGE KITCHEN CARDIAC ARREST ❸

11 King's Parade ☎01223 350 191 www.fudgekitchen.co.uk

Though Fudge Kitchen is a chain, that doesn't change the fact that employees here wear awesome hats and make the fudge fresh in front of throngs of people between 11am and 3pm daily before distributing samples of freshly-made chocolates. Get a Student Loyalty card—after three stamps, you get free fudge. An insider **tip:** pick up the card on your first purchase (any day but Friday) and get one stamp. Then, come in on Friday, buy a slice and say "fudge Friday." This gets you two stamps and then an extra slice of fudge. You're welcome.

King's Parade. 1 slice of fudge £4.25-4.85. Open M-Sa 10am-6pm, Su 10am-5:30pm.

AUNTIE'S TEA SHOP BRITISH TEA ❷

1 St. Mary's Passage ☎01223 870 144 www.auntiesteashop.co.uk

If you're searching for an authentic British tea, look no further than the calming quietude and lace table cloths of Auntie's Tea Shop. This is probably what your aunt's living room would look like if she liked tea and wanted you to call her "auntie."

Go up King's Parade toward Trinity St. and turn right onto St. Mary's Passage. Full tea £7.65. Sandwiches £4-4.50. Panini £5.50. Open M-F 9:30am-6pm, Sa 9:30am-6:30pm, Su 10:30am-5:30pm.

COPPER KETTLE BRITISH ❷

4 King's Parade ☎01223 365 068

A cozy breakfast place with traditionally English fare. Enjoy a full English breakfast (veggie option available) while basking in the beautiful architecture of King's College.

King's Parade. Lunch £7.50-8. Full English breakfast £5.

LA MARGHERITA GELATO ❷

15 Magdalene St. ☎01223 315 232

Though also an Italian restaurant, La Margherita excels at serving the largest section of delectable gelato in Cambridge. The Amaretto is especially fantastic.

Go up Bridge St. Small £1.70, medium £2.50, large £3.80. Open M-F 10am-4pm and 6-10:30pm, Sa 10am-11pm, Su 10:30am-8pm.

CHOCOLAT CHOCOLAT GELATO, CHOCOLATE ❹

21 St. Andrew's St. ☎01223 778 982

Chocolat Chocolat serves, surprisingly, a wealth of delicious, hand-crafted, French chocolate. They also have fantastic gelato. Try the Hazelnut—it's so legitimate you may even bite into a nut now and then. They're also known for their extra-thick hot chocolate and handmade chocolate sheets. It's *delicieux delicieux!*

Go up Regent St. until it becomes St. Andrew's St. ***i*** *Cash only for ice cream.* *1 scoop £2, 2 for £3, 3 for £4.* *Open M-Tu 9am-6pm, W 9am-8pm, Th-F 9am-6pm, Sa 9am-7pm, Su 10:30am-6pm*

CB2 ITALIAN BISTRO ❹

5-7 Norfolk St. ☎01223 508 503 www.cb2bistro.com

Though a little far from the center of town, CB2 is a great place to catch the occasional concert and the more consistent coffee. Come here if CB1 (see above) just ain't enough.

Go up East Rd. away from town and turn right on Norfolk St. *Cover usually £4-8. Entrees £12-14. Pasta £7.50-8.25. Beer £3.20 per bottle.* *Open M-Th 10am-10:30pm, F-Sa 10am-11pm, Su noon-10:30pm. Breakfast served M-Sa 10am-noon. Th-Sa live music starts 8pm.*

THE CAMBRIDGE CHOP HOUSE BRITISH FOOD ❹

1 King's Parade ☎01223 359 506 www.chophouses.co.uk

For anyone who wants to prove that British cuisine can be taken seriously, the Chop House is a necessary stop. The mostly local, fresh ingredients are brought together into carefully-prepared dishes like sausage and mash *(£10.50)* and roast chicken, sugar snaps, peas and carrots, poultry sauce and mash *(£14)*.

King's Parade. *Entrees £10-19. M-F 11am-7pm 2 courses £11.* *Open M-Th 11am-10:30pm, F-Sa 11am-11pm, Su 11am-9:30pm.*

t.g.i.f.

Fridays are often turn-around days for tour groups. Take advantage of the diminished crowds to see some of the busier sights.

LA TASCA TAPAS ❹

14-16 Bridge St. ☎01223 464 630 www.latasca.co.uk

Though a chain restaurant, La Tasca manages all the warm, candlelit intimacy of any good local Spanish restaurant and truly delivers on the delicious food. The frequent deals only sweeten the entire package.

Go up Sidney until it becomes Bridge St. ***i*** *Daily until 5pm 5 tapas for 2 people £10.* *T-W 5-9pm all-you-can-eat £10. Tapas £3.75-4.35, recommended for 3-4 people.* *Open daily noon-11pm.*

ANATOLIA TURKISH ❹

30 Bridge St. ☎01223 362 372 www.anatolia.uk.com

Within the very British town of Cambridge, Anatolia is a refreshingly ethnic treat priding itself on authentic Turkish cuisine. The set lunch, available until 2:30pm, provides a three-course meal *(£11.95)*.

Go up Sidney St. until it becomes Bridge St. *Entrees £12.50-12.95.* *Open daily noon-midnight.*

DE LUCA'S ITALIAN ❺

83 Regent St. ☎01223 356 666 www.delucacucina.co.uk

A modern Italian restaurant featuring mostly locally-sourced ingredients, an exposed kitchen, and a greenhouse-esque back dining area, De Luca's is a unique and pleasant dining experience. Those looking to save money should take full advantage of the bread, olive oil, and vinegar given free of charge to the table. Come during the express lunch times or order some of the cheaper pastas to feast well for cheap.

Regent St. *2-course express lunch £10, 3-course express lunch £14. Pasta £9.95-10.95. Entrees £16.95-17.95.* *Open M-Sa noon-10pm, Su noon-8pm. Express lunch M-F noon-4pm.*

THE COW

PIZZA ❸

Corn Exchange St. ☎01223 308 871 www.barroombar.com

Housed in an alternative bar, The Cow provides cheap, delicious pizzas in the heart of the city. If Cambridge weather behaves itself, you can enjoy your slices in the outdoor seating.

Go down Downing St. and turn right on Corn Exchange. 12 in. pizzas £8-8.25. Wraps £5-5.25. Burgers £8-8.25. Open M-Tu noon-11pm, W noon-1am, Th noon-1am, F-Sa noon-1am, Su noon-11pm.

CHARLIE CHAN CHINESE RESTAURANT

CHINESE ❸

14 Regent St. ☎01223 359 336

This calm, simple Chinese restaurant is a delicious place for a highly customizable and enjoyable Chinese meal. Select from a list of rice and noodles and choose an accompanying meat or seafood dish.

Regent St. Chicken, pork, and beef dishes £5.80-7.50. Seafood £7.80. Rice and noodles £1.80-6. Fried rice £3. Boiled rice £1.80. Open daily noon-11pm.

CÔTE BRASSERIE

FRENCH ❸

21-24 Bridge St. ☎01223 311 053 111.cote-restaurants.co.uk

One of a chain of restaurants, Côte Brasserie offers up fantastic French food in a pleasant environment for reasonable prices, especially if you come in for one of their lunch or early evening deals.

Go up Sidney St. until it becomes Bridge St. 2-course lunch and early evening deal £10. Open M-F 8am-11pm, Sa 9am-11pm, Su 8am-10:30pm. Lunch and early evening deal noon-7pm.

MAI THAI

THAI ❸

Park Terr. ☎01223 367 480 www.mai-thai-restaurant.co.uk

Mai Thai is seated on the edge of a popular cricket pitch, making for a bizarre and highly enjoyable cultural mashup in a calming atmosphere of clean white walls, floors and tabletops.

Go south on St. Andrew's St. toward Regent St. and turn left onto Park Terr. Lunch entrees £6.50, dinner entrees £8. Open daily noon-3pm and 5:30-11pm.

nightlife

THE FREE PRESS

PUB

Prospect Row ☎01223 368 337 www.freepresspub.com

This small pub is bursting at the seams with character. Cell phones and music are banned, making space for idiosyncratic, pubby conversation that's missing at many modern establishments. Deriving its name from its former life as a newspaper printing shop, the Free Press is a classic watering hole that's well worth the visit for any pub culture fanatic. Get some sun (or clouds) in the beer garden.

Left off Parkside (when heading away from town center) onto Warkworth Terrace. Left onto Warkworth St., right onto Prospect Row. Pints £3. Open M-F noon-2:30pm and 6-11pm, Sa noon-11pm, Su noon-3pm and 7-10:30pm.

THE EAGLE

PUB

8 Benet St. ☎01223 505 020

On a cool February 28th in 1953, **Francis Crick** and **James Watson** burst into the Eagle and announced to the scientists who were slowly killing their Nobel-prize-winning brain cells that they had discovered the "secret to life," the **double helix.** The history of this charming bar doesn't stop there. Toward the back, messages and squad numbers remain scorched on the ceiling where RAF men burnt them with lighters on the evenings before missions during the war. Furthermore, it's only a short distance from where the atom was first split. For your purposes, the bar has history, charm, and affordable alcohol.

Head toward Trumpington on King's Parade and turn left onto Benet St. i Credit card min. £5. Pints £3. Open M-Sa 10am-11pm, Su 11am-10:30pm.

CHAMPION OF THE THAMES

PUB

68 King St. ☎01223 352 043

The Champion of the Thames is the sort of pub with comfortably low ceilings and lamps that seem to shed only the warmest, most orange light. Decorated in oars and leather chairs and boasting two rotating guest pints which trend towards excellence, the Champion of the Thames is a great place to grab a brew.

Turn right off Sidney St. onto Jesus Ln., then turn right onto Malcolm St. and you'll hit King St. Carlsberg and IPA pints £2.45. Open M-Th noon-11pm, F-Sa 11am-11pm.

THE ANCHOR

PUB

Silver St. ☎01223 353 554

Situated near the river, The Anchor has beautiful bay windows that look onto the water. Get a beer and watch self-punters slowly crash into each other and occasionally sink. The stained glass in the pub is also nice.

Off Trumpington. Pints £3-4. Open M-Th 10am-11pm, F-Sa 10am-midnight, Su 10am-11pm.

THE SALISBURY ARMS

PUB

76 Tenison Rd. ☎01223 576 363 www.thesalisburyarms.com

The Salisbury Arms is packed with eight exciting different lagers as well as unique bottled beers (banana bread beer, anyone?) High on local charm, the bar also has one of the more popular pub dogs in the area, Max, an adorable pooch with hair completely covering his eyes. Check out his page on the website where other dogs write in and he responds, elucidating the pub rules. It's a little strange and highly entertaining.

*Go down Mill Rd. away from town center and turn right onto Tenison Rd. **i** Min. credit card £10. Pints £3. Open M-Th noon-2:30pm and 5-11pm, F noon-2:30pm and 5pm-midnight, Su noon-2:30pm and 7-10:30pm.*

MILL

PUB

14 Mill Ln. ☎01223 357 026

Mill is a great old-fashioned pub with excellent river views. They're known for their specialty sausages, all delicious local concoctions like lamb and rosemary. Choose your own sausage and then your own mash *(£6.50)*.

Go up Trumpington St. toward King's Parade and turn left onto Mill Ln. Pints £3.50. Open daily noon-11pm. Kitchen open M-Sa noon-5pm.

SOUL TREE

CLUB

1-6 Corn Exchange St. ☎01223 303 755 www.soultree.co.uk

Soul Tree is the biggest club in Cambridge, with an impressive three floors of stylishly-graffitied walls. Come enjoy the loud music and dancing in the hip environment.

*Go down Downing St. and turn right onto Corn Exchange. **i** Cover cash-only. Credit card over £10. M international student night: cover £3-4, tequila shots £1, bottled beer £1.80. F before 11pm cover £4, after £6. Sa before 11pm £6, after £8. Mixed drinks £6. Bottled beer £3.50. Open M 10am-4pm, F 10am-4pm, Sa 10pm-4am.*

FEZ CLUB CAMBRIDGE

CLUB

15 Market Passage ☎01223 519 224 www.cambridgefez.com

The Fez Club hosts the largest student night in Cambridge. With a striped cloth ceiling and faux-cave walls, it's exotically decorated and hopping with activity.

*Left onto Market St. off of Sidney St., right onto Market Passage. **i** Cover cash-only. Inquire about a free membership card from inside and ask about student discounts. M is the biggest student night in Cambridge. Tu is R and B. W is International. Th is Underground. F is a basic club night. Sa is house night. Cover M before 11pm students £3, after £4; before 11pm adults £4, after £5. Tu before 11pm £3; 11pm-midnight £4, after midnight £5. W £3 before 11pm, after £4; before 11pm international students £1, after £3. Th £6-8. F before midnight £5, after £7. Open M-Sa 10pm-3am, Su during term-time 10pm-3am.*

HIDDEN ROOMS

BAR, CLUB

7a Jesus Ln. ☎01223 514 777 www.hiddenthing.com

Tucked away under Pizza Express, the Hidden Rooms, while not as secretive as the name would suggest, is a hotspot for nightlife, especially for the more soul-oriented clubbers. With a killer laser light show and state of the art sound system, Hidden Rooms provides all the essentials. The curtained booths hearken back to the days when it was host to numerous clandestine meetings (included a heavily rumored meeting between Stalin and Churchill). It's the former site of the University's Pit Club which currently resides on the top level.

Head north on Sidney St. and turn right onto Jesus Ln. ***i*** *Credit card min. £10. Th is jazz night, F is soul night, Sa is house music. Cover for jazz £2 before 10pm, after £5. Open M-Sa 3pm-12:30am. Club open Th-Sa.*

THE GRANTA

PUB

14 Newnham Terr. ☎01223 505 016

The Granta has gorgeous river views, riverside outdoor seating, and, perhaps most beautiful of all, occasional deals on burgers and pints. Punting available from the dock just next to the pub.

Left onto Silver St. off of Trumpington, left onto Queen's Rd. ***i*** *Credit card min. £5. Pints £3. Burger and pint £7. Open M-Th 11am-11pm, F-Sa 11am-midnight, Su 11am-11pm. Kitchen open M-Sa noon-10pm, Su noon-8pm.*

THE MITRE

PUB

17 Bridge St. ☎01223 358 403

Founded in 1754, The Mitre wears its history with worn grace. Decorated by flickering candles and an ornately carved fireplace, The Mitre's happy customers sprawl out on thick leather couches as well as more traditional chairs. Between the warm atmosphere and the cheap pints, the Mitre's a great place to drink.

A continuation of Sidney St. ***i*** *Credit card min. £5. Pints £2.60. Open M-W 10am-11pm, Th 10am-midnight, F-Sa 10am-1am, Su 10am-11pm.*

KING STREET RUN

PUB

86-88 King St. ☎01223 328 900

A bustling pub where the music is as it should be: loud. The juke box offers customers choices from rock, hip-hop and soul, with albums from the likes of Muddy Waters, The Smiths, and the White Stripes.

Turn right off Sidney St. onto Jesus Ln., turn right onto Malcolm St. and you'll hit King St. Pints £3.30. Open M-Th 11am-11:30pm, F-Sa 11am-12:30pm, Su noon-11:30pm. Happy hour M-F 5-7pm.

THE CRICKETERS PUB

PUB

18 Melbourne Pl. ☎01223 305 544

The Cricketers Pub is a good old-fashioned Irish pub by day, even hosting the occasional Irish Jam session. By night, it hosts live music of different varieties, including jazz. Come for the music and stay for the pool and ale.

Turn right off Park Terr. onto Parkside and then left onto Melbourne Pl. ***i*** *Credit card min. £5. Pints £3.40. Open M-Th 11am-midnight, F-Su 11am-1am. Live music M and Th.*

THE FOUNTAIN INN

BAR

12 Regent St. ☎01223 366 540 www.fountaincambridge.co.uk

Though it strongly resembles a pub from the outside, the Fountain Inn stays open later and hosts a much younger, more excited crowd than most pubs. Couches in the back and cube chairs dotted around the spacious interior provide relief for club-weary feet.

Regent St. ***i*** *Credit card charge if under £10. Pints £3.50. Open M-Th 11:30am-2am, F-Sa 11:30am-3am, Su noon-1am.*

THE PICKEREL INN

PUB

30 Magdalene St. ☎01223 355 068

The first licensed pub in Cambridge, The Pickerel Inn is a solid, old-fashioned pub with **Being John Malkovich**-esque archways that lead from one part of the bar to the next. A worn old barrel keeps the door to the beer garden open.

Go up Sidney St. until it becomes Bridge St. Follow Bridge until it becomes Magdalene St. Pints £3. Open M noon-11pm, Tu-Sa noon-midnight, Su noon-11pm.

REVOLUTION CLUB, BAR

3-8 Downing St. ☎01223 364 895 www.revolution-bars.co.uk

Even with several floors, Revolution is one of Cambridge's most crowded clubs. Be sure to catch the Monday night "Tossers" deal, where you order a round, flip a coin, and, if you called it correctly, get an extra round free! There's a screen in the back of the bar area that projects a trippy montage of pop culture images. Plus, stone-baked pizzas are served whenever the place is open. Viva la Revolution!

Left off St. Andrew's St. onto Downing St. i Cover cash-only. Sa is 21+ night. Upstairs open Sept-May Tu-Sa. Cover M £3; Tu-Th free; F students £3, adults £4, Sa £5-6; Su free. Pints £3.80. Open M-Sa 11:30am-2am, Su noon-2am.

THE ZEBRA PUB

80 Maids Causeway ☎01223 308 465 www.thezebracambridge.com

The Zebra frequently hosts live music and DJ nights in its cluttered, alternative space. The curtains are zebra print, there's a picture of a zebra, and there are a few skeletal decorations lying around, all of which contribute to the off-beat feel of this solid pub.

Follow Newmarket Rd. toward town center; it will become Maids Causeway. i Credit card min. £3. Pints £3.20. Open M-Su noon-midnight. Last call 30min. before close.

THE BUN SHOP PUB

1 King St. ☎01223 327 274

This pub is a study in incongruities. An old punting boat named "The Oak Joke" rests retired in the wooden rafters. The juke box has a most-played playlist that features Rockstar by Nickelback, Best of You by the Foo Fighters and an M.I.A. song. A fun pub with good alcohol, the contradictions only get better with ale.

Turn right off Sidney St. onto Jesus Ln., turn right onto Malcolm St. and you'll hit King St. Pints £3.20. Open M-F 11am-11pm, Sa-Su 11am-midnight.

THE COUNTY ARMS PUB

Castle St. ☎01223 361 695

This pleasant neighborhood pub is brightly lit by the sun during the day, and features high-backed benches and a courtyard out back for the outdoorsman that sometimes comes out after your third pint.

Take Magdalene St. over the river until it becomes Castle St. at the intersection with Chesterton Ln. i Credit card min. £5. Ale £3, lager £3.50. Open M-F 11am-midnight, Sa 11:30am-midnight, Su noon-6pm.

CLARENDON ARMS PUB

35-36 Clarendon St. ☎01223 353 640

Another pub with quotes about being drunk on the walls, the Clarendon Arms is a solid neighborhood watering hole with a frequently changing selection of ales and a quiz night every Thursday. You can be drunk too!

Go down Park Terr. toward Parkside and continue onto Clarendon St. i Credit card min. £5. Ale £3.10. Open M-Th noon-11:30pm, F-Sa noon-midnight, Su noon-11pm.

arts and culture

SCUDAMORE'S RIVER CAM

Quayside ☎01223 359 750 www.punting.co.uk

Punting is one of those classic Cambridge activities that can't be skipped—not unlike getting soused on Pimm's and falling in the Cam. These vaguely rectangular boats (punts) can be rented for chauffeured tours up and down the river Cam.

More adventurous (or possibly idiotic) boaters can try their hand at punting. Simply stand at the back of the boat and thrust the pole into the bottom of the river. As you remove the pole (quant, in the old lingo, though if you're whipping out *that* vocabulary, you might also want to get your French navy sweater, corn-cob pipe, and massive harpoon, just in case you see Moby), twist it to ensure it doesn't get stuck and drag you into the water as your boat moves on without you. If you're reading this while a passenger in a self-powered boat, don't tell the punter, and watch in amusement as he or she figures it out. Scudamore's on Quayside offers both types of punting experiences.

Right off Bridge St. underneath Magdalene Bridge. Self-hire £18 per hr. plus a £90 deposit taken in the form of an imprint of your credit or debit card. With student card £14 and a £90 deposit. Guided tours £15, concessions £13.50, under 12 £7.50, no deposit. Open daily May-Aug 9am-10pm, Sept-Nov 9am-8pm, Nov-Easter 9:30am-5pm, Easter-mid-May 9am-6pm.

ARTS PICTURE HOUSE

CENTRAL CAMBRIDGE

38-39 St. Andrew's St. ☎0871 902 5720 www.picturehouses.co.uk

Just above one of the raging bars of Cambridge, the Arts Picture House screens art flicks, lesser known independent films, classics, and more popular films while its downstairs partner serves alcohol to kill the brain cells the APH's films would otherwise cultivate.

A continuation of Regent St. i Off-peak M-F until 5pm; peak is all day Sa and Su and every other day after 5pm. Adults M £7; Tu-F before 5pm £7, after £8; Sa-Su £8. Students £1 off. Box office opens 30min. before first show, closes 15min. after the start of the last. Line open 9:30am-8:30pm daily for phone booking.

ADC THEATRE

CHESTERTON

Park St. ☎01223 300 085 www.adctheatre.com

Short for "Arts Dramatic Club," the ADC was a student-run theater for a long time, specializing in new writing and university productions, including frequent performances by the Cambridge Footlights, the comedy group that launched **Hugh Laurie, Steven Fry,** and **John Cleese.** Both **Ian McKellen** and **Sam Mendes** played here while at Cambridge. It still hosts university performances as well as touring shows.

Left off Jesus Ln. when you're heading away from town center. M-F adults £8, concessions £6. Sa-Su adults £10, concessions £8. Prices subject to change. Box office open Tu 12:30pm-showtime, W 3pm-showtime, Th 12:30pm-showtime, F-Sa 3pm-showtime.

CAMBRIDGE ARTS THEATRE

CHESTERTON

Peas Hill ☎01223 503 333 www.cambridgeartstheatre.com

This popular Cambridge theater puts on a mix of music, straight plays, comedies, operas, ballet, contemporary dance, and occasional shows from the Cambridge Footlights. Basically, everything. The in-house pantomime group is also very popular.

Head towards Trumpington St. on King's Parade, turn left onto Benet St. and left onto Peas Hill. Tickets £12-35. Students £2 off. Open summer M-Sa noon-6pm, winter M-Sa noon-8pm.

CAMBRIDGE CORN EXCHANGE

CHESTERTON

Wheeler St. ☎01223 357 851 www.cornex.co.uk

Probably the largest music venue in Cambridge, the Cambridge Corn Exchange presents many big name musical acts coming through Cambridge.

Head toward Trumpington St. on King's Parade, turn left onto Benet St., and go straight until Benet becomes Wheeler St. Prices vary. Occasional student discounts, depending on the show. Open M-Sa 10am-6pm.

MAY WEEK

CENTRAL CAMBRIDGE

This is a Cambridge festival that originally marked the end of exams. May Week originally took place in May, but is now in June, lasting for ten days. Seven days just weren't enough to contain the revelry.

CAMBRIDGE FOLK FESTIVAL EDGE OF TOWN

☎01223 357 851 www.cambridgefolkfestival.co.uk

Paul Simon played at the first Folk Festival in 1965. Since then, this popular mid-July festival has gone on to include the likes of **Lucinda Williams, Mavis Staples, James Taylor,** and **Elvis Costello.** The festival is popular, so book in advance!

Full festival £108, concessions £80, 1-day only £30-50.

HEART OF THE WORLD FESTIVAL VARIOUS LOCATIONS

☎01223 457 555 www.cambridge.gov.uk/public/hotw

Relatively new to the Cambridge festival scene, the Heart of the World Festival features arts from cultures around the world and happens in mid-July. It's a multimedia experience featuring live music, film screening, art exhibitions, and more from international artists.

CAMBRIDGE SHAKESPEARE FESTIVAL CENTRAL CAMBRIDGE

☎07955 218 824 www.cambridgeshakespeare.com

Running from mid-July through August, the Cambridge Shakespeare Festival features the works of David Mamet. Kidding!—it's a Shakespeare festival. Many of the plays are performed in the colleges' beautiful gardens.

Tickets £14, concessions £10.

STRAWBERRY FAIR CENTRAL CAMBRIDGE

Midsummer Common www.strawberry-fair.org.uk

Begun in 1974, the Strawberry Fair is a free-wheeling music and arts festival held on Midsummer Common in the first week of June. It is an alternative to the May Week festivities, full of entertainment, arts, and crafts. The 2010 Strawberry Fair was unfortunately canceled, but the 2011 fair is in the works. Phew.

Midsummer Common.

MIDSUMMER FAIR CENTRAL CAMBRIDGE

Midsummer Common www.cambridge-summer.co.uk

One of the oldest fairs in the country, with a history reaching back to 1211. Midsummer Fair takes place in late June and involves carnival rides. We're in.

Midsummer Common.

shopping

shopping

BOOKS FOR AMNESTY BOOKS

46 Mill Rd. ☎01223 362 496 www.amnesty.org.uk/bookshops

This second-hand charity bookshop is cluttered with an eclectic selection of donated books. The prices are low, making this an excellent place to stock up on road reads. The shelf near the counter houses rare or unique books and is worth a look.

Mill Rd. Open M-F 11:30am-6pm, Sa 9:30am-6pm.

BRIAN JORDAN MUSIC BOOKS FACSIMILES SHEET MUSIC, BOOKS ON MUSIC

10 Green St. ☎01223 322 368 www.brianjordanmusic.co.uk

An old music store, Brian Jordan specializes in elegant editions of classical sheet music as well as a fantastic selection of musical literature.

Go up King's Parade until it becomes Trinity St. and follow it until it becomes St. John's St., turn right onto Green St. Open M-Sa 9:30am-6pm.

HAUNTED BOOKSHOP BOOKS, ANTIQUITIES

9 St. Edward's Passage ☎01223 312 913 www.sarahkeybooks.co.uk

Legend has it that a woman in white smelling of violets paces the stairway of the Haunted Bookshop. Fact has it that the bookshop contains a massive collection of age-old, elegant editions of a wide variety of literature and children's books. Well worth a look for any bibliophile.

Go up King's Parade toward Trinity St. and turn right onto St. Edward's Passage. Open M-Sa 10am-5pm.

ONE WORLD IS ENOUGH CLOTHING

31 Bridge St. ☎01223 361 102 www.one-world-is-enough.net

Probably the only store in the world to simultaneously promote fair trade while directly contradicting James Bond, One World is Enough ships in clothes from fair trade organizations in India, Nepal, Indonesia, and Thailand. The owner personally checks the establishments to make sure all producers of the goods are paid properly. Many of the items, such as silk saris, are handmade or totally unique.

A continuation of Sidney St. Open M-Sa 10:30am-6pm, Su 11am-5:30pm.

ARK VINTAGE CLOTHING

2 St. Mary's Passage ☎01223 363 372 www.arkcambridge.co.uk

There's always old-fashioned, prohibition-style jazz on an Ark, right? Hip retro and vintage clothes, home and garden items, and everything from old school icing pens to funny post cards and comfortable wool travel blankets grace the shelves here.

Go up King's Parade toward Trinity College, turn right onto St. Mary's Passage. Open M-Sa 9:30am-5:30pm, Su 11am-5pm.

TINDALL'S ART AND GRAPHICS ART SUPPLIES

15-21 King St. ☎01223 568 495 www.tindalls.co.uk

Tindall's has a comprehensive collection of notebooks and all things artistic. Come and stock up for the moment when the River Cam strikes inspiration in your nomadic, artistic heart.

Turn right off Sidney St. onto Jesus Ln., turn right onto Malcolm St. and you'll hit King St. Open M-Sa 9am-5:30pm.

KEN STEVENS AND MILLERS MUSIC CENTRE INSTRUMENTS

12 Sussex St. ☎01223 367 758 www.kenstevens.co.uk

A haven for any musician, Ken Stevens and Millers Music Centre (formerly two separate stores, now one fantastic joint) offer a wide selection of excellent instruments and gear that could readily serve any wandering minstrel.

Go up Sidney St. and turn right onto Sussex St. Open M-Sa 9:30am-5:30pm.

TALKING T'S T-SHIRTS

37 Bridge St. ☎01223 302 411 www.t-shirts.co.uk

If you're looking for a shirt that will simultaneously call everyone's attention to your torso and pick a fight with them, this is your shop. With T-shirts running the gamut from sassy to clever to official (Cambridge University shirts), Talking T's is an excellent place to shop for casualwear.

A continuation of Sidney St. Open M-Sa 9:30am-5:30pm, Su 10:30am-5:30pm.

THE MAGIC JOKE SHOP NOVELTY MAGIC

29 Bridge St. ☎01223 353 003 www.jokeshop.co.uk

The Magic Joke Shop is essentially a depository for things that couldn't really fit in any other store. Packed with novelty items like jumping putty, joke biscuits and golf-ball stickers that make it look like you shattered your window, The Magic Joke Shop provides loads of time-wasting items for the discerning customer.

A continuation of Sidney St. Open M-Sa 9am-5:30pm, Su 11am-5pm.

MOOK VINTGE CLOTHES

2a King St. ☎01223 316 001 www.mookvintage.com

Your one-stop, everything shop for vintage clothes and accessories. Come and check out the shoes, handbags, and sunglasses as well as the selection of track jackets.

Turn right off Sidney St. onto Jesus Ln., turn right on Malcolm St. and you'll hit King St. Open M-Sa 10:30am-6pm, Su 11am-4pm.

MARKET SQUARE MARKET OPEN-AIR MARKET

Market Hill

Keeping Market Sq. honest, the Market Square Market is open every day with different stands, serving a wide variety of tooth-melting sweets, instruments, shirts, food, and most other things you can imagine.

Turn right onto St. Mary's St. off of King's Parade. Open M-Su 9am-4pm.

SPICE GATE MARKET

14 Mill Rd. ☎01223 513 097

Spice Gate is a delectable and excellent Middle Eastern Market. Its products include date-filled cookies and juices hailing from the Mid-East.

Mill Rd.

essentials

PRACTICALITIES

- **TOURIST OFFICE: Tourist Information Centre** at Peas Hill sells National Express tickets, discounted punting tickets, sightseeing bus tickets and accommodations bookings. Disabled visitors to Cambridge can get an access guide for the city from the TIC. *(☎0871 226 8006 www.visitcambridge.org Open M-Sa 10am-5pm, Su 11am-3pm.)*
- **TOURS:** Several walking tours leave from the Tourist Information Centre. The Guided Tour features King's College and Queens' College. *(£11, concessions £9.50, children £6. Leaves M-Sa 11am and 1pm, Su and Bank Holidays 1pm.)* **City-Sightseeing** runs a bus with commentary available in nine languages *(Leaves from Silver St. ☎01223 423 578 www.city-sightseeing.com £13, concessions £9, children £7, family £32. Tours 1hr. 20min., in summer leave every 20min., in winter leave every 40min.)*

- **BUDGET TRAVEL OFFICE: STA Travel.** *(38 Sidney St. ☎0871 702 9809 www.statravel.co.uk Open M-Th 10am-7pm, F-Sa 10am-6pm, Su 11am-5pm.)*
- **BANKS: Banks** and **ATMs** line St. Andrew's St.
- **BIKE RENTAL: City Cycle Hire.** *(61 Newnham Road. ☎01223 365 629 www.citycyclehire.com £6 per 4 hr., £9 per 8hr., £10 per 24hr., £15 per 2-3 days, £20 per 4-7 days, £30 per 2 weeks, £65 per 9 weeks. Open Easter-Oct M-F 9am-5:30pm, Sa 9am-5pm; winter M-F 9am-5:30pm.)*
- **INTERNET ACCESS: Jaffa Net Cafe.** *(22 Mill Rd. ☎01223 308 380* £1 per hr. *Open daily noon-midnight.)*
- **POST OFFICE: Bureau de Change.** *(9-11 St. Andrew's St. Open M 9am-5:30pm, Tu 9:30am-5:30pm, W-Sa 9am-5:30pm.)*
- **POST CODE:** CB2 3AA.

EMERGENCY!

- **POLICE: Parkside Police Station** on Parkside *(☎0345 456 4564).*
- **HOSPITAL: Addenbrookes Hospital.** *(Hills Rd. by the intersection of Hills Rd. and Long Rd. ☎01223 245 151.)*

GETTING THERE

By Train

Trains depart from **Station Road** *(National Rail Enquiries ☎0845 7484 950 Ticket office open M-Sa 5:10am-11pm, Su 7am-10:55pm.)* Nonstop trains to **London King's Cross** *(£19.10. 48min., 2 per hr.)* and to **Ely** *(£3.70. 20min., 4 per hr.)*

By Bus

Bus station is on Drummer St. *(Ticket office open M-Sa 9am-5:30pm.)* Airport Shuttles run from Parkside. Trains to **London Victoria** *(£14.40. 2hr., every hr.)*; to **Gatwick** *(£32. 4hr., every 2hr.)*; to **Heathrow** *(£29.70. 3hr., every hr.)*; to **Stansted** *(£13. 50min., every hr.)*; to **Oxford** *(Stagecoach Express £11. 3hr., every 30min.)*

GETTING AROUND

By Bus

Buses run from **Stagecoach** *(☎01223 423 578).* **CitiBus** runs from stops throughout town, including some on **St. Andrew's Street, Emmanuel Street,** and the train station. **Dayrider Tickets** *(Unlimited travel for 1 day. £3.40)* can be purchased on the bus, but for longer stays, you can buy a **Megarider** ticket. *(Unlimited travel for 7 days. £11.50.)*

By Taxi

For a taxi, call **Cabco.** *(☎01223 525 555 Open daily 24hr.)*

EDINBURGH

It's a city that moves. Visitors are constantly streaming through Scotland's capital, and the population of the city swells by roughly one million during the month of August. Festival season, or **"Fest"** as it's known to locals, is a time of both great joy and chagrin, as free entertainment reigns supreme but walking down the street takes nearly half an hour. Even when Edinburgh isn't party central, its residents aren't afraid to sing its praises. The city's full of locals with an intense pride for both Scotland and Edinburgh, and you might have to coax information out of them over a **"pint and a blether"** (Scottish-speak for drink and a chat), as Edinburghers (yes, that's really what they're called) can be skeptical of tourists. A majestic city, it's one of those places where you watch the sun go down from the top of a hill and wonder just how you managed to wander into such a spectacular place. However you did it, keep going: Edinburgh was made for it.

greatest hits

- **RIDES AND LIQUOR.** Take a carnival ride in a keg at the Scotch Whisky Experience (p. 160).
- **FAR-OUT PASTRY.** Try the delectable macaroons at Madeleine (p. 168), the most futuristic cafe in town.
- **THE GORY STORY.** Feel a little bit like Dr. Frankenstein with a pit-stop at The Surgeon's Hall Museum (p. 179).
- **ONLY A QUID.** Enjoy the student scene and £1 drinks on Octopussy Club night at HMV Picture House (p. 180).

student life

Edinburgh may not have Glasgow's club scene, but that doesn't mean it isn't Scotland's capital for student life. **The University of Edinburgh** is home to over 24,000 students who, live, study, and drink just south of the **Royal Mile.** Yet the forward-thinking city also has some of Britain's most talented artists, so it's no wonder Edinburgh hosts the world's largest arts festival. Every August, mobs of students from around the globe arrive for **The Fringe,** where you too can hear great music, watch great theater and make some new best friends. Why settle for a pub?

orientation

Edinburgh's most famous neighborhoods **(Old Town, New Town)** are easily divisible, as they are separated by a large gully which houses **Waverley Station** and **Princes's Street Gardens.** This ravine is bisected by three bridges: **Waverley Bridge, North Bridge,** and **The Mound.** Stockbridge is to the north of **New Town** (walk as if you were heading to Leith and the sea) and **Haymarket** and **Dalry** are in the area west of New Town. **The Meadows, Tolcross,** and the **West End** are all over the hill from Old Town, off toward the south end of town.

OLD TOWN

Old Town is where it's at. It's heralded by the giant castle that sits atop the rocky crags that divide Old Town from New Town. Its winding streets are surrounded by four- and five-story Georgian buildings that house everything from storytelling centers to party-driven hostels. It's where you'll take the most pictures, it's where you'll drink, sleep, shop, and eat. You'll be hard pressed to find another neighborhood some days—there's just so much to do. However, everyone else knows this too, so make sure to hit up Old Town when you're feeling particularly ready for a tourist onslaught.

NEW TOWN

New Town isn't actually that new. It would have been new when it was designed by James Craig in the 1760s, but by this point it's down pat. Following a simple, grid-like pattern, it's bordered by **Queen Street** to the north and **Prince Street** to the south. **George Street,** a central thoroughfare, runs through the middle. The various intersecting thoroughfares have branches of their own, usually smaller streets with housing or shops. **Rose Street,** which houses the majority of the pubs in New Town, is one of these.

STOCKBRIDGE

Put on your best polo, because we're heading to the Edinburgh Country Club—Stockbridge. Full of the top tier of upper crust of society, it's a bit like a separate city, with its own restaurants, drinking, and way of life. Forgot your monocle? No worries: find one among the posh leftovers sold in the Stockbridge charity shops. As we always say, if you can't beat 'em, join 'em; if you can't join 'em, wear their cast-offs. When you're not scrounging through the thrift stores, you can meander through the streets, pop into a cafe, stop off at a nice restaurant, or just wander on down through the **Water of Leith.**

HAYMARKET AND DALRY

Haymarket and Dalry are not that pretty, at least compared to the rest of Edinburgh. This may be why they are home to some of the city's cheaper housing. A few good food stops are to be found, and those looking for a night out in this area will find cheap drinks. Be warned, there are some Old Guard pubs here that aren't the friendliest.

TOLLCROSS AND WEST END

Owned and dominated by the huge expanse of green that is the meadows, the West End is nevertheless right in the middle of the city. You'll be seeing far fewer tourists out this way, except during festival time, when it's impossible to open your eyes without seeing one. **Lothian Road** is home to several great pubs, and continuing up to **Home Street** will take you to the local cinema, **The Cameo.** The **University of Edinburgh** is isolated enough from the city that none of the pubs or bars in the area are student-dominated, but you'll find several full of a distinctly younger crowd. If you fancy it, take a putter and a chipping iron and head out to the **Bruntsfield Links,** where you can play on a 30+ chipping course. Get out to Tolcross and the West End. You'll feel better with fewer tourists around, and the locals will be more kindly disposed to you for the very same reason.

accommodations

Possibly more so than any other city in the UK, Edinburgh's accommodations options are defined by its neighborhoods. In New Town, you're looking at guesthouses and lodges on the upper end of the price range. Stockbridge has virtually no accommodations to speak of. Old Town is home to the majority of the hostels in town, all of which are right in the center of the action and, for those who wish to keep their distance from the Grassmarket, hostels and hotels fill Haymarket and Dalry, and Tolcross and the West End.

OLD TOWN

ART ROCH HOSTEL — HOSTEL ❶

2 Westport, Grassmarket ☎0131 228 9981 www.artrochhostel.com

The new kid on the block, the Art Roch is already showing everybody else how it's done. With cool, airy dorms featuring sturdy wooden bunks (instead of squeaking metal), this will be a comfortable place to hit the sack. However, you'll be *really* comfortable when you're hanging out, as the lounge and kitchen area is the size of a small airport and fits a kitchen, ping-pong table, TV, chairs and couches—even a teepee—all with plenty of room to spare.

i Wi-Fi available. $ High-season dorms £12, £80 per week. Low-season dorms £9 per night. Singles £20. Reception 24hr.

SMART CITY HOSTELS — HOSTEL ❸

50 Blackfriars St. ☎0131 524 1989 www.smartcityhostels.com

The Smart City Hostel is clean, white, and efficient. Unfortunately, so is a hospital. Catering to families and those looking to "stay at a hostel" without any of the backpackers, the SCH is large, modern and spotless, with an elevator up to every floor and a massive cafe and bar on the ground floor, often with kids chasing each other round the pool table.

Turn onto Blackfriars St. from High St. i Breakfast £4.50. Kitchen available. $ 10-to 12-bed dorm £17-30; 4-bed dorm £21-32. Add £2 on weekends. Reception 24hr.

BUDGET BACKPACKERS — HOSTEL ❷

37-39 Cowgate St. ☎0131 226 6351 www.budgetbackpackers.com

A surf-green hostel just a few drunken steps from the pub-filled Grassmarket, Budget Backpackers is a vibrant place that's bound to be packed during the summer with young travelers searching for the next party. If you are staying in (we're not going to say you'll be the only one, but...) there's a DVD and movie rental at the lobby.

i Breakfast £2. Wi-Fi £1 per week. Internet £1 per 30min. Book well ahead of Jul-Aug for summer reservations. $ High-season dorms £20-40; low-season dorms £10-20. Reception 24hr.

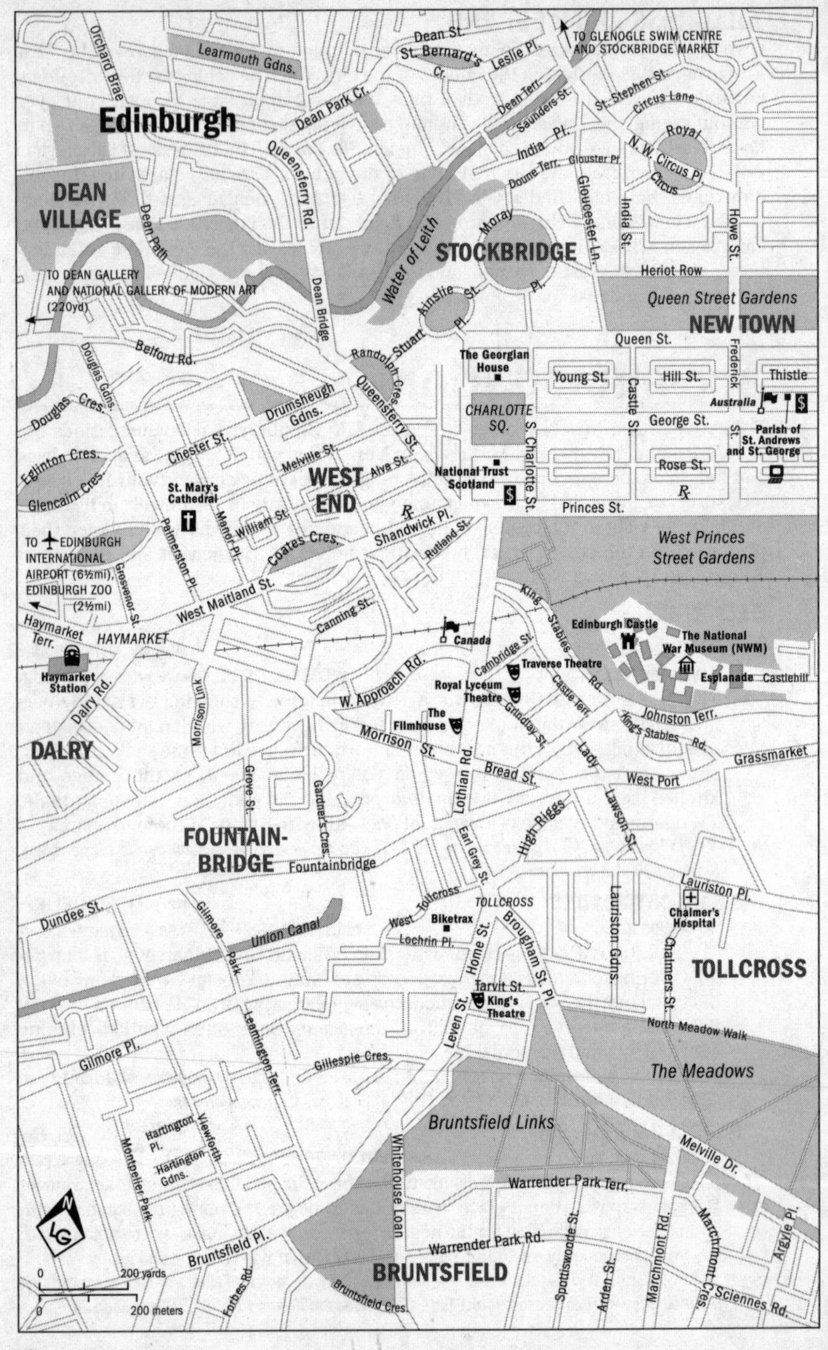
Edinburgh
DEAN VILLAGE
STOCKBRIDGE
NEW TOWN
WEST END
DALRY
FOUNTAIN-BRIDGE
TOLLCROSS
BRUNTSFIELD
TO GLENOGLE SWIM CENTRE AND STOCKBRIDGE MARKET
TO DEAN GALLERY AND NATIONAL GALLERY OF MODERN ART (220yd)
TO EDINBURGH INTERNATIONAL AIRPORT (6½mi), EDINBURGH ZOO (2½mi)
The Georgian House
CHARLOTTE SQ.
National Trust Scotland
Australia
Parish of St. Andrews and St. George
Thistle
St. Mary's Cathedral
Canada
Haymarket Station
HAYMARKET
Edinburgh Castle
The National War Museum (NWM)
Esplanade
Traverse Theatre
Royal Lyceum Theatre
The Filmhouse
Biketrax
TOLLCROSS
King's Theatre
Chalmer's Hospital
Queen Street Gardens
West Princes Street Gardens
The Meadows
Bruntsfield Links
Union Canal
Water of Leith
200 yards
200 meters

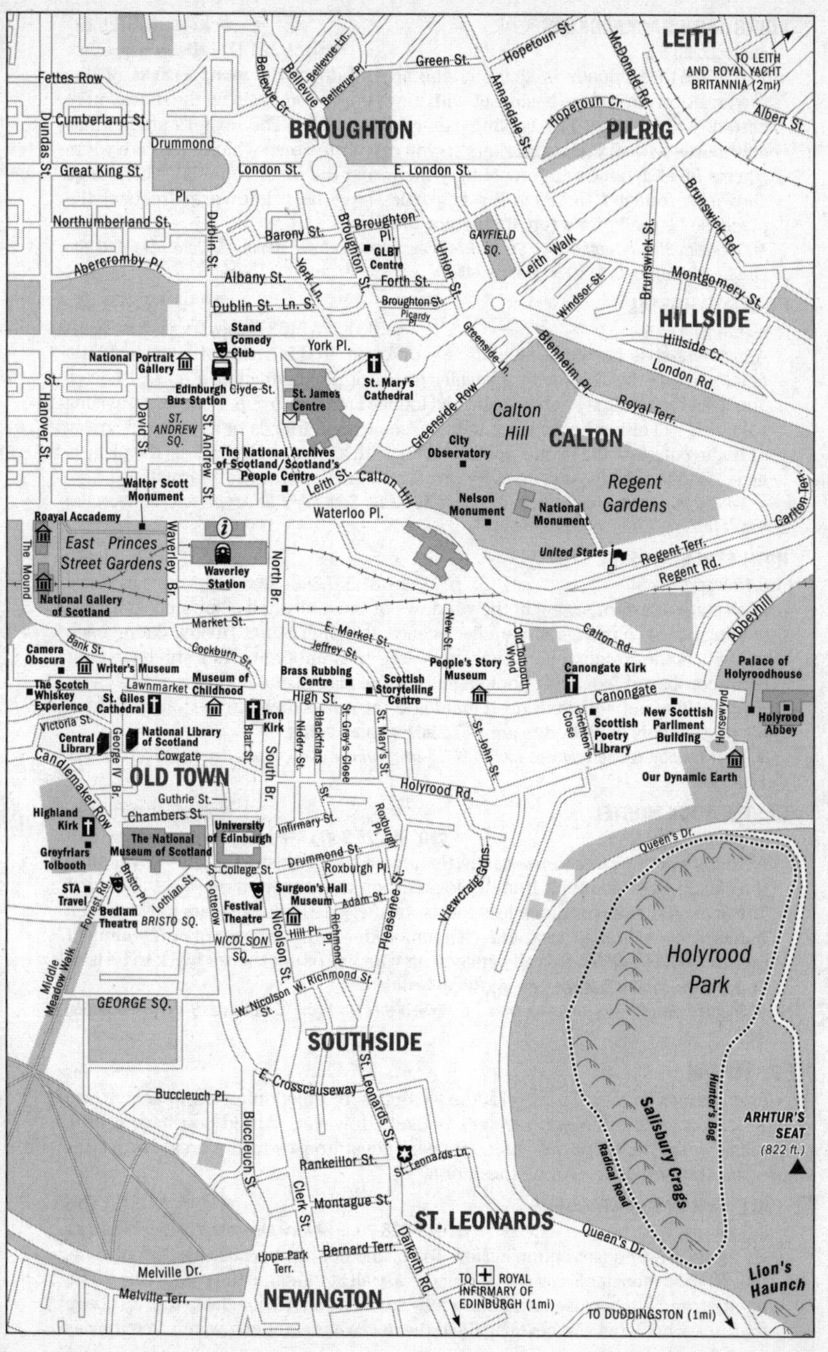
LEITH
TO LEITH AND ROYAL YACHT BRITANNIA (2mi)
BROUGHTON
PILRIG
HILLSIDE
CALTON
OLD TOWN
SOUTHSIDE
ST. LEONARDS
NEWINGTON
Fettes Row
Cumberland St.
Dundas St.
Drummond Pl.
Great King St.
London St.
E. London St.
Northumberland St.
Abercromby Pl.
Dublin St.
Barony St.
Broughton Pl.
GLBT Centre
Albany St.
York Ln.
Forth St.
Broughton St.
Dublin St. Ln. S.
Broughton St.
Picardy Pl.
Bellevue Pl.
Bellevue Ln.
Bellevue
Bellevue Cr.
Green St.
Hopetoun St.
McDonald Rd.
Annandale St.
Hopetoun Cr.
Albert St.
Union St.
GAYFIELD SQ.
Leith Walk
Brunswick St.
Brunswick Rd.
Montgomery St.
Windsor St.
Hillside Cr.
London Rd.
Royal Terr.
Blenheim Pl.
Greenside Ln.
Greenside Row
Stand Comedy Club
York Pl.
St. Mary's Cathedral
National Portrait Gallery
Edinburgh Bus Station
Clyde St.
St. James Centre
Hanover St.
David St.
ST. ANDREW SQ.
St. Andrew St.
The National Archives of Scotland/Scotland's People Centre
Calton Hill
City Observatory
Leith St.
Calton Hill
Regent Gardens
Walter Scott Monument
Nelson Monument
National Monument
Carlton Terr.
Roayal Academy
Waterloo Pl.
East Princes Street Gardens
The Mound
Waverley Br.
Waverley Station
North Br.
United States
Regent Terr.
Regent Rd.
National Gallery of Scotland
Market St.
E. Market St.
New St.
Old Tolbooth Wynd
Calton Rd.
Abbeyhill
Camera Obscura
Bank St.
Writer's Museum
Cockburn St.
Jeffrey St.
Brass Rubbing Centre
People's Story Museum
Canongate Kirk
Palace of Holyroodhouse
The Scotch Whiskey Experience
Lawnmarket
Museum of Childhood
Scottish Storytelling Centre
High St.
Canongate
St. Giles Cathedral
Tron Kirk
Horse Wynd
Holyrood Abbey
Victoria St.
Crichton's Close
New Scottish Parliment Building
Central Library
National Library of Scotland
George IV Br.
Blair St.
South Br.
Niddry St.
Blackfriars
St. Gray's Close
St. Mary's St.
St. John St.
Scottish Poetry Library
Our Dynamic Earth
Cowgate
Candlemaker Row
Guthrie St.
Holyrood Rd.
Chambers St.
Highland Kirk
University of Edinburgh
Infirmary St.
Roxburgh Pl.
Queen's Dr.
The National Museum of Scotland
Greyfriars Tolbooth
Drummond St.
S. College St.
Roxburgh Pl.
STA Travel
Forrest Rd.
Bristo Pl.
Lothian St.
Potterow
Festival Theatre
Surgeon's Hall Museum
Adam St.
Pleasance St.
Viewcraig Gdns.
Bedlam Theatre
BRISTO SQ.
Hill Pl.
Richmond Pl.
NICOLSON SQ.
Nicolson St.
Holyrood Park
Middle Meadow Walk
W. Nicolson St.
W. Richmond St.
GEORGE SQ.
E. Crosscauseway
St. Leonards St.
Buccleuch Pl.
Buccleuch St.
Hunter's Bog
Salisbury Crags
Radical Road
ARHTUR'S SEAT (822 ft.)
Rankeillor St.
St. Leonards Ln.
Clerk St.
Montague St.
Queen's Dr.
Hope Park Terr.
Bernard Terr.
Dalkeith Rd.
Melville Dr.
Melville Terr.
TO ROYAL INFIRMARY OF EDINBURGH (1mi)
Lion's Haunch
TO DUDDINGSTON (1mi)

EDINBURGH BACKPACKERS
HOSTEL ❶

65 Cockburn St. ☎0131 220 1717 www.hoppo.com

You'll get those quads in shape hiking up and down the many **stairs** of this tower. Dorms in EB are basic, but with new people coming in all the time, you're certainly not going to be lacking excursion partners. The hostel's kitchen has cupboards with dry erase markers so you can write down which foods are yours (threat level depends on how hungry the bro in the other room is). The lounge shows *Braveheart* (a *lot*) and stag parties have been known to frequent the place, so be ready for a fun, if raucous, time.

Cockburn St. winds off of High St. i Wi-Fi free. Internet £1 per 30min. Ⓢ Dorms M-F £10, Sa-Su £13-16; Singles £25. Reception 24hr.

COWGATE HOSTEL
HOSTEL ❷

96 Cowgate ☎0131 226 2153 www.cowgatehostel.com

Apartment-style hosteling—now *this* is different. In this series of individual little flats, you'll be bunking with a smaller group of people than at a normal hostel. You'll share the same kitchen, bath, and lounge area as a group. For those traveling solo, this will either be a chance to make some good friends or a really quick way of finding out that the people you're staying with are jerks. Regardless, the place is nice. Head to the blue and orange lobby for internet and tourist information.

i Wi-Fi free. Coffee and tea free. Ⓢ Dorms Aug £22, Sept-July £10 per person. Reception 8am-11pm.

HIGH STREET HOSTEL
HOSTEL ❷

8-18 Blackfriars St. ☎0131 557 3984 www.highstreethostel.com

With suits of armor sitting in the windows of the lobby and a spiraling staircase leading down to murals of paradise scenes, the High Street Hostel, dating back to 1985, is the "original backpackers hostel" of Edinburgh. They still have their character-based feel, with pool games on Tuesday nights and burger nights on Friday. Hang out with your hostel-mates at the tables down in the lounge, where it's pretty likely somebody's got a **drinking game** going.

i Wi-Fi in lobby. Laundry service £2.50. Ⓢ 15-bed dorms £14-15; 4-bed dorms £15-18; doubles £45-55.

CASTLE ROCK HOSTEL
HOSTEL ❷

15 Johnston Terr. ☎0131 225 9666 www.castlerockedinburgh.com

Actually much closer to the castle than most of the hostels on the Royal Mile, the Castle Rock benefits from its location on the smaller side street Johnston Terrace—it makes for much less tourist traffic. Castle Rock offers nice wooden bunks, a sweet lounge area, and—it's rumored—the option to work off your next night's stay. However, this all depends on whether or not there's work to be had. Make sure to ask before you show up broke.

South of West Princes Street Gardens. i Movie night daily 8pm. Ⓢ Dorms £13-15. Reception 24hr.

NEW TOWN

Accommodations in New Town, with the exception of Caledonian Backpackers, are usually far out of the budget traveler's pocket. However, should you have a little extra cash to spend, there are some fantastic guest houses in the area. No matter where you stay, you'll be near all the action.

CALEDONIAN BACKPACKERS
HOSTEL ❶

3 Queensferry St. ☎0131 226 2939 www.caledonianbackpackers.com

By far the best budget option in New Town, and not just because it's the only one, this 250-bed monster is comfortable and crazy all at the same time. With free Wi-Fi, internet, and kitchen use, as well as a fully stocked bar, it's not cheap fun, it's cheap *and* fun. Check out the beanbag-filled theater, where you can watch free movies anytime on a projector screen. The murals on the walls depict everything from rock stars to penguins, and the hostel has about as wide a range of people stop in.

West End of the city center, across from the Caledonian Hotel. Breakfast 6am-noon. Laundry: wash £1, dry £1. 18+ only. Female-only dorms available. Wi-Fi, Internet, and kitchen free. Dorms £13-20. Reception 24hr.

BALLANTRAE HOTEL — HOTEL ❹

8 York Pl. ☎0131 478 4748

The first thing to greet anyone walking in the door of this hotel is the winding staircase, complete with decorated wooden handrails. The rooms, all with high Victorian ceilings, are very nicely furnished. Big beds are a major plus. Some of the rooms even have fireplaces, though using them will get you in trouble.

Walk west along Queen St., which becomes York Pl. Full breakfast included. Singles £50-75; doubles £70-140; triples £80-160. Prices vary with season.

FREDERICK HOUSE HOTEL — HOTEL ❹

42 Frederick St. ☎0131 226 1999 www.townhousehotels.co.uk

Classy Frederick House has the furniture and the long hallway to prove its status. With nicely furnished rooms (and some really oddly-shaped bathrooms), it's a good choice if you can catch it when it's cheap: prices seem designed to prove just how much they can shift over the course of a year.

Wi-Fi available. Singles £30-160; doubles £50-180. Reception 24hr.

OSBOURNE HOTEL — HOTEL ❹

51-59 York Pl. ☎0131 556 5577 ww.osbournehotel.co.uk

An option that's feasible in the off-season, the Osbourne Hotel offers bare but comfortable rooms in an older building in Edinburgh's New Town. Occasionally you'll find a room that gets great natural light.

Walk west along Queen St., which becomes York Pl. Aug singles £65; doubles £80; triples £90; quads £100. Oct-Mar singles £35; doubles £50; triples £66; quads £78. Apr-Sept singles £50; doubles £65; triples £78; quads £90.

QUEEN'S GUESTHOUSE — GUESTHOUSE ❹

45 Queen St. ☎0131 226 2000 www.queensgh.com

This place is wicked expensive, but if you win the lotto and can afford it for a night, it's amazing. It's the only lodging in town the offers the five-star hotel atmosphere and comforts along with the amazingly friendly hospitality of a guesthouse. The managers will make sure that you're comfortable here, which isn't hard considering that your room (no matter which one it is) is gorgeous.

Along the south edge of Queen Street Gardens. Full breakfast included. Singles £60-120; doubles £170-300; family suite £145-199; executive suit £190-275.

ELDER YORK GUESTHOUSE — GUESTHOUSE ❸

38 Elder St. ☎0131 556 1926 www.elderyork.co.uk

Providing relatively constant prices throughout the year, the Elder York Guesthouse benefits from three distinct things: a prime location a few yards away from the bus station, a beautiful and shining breakfast area, and large, airy rooms. And then there's the wonderful hospitality of new owners Harry and his wife, who are doing a fine job of running the place.

Right off of York Pl. and St. James Pl. Cancellations in Jul-Aug should give 1 week notice. Aug £60 per person. Sept-Jul £40 per person.

HAYMARKET AND DALRY

THE HOSTEL — HOSTEL ❷

3 Clifton Terr. ☎0131 313 1031 www.edinburghcitycentrehostels.co.uk

Haymarket and Dalry's hostel, "The Hostel" (this is going to get confusing, isn't it?) is spotlessly clean. Having just undergone a massive renovation and refurbishment, its carefully color-coordinated lounge space has pool tables and a large flatscreen TV as well as free tea and coffee. Bear in mind, though, that The Hostel is intent on maintaining its stellar appearance, as evidenced by the long list of rules on the wall.

Right in Haymarket. i Continental breakfast £1. Towel rental £1, £5 deposit. $ 16-bed dorms £7-12; 5-bed dorms £12-14; 3-bed dorms £14-20. Reception 24hr. Lounge open 8am-11pm.

PIRIES HOTEL — HOTEL ❹

4-8 Coates Grdn. ☎0131 337 1108 www.pirieshotel.com

A nice, Georgian hotel located among a string of other similar ones, Piries has a small bar in the lobby and those paper rings that hold the pillows in place. It's the little things that count, right?

Right in Haymarket. i Wi-Fi available for a fee. $ Doubles in summer £80, in winter £60.

TOLLCROSS AND WEST END

ARGYLE BACKPACKERS — HOSTEL ❷

14 Argyle Pl. ☎0131 667 9991 www.argyle-backpackers.co.uk

Argyle is a great place for those who like to keep the party time outside and the cool, lounging-around time in the hostel. A beautiful red kitchen connects to a covered skylight area that in turn links to an outdoor seating area. The lounge space has two computers for guest use as well as a big-screen TV and wood-burning fireplace.

i In Aug, prices generally increase £5. In Aug, min. stay 3 days. $ M-F 10-bed dorms £13.50; 6-bed dorm £15; 4-bed dorms £16.50; doubles £48. Weekend 10-bed dorms £15.50; 6-bed dorms £17; 4-bed dorms £18.50; doubles £52. Reception 9am-10pm; call ahead to arrange a late check-in.

CRUACHAN GUESTHOUSE — GUESTHOUSE ❹

53 Gilmore Pl. ☎0131 229 6219 www.cruachanguesthouse.co.uk

Another nice guesthouse on Gilmore Place, the Cruachan has high-ceilinged, comfortable rooms. It may not be decorated with an eye for contemporary style, but the owner is nice. Plus, that floral pattern on your bed won't show up when you turn out the light.

i Breakfast included. $ Rooms £60-80.

KINGSVIEW GUESTHOUSE — GUESTHOUSE ❸

28 Gilmore Pl. ☎0131 229 8004 www.kingsviewguesthouse.com

You can look for hummingbirds buzzing about the entryway garden as you eat breakfast in the front room of this little Victorian guesthouse. The rooms are quaint but comfortable, with tiny desktop flatscreens.

i Dog-friendly. $ Low-season £27.50; high-season £40.

sights

OLD TOWN

THE SCOTCH WHISKY EXPERIENCE — TOUR

354 Castlehill, the Royal Mile ☎0131 220 0441 www.scotchwhiskyexperience.co.uk

Beginning with a carnival ride in giant barrels (it's a good thing that this happens before the drinking), you'll be shown the process of distilling single-malt whiskey by a ghostly apparition with a serious penchant for the elixir. Then after a short look at the barrel-making process, you'll be ushered into the tasting room, where an informed guide will offer you smells representative of each whiskey-making region in Scotland. At the end of that segment of the tour, you'll select the whiskey you want to taste and head to the display room, which houses the Diageo Claive Vidiz Collection of whiskeys, almost 3500 of them. There you'll learn how to properly enjoy your whiskey and have the opportunity to purchase a bottle from the store, should you find one that you really enjoy. Good luck walking home!

By the bottom of West Princes St. Gardens. Silver tour (basic): £11.50, students and seniors £20, children £6, family £27. Gold tour (advanced): £20, student and senior £17.45. The Collection Tour: £20. Open daily 10am-6:30pm. Last tour daily 5pm.

NATIONAL LIBRARY OF SCOTLAND — LIBRARY

57 George IV Bridge ☎0131 623 3700 www.nls.uk

Yes, it's a working research library and you can get a borrower's card (free with valid ID), but who wants to do that on holiday? Instead, make a stop to check out the exhibit space in the library's large entryway. Each focusing on a different author or theme, the different displays are put up in a large, attractive space that makes it a bit like a museum instead of a library.

i There's a cafe open in the library as well. Open M-F 9:30am-8:30pm, Sa 9:30am-1pm, Su (cafe only) 2-5pm.

BRASS RUBBING CENTRE — ARTS CENTER

Trinity Apse, Chalmers Close, 42 High St. ☎0131 556 4364

Located in what seems like a one-room cathedral complete with sky-high echoey ceilings and stone gargoyles, is this oddball activity. Pick out a brass plate of Pictish designs *(prices vary according to size)* and the center will supply you with all the materials you need to do a rubbing and create your own take-home artwork. Work on anything from a plate as big as your hand *(£1)* to a life-size Pictish knight *(£20)*.

Cash only. Open M-Sa 10am-noon and 1-5pm. Last rubbings at 4:15pm. During festival open Su noon-5pm.

ST. GILES CATHEDRAL — CATHEDRAL

St. Giles Cathedral, High St. ☎0131 225 9442

The stonework on the outside is finer than your granny's lace doily, and the inside's just as beautiful. With glowing stained-glass windows that cast enormous rainbows onto the walls in the late morning and a massive wooden organ near the center of the building, St. Giles is so photo-worthy that you'll find yourself looking like the ultimate tourist and trying to get a shot of everything. However, you won't be the only one, and the constant flow of tourist traffic means that St. Giles is hard-pressed for that calming atmosphere associated with cathedrals. Still, get someone to take your picture in front of a jewel-like window and you'll be more colorful than Captain Planet at Chuck E. Cheese's.

i Tours available, inquire inside. Free. Open May-Sept M-F 9am-7pm, Sa 9am-5pm, Su 1-5pm; Oct-Apr M-Sa 9am-5pm, Su 1-5pm and for services.

SCOTTISH STORYTELLING CENTRE — CULTURAL EXPERIENCE

43-45 High St. ☎0131 556 9579 www.scottishstorytellingcentre.co.uk

Possibly one of a kind, the Scottish Storytelling Centre is just that: a place where people tell tall tales. Featuring Scotsmen and women from all over as well as professional storytellers from Canada, Japan, Africa and beyond, the center also runs storytelling workshops in case you'd like to make sure you have something to say about your trip other than, "Yeah, Scotland. It was cool."

£4-10. Open Jul-Aug M-Sa 10am-6pm, Su noon-6pm; Sept-June M, Sa 10am-6pm. Open later when events are on.

THE WRITER'S MUSEUM — MUSEUM

Ladystairs House, Ladystairs Close, The Royal Mile — ☎0131 529 4901

Housed in the majestic Ladystairs mansion is a sanctuary of the works and personal belongings of three of Scotland's greatest authors: **Sir Walter Scott, Robert Burns,** and **Robert Louis Stevenson.** From mannequin displays to locks of hair and writing desks, it's great for a quiet wander whether you've read the collected works of all three or are simply interested in discovering why *Treasure Island* was so damn good.

Half-hidden in one of the small, tunneled "close" passages off of the Royal Mile. Free. Open M-Sa 10am-5pm. During the festival, also Su noon-5pm.

THE NATIONAL WAR MUSEUM (NWM) — MUSEUM

Hospital Square, Castle Hill — ☎0131 247 0413 www.edinburghcastle.gov.uk

Located inside the Castle grounds, the NWM is "free," but only after you've shelled out the cash for a ticket to the castle. Still, it's definitely worth a stop, whether your tastes run to old decorative swords or old, decorative admiral's pistols. It turns out that the evolution of the Scottish soldier and his weaponry is a smorgasbord of the instruments of death.

Free. Open summer 9:45am-5:45pm, winter 9:45am-4:45pm.

CAMERA OBSCURA AND THE WORLD OF ILLUSIONS — VISUAL ATTRACTION

Camera Obscura, Castlehill, The Royal Mile — ☎0131 226 3709 www.camera-obscura.co.uk

Just across the street from the Scottish Whisky Experience is this slightly more kid-friendly option. The actual "camera obscura," a combination of reflecting lenses and mirrors, presents a live-action, birds-eye view of the city. However, if it's overcast, your picture will be dimmer (heads-up: you're in Scotland), and if you're not on the bottom level of seating, chances are high that some little kid's noggin is going to be eagerly "obscuring" yours. The rest of the exhibition is a series of floors full of holograms, illusions, and distortions. They even have a maze of mirrors. This sight scores high on the "kids-take-ability" scale but might be a bit boring for the single traveler.

i Ask the desk for the next Camera Obscura showtime upon arrival. £9.25, students and seniors £7.25, ages 5-15 £6.25. Open daily first 2 weeks of June daily 9:30am-6pm, second 2 weeks of June 9:30am-7pm, Jul-Aug 9:30am-7:30pm, Nov-Mar daily 10am-5pm, Mar-May daily 9:30am-6pm.

THE NATIONAL MUSEUM OF SCOTLAND — MUSEUM

NMOS, Chambers St. — ☎0131 247 4422 www.nms.ac.uk

Housed in an enormous modern "castle" complete with winding staircases and enormous open spaces, this museum features nine floors to check out. Here's the crazy part: that's with half it closed for a massive, £46m renovation that is going to take it "into the 21st century." The exhibits here are as wide ranging as you would expect, from "The Kingdom of the Scots," featuring powder horns and ancient Pictish stonework, to "Scotland: A Changing Nation," showing Scotland in places you'd never expect—inventors, innovators and even Ewan MacGregors. (Seriously, who knew he was Scottish?) As a final stop, hit up the rooftop terrace for some awesome castle photo ops. But beware: you'll be fair game for the Camera Obscura tours up there. They're watching.

i 3 daily tours at 11:30am, 1;30pm, and 3:30pm. Free. Open daily 10am-5pm.

EDINBURGH CASTLE — CASTLE

Edinburgh Castle, Castle Hill — ☎0131 225 9846 www.edinburghcastle.gov.uk

It's the first thing you see on the skyline in Edinburgh and one of the most arresting structures on the planet: the Edinburgh Castle just can't be beat. From the top you'll get all sorts of brilliant photo ops, and there are several different places where you can snap that perfect pic. However, everyone else in town has the exact same idea, so don't be surprised if you find yourself jockeying for frame space. The **"Honours of the Kingdom"** (or the Scottish Royal Jewels) exhibit funnels you along a winding display of murals and mannequins before finally reaching the jewels. If the place is busy, this can take up to 40min., so be warned. Stop by at the top of the hour to see the changing of the guard at the front entrance.

Within West Princes Street Gardens. i Disabled-access patrons should phone in advance to set up a tour. £14, seniors £11.20, children £7.50. Open in summer 9:30am-6pm, winter 9:30am-5pm; last entry 45min. before close.

NEW TOWN

NATIONAL GALLERY OF SCOTLAND — MUSEUM

The Mound, just across Princes St. ☎0131 624 6200 www.nationalgalleries.org

At the National Gallery, even the rooms in which the artwork is hung seem designed to make you take your time. The place is octagonally designed and painted a royal red. You'll not want to rush your way through this collection of pre-1900 works, including some fantastic pieces by Raphael and El Greco.

i Free. Special exhibits £5-10. Open M-W 10am-5pm, Th 10am-7pm, F-Su 10am-5pm.

NATIONAL TRUST SCOTLAND — NATIONAL TRUST, GALLERY

28 Charlotte Sw. ☎0844 493 2100 www.nts.org.uk

The group in charge of conserving cultural sites, artifacts, and buildings in Scotland, National Trust Scotland keeps its head office here, where it also maintains a small gallery full of works by 20th-century Scottish artists, a bookshop, a restaurant and a cafe.

Gallery open M-F 9am-4:30pm. Cafe, bookshop, and restaurant open M-Sa 9:30am-5pm.

ST. ANDREWS SQUARE — PARK

At the end of George St.

It's not the most "interactive" of sights, but it is a perfectly enjoyable park with long benches, lots of grass and even a little coffee hut right there in the square. Check out the giant pillar (the **Melville Monument**) in the center. It was the first edifice erected with an iron balance crane, which crane enthusiasts will be pleased to learn.

Open daily 8am-8pm.

PARISH OF ST. ANDREW AND ST. GEORGE — CHURCH

13 George St. ☎0131 225 3847 www.standrewsandstgeorges.org.uk

Whether you're coming to pray, visit the stained glass, or simply escape the sounds of traffic, the Parish of St. Andrew and St. George offers a beautiful, calming atmosphere. An amphitheater-style church, it's got several rows of seating on the lower levels and a wrap-around balcony above.

Free. Open M-F 10am-3pm.

ST. MARY'S CATHEDRAL — CATHEDRAL

York Pl.

If nothing else, come to St. Mary's to see the beautiful kings with angel wings, and perhaps some of the biggest organ pipes we've ever seen.

Free. Open daily 8am-7pm.

THE NATIONAL ARCHIVES OF SCOTLAND — NATIONAL ASSEMBLY

2 Prince's St. ☎0131 535 1400 www.nas.gov.uk

A small collection about dusty old documents inhabits the much larger National Archives. Luckily, feather quills and old ink blotters are cooler than you would think. Look for the facsimile reproductions of government documents ascertaining the existence of the Loch Ness monster on the display boards.

i Water cooler available. Free. Open M-F 9am-4:30pm.

SCOTLAND'S PEOPLE CENTRE HERITAGE SITE

2 Prince's St. ☎0131 314 4300 www.gro-scotland.gov.uk

Do you have a kilt hiding in the underwear drawer for "special occasions?" Come find out for sure if you have some Scottish blood running through your veins at Scotland's People Centre, where you can access electronic birth, death, and marriage records to try and trace your family back to its roots.

i Records run 1855-2008. Geneology services £10. Open M-F 9am-4:30pm.

THE GEORGIAN HOUSE MUSEUM

7 Charlotte Sq. ☎0844 493 2100 www.nts.org.uk

Essentially the perfect replica of a Victorian household, the Georgian House tour starts in the basement, where you can see a 16min. introductory video that's as informative as it is boring. Move on to the kitchen and cellar to see old sugar and booze respectively. Moving up the stairs and floors you'll see drawing and dining rooms as well as a bedroom with so much floral print that the guys from the "Home and Design Network" would have a cardiac arrest.

£5.50, concessions £4.50, family £15, members free Open daily 10am-6pm. Last entry 30min. before close.

THE WALTER SCOTT MONUMENT SCALABLE MONUMENT

West Princes St. ☎0131 529 4068

The tower dedicated to Scotland's most famous author sticks up out of the ground and extends—well, a really long way up. You can make the climb to the top of this famous Edinburgh landmark, though it's worth bearing in mind that there are 287 steps to the top, and it's a squeeze as you near the summit. You also may have to wait for a while to get down from the top: there's only room for around six people on the stairs and no way to get down if people are coming up.

STOCKBRIDGE

GLENOGLE SWIM CENTRE SWIMMING

Glenogle Rd., Stockbridge ☎0131 343 6376 www.edinburghleisure.co.uk

Having just undergone an £18 million renovation, the Glenogle Swim Centre is totally state of the art, with a 25m pool, a sauna, and a steam room. The best part? It's all available for public use. The best best part? It's all available for public use, for cheap. They also have a gym and fitness classes. Makes you re-consider your wild idea to go down and swim in the freezing Atlantic, doesn't it?

Swim costs £4. Sauna and steam room £.60. Open M-F 7am-10pm, Sa-Su 8am-6pm.

STOCKBRIDGE MARKET MARKET ARCHWAY

At the junction of St. Stephens Pl. and St. Stephens St., Stockbridge

Before you go grab your all-hemp, recycled grocery bag and head off to get your fix of farmers' market veggies, it's worth knowing that the Stockbridge *Market* no longer exists—it's been replaced by houses. However, the **old archway,** with its engraved lettering and protruding lamp is still there, and it makes for quite a picturesque scene. Grab the camera, snap a few quick shots and stroll down through the pathway, now covered by trees. Or just head off to the art gallery next to the entrance.

WATER OF LEITH NATURE WALK

A beautiful way to spend an afternoon or a date is to take a walk along the paved paths that line this small river, flowing through New Town and Stockbridge. Green trees and foliage hang over the path, providing some shade for when you want to sit down on one of the many benches that line the water. If you follow it long enough, you'll come up underneath the massive, arched underbelly of the Dean Bridge.

THE ROYAL BOTANIC GARDENS BOTANIC GARDENS

20a Inverleith Row ☎0131 552 7171 www.rbge.org.uk

A center for plant research and conservation, this place is nuts (seeds, and spores too) for plants. The entrance and visitors center is beautifully impressive, with a glass facade and white, spinning windmill in front. Entrance to the gardens themselves is free, but to get in to the glasshouses for the real, misty green experience, you'll have to pay.

£4, concessions £3, children £1, family £8. Open daily Apr-Sept 10am-6pm, Mar-Oct 10am-5pm.

TOLLCROSS AND WEST END

THE MEADOWS — PUBLIC PARK

Located on the southwestern end of town, the Meadows are a beautiful, welcome respite from the honking cars and blabbing people inside the city. With wide-open, grass-covered fields intersected by paths covered by the shade of trees, it's no wonder that during the festival the Meadows become a hotspot for people to gather and throw frisbees, barbecue, and generally just have a great time. There are also 16 tennis courts and a playground on one end.

i If you want to make sure of your spot on a tennis court during the summer months, call ahead to reserve at ☎0131 444 1969. Courts open Apr-June M-F 4-9pm, Sa-Su 10am-6pm; July-Aug MoF 9am-9pm, Sa-Su 10am-7:30pm; Sept M-F 4-9pm, Sa-Su 10am-6pm.

food

Edinburgh, like any heavily touristy city, has just about any kind of cuisine you might be hankering for. So if you haven't quite gotten up the gumption to try haggis yet, try some fantastical veggie creations over at **David Bann's** or a huge plate of beef curry over at the **Mosque Kitchen.** You can do a wine and cheese night at the hostel if you stock up at **I. J. Mellis** in Stockbridge. In short, the possibilities are endless.

OLD TOWN

DAVID BANN — VEGETARIAN ❸

56-58 St. Mary's St. — ☎0131 556 5888 www.davidbann.com

At this all-vegetarian restaurant, you're not going be suffering through your salad. How's a watercress, beetroot, and goat cheese salad sound? Good? We thought so. Enjoy your meal and maybe one of the excellently spicy **Bloody Marys** in the attractive, modern interior.

Entrees £15-20. Open M-Th 11am-10pm, F 11am-10:30pm, Sa 10am-10:30pm, Su 10am-10pm.

LE CAFÉ ROYALE — CAFE ❷

274 Cannongate St. — ☎0131 652 3534

A people watcher's paradise, the entire front of this café swings open in good weather, leaving you with a covered fresh-air view of the street outside. A few quaint round tables, local artwork on the walls and a central support beam that looks like it was ripped out of the Titanic complete the ensemble. Grab a coffee—it's strong and fresh. Let the watch begin.

All coffee under £2. Open daily 8am-around 8pm.

ELEPHANT CAFÉ — CAFE, BAR ❸

21 George IV Bridge — ☎0131 220 5355 www.elephanthouse.biz

Harry Potter and company were birthed here on scribbled napkins. The cafe serves both coffee and booze, making you wonder which one **J.K. Rowling** was drinking when she had her "inspiration." Choose yours. They also have a selection of pastries and pies.

£5 minimum. Coffee £1.50-2.75. Beer £3 per bottle. Open M-F 8am-11pm, Sa-Su 9am-11pm.

RISTORANTE GENNARO ITALIAN ❸

64 Grassmarket St. ☎0131 226 3706

The best way to pick out an Italian restaurant is obvious—look for the one that's full. The second method requires a quick peek at the menu—is it in Italian? **Ristorante Gennaro** fulfills both of these requirements, seeing its tables fill every night and a menu that has English translations. Dim lighting and a deep red color scheme accentuate the fancy feel, but students as well as a pre-theater crowd are known to turn up.

Appetizers £1.50-9. Pizza £8-12. Fish entrees £12-14, meat entrees £14-19.50. Open daily noon-11pm.

CAFÉ TRUVA CAFE ❷

231-253 Cannongate St. ☎0131 556 9524 www.cafetruva.com

Cafes on the Royal Mile are many, but there may not be any that can rival Café Truva in terms of great outdoor seating. With small tables set out underneath the stone arches of the entryway, the cafe boasts a view that overlooks the Royal Mile along a row of picturesque houses. The food is Turkish and Mediterranean, but they also have a great selection of truffles and chocolates.

Coffee £1.50-2.10. Open M-Th 8am-9pm, F-Su 8am-10pm or 11pm.

THE LITTLE INN SANDWICHES ❶

1 Johnston Terr. ☎0775 661 4407

One of the smallest places on the Royal Mile (the only seating is a little bench outside the shop), it's probably so small because it's selling sandwiches at cheap prices on some prime real estate. Grab a soup and a baguette for just £1.90. Even the milkshakes (tasty!) are only £2.40.

Breakfast rolls £1.40-2.70. Open daily 6:30am-3pm. Open late during festival.

MAXIE'S BISTRO RESTAURANT ❸

5b Johnston Terr. ☎0131 226 7770 www.maxies.co.uk

To get to Maxie's you'll have to descend two sets of stairs flanked by paintings of old cigarette ads and one remarkably square-jawed woman (Maxie?) to the basement of the building. You can sit inside there, but if you're smart you'll immediately walk up another set of stairs to the terrace. Overlooking the city 50 feet above the ground, it's the perfect place to enjoy your well-cooked meal.

Starters £3.50-7. Entrees £8-17. Open daily 11am-11pm.

THE BOTHY SANDWICHES ❶

37 Grassmarket ☎0131 225 2322 www.thebothydeli.co.uk

Don't pass on the great toasted sandwiches *(£1-3)*—and they're big, guys—and amazing lemon-lime slushies *(£1-2)* from this small, easily passable place on Grassmarket. The owner is unduly kind to her customers, and you're sure to feel more than welcome from the time you arrive to the time you leave satisfied.

i 10% student discount with ID. American milkshakes £1.30. Coffee £1.25-1.75. Open daily 7am-5pm, with later hours during the summer.

NEW TOWN

THE UNDERGROUND CAFÉ (TUC) CAFE ❶

34 Eden St. ☎0131 624 7161

A surprisingly great local dive—you'll literally be going down some steep stairs to get to it—located just a few steps away from the Edinburgh bus station, TUC has a charming interior and delicious food. Check out the local artwork on the walls or browse through the festival information resting conveniently on top of an old piano in the entrance.

Soup with bread £1.75-2.75. Open M-F 7:30am-4pm, Sa 8:30am-4pm.

WOLFITS RESTAURANT, DELI ❶

200 Rose St. ☎0131 225 5096

We have no idea why this restaurant is called "Wolfits." What we do know is that this small establishment sells good food cheap. Soups and buttered baguettes go for under £3. There's not *really* an atmosphere, but you can watch music videos on the television while you wolf it down.

Open daily 7:30am-4pm.

INDIAN THALI RESTAURANT RESTAURANT ❸

1-3 York Pl. ☎0131 557 9899

With a deep, royal red interior filled with flower vases, this isn't your typical stop-off for a quick bite. The Bollywood music's playing, but if that doesn't drag you in, you can grab some takeaway—it comes with free rice.

Entrees £8-11. Breakfast sandwiches £1-3. Open Tu-Sa noon-2:30pm. Open daily 5:30-11pm.

THE CONAN DOYLE PUB GRUB ❷

71-73 York Pl. ☎0131 557 9539

In the neighborhood where **Sir Arthur Conan Doyle** himself used to live, there's memorabilia—Sherlock Holmes and otherwise—galore in this resto pub. A good value for a full cooked breakfast (veggie or not). Come by on the weekends when it's more of a pub and receive the same kind of value on drinks. Also, enjoy the comfy armchairs galore.

Breakfast from £5. Open M-Th 9am-11:45pm, F-Sa 9am-1am, Su 12:30pm-midnight.

BROWN SUGAR CAFE ❶

39 Queen St. ☎0131 623 7770

There aren't really any attention-grabbing words like "arresting" or "insane" to describe Brown Sugar. And that's what makes it great. Located on a corner just across the street from the park-like Queen's gardens, it's a spot where you can grab a nice coffee, sit back, munch on some homemade **banana bread** and watch the world go by. How's that for arresting?

Americano £1.90. Cadbury's hot chocolate £1.60. Open M-F 7am-3:30pm, Sa 10am-4pm.

MIRÓ CANTINA MEXICANA MEXICAN ❸

184 Rose St. ☎0131 225 4376

It's a *fiesta* in here! Or at least, that's what the paint job would have you believe. Bright yellows and wild patterns cover the inside (and outside) of this eatery. A little more "Mexican" than "Taco Bell," this place offers a big plate of nachos with beans, jalapeños, melted cheese, salsa, sour cream, and guacamole *(£5)*. Even the outdoor seating has a festive paint job.

Selection of Mexican beers £3.10-3.25. Open daily in summer noon-10:30pm. Open in winter noon-2:30pm and 5:30-10pm.

JUICE ALMIGHTY COFFEE, JUICE BAR ❸

7a Castle St. ☎0131 220 6879 www.juicealmighty.com

The bright, neon interior of this smoothie shop is matched by the equally bubbly staff. If the healthy fruit smoothies aren't fortifying enough for you, buy a large and receive a shot of wheatgrass *(£1)*. They also serve hot foods, such as soups and baked potatoes.

Coffee only £1 until noon. Open M-F 7:30am-7pm, Sa 8am-1am, Su 10:30am-6pm.

FINNEGAN'S SANDWICH SHOP SANDWICHES ❶

28 Queensferry St. ☎0131 226 5005

A great stop for a quick bite if you're hungry, you can get your food in one of two ways: quick or quicker. The quick way: order from the counter and have your food made on the spot. The quicker way: grab a freshly-made sandwich from off the shelf and take it to go.

Sandwiches £2-2.40. Homemade soups £1.50. Open M-F 7am-3pm.

MUSSEL INN SEAFOOD 3

61-65 Rose St. ☎0131 225 5979 www.mussel-inn.com

Serving mussels brought in from the west lochs of Scotland and the Shetland Isles, the Inn only dishes out food that's fresh and savory. As if the natural taste weren't enough, they serve pots with Moroccan, shallot, and bleu cheese flavors as well. It's a crowded place, so you may have to "mussell your way inn" on the weekends. Or book ahead.

1kg. pot of mussels £9.60-11.60. 0.5kilo pot of mussels £4.80-5.80. Open M-Th noon-3pm and 5:30-10pm, F-Sa noon-10pm, Su 12:30-10pm.

HENDERSON'S WINE BAR 3

94 Hanover St. ☎0131 225 2131 www.hendersonsofedinburgh.co.uk

What began in 1962 as a way for the Henderson family to sell off the surplus produce at their farm and earn a little cash has continued—and then some. Now featuring a deli, bistro, wine bar, and art gallery, Henderson's is a full-blown industry. However, they still maintain their organic, high quality standard.

i Check out their alternative location at John's Church at the end of Prince's St. Lunch specials £9-10. 2 side salads £2.40. Organic lager £3.10. Open M-Sa 8am-10:30pm.

STOCKBRIDGE

BELLS DINER DINER 3

7 St. Stephens St. ☎0131 225 4673

We at **Let's Go** are not picky about burgers. For us, as long as it's hot, has a bun, and isn't from a franchise with a "drive-thru," we're pretty happy. However, there are occasions in one's life when one is exposed to burger greatness, and eating at Bells Diner is one of those times. The burgers cost a bit more than you'd usually pay *(£8-10)* but are well worth the expenditure. Also, they come with a full plate of chips (fries) and a selection of six different dipping sauces.

i Reservations for weekend evenings recommended. Open M-F 6-10pm, Sa noon-10pm, Su 6-10pm.

MADELEINE CAFE 2

27b Raeburn Pl. ☎0131 332 8455

An intensely modern, intensely chic cafe with the most futuristic bathrooms you've ever seen (seriously, it's like NASA designed the loo...), Madeleine earns the **thumbpick** for the macaroons. These light wafery cookie sandwiches are sweet but tart, in flavors like vanilla, chocolate, raspberry, and mango *(all for £.80 each)*. You can't stop eating them. Seriously, we tried. You can't (mumble crunch yum!) stop.

Cakes and coffees £1.40-5. Open T-Sa 10am-5:30pm, Su 11am-5:30pm.

GREEN GROCER'S GROCERY 1

11 Deanhaugh St. ☎0131 332 7384

Get your fresh apples, nectarines, carrots and any other type of fresh munchable you may be interested in here. Head inside the store for the more sinful foodstuffs, such as chocolates and soft drinks.

Open daily 6:30am-9pm.

SAN MARCO ITALIAN 4

10-11 Mary's Pl. ☎0131 332 1569

An Italian bistro, San Marco's offers all your Italian staples, such as an *insalata caprese*, with sliced mozzarella and tomato with fresh basil and olive oil *(£4.95)*

and pizzas *(£10)*. The meat dishes will run you a bit more *(£15-25)*. This is a bank-buster, but you're sure to leave with a belly full of soul-satisfying pasta.
Open M-Th 5:30-11pm, F 5:30-11pm, Sa noon-2pm and 5:30-11pm, Su 12:30pm-midnight.

PIZZA EXPRESS PIZZA ❷
1 Deanhaugh St. ☎0131 332 7229 www.pizzaexpress.com
A pro in the art of family dining, Pizza Express always has children in high chairs with happy, pizza-filled faces. A large, airy blue and white establishment, this Pizza Express may have some of the best outdoor seating in Stockbridge, right along the water of Leith. Get out there to escape the constant calls of, "No, junior, we keep our napkins in our laps."
Pizza £6.50-10. Open M-Th and Su 11:30am-10:30pm.

I. J. MELLIS DELI ❸
6 Bakers Pl. ☎0131 225 6566 www.mellischeese.co.uk
Yeah, you may be paying the same for some cheese and cured meat as you would for a big plate of fish n' chips, but where else are you going to find *Pyrenees Chevre* goat cheese? Not at the Chippie's you aren't.
Open M-F 9am-6:30pm, Sa 9am-6pm, Su 10am-5pm.

PECKHAM'S DELI ❷
48 Raeburn Pl. ☎0131 332 8844 www.peckhams.co.uk
Half cafe with sit-down coffees and an outdoor terrace and half specialty food n' booze store, Peckhams' attractive warm interior is matched by the friendliness of the staff and the surprising affordability of its merchandise. Get a freshly-baked loaf of bread *(from £1)*, and then supplement it with any number of cheeses, salamis, or quiches.
Open M-Sa 8am-11pm, Su 9am-10pm.

CAFÉ PLUM CAFE ❶
96 Raeburn Pl. ☎0795 781 1703
Plum is a tiny, purple and white cafe down on Raeburn with one hell of a coffee and tea selection. In a country that plays cricket, a game in which taking a break for afternoon tea is actually part of the procedure, you'd think you'd usually be able to find a little variety; Café Plum provides this variety, with 12 different teas and coffee that are brought in weekly, ensuring their freshness.
House salad £2.75. Coffee £1.30-2.50. Full breakfast £5.50. Cash only. Open M-W 8am-5pm, Th-F 8am-6pm, Sa 9am-5pm, Su 10:30am-5pm.

HAYMARKET AND DALRY

GOOD SEED BISTRO BISTRO ❸
100-102 Dalry Rd. ☎0131 337 3803 www.goodseedbistro.com
The new kid on the block, the Good Seed Bistro is doing everything right: classy interior, a relaxed vibe. They serve weekday lunch specials *(2 courses, £7.95)*. Interested in coming during the mornings? Coffee and cakes go for just £4.50.
i Wi-Fi available. Open M-Th noon-10pm, F-Sa noon-11pm, Su noon-4pm.

CLIFTON FISH BAR FISH AND CHIPS ❶
10 Clifton Terr. ☎0131 346 8723 www.clifton-fish-bar.justeat.co.uk
A tiny fish 'n chips joint with two slap-happy fry cooks who are more than ready to play on the job, the Clifton Fish Bar sells cheap pizzas, calzones, and chips. Order the "munchy box," with chicken pakora, vegetable pakora, doner meat, chips and a can of soda *(just £8.99)*.
10in. calzone £4.-5.50. 7in. pizza £3. Open M-Th 4:30pm-1am, F-Sa 4:30pm-2am, Su 4:30pm-1am.

XIANGBALA HOTPOT RESTAURANT ❸
63 Dalry Rd. ☎0131 313 4408
A slightly different take on restaurant culture, the Xiangbala Hotpot is £15 per person all you can eat for 2hr. With a silver boiling pot in the middle of the

smooth black tables, meats, seafood, and veggies are introduced into boiling broths and then eaten.

Open daily 3-11pm.

SCOOBY'S SANDWICHES ❷

95 Morisson St. ☎0131 221 1877

A DIY (do-it-yourself) sandwich shop with a BWU (banter with us) attitude. Scooby's does a mean spicy tuna mayo or spicy meatball soup. Or if none of the stuff on the board strikes your fancy, just take a look at the ingredients and go nuts.

Soup and sandwiches from £2.50. Open M-F 6:30am-3pm.

PG'S SANDWICH BAR SANDWICHES ❶

127 Morrison St. ☎0131 228 8763

Another small shop that's seriously lacking in decor, but damn if it ain't cheap and delicious! Get a sausage and haggis roll or a sandwich. They also do mac n' cheese should you begin feeling nostalgic...

Sausage and haggis rolls £.85, sandwiches £3.50. Open M-F 7am-2pm.

MORISSON BAKERY BAKERY ❶

147 Morisson St. ☎0131 229 6471

You'll be able to know you're getting close to Morisson Bakery by the smell. However, unlike when you know you're getting close to someone who's had too much to drink, this smell is delicious. With fresh cakes and donuts as well as meat pies, it's an excellent stop at any time of the day or night (considering they're open for most of both, being a bakery and all).

All pastries under £1. Pies £1-2. Open daily 1am-5pm.

THE SIZZLING SCOT SCOTTISH ❸

103-105 Dalry Rd. ☎0131 337 7744 www.sizzlingscot.co.uk

A good local spot that fills with the smells of good food and the hum of conversation as the night goes on, this restaurant uses the best in Scottish ingredients—McSween's haggis, Aberdeen Angus, and Orkney Island ice cream. Try it with some toffee or hot fudge.

Soups £3. Burgers £9.50. Entrees £7.95-11.50. Open daily 5-10pm, T-Sa noon-2pm.

TOLLCROSS AND WEST END

THE MOSQUE KITCHEN CURRY ❶

19a West Nicholson St.

The guys at the Mosque Kitchen don't mess around. There's not "atmosphere" to speak of—just some covered outdoor cafeteria seating—but you don't need it, as you'll be too busy staring at your giant plate of delicious rice and curry to care.

Veggie curry plate £3.50, meat £4.50, chicken £3. Open daily noon-8pm, closed F 1-1:45pm for prayers.

VICTOR HUGO CONTINENTAL DELICATESSEN DELI ❷

26-27 Melville Terr. ☎0131 667 1827 victorhugodeli.com

A true combination of deli and cafe, Victor Hugo's has little booths along the walls perfect for snuggling up with a coffee. The inside is a great place to wonder when the pissing rain is going to stop. Or if you've got a slightly more benevolent attitude towards the weather, you can sit outside and enjoy the rain—from underneath the awnings of course. With locals who've been coming back since 1940 as well as students who come for the belly-filling mac 'n cheese, it's everybody's favorite. Try the award-winning Ramsay of Carluke bacon roll *(£2.85)*.

Teas £1.60. Open M-F 8am-10pm, Sa-Su 8am-8pm. During the festival, open daily 8am-11pm.

BRAZILIAN SENSATION BRAZILIAN ❶

117-119 Buccleuch St. ☎0131 667 0400 www.braziliansensation.co.uk

Brazilian Sensation is a smallish but elaborately decorated restaurant that can't get enough of it's South American namesake. Even the mannequin in the window is decked out in Brazilian gear. Serving rolls and sandwiches as well as a large variety of tropical fruit smoothies *(£3.50)*.

Baguettes £2.75. Open M-Sa noon-4pm, open Su during the festival.

PETER'S YARD CAFE ❸

27 Simpson Ln. ☎0131 229 5876 www.petersyard.com

Peter's Yard, a Swedish style cafe housed right in the heart of the University of Edinburgh, serves hot cinnamon buns as well as *Kladdkaka* (a Swedish chocolate cake). The cafe is housed in a clear glass box, so those sitting outside on the balcony may **spy** on those sitting inside and vice versa. Unfortunately, it seems that most of the people coming to Peter's Yard aren't interesting enough to spy on.

Kladdkaka £2.70. Coffee £1.75-2.95. Open M-F 7am-6pm, Sa-Su 9am-6pm.

TEA TREE TEA CAFE ❷

13 Bread St. ☎0131 228 3100 www.teatreetea.com

Ordering at Tea Tree Tea is a bit like seeing your grandmother for the first time in a long time: you'll be bombarded with questions about how you're doing. Except that the baristas here have fewer wrinkles and won't pinch your cheeks. Order yourself a fantastic chai latté, and sit down among the green walls while you try and remember what your grades were last semester so you can tell your new friend behind the counter.

A pot of tea, sandwich, and cake under £7. Open M-F 7am-7pm, Sa-Su 9am-7pm.

MADE IN FRANCE FRENCH CAFE ❷

5 Lochrin Pl. ☎0131 221 1184

"A cute little French place on the west end..." See? It even sounds adorable. With French posters and framed Monet prints, it's a nice place to enjoy the tiny quiches and tarts. You can also pick up some wine or preserves from their shelves and take them home. *La vie...c'est tres belle.*

Baguettes from £2.60. Open M-F 8am-4pm, Sa 10am-4pm.

MONSTER MASH CAFÉ BRITISH ❷

20 Forest Row ☎0131 225 7069

This one's a belly-buster. Seriously. The fare here's typical British staples—sausages and mash but cooked to perfection and served with one of several gravies. The big thing though is just that: the huge plates. Come by at dinnertime and skip breakfast the next day.

1 sausage and mash £7, 2 sausages and mash £9. Open daily 9am-10pm. During festival open until 11pm.

THE TREEHOUSE CAFÉ CAFE ❷

44 Leven St. ☎0131 656 0513

At this great local hangout for students, couples, and locals, sometimes the owner even comes by to sing a few tunes. It's no surprise then, that there are records and musical scores hung on the walls. More unexpectedly, there's great coffee and delectable cakes to be had with all that folky goodness. Come by on Sundays to hear live folk music *(from 3-4:30pm)*,

Coffee from £1.50-1.75. Open M-Sa 8am-5pm, Su 9am-5pm.

THE NEW LEAF ORGANIC GROCERIES ❸

23 Argyle Pl. ☎0131 228 8840

Featuring a selection of organic, natural, and fair-trade items ranging from juice blenders to granola bars, The New Leaf offers a 5% discount for students and even has a little play area in front. The latter's probably not for you though...

i Gluten- or dairy-free items available. Prices vary. Open M-Sa 9:30am-6pm.

Edinburgh, despite being the "prettier little sister" to Glasgow, has nowhere near the same club scene. This town full of **pubs and bars,** however, buzzes happily on the weekends, and skyrockets in intensity during the festivals in August. Each specific neighborhood will have its own variations on the classic pub, from the tourist-heavy areas along the Royal Mile, to the strange collection of odd and local watering holes on **Rose Street** in New Town, to the posh, hip new bars in Stockbridge.

Drinking in Scotland, and in Edinburgh especially, isn't about "going on the piss" (though that is a part of it), but about finding the right place for yourself, your group, your night, and your state of mind—no matter how much that last one may be altered throughout the night.

OLD TOWN

BANNERMAN'S

BAR, MUSIC VENUE

212 Cowgate ☎0131 556 3254 www.myspace.com/bannermanslive

With a subterranean, half-barrel auditorium for the live acts, the soundproofing in Bannerman's is so good that if you want to sit in the bar and have a friendly chat, you can...while a rock show goes on next door. A wide selection of beers and cask ales are available, but if you want to try the house special, go for the **"Jager U-boat."** What is a Jager U-boat, you ask? Just place your fingers in your ears, grab a small bottle of Jager with your teeth, tilt your head back and—*Whoosh!* hear the bubbles of the ocean as you descend...into a drunken stupor. Nah, you'll be fine, and Bannerman's is a kick-ass place to hang out.

i Live shows cost £4-8 entry. Jager U-boat £2. Pints £3.40-3.65. Open daily noon-1am. In Aug open daily noon-3am.

WHITE HART INN

PUB

34 Grassmarket ☎0131 226 2806

The Grassmarket's oldest pub (est. 1516), the White Hart Inn retains its olden feel, with faded photographs on the walls, beer steins hanging from the ceilings, and one slightly creepy bust of William Burke by the door. Famous patrons of the pub include Scotland's favorite poet, **Robert Burns.** Grab a pint and see if your poetical stylings are loosed.

Pints £2.85-4. Spirits £2.95-12.49. Open M-Th 11am-midnight, F-Sa 11am-1am, Su 11am-midnight.

GREYFRIARS BOBBY'S BAR

PUB

30-34 Candlemaker Row ☎0131 225 8328

Named after one of Edinburgh's local legends—Greyfriars Bobby, a terrier so faithful that it slept at his owner's grave for the next 14 years until his own death. The citizens here buried him next to his beloved owner and the loyal pooch entered annals of local legend. There's a statue of Bobby outside this pub, and it's a popular photo spot for tourists of all nationalities. The pub itself is a pretty standard alehouse, but if you want to contemplate Bobby's loyalty from across the street you can sit outside and have a beer.

Ales £2.80-3. Spirits £3. Open M-Sa 11am-midnight, Su 11:30am-midnight.

BLACK BULL

PUB

12 Grassmarket St. ☎0131 225 6636

The floors, the walls, and the ceiling make the place look like the inside of an oak tree. A really big oak tree. The Black Bull is enormous, with ample room for you and a party of any size to find seats in one of the warmly lit booths or on a plush leather sofa. Serving real cask ales, it's more a hang-out than a dance bar, but there are DJs on the weekends.

Folk session M. Live bands play most Th. Spirits £2-2.60. Pints £2.60-3.45. Open M-F 11am-1am, Sa-Su 10am-1am.

THE BANSHEE LABYRINTH CLUB

29-35 Niddry St. ☎0131 558 8209 www.thebansheelabyrinth.com

Built into the side of a hill and just above Edinburgh's famous "haunted vaults" (the Auld Reekie tours actually end here), the Banshee Labyrinth is a maze of stairs and tunnels, low-ceilinged cave-like rooms and Addams Family inspired bars. There are three bars and seven rooms, a pool hall and a cinema, plus a pole-dancing area. Note the sign that absolves the bar from any injuries you may sustain from your "sexy dancing."

Spirits with mixer £2.50. Pints £2.70-3.40. Open daily 12:30pm-3am.

SIN CLUB

207 Cowgate ☎0131 220 6176 www.club-sin.com

A recently-remade club and one of the Cowgate's newest nightlife options, Sin lives up to its name, getting crazy during the week, on the weekends, whenever. With more fog and spinning lights than that alien spaceship in *Men In Black* and a massive downstairs dance floor, you can head up to the mezzanine level if you—ahem—have just one sip too many and need to find your friends again.

Cowgate. Bottles £2. Pints £2.49. Open daily 10pm-3am. During festival open daily 1pm-5am.

WHISTLE BINKIES BAR, LIVE MUSIC

46 Southbridge ☎0131 557 5114 www.whistlebinkies.com

A popular place to see smaller live acts, Whistle Binkies has a sort of "pre-ripped jeans" feel—there are lots of old barrels and comfortable ratty stools, but the holes in the wall with brick underneath are definitely stylized. Framed photos of famous musicians are carefully hung and illuminated, though notably not behind the stage, where things might get messy.

Live music every night except Sa, when DJs come on. Pints £3.40-3.60. Spirits £1.60-3.30. Open M-Th 5pm-3am, F-Su 1pm-3am.

THE CITY CAFÉ BAR, MUSIC

19 Blair St. ☎0131 220 0125

A hotspot for students and young Edinburghers to party at before heading out to the clubs. Styled like a '50s soda fountain, it's got retro red countertops and a second bar downstairs if you just can't wait to really get your groove on.

Coffee and food available during the day. Wi-Fi available. Pints £3-4. Open daily 11am-1am. During the festival, open daily 11am-3am. DJs play W-Sa.

CABARET VOLTAIRE CLUB

36-38 Blair St. ☎0131 220 6176 www.thecabaretvoltaire.com

One of Edinburgh's most popular nightlife spots, Cabaret Voltaire has a line that begins leading out the door of the Cab Volt as soon as the club opens up around 11:30pm. The queue grows longer throughout the night. Located just above the "haunted vaults" used by the Ghost tours, the actual club has much of that low-ceilinged, brick, domed feel. Lots of red neon keeps things a little naughty without being strip-club worthy.

Cover up to £12. Open daily 7pm-3am.

round and round the kitty

I was out at a pub the other day and was talking to a few people I had met, well, at the pub. One of my new friends asked me about the drinking culture in the United States, particularly, college drinking culture. After struggling through a few awkward sentences, trying to find the right combination of "vodka...too much...sloppy" I finally just gave up, and said, "It's complicated." I then turned to enter the pub and get another beer. It was only my second, don't judge.

However, I hadn't taken a step before my newfound friend stopped me and said, "Whoa there, you're not going to buy a drink by yourself are ye?"

"Um, well, did you guys want anything?" I said.

"Let me tell you about drinking in a pub," was his answer. He then proceeded to tell me about the two modes of drinking. I pass them onto you.

- **THE ROUND:** In a somewhat random manner, a starter is selected from the group. That person takes orders from the rest of the people in his or her group and buys all of the drinks from the bar. Then, after those drinks are finished (you will not be waited for if you find yourself behind the group) the next person in line goes up to the bar and does the same thing. It's just rude to leave without having bought a round. Think about it, you're really only paying for as many drinks as you have, but if you cut out early before a complete buying circle has been made, you're losing money. The only way for you to break even is to stay and drink with the group. If the group is particularly large, you could be there for a while. Bear this in mind if you decide to head out with your entire hostel.
- **THE KITTY:** The Kitty works along essentially the same principles but with one major difference. Each person, instead of buying a round for the group, puts in a set amount (the "kitty") into an empty pint glass that sits in the middle of the table. It could be £5, £10 or, God forbid, £20. Drinks are then bought with money taken exclusively from the Kitty, and, while you can leave before the cash has been fully depleted, there's no way to get back what you've put in other than in drink. Again then, you're only getting your money's worth if you stay and sit through quite a few pints.

Then again, leaving early does have its health and sobriety benefits I suppose.

Asa Bush

NEW TOWN

CITIZEN SMITH

BAR ❸

168 Rose St. ☎0131 225 5979

The only independently owned and run bar on Rose Street, Citizen Smith is a haven for all things folk, blues, rock, alt rock, and indie. There's live music every night on the somewhat improvised stage, but try to show up in August for their own, private "Woodstock," where 50 bands play over the span of three days. Come in, sit down, and admire the giant cardboard arachnid on the ceiling.

Pints £3.30. Open daily 2pm-1am and in summer 4pm-1am. During festival, open daily 1pm-3am.

ROSE AND CROWN PUB ❸

170 Rose St. ☎0131 225 4039

In this decent bar with molded ceilings live music is on three nights a week. Other than that and the occasional DJ, however, it's a pretty chill place, simply a nice place to get a cider and sit out in the sun.

Pints £3-3.30. Spirits £3.15-4. Open daily 11am-1am.

JEYKLL AND HYDE BAR BAR ❸

112 Hanover St. ☎0131 224 2002 www.eeriepubs.co.uk

A dark and foreboding—who are we kidding, this place is meant to look creepy on purpose. It's called the Jeykll and Hyde Bar! Still, with iron chandeliers and high-backed "creeeeepy" chairs, they do an okay job. Dracula could have lived here, but he would have been drunk on Bloody Marys the whole time.

i Bring your passport, the license isn't going to work here. Pints £1.50-3. Mixed drinks £5, 2 £6. Open M-Sa noon-1am, Su 12:30pm-10pm.

QUEEN'S ARMS PUB ❸

49 Frederick St. ☎0131 225 1045

Having recently undergone a massive refurbishment, the Queen's Arms is classier than ever. It's still got that traditional feel, with a padded bar, bookshelf full of classics, and wiry chandeliers, but it's all got that new-pub smell. Take it all in over one of their hand-pulled ales. Can we say anymore about its classy classic-ness?

i The Queen's Arms is the 1st pub in Scotland to have Blue Moon on draft. Pints £3-3.50. Spirits £2.75 and up. Open M-Sa 11am-1am, Su 12:30pm-1am.

BLACK ROSE TAVERN BAR ❷

49 Rose St. ☎0131 220 0414 www.blackrosetavern.com

If you've ever grown a beard to impress the guys in Pantera or ever bought a guitar with more sharp ends than your Swiss Army knife, you'll enjoy the Black Rose. With "rock karaoke" on Wednesdays and a major skeleton obsession and various tattoos among the staff, the Black Rose is great for rockers of all types. **Jagermeister** is the self-proclaimed house wine. What more do you want?

i Open mic night on T, Quiz on W just before the karaoke. Pints £2.80-3.65. Spirits from £1.20-1.60. Open M-Sa 11am-1am, Su 12:30pm-1am.

EL BARRIO BAR, CLUB ❹

47 Hanover St. ☎0131 220 6818 www.elbarrio.co.uk

New Town's only club is rowdy enough on its own. Open until 3am everyday, this basement of brightly colored walls and Latin music becomes packed with people on the weekends, as the photos on the walls will attest. Laugh at the most intoxicated people you see on the walls and then come back next week to make sure you haven't joined their ranks.

Spirits and mixer £3-3.80. Pints £3.50. Open daily noon-3am.

ROSE STREET BREWERY PUB ❷

55-57 Rose St. ☎0131 220 1227

A local's pub, the Rose Street Brewery did actually used to be a brewery, but has since been promoted to a place where you can drink it rather than make it. The restaurant upstairs is a popular spot for tourists and serves a mean steak. A plain but comfortable interior, a wooden entry space will take you down a pair of step onto a strangely kilt-like carpet.

i 4 ales available, 2 constant, 2 rotating. Pints £2.70-3.40. Spirits £2.55. Bar open M-Th 11am-11pm, F-Sa 11am-1am, Su 11am-11pm. Restaurant open daily noon-10pm.

LORD BODO'S BAR BAR ❷

3 Dublin St. ☎0131 477 2563

You could walk by Lord Bodo's bar and say to yourself, "Why, that doesn't look like much of a bar." The exterior's not much to look at, it's true, but the inside is seriously classy, with brown suede chairs and stained wood all around. Grab a martini and get out the tux Bond fans.

Pints £2.70-3. Mixed drinks £3.50-4. Open M-Th 11am-11:30pm, F-Sa 11am-1:30am, Su 11am-11:30pm.

DIRTY DICK'S PUB ❸

159 Rose St. ☎0131 260 9920 dirtydicksedinburgh@gmail.com

I spy, among the bric-a-brac housed in Dirty Dick's: a sea of upside-down golf clubs, a picture of **Alfred Hitchcock,** somewhat creepy teddy bears, a full pint of beer stuck upside down on the ceiling, and an accordion.

Pints £3.30. Spirits £2.60. Open M-Sa 11am-1am, Su noon-1am.

STOCKBRIDGE

THE ANTIQUARIAN PUB ❷

68-72 St. Stephens St. ☎0131 225 2858 www.theantiquarybar.co.uk

Its entrance may be hidden at the bottom of a small stairwell in Stockbridge, but this bar lets its people and atmosphere do the talking. A great local crowd with a jovial attitude hangs out here, and if you come by on Tuesday night around 8pm you can get in on one hell of a poker game. You probably won't win (some of these guys are legit), but you will have a lot of fun at this bar.

Spirits £2.10-3.50. Pints £3-3.55. Open M noon-11pm, T-W noon-midnight, Th-Sa noon-1am, Su noon-12:30am.

AVOCA BAR BAR ❸

4-6 Dean St. ☎0131 315 3311 www.avocabarandgrill.co.uk

A regulars' watering hole, Avoca is your typical food 'n booze stop. The building is quite nice, with more of those Victorian moldings we've seen so much of, but the bar itself is fairly spare on decoration. A nice place to come in and have a private chat.

Pints £3-4.15. Spirits £2.70. Open M-Th 11am-midnight, F-Sa 11am-1am, Su 11am-midnight.

HAMILTON'S BAR ❸

16-18 Hamilton Pl. ☎0131 225 8513 www.hamiltonsedinburgh.co.uk

With lots of posh, leather couches and very "in" 60s pop art on the back wall, it's no surprise to see that everyone in Hamilton's is well-dressed, mild-mannered, and sipping on glasses of wine. Should you like to go and join them, you'd be wise, though it's certainly not necessary, to spiff yourself up a bit. Look at you, you need to wash behind those ears before you go out drinking!

Pints £3.30-4.50. Spirits £3.10. Open daily 9am-1am. In Aug and Dec open daily 9am-3am.

ST. VINCENT BAR BAR ❷

11 St. Vincent St. ☎0131 225 7447 www.stvincentbar.com

From the outside the St. Vincent Bar looks like a normal pub...and actually, it looks pretty normal from the inside as well. However, it's a *Let's Go* favorite in terms of pub quirks: St. Vincent's allows you to purchase two pints of your favorite ale "to go." That's right. Tell 'em you feel like drinking at home, and they'll give you a lovely carton of beer. Now that's brilliant.

Pints £3.04-3.85. Open M-Sa 11am-1am, Su 12:30pm-1am. During festival open until 3am.

HECTOR'S BAR ❸

47-49 Deanhaugh St. ☎0131 343 1735 www.hectorsstockbridge.co.uk

A hip, trendy bar in the heart of Stockbridge, Hector's burns the candles until the wax falls on the tables. It's got a classy yet laid-back feel, thanks to wraparound couches complete with funky pillows and dark purple interior. A heavily local patronage keeps things from getting too fancy-schmancy. Hector's stocks a wide selection of wines, ales, and beers as well as an organic cider.

Pints £3-3.50. Organic cider £3.10. Open M-W noon-midnight, Th-F noon-1am, Sa 11am-1am, Su 11am-midnight.

THE STOCKBRIDGE TAP PUB 2

2-6 Raeburn Pl. ☎0131 343 3000

A great local place right next to Hector's, the Stockbridge Tap sees everyone from old men to young girls come in to enjoy the hefty ale selection. If you've got the time and the liver for it, try to drink them all.

Spirits £2.40. Pints £3-3.30. Open M-Th noon-midnight, F-Sa noon-1am, Su 12:30pm-midnight.

HAYMARKET AND DALRY

CARTER'S BAR 3

185 Morrison St. ☎0131 228 9149

Unlike the concept pubs of Haymarket and Dalry, Carter's has an artsy feel accentuated by the candle wax dripping down the stairs and the mismatched couches and chairs in the loft. A place for live music, it sets up small shows in the downstairs space. Come on Wednesday for Bluegrass. As the sign painted on the wall says, "Are you gonna piss about all day?—Or are you coming in?" Do the latter.

i Music begins 9-9:30pm. Spirits £2.30-3.30. Pints £2.90-3.20. Open M-Sa noon-1am, Su 12:30pm-1am.

THE MERCAT BAR PUB 3

28 West Maitland St. ☎0131 225 8716 www.mercatbar.com

A pub that's renowned locally for it's grub, the Mercat Bar has owners that'll swear it's a bar before a restaurant. Still, with classy tables illuminated under an orange glow and only the lights from the taps to signal out the bar, that'll be up to you to decide.

i Be on the lookout for daily specials. Spirits from £2.20. Pints £3.20-3.70. Entrees £9-12. Open daily 9am-1am. During the festival open daily 7:30am-1am.

DIANE'S POOL HALL PUB, POOL HALL 2

242 Morrison St. ☎0131 228 1156

"Diane's" is a bit of a strange name for this pub, considering it's mostly men that frequent it. However, Haymarket could just be lacking in female pool sharks. With nine tables all for £.20 a game, it's a good place to get snookered.

Pints £2.10-2.60. Spirits around £1.55. Cash only. Open daily 8am-midnight.

RYRIE'S PUB 2

1a Haymarket Terr.

A traditional, old-fashioned bar, Ryrie's lays out its whiskeys in a long line in a glass case above the bar, making your choice even more difficult. If you're not in for booze, they serve pub grub until 7pm. People watching is not really an option, as the windows are old stained glass.

Pints £2-3.35. Spirits £3.25. Open M-Sa 9am-1am, Su 12:30pm-1am. Pub grub served until 7pm.

HAYMARKET BAR PUB 2

11-15a West Maitland St. ☎0131 228 2537

A strange combination of sports bar and tasteful gastropub, the Haymarket bar has pictures of muddy rugby players about to smash each others' faces hung next to tasteful pastel paintings of bucolic country scenes. Come by for a quiz on Sunday or for any sporting event on television. If you get there early enough you might be able to score one of the little booths by the windows or the small upstairs loft.

Pints £2-3. Spirits £2.09-3.09. Open M-Sa 9am-midnight or 1am, Su 12:30pm-midnight.

TOLLCROSS AND WEST END

THE LINKS BAR

SPORTS BAR ❷

2-4 Alvanley Terr. ☎0131 229 3854

A sports bar with all the typical trimmings—pool tables *(£1 per game)*, pictures of sports greats, cases full of old sporting memorabilia such as ancient golf clubs and stinky old shoes (thank God they're in a case), and a name like The Links Bar (what more do you need?). For those who really don't care what Jack Nicklaus's handicap was during the 1982 British Open, the other half of the bar is an ultra-modern, wooden tube with blue lighting.

Pints £2.95-3.75. Spirits £2-2.50. Open daily 9am-1am.

HENDRICKS

BAR ❸

1a Barclay Pl. ☎0131 229 2442

A classy young professionals bar with a decor that could be put up in an interior design catalogue. Thistle wallpaper and little black lamps above the bar illuminate the LBDs that show up on the weekends. No live music or quiz over here though guys. This place is fancy.

Pints £3.15-4.50. Mixed drinks 2x1 M-Th £5.49. Open M-Th 11am-11pm, F-Sa 11am-1am, Su 11am-11pm.

CUCKOO'S NEXT

BAR ❷

69 Home St. ☎0131 228 1078

A smaller, student bar with a tiki feel, the booths are lined by a row of bamboo pieces and the mirrors on the walls are framed by what looks to be a bird's nest gatherings. Unless you're really going nuts here though, it looks like the only thing making the name pertinent is the empty bird cage at the back of the bar. There's quiz on Mondays, musical bingo on Thursday and an open mic night the second Wednesday of every month.

Pints £2.50-3.50. Mixed drinks from £3.50. Open daily noon-midnight or 1am.

THE EARL OF MARCHMOUNT

BAR ❷

22 Marchmount St. ☎0131 662 1877

A talker's bar, the Earl of Marchmount fills up with students around 9pm during the year. There's also a really great outdoor covered seating area. We said talker's bar, but that must be when they're not playing music: Jazz on Sundays at 3:30pm, Celtic music every other Monday, Bluegass on the odd Tuesday and DJs on Saturday. Maybe you'll just shut up and listen to the music.

Pints £3. Thistle Cross (strong cider) £4.25. Open M-Sa 11am-1am, Su 11am-midnight.

THE BLUE BLAZER

PUB ❸

2 Spittal St. ☎0131 229 5030

A heavily local place, the Blue Blazer refuses to let rules cramp their sense of humor. As the sign above the door says, "We at the Blue Blazer take our drinking very seriously. Anyone who appears to be having fun will be asked to leave." We think they're kidding. When we were there, people laughed and talked in front of the wood fireplace.

Pints £3.10-3.40. Open M-Sa 11am-1am, Su 12:30pm-1am. In Aug open until 3am.

THE ILLICIT STILL

BAR, PUB ❷

2 Broughton St. ☎0131 228 2633 www.theillicitstill.com

Badass names accompany badass bars. Don't let the purple exterior fool you; the Illicit Still keeps its empty malt whiskey boxes on display like trophies of war. A small entrance opens up into a large bar with long red benches, where you can sit during the comedy show every Tuesday night at 8pm.

i Quiz Su 8pm. Bottled beer from £1.80. Spirits £2.50-3.50. Open daily 4pm-1am. During the festival open 4pm-3am.

BENNET'S BAR PUB ❷

8 Leven St. ☎0131 229 5143

A great local haunt right next to the **King's Theatre** (currently under renovation), Bennet's has seen actors act out pantomimes over pints (in preparation for an upcoming show) or nip in for a quick one during intermission (apparently the beer-laden rehearsals didn't turn out well). A beautiful older pub, it's separated from the busy street by a pair of double doors with flowered stained glass. A giant wooden gantry houses the booze behind the bar.

Spirits £1.70-2.20. Pints £2.80-3.20. Open M-Sa 11am-1am, Su 5pm-11pm or midnight.

arts and culture

Edinburgh becomes the world capital for arts and culture every August during the city's **Fringe Festival.** The Fringe publishes its own program of activities, available in hard copy from the Fringe office and online. A world-famous orgy of the performing arts, the Fringe Festival encompasses shows in theater, dance, comedy, opera, and more. The festival was begun in 1947 when eight rebellious theater groups not invited to perform at the International Festival decided that "the show must go on." The organization was formalized, and thus the world's largest arts festival was born. *(180 High Street. ☎131 226 0026. www.edfringe.com.)* For all listings and local events during the rest of the year, check out *The List* (£2.25. www.list.co.uk) available at newsstands.

MUSEUMS AND GALLERIES

SURGEON'S HALL MUSEUM OLD TOWN

Surgeon's Hall, Nicholson St. ☎0131 527 1649 www.rcact.ac.uk

Full of some of the nastiest body parts perfectly preserved in formaldehyde and the wickedest-looking tools you've ever seen, this museum showcases every little bit of the history of surgery, and some stuff that must just be there to shock. The exhibit detailing the gruesome story of **Burke** and **Hare,** who murdered innocent citizens in order to receive the cash for supplying early doctors with bodies, actually has a pocketbook made from Burke's very **human skin.** Before we had photography we had painting, and there are several *technically* beautiful oils of festering wounds. What can we say? It's great. Just don't come on a full stomach..

i Disabled visitors will want to call in advance to arrange a visit. £5, concession £3, family (2 adults, 3 children) £15. Open M-F noon-4pm. Aug open M-F 10am-4pm, Sa-Su noon-4pm.

HENDERSON GALLERY NEW TOWN

4 Thistle St. Ln. ☎0131 225 7464 www.hendersongallery.com

With around nine full rotating exhibitions a year, this isn't just some gallery set up by a sandwich shop, come check out the attractive loft space with paintings from all sorts of artists, from graffiti to fine art.

Out the back door of Henderson's. Ask a member of the staff. Open M-Sa 11am-6pm. In Aug open Tu-Sa 11am-6pm.

ALPHA ART NEW TOWN

52 Hamilton Pl. ☎0131 226 3066 www.alpha-art.co.uk

With a collection of original and limited-edition prints from artists that are local, UK-based and international, Alpha Art has a huge range of stuff. Great oils, silkscreens, and sculptures abound.

Open T-F 10am-6pm, Sa 10am-5pm, Su noon-5pm.

SCOTLANDART.COM NEW TOWN

1 St. Stephen Pl. ☎0131 225 6257 www.scotlandart.com

With over 1000 original pieces between their Glasgow and Edinburgh branches, as well an extensive online selection (they've got computers right there in the gallery if you want to check it out) the guys at www.scotlandart.com are there to make sure you find what you're looking for. For those of us on a traveler's budget, however, it may suffice simply to browse around.

Browsing free. Artwork expensive. Open T-F 10:30am-5:30pm, Sa 10am-5:30pm, Su noon-5pm.

RM ART NEW TOWN

51 St. Stephens St. 0797 357 4175 www.rosiemackenzieart.com

The most affordable of the art galleries in Stockbridge, Rosie Mackenzie Art has a nice selection of unique, handmade jewelry as well as sculptures and paintings from various local artists. That T-Rex with the Gibson Les Paul necklace that we picked up was fantastic.

Prices vary. Open W-Sa noon-5pm, Su 1-4pm.

MUSEUM OF CHILDHOOD OLD TOWN

42 High St. 0131 529 4142

This museum showcases a collection of old childrens' toys including building blocks and bassinets, plus one creepy "Kids Forever" sculpture. The kids in the Museum of Childhood, however, seem less interested in the exhibits and more interested in the toys at the gift shop. Go figure.

Free. Open M-Sa 10am-5pm, Su noon-5pm. Last entry 30min. before close.

MUSIC

HMV PICTURE HOUSE WEST END

31 Lothian Road 0131 221 2280 www.edinburgh-picturehouse.co.uk

A beautiful place to watch things get messy, the HMV Picture House sees the likes of Imogen Heap and Less Than Jake, plus other big names regularly. On Thursday nights they do the intense "Octopussy Club night," popular with students because of its £1 drinks. Who would have guessed?

Box Office M-F 12pm-2pm, Sa-Su 12pm-4pm.

THE BONGO CLUB CANONGATE

37 Holyrood Road 0131 558 8844 www.thebongoclub.co.uk

Half club, half live music venue, half arts space...wait, how many halves is that? Bongo does it all, throwing raging parties on the weekends in their jungle-esque main room, with a stage for bands and live DJ set-up. Head upstairs during the day to check out the revolving art exhibitions in the café.

Prices vary. Cover entrance F-Sa £3-12 depending on the act. Cafe open daily 1pm-7pm. Club open 11pm-3am. Open 7pm-10pm when music gigs are on.

THE JAZZ BAR OLD TOWN

1A Chambers St. 0131 220 4298 www.thejazzbar.co.uk

This is a perfect venue to hear blues, hip-hop, funk, and all that jazz. The Jazz Bar hosts not one, but three shows most nights: "Tea Time" *(Tu-Sa 6-8:30pm)* is acoustic, "The Early Gig" *(daily 8:30-11:30pm)* is jazzy and "Late N' Live" *(daily 11:30pm-3am)* is funky and electric.

Off of South Bridge St. i Cover cash only. Cover after Tea Time £1-5. No cover during Tea Time. Open M-F 5pm-3am, Sa 2:30pm-3am, Su 7:30pm-3am. Open until 5am during Fringe Festival in Aug.

DANCE

GHILLIE DHU WEST END 3

2-4 Rutland Pl. 0131 222 9930 ghillie-dhu.co.uk

A heavily-touristy bar in what used to be a church building, the room upstairs (with an organ, high columned ceilings, and 3 awesome chandeliers) still does weddings. More importantly, however, it's the space used for the **traditional Scottish jigs** and dancing that are put on. Head on over if you feel like getting down to some serious bagpipe music.

Pints £2.95-3.60. Spirits £2.75. Whiskeys £2.75-17.50. Open M-F 8am-3am, Sa 10am-3am, Su noon-3am.

THEATER

THE BEDLAM THEATRE — OLD TOWN ❶

116 Bristol Pl. ☎0131 225 9893 www.bedlamtheatre.co.uk

The oldest student-run theater in Great Britain, the Bedlam (named after a nearby mental institution) is full of fun and crazy performances, several by the **Edinburgh University Theatre Company (EUTC).** The "Improverts," the University Improv group, who play every Friday at 10:30pm and every night at 12:30am during the festival, shouldn't be missed.

i Those requiring disabled access should provide advance notice. Ⓢ Tickets £3.50-5, students usually receive a £1 discount. Closed June-July. Aug-May, just knock and someone will be there to greet you.

EDINBURGH PLAYHOUSE — OLD TOWN

18-22 Greenside Pl. ☎0844 847 1660 (24hr.) www.edinburghplayhouse.org.uk

Originally built to be a cinema, which it remained for 40 years, the Edinburgh Playhouse underwent a massive renovation in 1993 and now revels in its status as one of the most popular theaters in the city.

Ⓢ Ticket prices vary. Box office open M-Sa noon-6pm, show days noon-8pm.

USHER HALL — WEST END

Usher Hall, Lothian Rd. ☎0131 228 1155 www.usherhall.co.uk

The massive, white and royal-red concert hall has seen everyone from **Ella Fitzgerald** to Beck. Book online or visit their premises in person to inquire about upcoming shows.

Ⓢ Ticket prices vary. Box office open M-Sa 10am-5:30pm. Su shows open 1pm-1hr. before the event.

FESTIVAL THEATRE — OLD TOWN

13-29 Nicholson St. ☎0131 529 6000 www.eft.co.uk

Holding shows throughout the year, the Festival Theatre really gets going around festival season in August. With 1927 seats and the largest stage in Scotland, it's huge and a great deal for students who are able to score standby tickets for just £10. Call after noon the day of the show to inquire.

Ⓢ Average show tickets £20. Box office open M-Sa 10am-6pm, show nights 10am-8pm.

FILM

THE CAMEO — WEST END ❷

38 Home St. ☎0871 902 5723 www.picturehouses.co.uk

Scotland's second oldest cinema and one of the last to show independent, foreign, and cult flicks, the Cameo is a great place to see something other than the next steaming pile of whatever James Cameron has whipped up. Check the calendar to see when the monthly showing of the "so-bad-it's-good" cult classic, "The Room" is playing, then head off to the bar after the movie gets out.

Ⓢ £6.80, matinee £5.80, student concession £4.50-5.20. Open M-Th 11am-midnight, F-Sa 11am-1am, Su 11am-midnight.

shopping

CLOTHING

W.M. ARMSTRONG AND SONS VINTAGE EMPORIUM — OLD TOWN

83 Grassmarket ☎0131 220 5557 www.armstrongsvintage.co.uk

The largest vintage store in Britain has three physical shops and an online store. Still, if you're shopping online, you're likely to miss the giant paper-mâché trapeze artist dangling upside down in one of the Grassmarket location's crowded display rooms. You'll probably also miss out on the £1 box, full of all sorts of fun odds and ends. And you miss out on the sunglasses, boots, dresses—hell, just go to the store already.

i Student discounts available. Open M-Th 10am-5:30pm, F-Sa 10am-6pm, Su noon-6pm.

W.M. ARMSTRONG AND SONS VINTAGE EMPORIUM STOCKBRIDGE

64-66 Clark St. ☎0131 667 3056 www.armstrongsvintage.co.uk

Hey! You guys already did this one! Guess again: Armstrong's is so good they've got multiple stores, and their Clark street location is just as excellent as their Grassmarket spot. This one's got WWI military helmets next to tiny pairs of lederhosen and elevator shoes—you know the drill. Awesome.

Prices vary. Open M-W 10am-5:30pm, Th 10am-7pm, F-Su 10am-6pm.

ELAIN'E VINTAGE CLOTHING STOCKBRIDGE

55 St. Stephens St. ☎0131 225 5783

A well-known and fun establishment down in Stockbridge, Elaine's got herself a collection of vintage stuff ranging from the 1920's onward. A great selection of dresses and high-heels (we're not saying they're always there, but **Prada** shoes have been known to frequent this establishment) and a nice collection of men's shirts and jackets.

Prices vary. Open T-Sa 1pm-6pm.

ROHAN NEW TOWN

86 George St. ☎0131 225 4876 www.rohan.co.uk

A store that totally, completely, entirely devotes its time to crafting clothing for travelers. Now, before you think "camping gear," think again—this is normal clothing (they've even got sport coats) that has been amped up for the rigors of intense travel. It's light, breathable, packable, and full of secret pockets so you can transport your passport and—cough!—other materials safely across the border.

Good travel gear doesn't come cheap. T-shirts run up to £30. Open M-Sa 9:30am-5:30pm.

STATE OF MIND BOUTIQUE (SMB) CANONGATE

20 St. Mary's St. ☎0131 556 0215 www.stateofmindboutique.co.uk

Showcasing the hipstery-est and baggiest specialty clothing from NYC, LA, Tokyo, and Scotland, SMB sells button-ups and T-shirts as well as a large selection of Vans and Converse. Ask about brands that can't be found outside of Edinburgh or Scotland.

i 10% Student discount available. Open daily 11am-6pm.

BOOKS

THE OLD TOWN BOOKSHOP OLD TOWN

8 Victoria St. ☎0131 225 9237 www.oldtownbookshop.com

Walking into the Old Town Bookshop, a wonderful little bookstore in the middle of Victoria St., is like walking into an well-tended study. A small space with books rising up to the ceiling, this shop carries an impressive collection of rare and vintage books as well as old paperback books you always wanted to read but never did *(£1)*. Antique prints and maps are also available.

Prices vary. Open M-Sa 10:30am-5:45pm.

BLACKWELL BOOKS OLD TOWN

53-62 South Bridge ☎0131 622 8222 www.blackwell.co.uk

A retail chain selling lots of titles at retail prices, there's not a lot of character but you're likely to find that book you couldn't locate in the smaller local shops. Small sale section available.

Prices vary. Open M-F 9am-8pm, Sa 9am-6pm, Su noon-6pm.

ST. JOHN CHARITY BOOKS PLUS STOCKBRIDGE

20 Deanhaugh St. ☎0131 332 4911 www.stjohnbookshop.co.uk

A secondhand bookshop with the best of both worlds, St. John's has a collection of old penguin paperbacks *(£1-2)* or a large collection of antiquarian books for those looking to pick up that rare first edition of **Henry James** that you're sure is worth millions but have never actually finished.

Open M-Sa 10am-5pm, Su noon-4pm.

TRANS-REAL FICTION OLD TOWN

7 Cowgatehead ☎0131 226 2822 www.transreal.co.uk

Surrounded by the ancient castles of Edinburgh and Scotland, who wouldn't be craving a good sci-fi or fantasy novel? Trans-Real Fiction's got your fix, as well as a selection of **stuffed animals.** Have at you! Taste my sword!

Just at the end of Grassmarket. Open M-F 11am-6pm, Sa 10am-6pm, Su noon-5pm.

OXFAM BOOKS STOCKBRIDGE

25 Raeburn Pl. ☎0131 332 9632

A charity shop for secondhand books, they do everything from popular fiction to classics. It's for charity people! Buy yourself some reading material!

Prices vary. Open M-F 9:30am-5:30pm, Sa 10am-5:30pm, Su 12:30pm.

THE BOOK SHOP SOUTHSIDE

45 Clerk St. ☎0131 668 3142

This small shop offers mostly secondhand books at discount prices. What new stock they have immediately receives a 60% markdown. How's that for a sale? Used vinyl and antique book sections available as well.

Discounted prices. Open M-Sa 10am-6pm, Su noon-4pm.

THE WORKS OLD TOWN

63 Princes St. ☎0131 539 0007 www.theworks.co.uk

Housing a selection of books both popular fiction and classic, The Works sells them at factory outlet prices. If you see more than one you like, why not take two or three? *(3 for £5; £1.95 each).*

Open daily 8:30am-9pm.

OUTDOOR MARKETS

EDINBURGH FARMER'S MARKET OLD TOWN

Castle Terr. www.edinburghfarmersmarket.co.uk

With over 65 separate providers, the Edinburgh Farmers Market is a great place for face painting (for kiddies or you, if you're so inclined), slow cooking demonstrations *(first Sa of every month)*, and, of course, the freshest foodstuffs you can imagine.

Castle Terr. is just off Lothian Rd. at the end of Princes St. Open Sa 9am-2pm.

LIQUOR STORES

THE WHISKY STORE OLD TOWN

28 Victoria St. ☎0131 225 4666 www.whiskyshop.com

The end-all for whiskey drinkers (besides a hangover) the guys at the whiskey store really know their stuff. So much so that they'll take you on a "tutored tasting," *(introductory £12.50, specialized £25)* to help you find the perfect bottle. They also have live casks, right there, and you can fill up your own bottle with stuff that's guaranteed to be unique not just to Scotland, but to that very shop.

i Call ahead to set up tutored tasting. Prices vary. Open M-Sa 10am-6pm, Su 11am-6pm. Jul 10am-7pm, Aug 10am-8pm.

ROBERT GRAHAM WHISKY AND CIGARS NEW TOWN

194a Rose St. ☎0131 226 1874 www.robertgraham1874.com

It's a whiskey shop on the pub-filled Rose St.—whodathunkit? From the tiny bottles *(£4-20)* to the full-size models, the items sold at this shop vary in quality and price—but all have whiskey in them. Robert Graham also sells cigars, pipes, and all the accoutrements you could ever need to sit in your study and act like James Bond.

Whiskey prices vary between £20-500. Open M-W 10:30am-6pm, Th-F 10:30am-7pm, Sa 10:30am-7:30pm.

ELECTRONICS

LAPTOP REPAIR CENTRE

OLD TOWN

6 Greyfriars Pl.

A brand-new option for those seeking salvation for their slow or non-functioning computer, PC or Mac. They'll add RAM, clean out junk space, or reset your hard drive if necessary. If you're in the market, they also usually have a few second-hand laptops for sale.

All repairs under £69. Open M-Sa 9am-6pm.

FURNITURE

HABITAT

OLD TOWN

32 Shandwick Pl. ☎0844 499 1114 habitat.co.uk

A classy but reasonably priced option, Habitat has everything from couches and chairs to wall decorations and **kitsch.** Think of it as IKEA, but not.

Open M-W 10am-6pm, Th 10am-7pm, F 10am-6pm, Sa 9:30am-6pm, Su 11am-6pm.

INHOUSE LIMITED

NEW TOWN

28 Howe St. ☎0131 225 2888 www.inhouse-uk.com

With a selection of the most Modern of the Modern in furniture pieces, you could make your flat look like a **Samuel Beckett** play—minimalist. It'll cost you though.

Prices vary, but lean towards the high end. Open T-Sa 9am-5:30pm.

OMNI FURNISHING

NEW TOWN

6-10 Earl Grey St. ☎0131 221 1200 www.omnifurnishings.co.uk

Specializing in wooden pieces (and, from the lovely smell of fresh cut wood inside the display rooms, newly-made pieces at that), OMNI has a wide selection of tables, chairs, and other furnishings.

Prices vary. Open M-F 10am-6pm, Sa 9:30am-5pm, Su noon-5pm.

ANTIQUES

UNICORN ANTIQUES

NEW TOWN

65 Dundas St. ☎0131 556 7176

You may have to paw your way through a few doorknobs, but it'll be worth it when you find that awesome one of a kind souvenir you've been looking for. Bear in mind that this is a hodge-podge collection, so you're not going to find any signs pointing out where "cool 19th-century photographs" are. The best antique stores are all like this.

From Queen St., turn onto Dundas St. and follow for 3 blocks. Open M-Sa 10:30am-6:30pm.

CAVANAGH ANTIQUES

OLD TOWN

49 Cockburn St. ☎0131 226 3391

Specializing in metal knick-knacks and everything shiny, this shop has a large selection of coins, medals, and both costume and upper-end jewelry.

Cockburn St., off of High St. on Royal Mile.

HARLEQUIN ANTIQUES

OLD TOWN

30 Bruntsfield Pl. ☎0131 228 9446

A **clock** and watch specialist, Harlequin has lots of beautiful old wrist and pocket watches, as well as that gorgeous grandfather clock you've always wanted. The only question is how to get it home. They also do repairs.

Bruntsfield Pl., on the West edge of Meadow Park. Prices vary. Open M-Sa 10am-5pm.

DEPARTMENT STORES

ST. JAMES SHOPPING CENTRE

OLD TOWN

1 Leith St. ☎0131 557 0050 www.stjamesshopping.com

Get yer shop on at St. James's, with over 60 different shops of every genre, as

well as department stores, a food court, and an internet cafe.
‡ Off of Waterloo Pl., a 5min. walk from Waverley Station. i Internet cafe first floor. ⏰ Open M-W 9am-6pm, Th 9am-8pm, F-Sa 9am-6pm, Su 10am-6pm.

PRINCES MALL NEW TOWN
Princes Plaza, Princes St. ☎0131 557 9179 www.princesmall-edinburgh.co.uk
An underground mall that gets its natural light from the plaza above, it's got escalators connecting the floors, a food court, and more retail than you can shake a stick, or a pound sterling, at.
‡ On the south side of Princes St. at the east end. Side by side with Waverley Train Station. ⏰ Open M-W 8:30am-6:30pm, Th 8:30am-7:30pm, F-Sa 8:30am-6:30pm, Su 10:30am-5:30pm.

essentials i

PRACTICALITIES

- **TOURIST OFFICE: Visit Scotland Information Centre** is the largest tourist information center in Scotland. The friendly representatives from this Edinburgh branch will help you book accommodations, city tours, and coach and bus tours. The office also houses a souvenir shop and Internet center. *(3 Princes Street. ‡ Across from Waverley Station. ☎08452 255 121 www.visitscotland.com $ Credit cards accepted. ⏰ Open Sept-Jun M-Sa 9am-5pm, Su 10am-5pm; Jul-Aug M-Sa 9am-7pm, Su 10am-7pm.)*
- **POST OFFICE: Newington Branch.** *(41 S. Clark St. ☎0131 667 1154 ⏰ Open M-Sa 9am-5:30pm, Su 9am-12:30pm.)* **Forest Row Post Office** *(32 Forest Row. ☎0131 225 3957 ⏰ Open M-F 8:30am-6pm, Sa 8:30am-5pm.)* **St. Mary's Street Post Office** *(46 St. Mary's St. ☎0131 556 6351 ⏰ Open M-F 9am-5:30pm, Sa 9am-12:30pm.)*
- **POST OFFICE: Frederick St. Post Office.** *(40 Frederick St. ☎08457 740 740 ⏰ Open M-F 9am-5:30pm except Tu open at 9:30am, Sa 9am-12:30pm.)*
- **INTERNET CAFE: E-Corner Internet.** *(54 Blackfriars St. ☎0131 558 7858 info@e-corner.co.uk $ Internet £.50 per 10min., £1.80 per 1 hr. Printing £.29 per page. International calls £.10 per min. to landlines. ⏰ Open M-F 9am-10pm, Sa-Su 10am-9pm.)* **PC Emergency Internet.** *(13 Frederick St. ☎0754 363 3242 info@e-corner.co.uk $ Internet £2 per hr. Day pass 9am-9pm £6. Printing £.50 per page for first 5 pages, £.25 per page after that. ⏰ Open M-F 9am-10pm, Sa-Su 10am-9pm.)*
- **BANK: Barclays.** *(1 St. Andrews Sq. ☎0845 755 5555 www.barclays.co.uk $ Credit cards accepted. ⏰ Open M-F 9am-5pm, Sa 10am-2pm.)*
- **ATM: Barclays** has 24hr. ATM out front *(72 George St. ☎0131 470 6000 www.barclays.co.uk $ Credit cards accepted. ⏰ Open M-F 9am-5pm, Sa 10am-2pm.)*

EMERGENCY!

- **POLICE:** Headquarters at Fettes Ave. *(☎0131 311 3131 www.lbp.police.uk.)* Other stations at 14 St. Leonard's St. *(☎0131 662 5000)* and 188 High St. *(☎0131 226 6966)*. Blue police information boxes are scattered throughout the city center, with tourist information and an emergency assistance button.
- **PHARMACY: Boots** Pharmacy. *(32 West Maitlin St. ☎0131 225 7436 $ Credit cards accepted. ⏰ Open M-F 8am-6pm, Sa 9am-6pm.)* **Royal Mile Pharmacy** *(67 High St. ☎0131 556 1971 royalmilepharmacy@hotmail.com $ Credit cards accepted. ⏰ Open M-F 9am-6pm, Sa 9am-5pm.)*
- **HOSPITALS: Royal Infirmary of Edinburgh** *(51 Little France Crescent ☎0131 536 1000, emergencies 536 6000)*. **Royal Hospital for Sick Children** *(9 Sciennes Rd. ☎0131 536 0000)*.

GETTING THERE

By Train

Waverley Train Station *(between Princes St., Market St., and Waverley Bridge. ☎08457 484 950. www.networkrail.co.uk Open M-Sa 12:45am-4am, Su 12:45am-6am.)* has trains to **Aberdeen** *(£33.20. 2½hr. M-Sa every hr., Su 8 per day.)*; **Glasgow** *(£9.70. 1hr., 4 per hr.)*; **Inverness** *(£32. 3½hr., every 2hr.)*; **London King's Cross** *(£103. 4¾hr., every hr.)*; **Stirling.** *(£6.10 50min., 2 per hr.)* **Haymarket Train Station** is smaller, but has service to destinations throughout Scotland. *(Haymarket Terrace. www.scotrail.com. Open M-Sa 5:10am-12:30am, Su 7:45am-12:45am. Ticket office open 7:45am-9:30pm.)*

A UNESCO World Heritage sight and the first major steel bridge in the world, the **Forth Railway Bridge** connects central Edinburgh to the city of Fife to the northeast. This 2.5 km structure connects the northeast and southeast regions of Scotland. Check www.scotrail.co.uk for details.

GETTING AROUND

By Bus

Getting around in Edinburgh is always easiest on **foot,** so unless you've just completed your trip through the Himalayas, you shouldn't find you're too sore at the end of the day. However, for those who really dislike hoofin' it, **Lothian Buses** have routes zig-zagging all over the city.

LOTHIAN BUSES BUSES

Lothian Buses Plc., Annandale Street, ☎0131 555 6363 www.lothianbuses.com

The first thing you should note about the bus system in Edinburgh is that most bus stops will have both an electronic screen alerting you to which lines are in service and the ETA of their arrival at the stop. The second is that there is a ticket machine at the stop, so buying your ticket in advance will save the bus driver a lot of chagrin (and perhaps save you from a telling off). Major lines for Lothian buses include the **24, 29, and 42 buses**, running from Stockbridge, through city center all the way to Newington St. on the South End. The 24 Line heads off toward Mixto St. and Arthur's Seat, the 42 bends west to end at Portobello by Dynamic Earth, and the 29 ends at the Royal Infirmary. The **12, 26, and 31 buses** all come in from the Northwest and the Haymarket/Dalry area, the 12 bending off to the Northeast after passing through city center, the 26 heading south toward Newington and Mixto St., and the 31 pulling the same route but diverging to head Southwest into Liberton and Gracemount.

Daytime adult singles £1.20, child £.70; day pass adult £3, child £2.40; city singles (detachable day passes) 20 for £24. Night tickets: all-night ticket available for night buses £3.

By Taxi

CENTRAL TAXIS TAXIS

8 St Peter's Buildings, Gilmore Pl. ☎0131 229 2468 www.taxis-edinburgh.co.uk

With over 400 cabs and a 24/7 booking policy, Central cabs are by far the best taxi company to call when you need a lift. Book online if you're lacking in the phone department, and they'll amid within 5-10min.

Open 24hr.

ESSENTIALS

You don't have to be a rocket scientist to plan a good trip. (It might help, but it's not required.) You do, however, need to be well prepared, and that's what we can do for you. Essentials is the chapter that gives you all the nitty-gritty you need to know for your trip: the hard information gleaned from 50 years of collective wisdom (and that phone call to Britain the other day that put us on hold for an hour). Planning your trip? Check. Staying safe and healthy? Check. The dirt on transportation? Check. We've also thrown in communications info and meteorological charts, just for good measure. Plus, for overall trip-planning advice from what to pack (money and as little underwear as possible) to how to take a good passport photo (it's physically impossible; consider airbrushing), you can also check out the Essentials section of www.letsgo.com.

We're not going to lie—this chapter is tough for us to write, and you might not find it as fun of a read as 101 or Discover. But please, for the love of all that is good, read it! It's super helpful, and, most importantly, it means we didn't compile all this technical info and put it in one place for you (yes YOU) for nothing.

greatest hits

- **GET A VISA.** Put it on your spring-cleaning list, since you'll need to apply six to eight weeks in advance if you're staying more than 90 days (p. 188).
- **JUST THE TIP.** Service is sometimes included on restaurant bills. Double check your receipt to make sure you tip your waiter (p. 191).
- **USE A WEB-BASED EMAIL ACCOUNT.** Using an online service like Gmail will save you lots of time in internet cafes (p. 197).
- **NEVER PASS ON A BUS PASS.** Did someone say unlimited rides for $20 a month (p. 195)?
- **A PINT AIN'T SO PINT SIZED.** The Imperial Pint is 20 oz., as opposed to the traditional 16 oz. American pint. Chug accordingly (p. 200).

planning your trip

entrance requirements

- **PASSPORT:** Required for citizens of Australia, Canada, New Zealand and the US.
- **VISA:** Required for citizens of Australia, Canada, New Zealand and the US only for stays of longer than 90 days.
- **WORK PERMIT:** Required for all foreigners planning to work in the UK.

DOCUMENTS AND FORMALITIES

You've got your visa, your invitation, and your work permit, just like **Let's Go** told you to, and then you realize you've forgotten the most important thing: your passport. Well, we're not going to let that happen. **Don't forget your passport!**

VISAS

EU citizens do not need a visa to globetrot through Britain. Citizens of Australia, Canada, New Zealand, and the US do not need a visa for stays of up to 90 days, but this three-month period begins upon entry into any of the countries that belong to the EU's **freedom of movement** zone. For more information, see **One Europe** (below). Those staying longer than 90 days may purchase a visa at British consulates. A visa costs £65 and allows the holder to spend six months in the UK.

Double-check entrance requirements at the nearest embassy or consulate of Britain (listed below) for up-to-date information before departure. US citizens can also consult http://travel.state.gov.

A long-term multiple-entry visa usually costs £205 and allows visitors to spend a year or more in Britain. If you plan to work or study in Britain, these policy changes may affect your plans. Under the new visa policy, all visa applicants are divided into five tiers, with priority given to skilled workers. Introduced in February of 2008, the new visa system will be implemented on a staggered basis. Consult the UK Visa Bureau website (*www.visabureau.com/uk*) to determine your visa eligibility.

Entering Britain to study requires a special visa. For more information, see the **Beyond Tourism** chapter.

essentials

one europe

The EU's policy of freedom of movement means that most border controls have been abolished and visa policies harmonized. Under this treaty, formally known as the Schengen Agreement, you're still required to carry a passport (or government-issued ID card for EU citizens) when crossing an internal border, but, once you've been admitted into one country, you're free to travel to other participating states. Most EU states are already members of Schengen (excluding Cyprus), as are Iceland and Norway.

WORK PERMITS

Entry to the UK as a traveler does not include the right to work, which is authorized only with a work permit. For more information, see **Beyond Tourism**.

TIME DIFFERENCES

Great Britain is on Greenwich Mean Time (GMT) and observes Daylight Saving Time. This means that it is 5hr. ahead of New York City, 8hr. ahead of Los Angeles, 10hr. behind Sydney, and 11hr. behind New Zealand (note that Australia observes Daylight Savings Time from October to March, the opposite of the Northern Hemispheres—therefore, it is 9 hours ahead of Britain from March to October and 11 hours ahead from October to March, for an average of 10 hours).

embassies and consulates

For addresses of British embassies in countries not listed here, consult the Foreign and Commonwealth Office (☎020 7008 1500; wwww.fco.gov.uk). Some cities have a British consulate that handle most of the same functions as an embassy.

UK CONSULAR SERVICES ABROAD

- **AUSTRALIA:** *Commonwealth Ave., Yarralumla, ACT 2600 (☎61 026 270 6666 http://ukinaustralia.fco.gov.uk). Consular section (UK passports and visas), Piccadilly House, 39 Brindabella Circuit, Brindabella Business Park, Canberra Airport, Canberra ACT 2609 (☎61 1902 941 555). Consulates-general in Brisband, Melbourne, Perth, and Sydney; Consulate in Adelaide.*
- **CANADA:** *80 Elgrin St., Ottowa, ON K19P 5K7 (☎613 237 1530 www.britainincanada.org). Consulate-General, 777 Bay St., Ste. 2800, Toronto, ON M5G 2G2 (☎416-593-1290). Other consulates-general in Montreal and Vancouver; Honorary Consuls in Quebec City, St. John's, and Winnipeg.*
- **IRELAND:** *29 Merrion Rd., Ballsbridge, Dublin 4 (☎353 01 205 3700 www.britishembassy.ie).*
- **NEW ZEALAND:** *44 Hill St., Thorndon, Wellington 6011 (☎64 04 924 2888 www.britain.org.nz); mail to P.O. Box 1812, Wellington 6140. Consulate-General: 151 Queen St., Auckland (☎64 09 303 2973); mail to Private Bag 92014, Auckland.*
- **US:** *3100 Massachusetts Ave. NW , Washington, D.C. 20008 (☎202 588 7800 www.britainusa.com). Consulate-general: 845 Third Ave., New York, NY 10022 (☎212 745 0200). Other offices in Atlanta, Boston, Chicago, Houston, Los Angeles and San Francisco. Consulates in Dallas, Denver, Miami and Seattle.*

money

GETTING MONEY FROM HOME

Stuff happens. When stuff happens, you might need some money. When you need some money, the easiest and cheapest solution is to have someone back home make a deposit to your bank account. Otherwise, consider one of the following options.

Wiring Money

Arranging a **bank money transfer** means asking a bank back home to wire money to a bank in Britain. This is the cheapest way to transfer cash, but it's also the slowest and most agonizing, usually taking several days or more. Note that some banks may only release your funds in local currency, potentially sticking you with a poor exchange rate; inquire about this in advance. Money transfer services like **Western Union** are faster and more convenient than bank transfers—but also much pricier. Western Union has many locations worldwide. To find one, visit www.westernunion.com or call the appropriate number: in Australia ☎1800 173 833, in Canada and the US ☎800-325-6000, in the UK ☎0800 735 1815, or in Ireland, ☎353 66 979 1843. To wire money using a credit card in Canada and the US, call ☎800-CALL-CASH; in the UK, ☎0800 731 1815. Money transfer services are also available to **American Express** cardholders and at selected **Thomas Cook** offices. You need an ID to receive the money.

pins and atms

To use a debit or credit card to withdraw money from a cash machine (ATM) in Europe, you must have a four-digit Personal Identification Number (PIN). If your PIN is longer than four digits, ask your bank whether you can just use the first four or whether you'll need a new one. Credit cards don't usually come with PINs, so if you intend to hit up ATMs in Europe with a credit card to get cash advances, call your credit card company before leaving to request one.

Travelers with alphabetic rather than numeric PINs may also be thrown off by the absence of letters on European cash machines. Here are the corresponding numbers to use: 1 = QZ; 2 = ABC; 3 = DEF; 4 = GHI; 5 = JKL; 6 = MNO; 7 = PRS; 8 = TUV; 9 = WXY. Note that if you mistakenly punch the wrong code into the machine multiple (often three) times, it can swallow (gulp!) your card for good.

US State Department (US Citizens only)

In serious emergencies only, the US State Department will forward money within hours to the nearest consular office, which will then disburse it according to instructions for a US$30 fee. If you wish to use this service, you must contact the Overseas Citizens Services division of the US State Department. *(☎1 202 501 4444, from US ☎888 407 4747)*

TIPPING AND BARGAINING

Tips in restaurants are often included in the bill (sometimes as a "service charge"). If gratuity is not included, you should tip your server about 12.5%. Taxi drivers should receive a 10% tip, and bellhops and chambermaids usually expect£1-3. To the great relief of many budget travelers, tipping is not expected at pubs and bars in Britain. Bargaining is generally unheard of in UK shops.

TAXES

The UK has a 17.5% value added tax (VAT), a sales tax applied to everything but food, books, medicine, and children's clothing. The tax is included in the amount indicated on the price tag. The prices stated in **Let's Go** include VAT. Upon exiting Britain, non-EU citizens can reclaim VAT (minus an administrative fee) through the Retail Export Scheme, although the complex procedure is probably only worthwhile for large purchases. You can obtain refunds only for goods you take out of the country (not for accommodations or meals). Participating shops display a "Tax-Free Shopping" sign and may have a minimum purchase of £50-100 before they offer refunds.

To clam a refund, fill out the form you are given in the shop and present it with the goods and receipts at customs upon departure (look for the Tax-Free Refund desk at the airport). At peak times, this process can take up to an hour. You must leave the country within three months of your purchase in order to claim a refund, and you must apply before leaving the UK.

safety and health

GENERAL ADVICE

In any type of crisis, the most important thing to do is **stay calm.** Your country's embassy abroad is usually your best resource in an emergency; registering with that embassy upon arrival in the country is a good idea. The government offices listed in the **Travel Advisories** feature at the end of this section can provide information on the services they offer their citizens in case of emergencies abroad.

travel advisories

The following government offices provide travel information and advisories by telephone, by fax, or via the web:

- **AUSTRALIA: Department of Foreign Affairs and Trade.** *(☎61 2 6261 1111 www.dfat.gov.au)*
- **CANADA: Department of Foreign Affairs and International Trade (DFAIT).** Call or visit the website for the free booklet *Bon Voyage...But.* *(☎1 800 267 8376 www.dfait-maeci.gc.ca)*
- **NEW ZEALAND: Ministry of Foreign Affairs.** *(☎64 4 439 8000 www.mfat.govt.nz)*
- **UK: Foreign and Commonwealth Office.** *(☎44 20 7008 1500 www.fco.gov.uk)*
- **US: Department of State.** *(☎888 407 4747 from the US, 1 202 501 4444 elsewhere http://travel.state.gov)*

Local Laws And Police

Police presence in cities is prevalent, and most small towns have police stations. There are two types of police officers in Britain: regular officers with full police powers, and police community support officers (PCSO) who have limited police power and focus on community maintenance and safety. The national emergency numbers are ☎999 and ☎112. Numbers for local police stations are listed under each individual city or town.

Drugs And Alcohol

Remember that you are subject to the laws of the country in which you travel. If you carry insulin, syringes, or prescription drugs while you travel, it is vital to have a copy of the prescriptions and a note from your doctor. The Brits love to drink, so the presence of alcohol is unavoidable. In trying to keep up with the locals, remember that the Imperial pint is 20 oz., as opposed to the 16oz. US pint. The drinking age in the UK is 18 (14 to enter, 16 for beer and wine with food). Smoking is banned in enclosed public spaces in Britain, including pubs and restaurants.

SPECIFIC CONCERNS

Northern Ireland

Border checkpoints in the UK have been removed, and armed soldiers and vehicles are less visible in Belfast and Derry. Do not take photographs of soldiers, military installations, or vehicles; the film will be confiscated and you may be detained for questioning. Taking pictures of political murals is not a crime, although many people feel uncomfortable doing so in residential neighborhoods.

Terrorism

The bombings of July 7, 2005 in the London Underground revealed the vulnerability of large European cities to terrorist attacks and resulted in the enforcement of stringent safety measures at airports and major tourist sights throughout British cities. Allow extra time for airport security and do not pack sharp objects in your carry-on luggage—they will be confiscated. Unattended luggage is always considered suspicious and is also liable to confiscation. Check your home country's foreign affairs office for travel information and advisories, and be sure to follow the local news while in the UK.

PRE-DEPARTURE HEALTH

Matching a prescription to a foreign equivalent is not always easy, safe, or possible, so if you take **prescription drugs,** carry up-to-date prescriptions or a statement from your doctor stating the medications' trade names, manufacturers, chemical names, and dosages. Be sure to keep all medication with you in your carry-on luggage.

Immunizations And Precautions

Travelers over two years old should make sure that the following vaccines are up to date: MMR (for measles, mumps, and rubella); DTaP or Td (for diphtheria, tetanus, and pertussis); IPV (for polio); Hib (for *Haemophilus influenzae* B); and HepB (for Hepatitis B). For recommendations on immunizations and prophylaxis, check with a doctor and consult the **Centers for Disease Control and Prevention (CDC)** in the US or the equivalent in your home country. *(☎1 800 CDC INFO/232 4636 www.cdc.gov/travel)*

STAYING HEALTHY

Diseases And Environmental Hazards

Common sense is the simplest prescription for good health while you travel. Drink lots of fluids to prevent dehydration and constipation, and wear sturdy, broken-in shoes and clean socks. The British Isles are in the gulf stream, so temperatures are mild: around 40°F in winter and 65°F in summer. In the Scottish highlands and mountains temperatures reach greater extremes. When in areas of high altitude, be sure to dress in layers that can be peeled off as needed. Allow your body a couple of days to adjust to decreased oxygen levels before exerting yourself. Note that alcohol is more potent and UV rays are stronger at high elevations.

Many diseases are transmitted by insects—mainly mosquitoes, fleas, ticks, and lice. Be aware of insects in wet or forested areas, especially while hiking and camping. Wear long pants and long sleeves, tuck your pants into your socks, and use a mosquito net. Use insect repellents such as DEET and soak or spray your gear with permethrin (licensed in the US only for use on clothing). Mosquitoes—responsible for malaria, dengue fever, and yellow fever—can be particularly abundant in wet, swampy, or wooded areas. Ticks—which can carry Lyme and other diseases—can be particularly dangerous in rural and forested regions of Britain.

getting around

For information on how to get to Britain and save a bundle while doing so, check out the Essentials section of **www.letsgo.com.** (In case you can't tell, we think our website's the bomb.)

BY PLANE

When it comes to airfare, a little effort can save you a lot of cash. If your plans are flexible enough to deal with the restrictions, courier fares are the cheapest. Tickets bought from consolidators and for standby seating are also good deals, but last-minute specials, airfare wars, and charter flights often beat these fares. The key is to hunt around, to be flexible, and to ask persistently about discounts. Students, seniors, and those under 26 should never pay full price for a ticket. Beware of the extremely exorbitant fees often tacked on to your ticket price. They can sometimes be equal to the cost of the ticket.

Commercial Airlines

For small-scale travel on the continent, *Let's Go* suggests **budget airlines** (below) for budget travelers, but more traditional carriers have made efforts to keep up with the revolution. The **Star Alliance Europe Airpass** offers low economy-class fares for travel within Europe to 220 destinations in 45 countries. The pass is available to non-European passengers on Star Alliance carriers, including United and Continental Airlines *(www.staralliance.com).* **EuropebyAir's** snazzy FlightPass also allows you to hop between hundreds of cities in Europe and North Africa. *(☎1 888 321 4737 www.europebyair.com Ⓢ Most flights US$99.)*

budget airlines

The recent emergence of no-frills airlines has made hopscotching around Europe by air increasingly affordable. Though these flights often feature inconvenient hours or serve less popular regional airports, with ticket prices often dipping into single digits, it's never been faster or easier to jet across the continent. The following resources will be useful not only for crisscrossing Britain but also for those ever-popular weekend trips to nearby international destinations.

- **BMIBABY:** Departures from multiple cities in the UK to Paris, Nice, and other cities in France. *(☎0871 224 0224 for the UK, 44 870 126 6726 elsewhere www.bmibaby.com)*
- **EASYJET:** London to Bordeaux and other cities in France. *(☎44 871 244 2366, 10p per min. www.easyjet.com Ⓢ UK£50-150.)*
- **RYANAIR:** From Dublin, Glasgow, Liverpool, London, and Shannon to destinations in France. *(☎0818 30 30 30 for Ireland, 0871 246 0000 for the UK www.ryanair.com)*
- **STERLING:** The first Scandinavian-based budget airline connects Denmark, Norway, and Sweden to 47 European destinations, including Montpellier, Nice, and Paris. *(☎70 10 84 84 for Denmark, 0870 787 8038 for the UK www.sterling.dk)*
- **TRANSAVIA:** Short hops from Krakow to Paris. *(☎020 7365 4997 for the UK www.transavia.com Ⓢ From €49 one-way.)*
- **WIZZ AIR:** Paris from Budapest, Krakow, and Warsaw. *(☎0904 475 9500 for the UK, 65p per min. www.wizzair.com)*

In addition, a number of European airlines offer discount coupon packets. Most are only available as tack-ons for transatlantic passengers, but some are standalone offers. Most must be purchased before departure, so research in advance. For example, **oneworld,** a coalition of 10 major international airlines, offers deals and cheap connections all over the world, including within Europe. *(www.oneworld.com)*

BY TRAIN

Trains in Britain are generally comfortable, convenient, and reasonably swift, crisscrossing the length and breadth of the island. Second-class compartments, which seat from two to six, are great places to meet fellow travelers. Make sure you are on the correct car, as trains sometimes split at crossroads. Towns listed in parentheses on European train schedules require a train switch at the town listed immediately before the parentheses. In cities with more than one train station, the city name is given first, followed by the station name (for example, "Manchester Piccadilly" and "Manchester Victoria" are Manchester's two major stations).

In general, traveling by train costs more than by bus. You can either buy a **railpass,** which allows you unlimited travel within a particular region for a given period of time, or rely on buying individual **point-to-point** tickets as you go. Almost all countries give students or youths (under 26, usually) direct discounts on regular domestic rail tickets, and many also sell a student or youth card that provides 20-50% off all fares for up to a year.

rail resources

- **WWW.RAILEUROPE.COM:** Info on rail travel and railpasses.
- **POINT-TO-POINT FARES AND SCHEDULES:** www.raileurope.com/us/rail/fares_schedules/index.htm allows you to calculate whether buying a railpass would save you money.
- **WWW.RAILSAVER.COM:** Uses your itinerary to calculate the best railpass for your trip.
- **WWW.RAILFANEUROPE.NET:** Links to rail servers throughout Europe.
- **WWW.LETSGO.COM:** Check out the Essentials section for more details.

BY BUS

The British distinguish between buses (short local routes) and coaches (long distances). *Let's Go* uses the term "buses" for both. Regional passes offer unlimited travel within a given area for a certain number of days; these are often called Rovers, Ramblers, or Explorers, and they usually offer cost-effective travel. Plan ahead and book tickets online in order to take advantage of discounts.

Though European trains and railpasses are extremely popular, in some cases buses prove a better option. In Britain, long-distance travel is extensive and cheap. Often cheaper than railpasses, **international bus passes** allow unlimited travel on a hop-on, hop-off basis between major European cities. **Busabout,** for instance, offers three interconnecting bus circuits covering 29 of Europe's best bus hubs. *(☎+44 8450 267 514 www.busabout.com 1 circuit in high season starts at US$579, students US$549.)* **Eurolines,** meanwhile, is the largest operator of Europe-wide coach services. We get misty-eyed just thinking about their unlimited 15- and 30-day passes to 41 major European cities. *(☎08717 818 181 www.eurolines.com High season 15-day pass €345, 30-day pass €455; under 26 €290/375. Mid-season €240/330; under 26 €205/270. Low season €205/310; under 26 €175/240.)* **National Express** *(☎08705 808 080; www.nationalexpress.com)* is the principal operator of long-distance bus services in Britain, although **Scottish Citylink** (☎08705 505 050 www.citylink.co.uk) has extensive coverage in Scotland with

discounts available for seniors (over 50), students, and young persons (16-25). The Brit Xplorer passes offer unlimited travel for a set number of days (7 days £79, 14 days £139, 28 days £219; www.nationalexpress.com). For those who plan far ahead, the best option is National Express's Fun Fares, only available online, which offer a limited number of seats on buses from London starting at, amazingly, £1. Tourist Information Centers carry timetables for regional buses and will help befuddled travelers decipher them.

Ulsterbus (☎028 9066 6630 www.ulsterbus.co.uk) runs extensive and reliable routes throughout Northern Ireland. Pick up a free regional timetable at any station. The Emerald Card, designed for travel in the Republic of Ireland as well as Northern Ireland, offers unlimited travel on Ulsterbus. The card works for eight days out of 15 (£115, under 16 £58) or 15 out of 30 consecutive days (£200/50).

BY BOAT

Most European ferries are quite comfortable; the cheapest ticket typically still includes a reclining chair or couchette. Fares jump sharply in July and August. Ask for discounts; ISIC and Eurail Pass holders get many reductions and free trips. You'll occasionally have to pay a port tax (under US$10).

Many of Britain's northern and western islands are inaccessible except by ferry. Ticket fares vary but almost always increase for automobiles. Be sure to board at least 15min. prior to departure. A directory of UK ferries can be found at www.seaview.co.uk/ferries.html.

BY BICYCLE

Much of the British countryside is well-suited for cycling. Consult tourist offices for local touring routes and always bring along the appropriate Ordinance Survey maps. Some youth hostels rent bicycles for low prices, and in Britain train stations rent bikes and often allow you to drop them off elsewhere. Keep safety in mind—even well-traveled routes cover uneven terrain, which might prove difficult to you easy riders. In addition to **panniers** (US$40-150) to hold your luggage, you'll need a good **helmet** (US$10-40) and a sturdy **lock** (from US$30). For more books on biking through the UK, try **Mountaineers Books.** *(1001 SW Klickitat Way, Ste. 201, Seattle, WA 98134, USA ☎1 206 223 6303 www.mountaineersbooks.org)*

keeping in touch

BY EMAIL AND INTERNET

Hello and welcome to the 21st century, where you can check your email in most major European cities, though sometimes you'll have to pay a few bucks or buy a drink for internet access. Although in some places it's possible to forge a remote link with your home server, in most cases this is a much slower (and thus more expensive) option than taking advantage of free **web-based email accounts** (e.g., **www.gmail.com**). **Internet cafes** and the occasional free internet terminal at a public library or university are listed in the **Practicalities** sections of cities that we cover. For lists of additional cybercafes in Britain, check out www.cybercaptive.com.

Wireless hot spots make internet access possible in public and remote places. Unfortunately, they also pose security risks. Hot spots are public, open networks that use unencrypted, unsecured connections. They are susceptible to hacks and "packet sniffing"—the theft of passwords and other private information. To prevent problems, disable "ad hoc" mode, turn off file sharing and network discovery, encrypt your email, turn on your firewall, beware of phony networks, and watch for over-the-shoulder creeps.

BY TELEPHONE

Calling Home From Britain

Prepaid phone cards are a common and relatively inexpensive means of calling abroad. Each one comes with a Personal Identification Number (PIN) and a toll-free access number. You call the access number and then follow the directions for dialing your PIN. To purchase prepaid phone cards, check online for the best rates; www.callingcards.com is a good place to start. Online providers generally send your access number and PIN via email, with no actual "card" involved. You can also call home with prepaid phone cards purchased in Britain.

If you have internet access, your best—i.e., cheapest, most convenient, and most tech-savvy—bet is probably our good friend **Skype.** (*www.skype.com)* You can even videochat if you have one of those new-fangled webcams. Calls to other Skype users are free; calls to landlines and mobiles worldwide start at US$0.021 per minute, depending on where you're calling.

Another option is a **calling card,** linked to a major national telecommunications service in your home country. Calls are billed collect or to your account. Cards generally come with instructions for dialing both domestically and internationally.

Placing a collect call through an international operator can be expensive but may be necessary in case of an emergency. You can frequently call collect without even possessing a company's calling card just by calling its access number and following the instructions.

Cellular Phones

Cell phones are everywhere in the UK, although the Brits call them "mobile phones." Competitive, low prices and the variety of calling plans make them accessible even for short-term, low-budget travelers. Also, Britain has developed a text-messaging culture. For most visitors to the UK, a pay-as-you-go plan is the most attractive option. Pick up an eligible mobile (from £25) and recharge, or top up, with a card purchased at a grocery store, online, or by phone. Incoming calls and incoming text messages are always free. **Vodaphone** (*www.vodaphone.co.uk*) and **T-Mobile** (*www.t-mobile.co.uk*) are among the biggest providers.

international calls

To call Britain or Ireland from home or to call home from Britain, dial:

- **1. THE INTERNATIONAL DIALING PREFIX.** To call from **Australia,** dial ☎0011; **Canada** or the **US,** ☎011; **Ireland, New Zealand,** or the **UK,** ☎00.
- **2. THE COUNTRY CODE OF THE COUNTRY YOU WANT TO CALL.** To call **Australia,** dial ☎61; **Canada** or the **US,** ☎1; **Ireland,** ☎353; **New Zealand,** ☎64; the **UK,** ☎44.
- **3. THE CITY/AREA CODE.** *Let's Go* lists the city/area codes for cities and towns in Britain opposite the city or town name, next to a ☎, as well as in every phone number. If the first digit is a zero (e.g., ☎020 for London), **omit the zero** when calling from abroad (e.g., dial ☎20 from Canada to call London).
- **4. THE LOCAL NUMBER.**
- **5. EXAMPLES:** To call the US embassy in London from New York, dial ☎011 44 20 7499 9000. To call the British embassy in Washington from London, dial ☎00 1 202 588 7800. To call the US embassy in London from London, dial ☎020 7499 9000.

The international standard for cell phones is **Global System for Mobile Communication (GSM).** To make and receive calls in Britain,you will need a GSM-compatible phone and a **SIM (Subscriber Identity Module) card,** a country-specific, thumbnail-size chip that gives you a local phone number and plugs you into the local network. Many SIM cards are prepaid, and incoming calls are frequently free. You can buy additional cards or vouchers (usually available at convenience stores) to "top up" your phone. For more information on GSM phones, check out 🖳www.telestial.com. Companies like **Cellular Abroad** *(🖳www.cellularabroad.com)* and **OneSimCard** *(🖳www.onesimcard.com)* rent cell phones and SIM cards that work in a variety of destinations around the world.

BY SNAIL MAIL

Sending Mail Home From Britain

Airmail is the best way to send mail home from Britain. **Aerogrammes,** printed sheets that fold into envelopes and travel via airmail, are available at post offices. Write "airmail" or "*par avion*" on the front. Most post offices will charge exorbitant fees or simply refuse to send aerogrammes with enclosures. Surface mail is by far the cheapest and slowest way to send mail. It takes one to two months to cross the Atlantic and one to three to cross the Pacific—good for heavy items you won't need for a while, like souvenirs that you've acquired along the way.

Sending Mail To Britain

In addition to the standard postage system whose rates are listed below, **Federal Express** handles express mail services from most countries toBritain. *(☎1 800 463 3339 🖳www.fedex.com)* Sending a postcard within Britain costs 24p, while sending letters (up to 100g) domestically requires 27p.

There are several ways to arrange pickup of letters sent to you while you are abroad. Mail can be sent via **Poste Restante** (General Delivery) to almost any city or town in Britain with a post office. Address Poste Restante letters like so:

William SHAKESPEARE
Poste Restante
2/3 Henley St.
Stratford-upon-Avon CV37 6PU
United Kingdom

The mail will go to a special desk in the central post office, unless you specify a post office by street address or postal code. It's best to use the largest post office, since mail may be sent there regardless. It is usually safer and quicker, though more expensive, to send mail express or registered. Bring your passport (or other photo ID) for pickup; if the clerks insist that there is nothing for you, ask them to check under your first name as well. *Let's Go* lists post offices in the **Practicalities** section for each city and most towns. **American Express** has travel offices throughout the world that offer a free **Client Letter Service** (mail held up to 30 days and forwarded upon request) for cardholders who contact them in advance. Some offices provide these services to non-cardholders (especially AmEx Travelers Cheque holders), but call ahead to make sure. For a complete list of AmEx locations, call ☎1 800 528 4800 or visit 🖳www.americanexpress.com/travel.

climate

We'd love to tell you that everything you've heard about British weather is false...but we're not here to lie to you. Britain is traditionally cool and precipitation is considerably higher than other European destinations. Don't let the weather keep you from traveling to this wonderful country, but be prepared for some damp, chilly days during your stay.

AVG. TEMP. (LOW/ HIGH), PRECIP.	JANUARY			APRIL			JULY			OCTOBER		
	°C	°F	mm	°C	°F	mm	°C	°F	mm	°C	°F	mm
London	2/6	36/43	54	6/13	43/55	37	14/22	57/72	57	8/14	46/57	57
Edinburgh	1/6	34/43	57	4/11	39/52	39	11/18	52/64	83	7/12	45/54	65

To convert from degrees Fahrenheit to degrees Celsius, subtract 32 and multiply by 5/9. To convert from Celsius to Fahrenheit, multiply by 9/5 and add 32.

°CELSIUS	-5	0	5	10	15	20	25	30	35	40
°FAHRENHEIT	23	32	41	50	59	68	77	86	95	104

measurements

Like the rest of the rational world, Britain uses the metric system. The basic unit of length is the meter (m), which is divided into 100 centimeters (cm) or 1000 millimeters (mm). One thousand meters make up one kilometer (km). Fluids are measured in liters (L), each divided into 1000 milliliters (mL). A liter of pure water weighs one kilogram (kg), the unit of mass that is divided into 1000 grams (g). One metric ton is 1000kg. Gallons in the US and those in Britain are not identical: one US gallon equals 0.83 Imperial gallons. Pub aficionados will note that an Imperial pint (20 oz.) is larger than its US counterpart (16 oz.).

MEASUREMENT CONVERSIONS	
1 inch (in.) = 25.4mm	1 millimeter (mm) = 0.039 in.
1 foot (ft.) = 0.305m	1 meter (m) = 3.28 ft.
1 yard (yd.) = 0.914m	1 meter (m) = 1.094 yd.
1 mile (mi.) = 1.609km	1 kilometer (km) = 0.621 mi.
1 ounce (oz.) = 28.35g	1 gram (g) = 0.035 oz.
1 pound (lb.) = 0.454kg	1 kilogram (kg) = 2.205 lb.
1 fluid ounce (fl. oz.) = 29.57mL	1 milliliter (mL) = 0.034 fl. oz.
1 gallon (gal.) = 3.785L	1 liter (L) = 0.264 gal.

let's go online

Plan your next trip on our spiffy website, www.letsgo.com. It features full book content, the latest travel info on your favorite destinations, and tons of interactive features: make your own itinerary, read blogs from our trusty Researcher-Writers, browse our photo library, watch exclusive videos, check out our newsletter, find travel deals, follow us on Facebook, and buy new guides. Plus, if this Essentials wasn't enough for you, we've got even more online. We're always updating and adding new features, so check back often!

LONDON, OXFORD, CAMBRIDGE & EDINBURGH 101

During your time in London, Oxford, Cambridge, or Edinburgh, you're probably going to want to walk the walk and talk the talk of the locals—whether you're volunteering at the Fringe in Edinburgh, studying for a semester at Oxford or Cambridge, or gallivanting through the posh shops of London. You're just dying to know about the everyday happenings—what sports teams to root for, what to read, what to eat. Well, here's the skinny—though you won't stay that way if you spend too much time around British cuisine (see Food and Drink).

facts and figures

- **NUMBER OF UMBRELLAS LOST ON THE TUBE EVERY YEAR:** 80,000
- **YEARS IT TOOK TO REBUILD LONDON AFTER THE GREAT FIRE OF 1665:** 10
- **NUMBER OF PEOPLE WHO DIED IN THE GREAT FIRE:** 6
- **YEAR UNIVERSITY OF CAMBRIDGE WAS FOUNDED:** 1209
- **YEAR UNIVERSITY OF OXFORD BEGAN ADMITTING WOMEN:** 1878
- **NUMBER OF MILES BETWEEN CAMBRIDGE AND LONDON:** 50

people and customs

MOTHER TONGUES

"Native" Brits come in four basic flavors–English, Irish, Scottish, and Welsh, and the corresponding languages are all still spoken, although English is the dominant tongue in all four countries. Wales has preserved their native tongue the best, with Welsh translations on every sign and official document and a reasonable percentage of fluent speakers. Irish Gaelic is being aggressively preserved by the Irish government, with classes taught in primary schools. Scottish Gaelic is not as widely taught, and lingers mainly in the outer islands.

JUST DUCKING AROUND

When it comes to slang, you might think the British just make it up on the spot. Poultry inspires affectionate names for girls, which include "bird" and "duck." Derogatory language is particularly entertaining. Let's be honest: if you're called a "big girl's blouse" or "namby pamby" (translation for both: wimp) will you be able to keep a straight face?

food and drink

LET'S GO PUBBIN'

Bars constitute a huge part of culture all over Great Britain, especially tourist-filled London. Pub-goers won't have to tip, but that's only because there's no table service, so sidle up to the bartender for some shots. Ordering at the bar usually proves an exciting way to meet a fellow Carlsberg connoisseur. England predominantly brews ales, and there's always a feisty crowd looking to down some premium bitter pale ale.

KNOW YOUR MEATS

Fish and chips, to be eaten with malt vinegar rather than ketchup, continue as the go-to "experience" of eating in England. Order "bangers and mash" if you're craving some sausage slathered in onion gravy and mashed potatoes. For the pork lovers, a pork pie cooked from lard pastry with chopped pork bits topped off with pork jelly should satisfy your porker. The more carnivorous traveler may also enjoy shepherd's pie, a lamb casserole dish covered with a layer of mashed potatoes.

ARE THEY PUDDING US ON?

Bread and butter, sticky toffee, spotted dick suet—just a few of the pudding varieties on the menu in Britain. The Brits hold pudding in a special place (and it's not their hearts). Mind you, English pudding is not simply sweet and jiggly. In Britain, the term refers to any rich, dairy-based dessert. Other non-sweet savory dishes also take the name, like Yorkshire pudding, black pudding, and blood pudding.

TEA FOR TWO

Avoid stuffing yourself too much during lunch time in order to make room for afternoon tea, the light English meal eaten a few hours before dinner. Catherine of Braganza brought the custom over from Portugal in the 17th century, it is now make it an essential part of the day. Loose tea served with milk and sugar accompanies cucumber and cress sandwiches, scones, and other jam pastries. Some Brits prefer High Tea to replace afternoon tea and dinner. This informal meal usually consists of cold meats, sandwiches, and small desserts. Don't think it's an elaborate, high-class tea party; it originated when the family was too lazy to cook anything substantial.

GASTRONOMIC MULTICULTURALISM

London's Chinatown, located just beyond Leicester Square, houses various supermarkets, as well as cheap restaurants for a meal with a little bit of (Kung) Pao. Indian food is readily accessible on Brick Lane in East London, where the potent smell of spices and curry is impossible to avoid. Middle Eastern fare is represented as well.

town and gown

Forget about the minor differences between America and Britain—the Oxbridge rivalry is the great divide of the English-speaking world. As the two oldest universities in the UK, Oxford and Cambridge continue to battle with each other in scholarship and athletics. When scholars sought academic sanctuary after being forced out by the angry townsfolk of Oxford in 1209, they formed a new university. With Oxford producing more British prime ministers, Oxonians feel no qualms about stirring up the debate at dinner parties, and as the institute that calls itself home to all Rhodes Scholars, including Bill Clinton, Oxford holds some severe scholarly bragging rights. Not that Cambridge doesn't rebut with equally impressive braggadocio: Isaac Newton, Charles Darwin, and Stephen Hawking, all graduated from the 'Bridge. But perhaps the biggest, most satisfying carrot that Oxford dangles in its counterpart's face is the fact that Harry Potter scenes were shot on its university grounds. *Expelliarmus!*

sports and recreation

FOOTBALL

Football is by far the most popular sport in Britain, and by "football" we mean soccer—you know, that game you actually play with your feet. Britain's most famous (and sexiest) player is, of course, David Beckham, but close runners-up are Wayne Rooney, Ashley Cole, and John Terry. Play is divided into FIFA/World Cup and Premiere League categories, with many Premiere Leaguers playing for their countries in the Cup. Well-known British Premiere League clubs include Arsenal, Celtic, Chelsea, Liverpool, Manchester United, and West Ham. Club preference is usually regional, although there will occasionally be the odd Arsenal fan in Chelsea neighborhoods. Devotion to clubs is often passionate and occasionally violent; the term "soccer hooligan" is a reference to the post-game behavior of some rowdy fans.

RUGBY

As a cousin of British football, rugby was allegedly created by William Webb Ellis in 1823, a then-student at the Rugby School. Although the sport has now spread to France, Russia, and beyond, it remains most popular in the United Kingdom. The Rugby Football League oversees all professional competitions in England, dealing with all major competitions in the country, such as the Anglo-Welsh EDF Energy Cup and the English Guinness Premiership. The London Wasps regularly compete in these along with other major European championships, including the Heineken Cup, which they won in the 2006-07 season. We'll drink to that.

CRICKET

Thousands of English play this summertime sport, though professional teams usually play in the Oval in Kensington in south London and Lord's in the St. John's Wood area. Each team consists of eleven players with around six specializing batsmen and the other as bowlers, as well as a wicket-keeper. The bowler runs up to the pitch to toss the ball; the batsman can only score after hitting the ball and running to the other side of the oval cricket pitch, getting past the crease. Like baseball, the runner can be taken out via fielders; unlike baseball, you have to wear clownish hockey padding. True MVPs of the game, called all-rounders, pop up in a game every now and then to show off their mastery at the game, making all the other mere batters hate them. The London Cricket Club, formed in 1722 by members of what was known as a "Gentlemen's Club," still hosts games at the Artillery Club against international competitors. It's unclear whether the pompousness of the "Noblemen"—their other moniker of said social organization—has ceased.

TENNIS

Held in the London suburb of the same name, Wimbledon remains the oldest tennis tournament in the world, and attracts hoards of Andre Agassi groupies annually. The championship begins in late June and runs into July with five events held in competition. Besides a strict dress code of all white for tournament players, more bizarre customs during Wimbledon include eating strawberries and cream and drinking Pimm's spritzers, a type of gin-based summer cocktail.

HURLING

Hurling, an almost solely Irish game, can best be described as an extremely violent cross between American football, lacrosse, golf, and field hockey. A stick (the hurley) is used to propel the ball toward a goal. The ball may be picked up, however, and carried in the hand for several steps, at which point it can be bounced off the ground or the hurley and then carried again. Tackling is encouraged.

did you know?

- **DON'T SWEAT IT.** In 1517, the sweating sickness, a disease that swept over Great Britan through the course of a century and whose cause is still unknown today, annihilated half of the population in each city.
- **WRONG ADDRESS.** Despite popular belief, the Muffin Man does not live in Drury Lane—it's actually the location of London's oldest theater, opening in 1663 as the "Theatre Royal in Bridges Street."
- **SAFE ZONE.** During World War II, because Hitler had planned on using Oxford as his new capital if he succeeded in capturing England, no attacks struck the city during a time when bomb shelters were commonplace in the country. Hurrah.

HORSEMANSHIP

With over 60 racecourses in Great Britain alone, the equestrian-obsessed Brits never seemed to have gotten over their pony phase. The National Hunt, in which horses jump over fences and hurdles, along with flat racing mark the two major forms of racing in the country. The Ascot Racecourse in the Berkshire suburb of London remains one of the most popular venues for gamblers. Along with racing, horse showing recently picked up in equestrian recreational activities with the London International Horse Show at the Olympia Grand and National Halls. Pony fanatics enter their steeds in agility tests and dressage competitions for the hopes of glory at this annual competition.

BRINGING HOME THE GOLD

As host to the most hyped-up international sporting event for the third time in its history, London defeated Paris, Madrid, and New York as the location for the XXX Olympiad. As the city dolls itself up for the onslaught of spectators in 2012, much of its current urban design is in consideration for revamping. City officials continue to fuss over the Tube. Simultaneously, Olympic planners worry over leaving London in a financial ruin with elaborate buildings that have no use after the flags have come down. But perhaps the most controversial debate about the London Games has nothing to do with sports itself. When Wolff Olins revealed the logo he designed in 2007, the geometric emblem of "2012" was met with sheer horror. Despite the overwhelmingly negative reaction to the logo, however, Londoners swallowed their opposition for the sake of national pride; in October 2008, 20% of clothing sold at the Adidas London flagship store bore the symbol.

media

TABLOIDS

London remains notorious for its psychotic paparazzi. *The Sun*, one of the most read gossip publications, regularly reports (read: stalks) on the activities of international celebrities in London. Their friendliness toward the famous has gotten them into legal snafus more than once—Ewan McGregor took them to court and won $75000 in damages when they published vacation photos of him and his family. The *Daily Mirror*, another publication specializing in scandals, had to shy away from the public eye itself when the rag mag published doctored photos of British soldiers harassing Iraqi soldiers. Causing then-editor Piers Morgan—who was also ironically a competitor on Donald Trump's "The Apprentice"—to step down from his position, the hoax dramatically tarnished what little reputation remained of the paper.

Of course, if you're looking for some serious reading, you've got plenty to chose from—though we can't promise you'll steer clear of celebrity gossip. London's major newspapers are the *Times*,the *Guardian*, and the *Telegraph*,while the *Monitor*, *Edinburgh Evening News*, and the *Scotsman* are among the leading papers in Scotland.

FILM AND TELEVISION

Lights in London

Besides serving as the setting for multiple international blockbusters like *Love Actually* and *Notting Hill*, London's various neighborhoods almost act as their own characters in various movies throughout film history. The image of "Swinging London" began the huge cinematic boom in the 1960s, as foreign filmmakers began to capitalize on its appeal, churning out quirky classics like *Alfie* **(Michael Caine)** and *Bedazzled* **(Raquel Welch)**. With its rich history of royal melodrama and Shakespearean men in tights, London offers itself as a historical place for period projects, its old monuments acting as the real deal in BBC miniseries that usually end up going straight to DVD. Perhaps competing for Paris for the sappiest city prize, the city also promulgates its romantic charm in films, featured as a posh place to fall in love, usually with the help of a lofty, fetishized accent. Most recently, comedies have found success after wrapping up shooting in London, such as *Bend It Like Beckham* **(Keira Knightley)** and *About A Boy* **(Hugh Grant)**.

British film has recently become synonymous with subtle, well-acted period pieces, but film made in Britain by Brits can be as silly as Monty Python, as action-packed as James Bond, or as classic as the Royal Shakespeare Company's filmed theatrical productions. Films are often infused with the notoriously dry, sarcastic brand of British humor. Chick flicks and bombastic, explosive action films are few and far between.

The Other Tube

Television is an interesting blend of original, uniquely British shows (full of inside jokes about the NHS and council housing) and imports from America. The typical British television season consists of either six or thirteen episodes, much shorter than the full American television season of twenty-one or twenty-two episodes. While a number of originally British shows have been brought to America and remade, translation between the two cultures is hit or miss, with the misses *(Life on Mars, Coupling, Red Dwarf)* vastly outnumbering the hits *(The Office, Pop Idol/ American Idol, Antiques Roadshow).* The evening soap-opera has remained popular in Britain, with *Coronation Street*, *Eastenders*, *Neighbours*, and *Hollyoaks* holding on to respectable viewerships even after decades on the air.

fine arts

LONDON'S GOTHICISM

Westminster Abbey in London still stands as one of the most ornate—and borderline garish—examples of medieval Gothic architecture in Britain, with exquisitely refined stained glass and structural columns running vertically. The **Tower of London,** built in the late 11th century, also exemplifies the Medieval English style of concentric interiors, serving as a castle, fortress, and prison during the last millennium.

ELIZABETHAN VERNACULAR

Beginning in 1599, the construction of the **Globe Theater**, home of Shakespeare and his acting troupe, the Lord Chamberlain's Men, marked the start of early Renaissance style architecture. You'll know the building by its octagonal shape and a timber frame, Tudor wings, symmetrical towers, and a gratuitous number of mullioned windows.

THE GEORGIAN ERA

During the 18th century, London expanded to include several villages nearby, taking in much Georgian architecture along with it. Rectangular sash windows decorate brick houses, setting Georgian houses apart from Victorian ones that donned arched or pointed windows. Parapets also make Georgian houses within inner London easy to spot.

HISTORY PAINTING

As the most definable movement of Great Britain, representations of momentous historical events trumps all other genres in English art history. Prominent artists of the 1700s include **Sir James Thornhill** and **William Hogarth.** Thornhill, influenced by Italian baroque artists, served as court painter for George I and later rose to become a member of Parliament. Revered for his astute inclusion of English habits and temperaments of the time, Hogarth constructed his image as a legitimate portrait artist, a story painter, and a political cartoonist who poked fun at the arranged marriages of the British upper class in a series called *Marriage à-la-mode*. Depicting suicides and murders committed by unhappy wives, Hogarth shows how things, even in posh British society, can get too real.

THE GOTHIC REVIVAL

Beginning in the 1740s, Victorian Gothic aesthetics grew in popularity as the English sought to revive old medieval styles, and **A.W.N. Pugin,** who headed the construction of the House of Parliament, that Gothic style acted as a symbol of a purer society. Also known as **Westminster Palace,** this city landmark gives the architectural aficionado a titillating experience, including **Big Ben** and **Victoria Tower**.

UNIVERSITY OF CAMBRIDGE

The university's long history has given way to a mixture of various architectural styles, mixing and often clashing both ancient and modern characteristics. **King's College** steals the thunder from most other buildings on campus as a model of Gothic architecture from the 15th century. Inside, vaults, stained glass, and woodcarvings spanning several hundred years combine to create a unique and historical atmosphere. The Bridge of Sighs, designed by **Henry Hutchison** in 1831, occupies a romantic span across the **River Cam** in St. John's College. The imposing University Library, designed by Sir Giles Gilbert Scott in the 1930s who also built the Tate Modern, presides over the grounds like an overbearing foreman; it's most notable for Scott's signature industrial style.

GET CULTURED

Art and history zealots usually find it difficult to break away from the museum scene of London even for happy hour at a pub in Kensington. With free admissions into some of the world's most well curated galleries, London provides a lot of culture for not even a tuppence. Located in Bloomsbury on the northeastern edge of the city, the **British Museum** houses an astonishing collection of anthropological and cultural artifacts. Established through the will of physician Sir Hans Sloane, the museum's original "collection of curiosities" has expanded into far-reaching exhibits of Greek, Roman, and Egyptian objects. The **Tate Modern,** a part of the Tate museum group in Britain, owns some of the most rare Rothko and Matisse works on the planet, which are perhaps trumped by the building itself. Designed by Herzog and de Meuron—the same firm who led the construction of the Bird's Nest for the Beijing Olympics—the Tate was converted from a former power station. The industrial capacity of the building's former life proved appropriate for its current use, as the Turbine Hall, once a storage area for electricity generators, now houses new sprawling exhibitions by contemporary artists. Most classical art historians prefer to trek over to Trafalgar Square to the **National Gallery.** With paintings dating back as early as the 13th century, the museum has faced severe opposition to its overzealous restoration techniques. Prestigious art historians such as Ernst Gombrich have fervently criticized the gallery for disrupting the original tone and appearance of certain works, somehow managing to make cleaning seem like a bad thing.

holidays and festivals

BOXING DAY

December 26th is now just a practical post-Christmas day off to be spent lazing in pajamas or traveling home from holiday trips. Originally it was celebrated by the servant classes that were required to work on Christmas Day; the "boxing" part of the name refers to the practice of rich families boxing up their unwanted clothes or gifts and sending them home with the servants. The origin of regifting!

THE QUEEN'S BIRTHDAY

Her Majesty's day of birth is celebrated on varying Saturdays in June. The current Queen's actual date of birth is April 21st, but the holiday is celebrated in the summertime in the hopes that the weather will cooperate with the agenda of parades, picnics, and announcement of the Birthday Honors or, "who's getting knighted."

BANK HOLIDAYS

These are public holidays declared each year by the Queen. Bank Holidays occur each year in May and August, as well as several other statutory days, depending on region. St Patrick's Day, for example, is a Bank Holiday in Northern Ireland, but not in England, Scotland, or Wales.

GUY FAWKES' DAY

"Remember, remember the fifth of November, the gunpowder, treason and plot." This day commemorates Guy Fawkes' failed attempts to blow up the houses of Parliament. Lots of bonfires, lots of fireworks, lots of burning in effigy.

CAMBRIDGE FOLK FESTIVAL

Held in Cherry Hinton Hall in one of Cambridge's suburban villages, the annual music gathering brings together a widespread variety of folk musicians. Broadcast live on BBC Radio, the festival's two main stages serve as host to burgeoning figures in the British music industry. With previous performers including Paul Simon and Joan Baez, the venue acts as somewhat of a career launcher. Folk lovers usually grab umbrellas and lounge chairs to shelter themselves from weather and relax during the long three-day weekend in late July. Since gaining popularity from its inception in 1964, the festival has sold out immediately in most recent years.

LORD MAYOR'S SHOW

When King John granted a charter for the citizens of London to elect their own Lord Mayor in 1215, he may not have imagined the pageantry that would follow Londoners into the modern era, where flamboyant floats and garish costumes decorate the streets each year on the second Saturday in November. Historically, the proceedings took place via horseback or barges on the River Thames—the parade term "floats" was actually derived from the Lord Mayor's traditional romp through the city by boat. In 1710, a drunken flower girl uprooted then-Lord Mayer Sir Gilbert Heathcote from his horse, initiating a change to a state coach procession known for its six-horse coach (only to be outdone by the Queen, who has eight steeds during formal public outings). At 11pm, the parade takes off after swinging by the Mansion House, the Lord Mayor's official residence, to pick the old chap up, stopping by St. Paul's Cathedral to receive the Dean's blessing. The showy ordeal, including the Twelve Great Livery Companies (Merchant Taylors, Haberdashers, Ironmongers and more), usually ends more than three hours later after the procession winds down along the river, and is followed by an evening spectacle of fireworks.

BEYOND TOURISM

If you are reading this, then you are a member of an elite group—and we don't mean "the literate." You're a student preparing for a semester abroad. You're taking a gap year to save the trees, the whales, or the dates. You're an 80-year-old woman who has devoted her life to egg-laying platypuses and figuring out what the hell is up with that. In short, you're a traveler, not a tourist; like any good spy, you don't observe your surroundings—you become an active part of them.

Your mission, should you choose to accept it, is to study, volunteer, or work in London, Oxford, Cambridge, or Edinburgh as laid out in the dossier—er, chapter—below. More general wisdom, including international organizations with a presence in many destinations and tips on how to pick the right program, is also accessible by logging onto the Beyond Tourism section of www.letsgo.com. We leave the rest (when to go, whom to bring, and how many changes of underwear to pack) in your hands. This message will **self-destruct** in five seconds. Good luck.

greatest hits

- **SUPPLY AND DEMAND.** Become an economist extraordinaire at LSE (p. 212).
- **TEACH THE TOTS.** With the right qualifications, you may be able to snag a teaching gig in England or Scotland (p. 216).
- **READING, WRITING, ROWING.** Study at Oxford or Cambridge, where your classes are one-on-one tutorials—and stay for The Race (p. 212).

studying

Not surprisingly, English-language countries are among the most popular destinations for American travelers, with the United Kingdom alone attracting tens of thousands of study abroad students each year. If you're looking for a true cultural immersion experience but that high-school Spanish is beyond rusty, don't despair. Great Britain beckons. You get the adorable foreign accents without needing to awkwardly stumble through phrasebooks.

Whether you're lusting after Prince William (sorry, ladies, he already graduated) or looking to experience the famed Oxbridge tutorial system, English universities offer something for everyone. Before you jet off, do your research to figure out what program best fits your needs and your budget. **The British Council** is an excellent resource for choosing the right institution and preparing to study in the UK. *(www.educationuk.org)* Devoted to international student mobility to and from the UK, the **Council for International Student Affairs** is another important resource for the practical aspects of living abroad. *(9-17 St. Albans Pl., London N1 ONX ☎020 7288 4330 www.ukcisa.org.uk)*

visa information

If you're planning to stay for more than a short trip, chances are you need a visa. Find out online at www.ukvisas.gov.uk. As of March 31, 2009, foreigners planning to study abroad in the UK are required to apply for a visa under Tier 4: (General) Student and (Child) Student of the new points-based immigration system. Immigration officials will request a letter of acceptance from your UK university and proof of funding for your first year of study, as well as a valid passport, from all people wishing to study in the UK. Student visas cost £199, and application forms can be obtained online at the website above.

UNIVERSITIES

England is the only country in the world that attracts more international students than the United States, and it's no surprise when you consider that University of Cambridge, University of Oxford, University College London, and Imperial College London all ranked in the top ten world universities in 2009, according to the *Times Higher Education*—ok, so the *Times Higher Education* is a British publication, but they have reason to toot their own horn. England isn't the only bastion of academia, however. The University of Edinburgh in Scotland boasts an excellent program for international students. For those looking to enroll directly in a British university, the **Universities and Colleges Admissions Service (UCAS)** offers listings geared toward international applicants, and can be searched by subject area *(www.ucas.com)*. If you're already a college student and planning to study abroad, visit your study abroad office or check out www.studyabroad.com. Be sure to apply early, as larger institutions fill up fast.

International Programs

AMERICAN INSTITUTE FOR FOREIGN STUDY (AIFS)

River Plaza, 9 West Broad Street Stamford, CT 06902 ☎800-727-2437 www.aifs.com

With programs in 17 different countries and over 50,000 participants each year, AIFS is one of the oldest and largest cultural exchange organizations out there. Offers semester, year-long, and summer programs in London, as well as internship opportunities.

$ Semester $14,495-15,995; 3- to 12-week summer programs $5,495-10,995.

INSTITUTE FOR STUDY ABROAD BUTLER UNIVERSITY (IFSA)

1100 W. 42nd St. 305, Indianapolis, IN 46208 ☎800-858-0229 www.ifsa-butler.org

IFSA organizes semester and full year programs; students directly enroll at their choice of dozens of universities throughout England and Scotland.

i Some programs have required minimum GPAs. ⓢ *Semester up to $23,275.*

ARCADIA UNIVERSITY

450 S. Easton Rd., Glenside, PA 19038 ☎866-927-2234 www.arcadia.edu/abroad

Arcadia offers dozens of semester and full-year programs in England and Scotland. Summer programs, internship opportunities, and even graduate summer programs in literature and creative writing.

ⓢ *Semester fees, excluding meals, up to $22,450.*

INSTITUTE FOR THE INTERNATIONAL EDUCATION OF STUDENTS

33 N. LaSalle St., 15th fl. Chicago, IL 60602 ☎800-995-1750 www.iesabroad.org

IES offers summer, semester, and year-long programs in London and term-time programs at St. Catherine's College at Oxford. In London, students can either take IES courses or enroll in one of seven London universities, including the Courtauld Institute of Art and the Mountview Academy of Theater Arts.

ⓢ *Semester programs $13,885-$21,320; 7- to 9-week summer program $6,995-7,340.*

CULTURAL EXPERIENCES ABROAD (CEA)

2005 W. 14th St., Suite 113, Tempe, AZ 85281 ☎800-266-4441 www.gowithcea.com

CEA offers summer, semester, or academic year programs in London affiliated with Goldsmiths College, University of Westminster, and the Foundation for International Education. Students live in residence halls at their university.

ⓢ *Semester $14,495 to $16,595; 3-week summer program $4,295.*

CCIS STUDY ABROAD

2000 P St., NW, Suite 503 Washington, DC 20036 ☎800-453-6956 www.ccisabroad.org

The College Consortium for International Studies (CCIS) is a partnership of colleges and universities that sponsors study abroad programs around the world. Students can choose a summer or term-time program in London.

ⓢ *Semester, excluding meals, up to $13,500.*

AHA INTERNATIONAL

70 NW Couch St. Ste. 242 Portland, OR 97209 ☎800-654-2051 www.ahastudyabroad.org

Participate in summer, quarter-, and semester-long study abroad programs in London. Students live in home stays or residence halls and take courses in literature, politics, theater, history, and art history at AHA's London Centre.

ⓢ *Semester $14,300.*

COUNCIL ON INTERNATIONAL EDUCATIONAL EXCHANGE

300 Fore Street, Portland, ME 04101 ☎800-407-8839 www.ciee.org

CIEE has 4 different semester- or year-long programs in London oriented towards a range of interests, from Asian and African studies to media, arts, and design.

ⓢ *Semester $17,100-$18,500.*

GREAT BRITAIN PROGRAMS

The universities listed below are only a few of the many UK institutions that open their gates to foreign students for summer, single term, or year-long study. Prices listed are an estimate of fees for non-EU citizens. In most cases, room and board are not included. Almost all of these universities offer summer programs as well; check online for more details.

LONDON SCHOOL OF ECONOMICS (LSE)

Houghton Street, London, WC2A 2AE ☎20 7405 7686 www.lse.ac.uk

LSE accepts international students who have completed at least two years of undergraduate study for a year-long general course, running from October to July.

i Minimum GPA requirements vary by department. Ⓢ Tuition £14,426.

KING'S COLLEGE LONDON

Strand, London WC2R 2LS ☎020 7836 5454 www.kcl.ac.uk

Main campus on the Strand; Guy's and Waterloo campuses located across Thames. World-renowned War Studies Department. In conjunction with the Globe Education Practitioners and Courses Faculty, the English Department at KCL offers a 2-week course at Shakespeare's Globe Theatre to international students only.

Ⓢ Fall semester £5,700-8,374; spring semester £7,100-10,238; full year £12,800-16,700.

UNIVERSITY OF CAMBRIDGE

The Old Schools, Trinity Lane, Cambridge CB2 1TN ☎12 23 33 3308 www.cam.ac.uk

Unlike your typical American university, Cambridge comprises 29 undergraduate colleges. Your college is where you eat, sleep, and have your "supervision"—Cambridge-speak for one-on-one or small group lessons with a professor. Lectures are optional, so you can sleep in and not even feel guilty about it.

Ⓢ Full year £15,000-19,000.

UNIVERSITY OF OXFORD

University Offices, Wellington Square, Oxford, OX1 2JD ☎18 65 27 0000 www.ox.ac.uk

Like Cambridge, Oxford operates on the tutorial system and has 38 independent, self-governing colleges. (Sorry—Gryffindor isn't one of them, but the Great Hall in Harry Potter was based on Christ Church, one of the Oxford colleges.) Check individual college and departmental websites for more information.

Ⓢ Full year up to £19,700.

UNIVERSITY OF EDINBURGH

Old College, South Bridge Edinburgh EH8 9YL ☎13 16 50 4296 www.ed.ac.uk

Edinburgh offers a number of opportunities for American students wishing to study abroad, including a year-long program for high school graduates and a parliamentary program in which you study with MSPs in the Scottish Parliament. Admissions requirements vary by degree program; check online for more details.

Ⓢ Full year £11,100-11,600.

UNIVERSITY COLLEGE LONDON

Gower Street, London WC1E ☎13 34 47 6161 www.ucl.ac.uk

Located in the center of London, UCL hosts students from nearly 140 different countries.

Ⓢ Full year £12,770-16,725.

COOKING SCHOOLS

We know the old adage: "Heaven is where the police are British, the chefs are Italian, the mechanics are German, the lovers are French, and the organizers are Swiss. Hell is where the police are German, the chefs are British, the mechanics are French, the lovers are Swiss, and the organizers are Italian." But British food has improved over the years, and so have the opportunities for studying British and ethnic cuisine.

COOKERY SCHOOL

15B Little Portland Street London W1W 8BW ☎20 76 31 4590 www.cookeryschool.co.uk

Courses at the Cookey School cater to all experience levels. Day-long classes ranging from "Seasonal English" to "Thai All Day."

Ⓢ Classes £90-130.

EAT DRINK TALK

Unit 102, 190 St John St, London ☎20 76 89 6693 www.eatdrinktalk.co.uk

Reputedly offers "the best cooking classes in London." Unlike some of its traditional counterparts, this culinary school emphasizes modern, stylish cooking.

Ⓢ Day-long classes £85-115.

TEASMITH

6 Lamb St, London E1 6EA ☎20 72 47 1333 www.teasmith.co.uk

Learn the art of tea, perfected long ago by the British, and enjoy perfectly matched tea cakes at a tea masterclass, Thursdays 7-9:30pm.

Ⓢ Classes £35 per person.

volunteering

Just because you're traveling in a first-world country, home to high tea and posh accents, don't think there isn't service work to be done. If you're looking to volunteer, start by searching online for charities that match your interests and schedule. **CharitiesDirect.com** offers extensive listings on hundreds of Britain-based charities, while **Volunteer Now** *(www.volunteernow.co.uk)* features listings of volunteer opportunities in England, specifically for volunteers ages 16-25. The **Volunteer Development Agency in Northern Ireland** *(☎28 90 23 6100 www.volunteering-ni.org)* offers training and assistance for volunteers. International websites like **www.idealist.org**, **www.volunteerabroad.com**, and **www.servenet.org** are all excellent resources. The **Council on International Educational Exchange** *(☎20 75 53 7600 www.ciee.org)* allows you to search volunteer opportunities by region and project type. Lastly, the parent organization **Volunteers for Peace** *(www.vfp.org)* can facilitate your search, offering placements in International Voluntary Service projects across Britain.

PEACE PROCESS

Tensions in Ireland have eased since the Good Friday Agreement was signed in 1998, but reconciliation is an ongoing project. Volunteering with the organizations listed below serves as a good opportunity for foreigners looking to advance political and social change in Northern Ireland.

- **KILCRANNY HOUSE:** A residential center that provides a safe space for Protestants and Catholics to explore nonviolence and conflict resolution. *(☎28 70 32 1816 www.kilcrannyhouse.org)*
- **CORRYMEELA COMMUNITY:** A residential Christian community designed to bring Protestants and Catholics together to work for peace. Over 6,000 people participate in Corrymeela programs each year. Meals and accommodation provided for volunteers. *(☎28 70 32 1816 www.corrymeela.org)*

DISABILITIES AND SPECIAL NEEDS

Despite the 2002 Disability Rights Commission and Britain's Educating for Equality campaign, discrimination against the physically and mentally handicapped persists. The organizations below take on volunteers to aid individuals with special needs and to help foster a culture of mutual respect.

- **KITH AND KIDS:** The Irish Centre, Pretoria Rd. London N17 8DX *(☎020 8801 7432 www.kithandkids.org.uk). Tasks include helping disabled youth during community outings, leading sports and art activities, and helping 18+ members find employment.*
- **LEONARD CHESHIRE DISABILITY, HEAD OFFICE:** 66 South Lambeth Rd., London SW8 1RL *(☎020 3242 0200 www.lgdisability.org.)* **Scotland Office,** Murrayburgh

House, 17 Corstorphine Road, Edinburgh, EH12 6DD (☎*0131 346 9040).* Volunteer opportunities include mentoring and participating in outdoor activities with disabled people.

- **SKILL:** National Bureau for Students with Disabilities, Unit 3, Floor 3, Radisson Court, 219 Long Ln., London SE1 4PR (☎*020 7450 0620* *www.skill.org.uk).* Promotes opportunities for people with any disability in learning and employment.
- **VITALISE, LONDON OFFICE:** 12 City Forum, 250 City Rd., London EC1V 8AF *(☎0845 345 1972 www.vitalise.org.uk).* Residential volunteers care for disabled people. Nearly all opportunities 16+.

YOUTH AND THE COMMUNITY

Youth and community-based volunteer work will probably be one of the most rewarding and challenging experiences you have abroad. Most of the listings below involve working directly with low-income families, at-risk youth, or inmates.

- **PRISON ADVICE AND CARE TRUST (PACT):** PACT recruits volunteers for a wide range of projects including advising visiting families, playing with children and serving refreshments at the visitors' center, lending support to prisoners during their first night in prison, and helping ex-prisoners transition back into the community. *(☎20 77 35 9535 www.prisonadvice.org.uk)*
- **BARNARDO'S:** Volunteers can work either directly with abused and underprivileged children or in one of Barnardo's retail outlets. Also offers a 12-week summer volunteer program. International volunteers only accepted with support of government agency in your home country. *(☎20 85 50 8822 www.barnardos.co.uk)*
- **CITIZENS ADVICE BUREAU:** The Citizens Advice Bureau started out as an emergency war service when World War II broke out. Today, trained volunteers at the 438 bureaus across the country give free advice on legal, financial, and other issues. *(☎20 78 33 2181 www.citizensadvice.org.uk)*
- **COMMUNITY SERVICE VOLUNTEERS:** Over 150,000 people volunteer each year with CSV on issues such as child protection services and adult education. Full-time volunteers spend 4 months to a year volunteering and are provided with meals, accommodation, and a weekly stipend. *(☎20 72 78 6601 www.csv.org.uk)*

REFUGEE AND IMMIGRANT ISSUES

Immigration is as much a hot-button issue in Britain as it is in the United States, particularly since the creation of the European Union. Net migration has risen from just a few tens of thousands per year in the early 90s to over 200,000 in recent years. The issue is particularly affecting cities: nearly 50% of all births in London in 2008 were to foreign-born mothers. The British immigration minister has promised a clampdown on the number of immigrants and asylum-seekers, while human-rights organizations like Amnesty International have fought against detention centers and raids on undocumented workers. The **Association of Visitors to Immigrant Detainees (AVID)** is the national umbrella organization for charities working to assist immigration detainees. The organizations listed below also provide information, legal assistance, and material aid to immigrants and refugees. Note that because of the nature of the work, most of these volunteer opportunities require a long-term commitment.

- **ASYLUM WELCOME:** Volunteers provide advice on social, legal, and health services, help run summer sports and activities for young refugees, and work to raise awareness of the issues faced by asylum seekers and immigration detainees. *(☎18 65 72 2082 www.asylum-welcome.org)*
- **HASLAR VISITORS GROUP:** Trained volunteers commit to weekly afternoon visits to immigration detainees at the Haslar Immigration Removal Centre, operated by the

prison service. Volunteers offer warmth, conversation and, occasionally, help finding solicitors and people to put up bail.*(☎23 92 83 9222 🖳www.haslarvisitors.org.uk)*

- **LONDON DETAINEE SUPPORT GROUP:** LDSG offers support and mentorship to detainees in London. Volunteers work at detention centers in Colnbrook and Harmondsworth and are required to make a 6-mo. commitment. *(☎20 72 26 3114 🖳www.ldsg.org.uk)*
- **REFUGEE ACTION:** Volunteers take on specific roles, including interpreting, mentoring refugees, and providing employment or career advice. Contact a local Refugee Action office for more information on volunteer opportunities. *(☎20 76 54 7700 🖳www.refugee-action.org.uk)*

LONDON 2012 OLYMPIC GAMES

The Olympic Games themselves last less than three weeks, but preparations and planning take years. London 2012 will need up to 70,000 volunteers and many are already signing on to get involved.

- **OLYMPIC DELIVERY AUTHORITY (ODA):** Volunteers at the games will assist with a range of tasks, from spectator services to language translation and medical care. In the meantime, Trailblazer volunteers work 1 day a week in the Organizing Committee offices, carrying out various administrative duties.*(☎20 02 01 2000 🖳www.london-2012.co.uk)*

working

In 2008, the UK Border Agency switched from a work-based system to a points-based immigration system. In other words, the good news is you don't need a job offer when you apply to enter or stay in the UK. The bad news is you need to pass a points-based assessment. Points are allotted based on your personal background (age, qualifications, previous earnings, and experience in the UK), English fluency, and whether you have funds available. Foreign students with a valid student visa can work up to 20 hours per week, except during official school or university vacations. Recent grads looking to work in the UK should check out the information provided by the UK Council for International Student Affairs. *(🖳www.ukcisa.org.uk/student/working_after.php)* Of course, those lucky souls who are citizens of most countries in the European Economic Area or Switzerland are free to live and work in the UK.

LONG-TERM WORK

If you're planning to work long enough in Britain to start spewing "righty-o" and "jolly good!" (read: more than 3 months), we recommend that you start your search well in advance. International placement agencies are often the easiest way to find employment abroad, especially for those interested in teaching. Although they are often only available to college students, internships are a good way to ease into working abroad. Be wary of advertisements for companies claiming to be able get you a job abroad for a fee—often the same listings are available online or in newspapers. Some reputable organizations are listed below.

- **INTERNATIONAL ASSOCIATION FOR THE EXCHANGE OF STUDENTS FOR TECHNICAL EXPERIENCE (IAESTE):** Positions available for students currently enrolled full-time in a Bachelor's or Master's degree program in scientific disciplines, engineering and technology, agriculture, and applied arts. Most placements for 8-12 wks. during the summer, but some longer-term placements are also available. Apply through your home country's IAESTE branch. *(☎20 73 89 4771 🖳www.iaeste.org)*

- **INTERNATIONAL COOPERATIVE EDUCATION:** Geared specifically toward American students looking for summer or term-time employment throughout the globe. Opportunities in England and Scotland include working at the Mini Cooper plant in Oxford, a medical software company in Edinburgh, or the commerce department of the US Embassy in London. *(☎1-650-323-4944 www.icemenlo.com Ⓢ Costs include a $250 application fee and a $900 placement fee.)*
- **HANSARD SCHOLAR PROGRAMME:** A non-partisan political research charity devoted to promoting public involvement in politics, the Hansard Society runs a summer program for international students that combines classes at the London School of Economics with internships in British government. *(☎20 74 38 1223 www.hansard-society.org.uk Ⓢ Summer program £7630.)*

more visa information

Swiss and European Economic Area (EEA) nationals (excluding Bulgarians and Romanians) do not need a visa to work in the UK. If you live in a Commonwealth country (including Australia, Canada, and New Zealand) and if your parents or grandparents were born in the UK, you can apply for UK Ancestry Employment and work without a visa (make sure you have all the relevant birth certificates that can prove your connection to the UK). Tier 5 youth mobility and temporary worker visas allow citizens of Australia, New Zealand, Canada or Japan aged 18 to 30 to work in the United Kingdom for a limited period to satisfy primarily non-economic objectives.

Teaching

No one ever went into teaching to strike it rich, and teaching in Britain is no exception. There are three types of British schools. State schools are government-funded and correspond to what we would call public schools in the States, while public schools are, confusingly, privately funded independent schools. International schools can be either state or public and cater largely to children of ex-pats. The academic year is divided into autumn (September to Christmas), spring (early January to Easter), and summer (Easter to late July) terms. Applications to teach at state schools must pass through local governments, while public and international schools must be applied to individually.

Foreigners looking for a permanent teaching position at a state school in England or Wales must have **Qualified Teacher Status (QTS),** which involves postgraduate teacher training or a teaching assessment for those with extensive experience outside of the UK. For more information on the **Initial Teacher Training (ITT),** see www.tda.gov.uk. The **General Teaching Council for Scotland** *(www.gtcs.org.uk)* regulates the teaching profession in Scotland and requires different qualifications for primary- and secondary-school certification. The **Scottish Education Department** has more information on teaching opportunities and certification requirements for internationals at www.teachinginscotland.com. The **British Council** *(www.britishcouncil.org)* has extensive information for prospective teachers in the UK generally. Placement agencies or university fellowship programs are the best resources for finding teaching jobs. The alternative is to contact schools directly or to try your luck once you arrive in Britain. In the latter case, the best time to look is several weeks before the start of the academic year. The following organizations are extremely helpful in placing teachers in Britain.

- **COUNCIL FOR INTERNATIONAL EXCHANGE OF SCHOLARS:** An American organization that administers the Fulbright program for faculty and professionals. *(☎1-202-686-4000 www.cies.org)*

- **ETEACH:** UK-based online recruitment service for teachers that allows you to search by the subject you want to teach.*(☎84 54 56 4384 www.eteach.com)*
- **EUROPEAN COUNCIL OF INTERNATIONAL SCHOOLS (ECIS):** Runs recruitment services for international schools in the UK and elsewhere. Check their website for more information on obtaining an International Teacher Certificate (ITC). *(☎17 30 26 8244 www.ecis.org)*
- **INTERNATIONAL SCHOOLS SERVICES (ISS):** A New Jersey-based organization, ISS hires teachers for more than 200 overseas schools, including some in Britain. Candidates should have teaching experience and a bachelor's degree. *(☎1-609-452-0990 www.iss.edu* $185 application fee*)*

Au Pair Work

Au pairs are typically women (although sometimes men) aged 18-27 who work as live-in nannies, caring for children and doing light housework in foreign countries in exchange for room, board, and a small spending allowance or stipend. One perk of the job is that it allows you to get to know Britain without the high expenses of traveling. Drawbacks, however, can include mediocre pay and long hours. In the UK, the recommended salary for an au pair is approximately £50 per week for 25 hours. Some families will also defray travel expenses to and from Britain. Much of the au pair experience depends on the family with which you are placed. Au pairs from outside the European Economic Area need a letter of invitation from their host family to obtain a visa. The agencies below are a good starting point for looking for employment as an au pair. EU nationals can work as an au pair in the UK without any formalities, but the Youth Mobility Scheme, which has replaced the au pair visa program, is only open to citizens of Australia, New Zealand, Canada, and Japan.

- **AU PAIR UK:** Connects host families with prospective au pairs. *(☎20 85 37 3253 www.aupair.uk.com)*
- **ALMONDBURY AU PAIR AGENCY:** Lists job openings in the UK. *(☎18 03 38 0795 www.aupair-agency.com)*
- **CHILDCARE INTERNATIONAL:** British employment agency that pairs au pairs with host families. *(☎20 89 06 3116 www.childint.co.uk)*

SHORT-TERM WORK

Don't be discouraged by the difficulty of obtaining a short-term work permit. Many travelers work odd jobs for a few weeks at a time to help cover the next leg of their journey, while others work a few hours a day at a hostel in exchange for free or discounted room and/or board. Most often, these short-term jobs are found by word of mouth or by expressing interest to the owner of a hostel or restaurant. Due to high turnover in the tourism industry, many places are eager for help, even if it is only temporary.

- **BRITISH UNIVERSITIES NORTH AMERICA CLUB (BUNAC):** Lists establishments that have hired short-term workers in the past. *(☎20 72 51 3472 www.bunac.org)*
- **YHA (YOUTH HOSTEL ASSOCIATION):** Lists job openings on website and hires short-term workers from a pool of globetrotters. Ask at individual hostels as well. *(www.yha.org.uk, in Scotland www.syha.org.uk)*

Other Opportunities By Region

England

Most English cities and larger towns have job spaces to fill, especially during the high season, mainly in pubs or restaurants. Brighton is especially accommodating to people looking for temporary work. Job hunting may be harder in the northern cities, where unemployment is higher. Check newspapers for listings or get in touch with a job placement organization like **AgencyCentral** (*www.agencycentral.co.uk*).

Scotland

The **Edinburgh Fringe Festival** in August is the world's largest arts festival and provides many job opportunities. Glasgow is also lively during the summer and temporary domestic and food service jobs may be available. Thousands of employment opportunities in Scotland can be searched online at www.s1jobs.com.

tell the world

If your friends are tired of hearing about that time you saved a baby orangutan in Indonesia, there's clearly only one thing to do: get new friends. Find them at our website, www.letsgo.com, where you can post your study-, volunteer-, or work-abroad stories for other, more appreciative community members to read. There's also a Beyond Tourism section that elaborates on non-destination-specific volunteering, studying, and working opportunities. If you liked this chapter, you'll love it; if you didn't like this chapter, maybe you'll find the website's more general Beyond Tourism tips more likeable, you non-likey person.

INDEX

a

Apsley House 39
au pair work 217

b

Beyond Tourism 6, 209
- studying 210
- volunteering 213
- working 215

Brass Rubbing Centre 161
bridges
- Bridge of Sighs (Oxford and Cambridge) 3
- Forth Bridge 3
- Mathematical Bridge 3
- Millenium Bridge 3
- Tower Bridge 3, 45

budget airlines 194

c

Cambridge 133
- accommodations 135
- essentials 151
- food 141
- nightlife 144
- shopping 149
- sights 136

Camera Obscura and the World of Illusions 162
castles
- Edinburgh Castle 162
- Oxford Castle 119

cathedrals and churches
- Brompton Oratory 40
- Chelsea Old Church 35
- Great St. Mary's Church 140
- Parish of St. Andrew and St. George 163
- Round Church 140
- Saint Mary-Le-Bow 46
- St. Benet's Church 140
- St. Giles Cathedral 161
- St. Martin-in-the-Fields 53
- St. Mary Abbots 39
- St. Mary's Cathedral 163
- St. Mary Woolnoth 47
- St. Paul's Cathedral 41
- St. Stephen Walbrook 47

climate 199
colleges 113
- All Souls, Oxford 114
- Balliol, Oxford 115
- Christ Church, Oxford 113
- Christ's, Cambridge 138
- Clare, Cambridge 138
- Jesus, Cambridge 138
- King's, Cambridge 137
- Magdalene, Cambridge 138
- Magdalen, Oxford 116
- Merton, Oxford 116
- New, Oxford 116
- Queens', Cambridge 139
- Queen's, Oxford 116
- St. John's, Cambridge 138
- Trinity, Cambridge 136
- Trinity, Oxford 117
- University, Oxford 118

commercial airlines 194
concessions 32
cricket
- Lord's Cricket Ground 5

d

diseases and environmental hazards 193
drugs and alcohol 192

e

Edinburgh 153
- accommodations 155
- essentials 185
- food 165
- nightlife 172
- shopping 181
- sights 160

embassies and consulates 190

f

festivals
- BBC Proms 94
- Blaze 94
- Cambridge Folk Festival 149
- Cambridge Shakespeare Festival 6, 149
- Edinburgh Fringe Festival 6
- Glastonbury Festival 94
- Heart of the World Festival 149
- London Literary Festival 94
- May Week 148
- Midsummer Fair 149
- Strawberry Fair 149

g

Georgian House 164
Glenogle Swim Centre 164

h

Harry Potter 2, 113, 165
holidays 207

i

international calls 198

k

Keats's House 57
Kenwood House 57

l

libraries
- Bodleian Library 118
- King's Library, The British Museum 33
- National Art Library, Victoria and Albert Museum 38
- National Library of Scotland 161
- The British Library 33
- Wren Library, Cambridge 137

local laws and police 192
London 13
- accommodations 21
- essentials 101
- food 59
- nightlife 72
- shopping 95
- sights 31

London Eye 49

m

measurements 200
media 205
money 190

wiring from home 191
museums and galleries
Alexander Fleming Museum 32
Alpha Art 179
Ashmolean Museum 118
Cambridge County and Folk Museum 140
Churchill Museum and Cabinet War Rooms 55
Clockmakers' Museum 46
Design Museum 48
Fitzwilliam Museum 137
Flying Colours 36
Gagliardi Art Gallery 36
Guildhall Art Gallery 45
Hayward Gallery 48
Henderson Gallery 179
Imperial War Museum 47
Institute of Contemporary Art 53
Kettle's Yard 140
Museum of Archaeology and Anthropology 139
Museum of Childhood 180
Museum of London 44
Museum of Zoology 139
National Army Museum 35
National Gallery, London 51
National Gallery of Scotland 163
National Maritime Museum 58
National Museum of Scotland 162
National Portrait Gallery, London 52
National Trust Scotland 163
National War Museum (NWM) 162
Natural History Museum 39
Oxford Museum of Natural History 120
Polar Museum 137
RM Art 180
Saatchi Art Gallery 34
Science Museum 38
Scotlandart.com 179
Sedgwick Museum 139
Subway Gallery 32
Surgeon's Hall Museum 179
Tate Modern 48
The British Museum 32
The Victoria and Albert Museum 38
Wallace Collection 41
Whipple Museum of the History of Science 139
Whitechapel Gallery 58
Writer's Museum 162
music and dance
London Coliseum 88
Royal Albert Hall 88
Royal Opera House 87
Southbank Centre 88

National Archives of Scotland 163

Oxford 105
accommodations 110
essentials 130
food 120
nightlife 124
shopping 127
sights 113

p

palaces
Buckingham Palace 56
parks and gardens
Cambridge University Botanic Garden 140
Chelsea Psychic Gardens 35
Hampstead Heath 57
Potters Fields Park 44
Regent's Park 40
Royal Botanic Gardens, Edinburgh 164
St. James's Park 55
St. Luke's Gardens 35
The Meadows 165
University of Oxford Botanic Garden 119
people and customs 202
performance spaces
Speaker's Corner 32
phone cards 198
pins and ATMs 191
pre-departure health 193
punting and boating
Serpentine Boating Lake 40

Royal Courts of Justice 37
Royal Observatory 58

safety and health 192
Scotland's People Centre 164
Scottish Storytelling Centre 161
Seven Dials 54
Shakespeare's Globe 49
shopping
Covent Garden Piazza 53
sports and recreation 203
squares
St. Andrews Square 163
St. John's Square 37
Trafalgar Square 52
Stockbridge Market 164
St. Paul's Cathedral 41

taxes 191
terrorism 193
theaters
Bedlam Theatre, Edinburgh 181
Donmar Warehouse 92
Edinburgh Playhouse 181
National Theatre 92
Old Vic 92
Royal Court Theatre 92
Shakespeare's Globe 92
Young Vic 92
The Charterhouse 37
The Eagle 144
The Eagle and the Child 124
The Monument 47
The Scotch Whisky Experience 160
The Temple, London 36
time differences 190
tipping and bargaining 191
Tower of London 45
towers
Carfax Tower 119
Saxon Tower 119
trains 195

visas 188

Walter Scott Monument 164
Water of Leith 164
Wellington Arch 40
Westminster Abbey 54
work permits 188

MAP INDEX

Cambridge *134*
Edinburgh *156-157*
London *16-17*
Oxford *106-107*
West End *50*
Westminster *54*

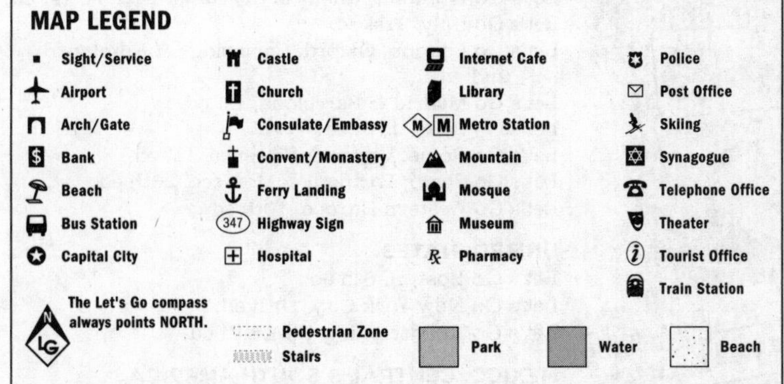

ACKNOWLEDGMENTS

MEAGAN THANKS: Matt for his unwavering dedication and fresh-to-deathness, even when *Rocky* ate my life; you're the best RM an Ed could ask for. Our RWs for their tireless work and adventurous spirits. DBarbs for MEdits and chop-busting. Marykate for calming my crazy. Sara and DChoi, who kept me rollin' on the RIVER. Joe for his marketing prowess, but mostly his smiles. Nathaniel for flawless editorial *and* ticket management. Ashley for teaching Meags how to make moves in the roughest times. I'm not really tryna forget Colleenie Bear and Sarah for making Fun Pod the best. Joey G. for hugs and *Glee*. Bronwen for flawless paper edits. Thanks to Betty White, Leslie Uggams, Cher, Meryl, Marge, and all the other deeves. HRST 2010 for Tater Tots and fishnet therapy. Matt and Chris for being so sweet when Maj had to edit. Here's to Billy Shakes, Ginny Woolf, and Jude Law. Thank you to Mrs. O'Brien and Nicole. Finally, thank you, mom, for your constant support.

MATT THANKS: Our RWs, for their terrific work on the road. Meg, for being a friend, a grandma, a wordsmith and an Anglophile. Daniel, for his multilingual motivational speaking. Marykate, for answering my XV hourly questions. Colleen, for being the best. Colleen, for being not the worst. Sarah, for sharing my favorite corner of 67 Mt. Auburn. Ashley, for helping me lock it up by day and rip it up by night. Nathaniel and Sara, for all the late-night help and snack foods. Joe Molimock, for making marketing moves. DChoi, for his technological wizardry. Joe Gaspard, for assisting my caffeine addiction. Bronwen, for putting the number one in P1. Hasty Pudding Theatricals. Not floods. Anybody who brought me from homeless to Harvard. Elisandre, for starting the week off right. Drake. Snuggies. Bolt Bus. Mom, dad, Rachel, Edna, and the rest of my family. And of course, Fun Pod: make big love, not war.

LET'S GO masthead

DIRECTOR OF PUBLISHING Ashley R. Laporte
EXECUTIVE EDITOR Nathaniel Rakich
PRODUCTION AND DESIGN DIRECTOR Sara Plana
PUBLICITY AND MARKETING DIRECTOR Joseph Molimock
MANAGING EDITORS Charlotte Alter, Daniel C. Barbero, Marykate Jasper, Iya Megre
TECHNOLOGY PROJECT MANAGERS Daniel J. Choi, C. Alexander Tremblay
PRODUCTION ASSOCIATES Rebecca Cooper, Melissa Niu
FINANCIAL ASSOCIATE Louis Caputo

DIRECTOR OF IT Yasha Iravantchi
PRESIDENT Meagan Hill
GENERAL MANAGER Jim McKellar

ABOUT LET'S GO

THE STUDENT TRAVEL GUIDE

Let's Go publishes the world's favorite student travel guides, written entirely by Harvard students. Armed with pens, notebooks, and a few changes of clothes stuffed into their backpacks, our student researchers go across continents, through time zones, and above expectations to seek out invaluable travel experiences for our readers. Because we are a completely student-run company, we have a unique perspective on how students travel, where they want to go, and what they're looking to do when they get there. If your dream is to grab a machete and forge through the jungles of Costa Rica, we can take you there. If you'd rather bask in the Riviera sun at a beachside cafe, we'll set you a table. In short, we write for readers who know that there's more to travel than tour buses. To keep up, visit our website, www.letsgo.com, where you can sign up to blog, post photos from your trips, and connect with the *Let's Go* community.

TRAVELING BEYOND TOURISM

We're on a mission to provide our readers with sharp, fresh coverage packed with socially responsible opportunities to go beyond tourism. Each guide's Beyond Tourism chapter shares ideas about responsible travel, study abroad, and how to give back to the places you visit while on the road. To help you gain a deeper connection with the places you travel, our fearless researchers scour the globe to give you the heads-up on both world-renowned and off-the-beaten-track opportunities. We've also opened our pages to respected writers and scholars to hear their takes on the countries and regions we cover, and asked travelers who have worked, studied, or volunteered abroad to contribute first-person accounts of their experiences.

FIFTY-ONE YEARS OF WISDOM

Let's Go has been on the road for 51 years and counting. We've grown a lot since publishing our first 20-page pamphlet to Europe in 1960, but five decades and 60 titles later, our witty, candid guides are still researched and written entirely by students on shoestring budgets who know that train strikes, stolen luggage, food poisoning, and marriage proposals are all part of a day's work. Meanwhile, we're still bringing readers fresh new features, such as a student-life section with advice on how and where to meet students from around the world; a revamped, user-friendly layout for our listings; and greater emphasis on the experiences that make travel abroad a rite of passage for readers of all ages. And, of course, this year's 16 titles—including five brand-new guides—are still brimming with editorial honesty, a commitment to students, and our irreverent style.

THE LET'S GO COMMUNITY

More than just a travel guide company, *Let's Go* is a community that reaches from our headquarters in Cambridge, MA, all across the globe. Our small staff of dedicated student editors, writers, and tech nerds comes together because of our shared passion for travel and our desire to help other travelers get the most out of their experience. We love it when our readers become part of the *Let's Go* community as well—when you travel, drop us a postcard (67 Mt. Auburn St., Cambridge, MA 02138, USA), send us an email (feedback@letsgo.com), or sign up on our website (www.letsgo.com) to tell us about your adventures and discoveries.

For more information, updated travel coverage, and news from our researcher team, visit us online at www.letsgo.com.

THANKS TO OUR SPONSORS

notes